Library of
Davidson College

Cambridge Archaeological and Ethnological Series

KINDRED AND CLAN

KINDRED AND CLAN

IN THE MIDDLE AGES AND AFTER

A STUDY IN THE SOCIOLOGY OF THE TEUTONIC RACES

BY

BERTHA SURTEES PHILLPOTTS, M.A.

Late Pfeiffer Student of Girton College, Cambridge ; Fellow of
the Royal Society of Northern Antiquaries, Copenhagen

OCTAGON BOOKS

A DIVISION OF FARRAR, STRAUS AND GIROUX

New York   1974

First published 1913

Reprinted 1974
by permission of Cambridge University Press

OCTAGON BOOKS
A Division of Farrar, Straus & Giroux, Inc.
19 Union Square West
New York, N. Y. 10003

Library of Congress Cataloging in Publication Data

Phillpotts, Dame Bertha Surtees, d. 1932.
    Kindred and clan in the Middle Ages and after.

    Reprint of the 1913 ed. published by the University Press, Cambridge, Eng., in series: Cambridge archaeological and ethnological series.

    1. Teutonic race. 2. Kinship. 3. Civilization, Medieval. I. Title. II. Series: Cambridge archaeological and ethnological series.

HN11.P5   1974   301.42′1′0902   74-9734
ISBN 0-374-96433-5

Manufactured by Braun-Brumfield, Inc.
Ann Arbor, Michigan

Printed in the United States of America

To
M. A. C. and M. C.
in whose house this book was planned and written.

PREFACE

THE aim of this book is to discover how long the solidarity of the kindred survived as a social factor of importance in the various Teutonic countries. The lack of accessible information on the subject was brought home to me by the difficulty I experienced in qualifying my own ignorance with regard to it,—an ignorance of which I only became aware through reading Dr Brunner's *Sippe und Wergeld nach altniederdeutschen Rechten*. I had just worked out the results embodied in the first chapter of this book, and the startling contrast between their negative character and the ample evidence set forth by Dr Brunner evoked a desire to know why the kindreds should have endured so long in North Germany, where they were assailed by so many adverse influences, while I had found but the faintest traces of their survival in Iceland. The present work is nothing more than an attempt at answering my own questions. In the course of a general survey of the field it became obvious that neglect of the evidence furnished by judicial records and charters had led scholars to attribute too long a lease of life to the system in some countries, and to under-estimate its duration in others; and that the causes usually adduced for its break-up only serve to complicate the problem still further. Finally there arose the suspicion that even in the later Middle Ages the institution played a part, obscure but not negligible, in the making of history. Thus I was lured on by successive problems, until the book was written, and I had never so much as asked myself whether my stock of legal and linguistic knowledge was equal to the demands made upon it.

Where I have been guilty of errors I can only ask for the indulgence of my critics.

Since the field was far too wide in any case, I have circumscribed it as much as possible by restricting myself to districts continuously occupied by the Teutonic races since the Age of National Migrations or the Viking Age. Further, I have been reluctantly obliged to forego any serious investigation of central and south German conditions. Such meagre scraps of evidence as presumably exist for those regions could only be gleaned by an exhaustive search through all the published collections of mediæval charters and chronicles. The search would be attractive, however slightly rewarded, but it must be the task of some student who has longer daily access to books than has fallen to the lot of the present writer.

In view of the fluctuations of boundaries in the later Middle Ages it has seemed best to discuss the various districts in terms of modern political divisions, though it must be admitted that such a method has its drawbacks.

With regard to terminology, I must apologize to the anthropologists for using the term 'clan' in its Scottish connotation, for large groups of kindred organized on an agnatic basis, regardless of the fact that they were probably not exogamous. 'Agnatic' and 'cognatic' I employ in the usual dictionary sense: 'agnatic' to denote kinship reckoned exclusively through males, 'cognatic' for all other blood-relationships, whether on the paternal or maternal side. In the concluding chapter I felt the need of a term signifying kinship reckoned exclusively through females, and I have there used the word 'matrilinear.' It would consequently have been more consistent to have substituted 'patrilinear' for 'agnatic' throughout the book, had that been feasible. As regards legal terminology, I am aware of the dangers of translating foreign mediæval technicalities into modern English, and have perhaps gone to the other extreme in using only the most general terms.

PREFACE ix

The difficulty which such combinations of sounds as *ldr*, *rðr* present to the non-Icelandic reader may, it is hoped, justify a certain inconsistency in my treatment of Old Norse proper names. Where a nominative final *r* is preceded by any other consonant the accusative form is used, in all other cases the nominative. Thus I write Thórð, Harald, Sæmund, but Njáll, Thorgeirr, Snorri. The Old Norse þ is of course rendered by *th*, but ð (with the sound of *th* in 'the') has been allowed to stand.

It is a pleasure to record some of the obligations I have incurred during a two-months' visit to Copenhagen and a month spent in German libraries and archives. Especially I would mention my debt of gratitude to Professor J. H. C. Steenstrup, of Copenhagen, for much kindness and advice. My thanks are also due to the staff of the Rigsarkiv, to Dr Louis Bobé of Copenhagen University, to Professor Poul Jørgensen for kindly allowing me to read an unpublished essay on Danish criminal law, and to my friend Mr Sigfús Blöndal of the Royal Library in Copenhagen. I owe much of the measure of success which attended my researches in Schleswig to the kindness of the Director of the Staatsarchiv, Geheimrath Dr de Boor, who has since added to my obligations by collating one of my transcripts with the original MS. For help in obtaining admission, at a day's notice, to the town archives of Hamburg, as well as for many useful hints, I have to thank Professor Borchling and Dr Reincke; and I have a most grateful memory of the kindness of Geheimrath Dr Wachter, Director of the Staatsarchiv at Aurich.

I find it difficult to express my sense of indebtedness to Professor Chadwick, who has most kindly read the greater part of the book either in proof or in manuscript; but other old pupils of his will know from their own experience in like case how much I owe to his criticisms and suggestions, and how lavish he has been of his own time and trouble. I should add that for the theories contained in the book, the author is alone responsible, as also for the errors.

For the calculations respecting wergilds I am greatly indebted to my friend Miss Cave-Browne-Cave of Girton, who is however not to be held accountable for any inaccuracies that may have crept into them. I must also thank Miss Kirchberger, of Girton, and Dr Braunholtz, for help in construing Old French legal phrases. Nor must I forget my obligation to Professor Vinogradoff, for criticism of certain chapters of the book at an early stage. My thanks are also due to the Syndics of the University Press for undertaking the publication of the book, and to their staff for their great care and skill.

Finally, I must make grateful acknowledgment to the Managers of the Frederick William Maitland Memorial Fund, for their grant of £40 towards the publication of this work.

B. S. P.

CAMBRIDGE
September 1913

CONTENTS

	PAGE
INTRODUCTION	1

CHAP.
I.	ICELAND	11
II.	NORWAY	47
III.	SWEDEN	68
IV.	DENMARK	79
V.	NORTH GERMANY AND HOLLAND	102
VI.	BELGIUM AND NORTHERN FRANCE	173
VII.	ENGLAND	205
VIII.	CONCLUSION	245
	I. Summary of previous chapters	245
	II. The influence of the kindreds on social conditions	246
	III. Causes of the decline of the kindreds	257
	IV. The pre-historic group	265

APPENDIX I. The 'hundred of silver' in Iceland . . 277

II. Documents:

1. Norway, 1348. Deed of reconciliation in a slaying-case 284
2. Norway, 1585. Plea to the king concerning wergild 285
3. Denmark, 1513. Deed of reconciliation . 286
4. Denmark, 1542. Wergild of Niels Mogensen 287
5. Denmark, 1602. Deed of reconciliation . 288
6. Schleswig, 1693. Court record of wergild-distribution 289
7. Schleswig-Holstein, 1588. Deed of reconciliation 291
8. Friesland, 1443. Notification of sums offered for the slaying of a slayer . . . 293
9. Holland, 1392. Official adjudication in a slaying-case 294

INDEX 297

ADDENDA ET CORRIGENDA

p. 1, l. 9 from bottom. *For* country *read* century.

p. 24, ll. 6–7. These words have been accidentally overlooked in revision. Since the publication of Heusler's *Strafrecht der Isländersagas* (1911) they are no longer true.

p. 48, l. 5 from bottom. *For* Bárðr *read* Bárð.

pp. 50–52. It is worthy of notice that the Frostuthing wergild does not include the ordinary class of *sakaukar*—father-in-law, brother-in-law and son-in-law.

p. 69, l. 12. *For* Teutonic *read* Scandinavian.

p. 101, l. 1. *For* Knud the Great *read* Knud VI.

p. 165, l. 1. *For* Exactly *read* More than.

p. 172, l. 4. *For* slayer *read* slain.

p. 181, l. 11 and l. 2 from bottom. *For* Henricourt *read* Hemricourt.

p. 237, l. 2. *For* Aeschere *read* Hondscioh, *and for* Grendel's mother *read* Grendel.

p. 249, l. 2. In Wursten the kindred-system was still strong up to 1525: see v. d. Osten, *Gesch. des Landes Wursten*, Th. I. pp. 46, 66 ff.

p. 251, l. 3. *For* kingdom *read* settlement.

p. 273, l. 2 from bottom. *For* the Netherlands *read* Holland.

INTRODUCTION

DURING the past few years an immense amount of valuable work has been done towards the elucidation of the ancient Teutonic tribal system. Ficker, Brunner, von Amira, Vinogradoff and many others have thrown light on its manifestations in Germany and Scandinavia, and in his *Tribal Custom in Anglo-Saxon Law* Seebohm has shown how shreds of tribal custom surviving in Old English law can be pieced together to give some idea of a time when tribal custom was the only law.

The object of all these scholars has been to disengage the original features of the tribal organization from the later and accidental accretions. Hence they have usually sought enlightenment in the earliest sources, and even then have had their eyes turned on the still remoter past. The result of this pre-occupation has been to give us a remarkably vivid picture of pre-historic society, of the organization of inter-related groups for agricultural as well as for offensive and defensive purposes. But it must be confessed that we are left with a curious vagueness in our knowledge when we turn to historical times and places. It is easy to acquaint ourselves, through many modern works, with details of the life and work of a typical freeman or villein in any mediaeval state: the dues he pays, the crops he grows, and so forth. But if we ask whether this typical freeman of such and such a country, of such and such a state, was still a member of a cohesive kindred, and if so, what it did for him, we too often ask in vain, for on this point our authorities are apt to be silent, or even to contradict one another. Yet, in forbearing to ask, are we not acting much as one who should read, a thousand years hence, of the minutiae of factory life and factory inspection in the 19th century, and should take no heed of the presence or absence of trade-unions? But for the fact that kinship-solidarity had no future before it, the comparison is not entirely fanciful.

How long did the solidarity of the kindred, the distinguishing feature of the tribal system, survive in the mediaeval States: and where did it survive longest and thrive best? These questions are not so important as the vast earlier problems, but they need an answer. Moreover there is something to be said for the plan of "reading our history backwards as well as forwards, of making sure of our middle ages before we talk about the 'archaic,' of accustoming our eyes to the twilight before we go out into the night[1]"; and it may be that our attempts, however partial and imperfect, at answering these questions will be found to throw light at any rate on one other question: 'What was the cause of the break-up of the kindreds?' This question, however, like the previous ones, is seldom asked. Conquest, Roman law, Christianity are usually considered to combine into so powerful a solvent that the attitude of historians is rather one of wonder that tribal custom should have survived them at all.

Before we proceed further it is necessary to define our terms. 'Clan' may fitly be used to describe large groups of kindred organized on an agnatic basis, such as we find in Dithmarschen. A clan system, however, is impossible where kinship is reckoned through both parents[2], as among the overwhelming majority of the Teutonic races in historical times. Here, to use Maitland's words[3], each individual[4] is himself the trunk of an *arbor consanguinitatis*, and it is this fluctuating group which we would designate by the word 'kindred.' It is a *wechselnde Sippe* rather than a gens, for it can have no name, no permanent organization, and no chief.

We must next consider what we shall regard as satisfactory evidence for the solidarity of the kindred. And here we shall do well to make quite sure what we mean. When we speak of the solidarity of kindreds in early or mediaeval times, we mean

---

[1] Maitland, *Domesday Book and Beyond*, p. 356.
[2] It is true that Welsh and Irish laws give some share of *wergild* to the relatives of the mother, but the whole organization of their groups of kinsmen in war is pre-eminently agnatic, as are also the laws of inheritance. The fact that kinship through the mother was recognized in ancient Rome in no way alters the fact that the *gens* is an agnatic organization.
[3] Pollock and Maitland, *Hist. of Eng. Law*, II. p. 238.
[4] Or rather each group of brothers and sisters.

something definitely more than the solidarity frequently exhibited among kinsmen of to-day. It is obvious that kinship-solidarity is often a considerable motive force in modern social conditions. It is not unknown, for instance, that a man in a position of influence should use that influence to press the claims of a nephew, or a cousin, or even, less ardently perhaps, of a second cousin; nor is it out of the range of our modern experience that the family of some delinquent should make great and not always entirely unsuccessful efforts to hush up the criminal action of a relative, even to the extent of straining every nerve to produce the sum for which a ne'er-do-well kinsman has forged a cheque. And it is still customary for relatives to act as guardians and trustees for minors, and to interest themselves in marriage settlements and so forth. This degree of solidarity exists to-day in all Teutonic countries, though perhaps least in our own. But when we speak of the 'kindreds' of earlier times, we imply, by the mere use of that comprehensive term, something more than this. We imply that not only do individual kinsmen act on occasion so as to further a kinsman's prospects or shield him from a penalty, but that this kinsman becomes the centre of a united group of kindred, who act on his behalf, partly perhaps because they have his prospects at heart, but mainly because public opinion, the law, and their own views of life, make them guilty with him, and almost equally liable to penalty; or, in the event of his death by violence, throw the responsibility for vengeance or satisfaction upon the whole group, not only on a few near kinsmen. Apparently the Teutonic kindred is not a corporation in the technical sense of that term[1], for it is not permanently organized, and each time that it organizes itself its centre, and therefore its circumference, varies; but nevertheless it is this *corporate* aspect of the kindred which really differentiates the kinship-solidarity of the past from that of to-day. Thus if we are to treat of kindreds, we must bear in mind that we mean something *more* than present-day society exhibits, and we must therefore resolutely dismiss, as affording no evidence, all manifestations of solidarity among kinsfolk which do not show this corporate character to a greater or less extent. It has been

---

[1] For the contrary view see Gierke, *Genossenschaftsrecht*, I. pp. 17 ff.

necessary to insist on this point, because it is so often overlooked, with the result that what we should to-day call normal manifestations of kinship-solidarity are used as evidence for the existence of a real kindred system. To make our case quite clear we will take an instance. The Anglo-Saxon, in his oath of fealty to the king, has to declare that he will not conceal breaches of the oath by his brother or near kinsman any more than those committed by a stranger[1]. Now to this day it is much less likely that a man will publish a serious lapse on the part of his brother or relative than if the delinquent were a stranger; and therefore we consider this passage (which moreover entirely lacks any sign of the corporate idea of the kindred) as revealing no more sign of the solidarity of the kindred than exists to-day. Yet the greatest living authority on Anglo-Saxon law thinks it worth while to quote this passage in his summary on the kindred[2], and to observe: "Das Sippenband droht die Staatspflicht zu ersticken[3]."

I. *Guardianship by Kinsmen.* For the reason just stated we shall be chary of attributing much value, as evidence for our purposes, to provisions in the laws vaguely assigning the charge of minors and so forth to the care of kinsmen. Here we cannot do better than quote Maitland on the clauses in the Anglo-Saxon laws concerning guardianship by kinsmen. These texts, he says, "do not authorize us to call up the vision of a *mægð*[4] [kindred] acting as guardian by means of some council of elders; the persons who would inherit if the child died may well be the custodians of the ancestral property. When Bracton, f. 87 b, says that an infant sokeman is *sub custodia consanguineorum suorum propinquorum*, we do not see a family council; why should we then see one when a similar phrase occurs in an Anglo-Saxon doom[5]?" It is only when we find the distant kinsmen's participation actually vouched for, as in Holland[6],

---

[1] III. Eadmund, 1.
[2] Liebermann, *Gesetze der Angelsachsen*, II. 2, s.v. *Sippe*, 6 a.
[3] Ib. s.v. *Königstreue*, 7 b.
[4] As a matter of fact the passages to which he refers (Hloth. and Ead. 6, Ine 38) do not use the word 'kindred.'
[5] Pollock and Maitland, *Hist. of Eng. Law*, II. p. 242.
[6] See below, ch. v.

that we can consent to see any evidence for the solidarity of the kin in such cases.

II. *Use of the word 'kindred.'* This leads us to a further point. The mere use, in the sources, of a word whose original meaning is 'kindred' must not be taken as evidence in itself for the existence of large groups of kinsfolk. Legal documents are conservative, and if custom prescribes the use of the word 'kindred' in a reconciliation-formula or elsewhere, it will continue to be used even though the kinsmen concerned include only the immediate family. An amusing instance of this occurs in the account of a Danish slaying-suit of 1630, in which reference is made to a deed of reconciliation between the slayer and the dead man's 'kindred[1].' We conjure up a vision of a large group of relatives, but the document goes on to say, without any sense of incongruity—"namely, Peder Trulsen of Sandby[2]." Many more instances of the same type could be adduced, but this example should be sufficient to warn us against building on the occurrence of a word meaning 'kindred,' unless some indication is given of the extent of that kindred. This caution seems all the more necessary when we reflect that in most Teutonic languages the word for 'kindred' has also to do duty for 'family' until a very late date, so that it is unsafe to assume that it invariably refers to the larger group.

III. *Consent of kin in marriage.* For the same reason we dismiss clauses providing vaguely for the consent of kin in marriage negotiations: we do not know, without further evidence, that this means very much more than the approval of the immediate family.

IV. *Tenure of land.* All restrictions of ancestral land to persons belonging to the kin are of interest as survivals of tribal ideas, but their actual tribal significance is negligible, little greater than that of the English entail, for the only evidence such laws usually afford is of the importance of descent.

---

[1] "dend dødis slegt."
[2] *Herredags Dombog* (Rigsarkiv in Copenhagen), Anno 1630, No. 33, 19 June, ff. 263-6.

If we now pass on to more convincing manifestations of kindred-cohesion, we shall see that these possess the distinguishing characteristic that the kindred appears as a group, not as a haphazard collection of individuals.

V. *Wergilds.* There can be no doubt that wergilds are an admirable criterion for judging of the solidarity of the kindred. It is clear that if every relative of a slayer, up to his second or third cousins, actually pays a sum in proportion to the degree of his relationship with the culprit, the solidarity of the kin cannot be called in question. And this is, as we shall see, very frequently the case. But when we find that the slayer alone is liable, or primarily liable, for the wergild, and payment is made vaguely to the 'kinsmen of the slain,' we shall do well to doubt whether such evidence indicates any real degree of kinship-solidarity. The phrase 'kinsmen of the slain' tends to suggest the idea of kindreds, but of course it is obvious that it must be used, however small the number of recipients may be, since the slain man cannot himself receive wergild—a point which is sometimes overlooked.

VI. *Blood-vengeance.* Organized blood-feuds, in which definite groups of kindred take part, show of course considerable cohesion of the kindred. But it is necessary to make a distinction between these and mere acts of blood-vengeance. Though the blood-feud between kindreds, unappeasable by any compensation, actually dates from an earlier stage of tribal society than wergild, mere acts of blood-vengeance by an individual may sometimes be even a sign of the breaking-up of the kindred, showing that though this primary duty is still acknowledged, the injured kinsmen have not sufficient solidarity to act together in a body and secure their just rights. The exercise of blood-vengeance by a near relative, though obviously a survival of tribal ideas, affords no proof that the kindred has not been narrowed down to something more like the modern family.

VII. *Oath-helpers of the kindred.* The system of oath-helpers of the kindred is well fitted to afford a criterion of kin-solidarity. This seems originally to have been entirely an affair within the kindred. The most common form of the institution is the oath of compurgation : the defendant in a case is required to clear himself of the accusation against him by an oath, and a certain number of his kindred have to swear with him, in order, apparently, that they shall be involved in the consequences of perjury if the accused is lying. At least the custom is thought to have originated in some such characteristically tribal idea. Where we find a considerable number of kindred required to take this oath, we may fairly assume some degree of solidarity among them.

VIII. *Maintenance of paupers.* Laws regulating the responsibility of kinsmen towards their pauper relatives can be divided into two classes : (1) where the liability extends to the whole kindred, the degree of relationship determining the contribution of each kinsman, and (2) where the maintenance of the pauper falls upon the nearest relative who has the means to support him. The former case exhibits strong tribal solidarity : the latter, where the liability is not corporate, differs after all only in degree from the moral responsibility attaching to relatives in the modern code of ethics.

IX. *a. Repudiation by the kindred.* It is perhaps paradoxical that a satisfactory proof of the solidarity of the kindred should be afforded by the formal repudiation, by the whole kindred, of an offending member. Yet it is clear that there would be no object in such a public repudiation unless membership of the kindred was a definite and acknowledged fact, involving the kindred in responsibilities.

b. Renunciation of the kindred. Conversely, it may be termed good evidence for cohesive kindreds if we find measures taken to allow an individual to renounce his membership of a kindred, if he should find that his responsibilities towards it are too heavy for him to bear.

Having decided what to look for, we must now make up our minds where to look. And here we must definitely part company with the seekers after origins. The ancient customary laws—English, Continental, Scandinavian, have long been recognized as the best place to seek for the remains of the tribal system, for it often happens that the laws of a country may preserve for centuries some *caput mortuum*, some archaic fragment of a tribal way of life, much as the chalk preserves the fossil, a scrap of wreckage from an earlier world, often meaningless save to those who hold the clue. But for this very reason, that the existence of a law can never be taken as safe evidence for the actual continuance of a custom, we shall do well to depend on other evidence as far as possible. Even in modern times laws remain on the statute-book which practice has abrogated centuries ago[1], and in ancient times law is almost as conservative as religious ritual[2], a fact which must always be borne in mind by those who wish to ascertain the actual conditions of a given period.

Laws are misleading in various ways. The local customary laws mislead by clinging to antiquated formulae, and quite often by omitting to incorporate a royal edict bearing on one of their clauses, even when it is actually in force in the district. Royal edicts, again, are misleading in the other direction, often emphatically annulling an old law which nevertheless continues to be practically valid, sometimes for centuries after its official repeal. Sometimes we can arrive at an approximate idea of the actual conditions by comparing a series of royal edicts or noting how often some clause is repeated in successive reigns. But for our purposes the most satisfactory form of legal monument is a customary law committed to writing or edited by a responsible official, who is consciously aiming at setting down actual custom, as for instance the sieur de Beaumanoir, for Northern France, or Ghis l'escrinewerkere of St Omer, or the town clerk of Briel, Jan

---

[1] Cp. Maitland, *Coll. Pap.* vol. III. pp. 3 f.

[2] It would be interesting to investigate how obsolete laws do perish in early times, especially when, as in Iceland and probably all over Teutonic Europe, some person is charged to repeat the law, verbally and unaltered, in the course of every three years or so. Even the Icelandic Sagas, with their strong interest in legal matters, give us no hint how a law could be annulled, though we hear of the passing of a clause to restrict the operation of a law (women no longer allowed to be plaintiffs in slaying-suits). Even in modern times, popular memory will sometimes cling for a long period to a law which has been repealed or fallen into desuetude, cp. Gomme, *Folk-lore as an hist. science*, pp. 196 f.

INTRODUCTION 9

Matthijssen. Both these last adduce cases in which the law, as they state it, has been actually applied in recent years. For their own period—but not, in spite of re-issues, for later times—their evidence is to be considered trustworthy. But where such evidence is lacking, we must turn to other sources, and it is here that the difficulties of our task become apparent. For the seekers after origins the laws are the best possible source, and they find these ready to hand in accessible editions. But we must rely, where we can find them, on contemporary literature, on the records of local courts, on registers of fines, on deeds of reconciliation and the like, and these are not always very accessible. As regards our first section, Iceland, we are indeed well provided with sources of the first-named class, and have little reason to lament the absence of other documents. In Norway, a number of wergild-receipts are available in printed form, and some of the Court records of the 16th century have been published. Sweden is publishing collections of charters in chronological order, but has so far only reached the first half of the 15th century. Recently a very small selection of Court records of the year 1608 has been published, but it is to be feared that most protocols of this kind are of too late a date to throw much light on our problem. Denmark has been fully alive to the value of her earlier judicial records, and has published several volumes of cases from the High Court; but little has so far been done with a view to making the records of local Courts available; and the example of Stemann, who edited extracts from the records of the rural jurisdictions of Schleswig, has not yet been followed. In Holland and Belgium much material of importance has been made accessible in various forms. But in Germany, though German scholars have edited and re-edited not only their own early laws but also ours, almost nothing has been done towards rendering accessible the material relative to the actual administration of justice, stored in innumerable bulky volumes in provincial archives. There can be little doubt that, in the North, these would be found to throw much light on kinship solidarity. Not only are they unpublished, however, but their contents are not indexed, and it would need the labour of a lifetime to extract from them sufficient material for more than a tentative treatment of the subject. The sketch contained in the present work is little more than a declaration of *non possumus*, and a similar admission must be made with regard to France, though in this case the shortcomings are partly due to the actual lack of material. For England, thanks to the two monumental editions of the Anglo-Saxon laws, and to the labours of Kemble and Birch, almost all the extant evidence is available in printed form.

In the following pages we attempt to trace the varying fate of the kindreds in the various Teutonic countries. Our survey, however, does not include those parts of Europe which were originally, or for a time, Teutonic, but were overrun during the Middle Ages by other peoples.

The plan followed in every chapter is more or less the same: a preliminary discussion of the laws, followed by an examination of such other evidence as has been available. At the end of the book, Appendix II. gives such longer excerpts from the sources as serve to illustrate the main theme.

CHAPTER I

ICELAND

IN selecting Iceland as the first of these studies, we are guided not so much by the prevalent opinion that Icelandic society rested on a basis of kindreds, as by the fact that a great wealth of sources is at the disposal of the student, so that it is possible to control the evidence afforded by the laws.

Besides Landnámabók, the Book of the Settlement, and the more or less historical Sagas, which deal with the lives of petty chiefs and landowners up to the middle of the 11th century, there is the group of later Sagas, known as the Sturlunga, which affords a contemporary view of Iceland for the greater part of the 13th century. From a study of Landnáma in conjunction with the Sagas a great store of genealogical information can be deduced, which we shall find of great value in estimating the solidarity of the kindreds. Both Sturlunga and the other Sagas abound in references to the laws, and we are fortunate in possessing some private person's collection of the whole body of Icelandic law, known as Grágás.

The main justification for the view which regards Iceland as almost a federation of kindreds is to be found in the section of the laws dealing with the division of wergild, entitled Baugatal[1], which all scholars agree in regarding as the oldest part of the laws[2], as indeed its archaic style testifies. It is probably unchanged since 930, when Úlfljót brought the laws to Iceland.

In Baugatal the wergild as a whole is called *bætr*, compensation (pl.), or *sakar-bætr*, compensation for [slaying-]suit, or

---
[1] Grág. I. pp. 193—207.
[2] B. M. Ólsen, *Um silfurverð og vaðmálsverð*, Skírnir, 1900, p. 6.

niðgjǫld, 'kindred payments,' and it is divided into three main parts: (1) the *baugr*, to near kinsmen, (2) payments to a wider circle of kindred, (3) payments to 'increasers of fines,' *sakaukar*. Agnatic Baug-recipients also get an extra payment, called *Baugþak*.

I. *Baug*.

		Baug (aurar).	Baugþak (aurar).
(1)	For father, son [or only unmarried daughter] and brother of the slain (3 mks.[1] =)	24 +	6
(2)	Grandfathers and grandsons	20 +	4
(3)	Uncles and nephews	16 +	3
(4)	Male first cousins	12 +	2
	"Here end the baugar."	72 +	15
		(i.e. 87 aurar)[2].	

II.

		Örtugar.
(1)	Male 1st cousins once removed (1 mk =)	24
(2)	„ 2nd cousins (5 aurar, 1 örtug =)	16
(3)	„ „ „ once removed (3½ aur.)	10½
(4)	„ 3rd cousins (2 aurar, 1 örtug)	7
(5)	„ „ „ once removed (1½ aurar)	4½
(6)	„ 4th cousins (1 eyrir)	3
		65
	(i.e. 21 aurar, 2 örtugar).	

III. Increasers of fines:
   (*a*) Illegitimate son, or son by thrall-woman.
   (*b*) Stepson.
   (*c*) Stepfather.
   (*d*) Son-in-law.
   (*e*) Brother-in-law.

                                12 aurar, 5 penningar.

	aur.	ört.	pen.
Totals	87		
	21	2	
	12		5
	120	2	5

---

[1] 3 örtugar = 1 eyrir (ounce, pl. aurar); 8 aurar = 1 mark.
[2] In this table the *þveiti* (doits), which are evidently of infinitesimal value, are omitted.

Excluding the örtugar and penningar we thus get a total of the old 'hundred' (120) of aurar. Each class pays to the corresponding class of the opposite side, thus the father, son and brother of the slayer pay to the corresponding kinsmen of the slain. It is to be observed that the slayer pays nothing, the assumption being that he was exiled and his goods forfeited. The kinsmen through females pay and receive one-fifth less than the agnates, and the agnates alone are concerned in the *baugþak*.

There are a great many regulations as to what is to happen if one class of recipients or payers does not exist. Roughly we may say that even if only one of the baug-*payers* exists, the payment of all four baugar devolves on him alone, but with certain reductions. If, on the other hand, there are no other legal *recipients*, the baug payment would be reduced to 63 aurar, including *baugþak*, instead of 87, thus reducing the total to 96 aurar instead of 120.

The outer circle payments (II.) are *per stirpes*, not *per capita*, and if any class of payers is non-existent, the class more remote pays the missing share, less a third, as well as its own. However there is nothing to show that any class could be responsible for more than one of the others, and supposing classes 2—6 were all non-existent, the total paid by II. would presumably be reduced to $13\frac{1}{3}$ aurar instead of $21\frac{2}{3}$.

The reciprocal payments seem to indicate a meeting of both kindreds, but there is no provision to ensure that all the kin pay their share, and no penalty mentioned if they omit to do so.

If we compare these regulations with Saga wergilds the result is somewhat baffling. According to Baugatal the maximum wergild, only paid if all classes of relatives exist, is 120 aurar, but this maximum may be reduced to as little as 90 aurar by the absence of grandfathers and grandsons and of all cousins more remote than second cousins once removed. In view of these facts, it is surprising to find that the only wergild mentioned in the Sagas is a *fixed* sum, viz. a 'hundred of silver,' which may well represent 120 aurar[1]; and that in the whole of the Saga literature we never come across this sum diminished by the

---
[1] See Appendix I.

absence of any class of kinsmen[1]. This is remarkable enough, but it is still more remarkable that we never hear of any division of wergild, on Baugatal lines, between various classes of kindred, nor of any dispute about wergild shares, either between kinsmen of the two opposing parties, or among the recipients or payers themselves. Kinsmen are ready enough to quarrel with one another, as we shall presently show, but there is not even a hint of a dispute about the division of wergild in any Saga, though one would have supposed that its arbitrary amount, fixed without respect to the existence or non-existence of classes of payers or payees, would have been a source of endless friction, if indeed it could ever have been exacted. Not a single quarrel in all the range of Icelandic literature turns on the division of wergild, though, as we shall see later, such disputes were common in other countries where the wergild was paid to the kindred. This absence of dispute as to the division of wergild might possibly be attributed to the extraordinary solidarity of the kindred, save for the enormous proportion of quarrels between relatives, on other points, mentioned in the Sagas. We often find that persons who should be receiving wergild, as relatives of the slain, had been in the fight on the side of the slayer, or that kinsmen of the slayer, who should help to pay his wergild, had been on the opposite side in the battle. In view of the large number of such cases, adduced below, and of the entire absence of any question as to the distribution of wergild in the sequel, the argument *ex silentio* becomes very strong indeed. The following instances may suffice:

[1] Professor Björn Ólsen, in a very interesting paper in the *Árbók hins ísl. fornleifafélags* for 1910, attempts to meet this difficulty (which he is the first to see), by distinguishing between *manngjöld*, the compensation paid for slaying, which we hear of in the Sagas, and *niðgjöld*, as described in Baugatal. He considers the former to consist of *réttr*, a fine of six marks, plus a payment made by the slayer to the plaintiff to avert outlawry; while each relative secured his share of *niðgjöld* by his own exertions. Apart from the fact that such individual action on the part of each relative involves grave difficulties, and is found nowhere else in Teutonic territory, this theory is open to two main objections: (1) the absence of any mention whatever of *niðgjöld* in the Sagas in spite of the number of individuals who would be concerned, and (2) the payment in lieu of outlawry would, as Prof. Ólsen himself remarks, vary according to the wealth of the slayer, so that the fixed *manngjöld* remains as inexplicable as ever.

In the West:

Harðar Saga is chiefly concerned with the enmity between Hörð and his uncle Torfi, and then with Hörð's strife with his brothers-in-law, who finally lure him to his death.

Bjarnar Saga hitdælakappa. Thorsteinn Kuggason makes friends witn Björn, and they agree that whichever of them survives the other shall take compensation for the other's slaying (ch. 29). Now it is already certain that if Björn falls it will be at the hands of his deadly enemy, Thórð Kolbeinsson, and so it turns out. Thórð is Thorsteinn's third cousin[1], but nevertheless Thorsteinn is the most eager of all against Thórð, and presumably takes his share of the enormous compensation extracted from him.

Eyrbyggja Saga. In ch. 24, Víga-Stýrr, third cousin once removed of Thórd gellir's sons[2], supports their slayer, Eirík rauði, against their surviving brothers. In ch. 44 Víga-Stýrr is on the opposite side to his son-in-law Snorri in a battle in which Snorri's son, Víga-Stýrr's grandson, was mortally wounded.

Laxdæla Saga is a well-known instance of feuds within the family. They begin with Höskuld's quarrel with his half-brother Hrút, in which four of the former's house-carles are killed. An actual encounter between the half-brothers is only averted by Höskuld's wife (ch. 19), who points out that Hrút would hardly be so bold if he were not sure of the support of Thórð gellir, Höskuld's first cousin[3]. Later (ch. 49) Bolli Thorleiksson kills his first cousin and foster-brother Kjartan Óláfsson: his brothers-in-law, the sons of Ósvíf (themselves fourth cousins of Kjartan[4]), are the instigators of the crime and force Bolli to carry it out. Kjartan's father Óláf gets the sons of Ósvíf outlawed, but cannot find it in his heart to outlaw Bolli, his foster-son and nephew, and asks him to pay compensation. But Bolli's payment is in vain, for a few chapters later (ch. 55) the sons of Óláf attack him (he is their first cousin) and he is killed by one of their followers, Helgi Harðbeinsson. In ch. 61 Helgi's brother-in-law Thorsteinn is intimidated by Thorgils Hölluson into joining a party which attacks and kills Helgi Harðbeinsson; and (ch. 67) Thorgils *and Thorsteinn* pay compensation. Thorsteinn paid two-thirds of the sum to Helgi's sons (his own nephews) and Thorgils paid the remaining third.

Gísla Saga. To avenge Vésteinn, his brother-in-law and sworn foster-

---

[1] Thorsteinn's great-grandfather, Óláf feilan, was brother of Thórð's great-grandmother Thórhild, *d.* of Thorsteinn rauð.

[2] Ketill flatnef ⟨ Auð—Thorsteinn rauð—Óláf feilan—Thórð gellir / Björn austræni—Kjallak—Thórgrím—Víga-Stýrr.

[3] Höskuld's mother Thorgerð was sister of Óláf feilan, Thórð gellir's father.

[4] Ketill flatnef ⟨ Auð—Thorsteinn rauðr—Thorgerð—Óláf pái—Kjartan / Björn austræni—Óttarr—Helgi—Ósvíf—sons of Ósvíf.

brother, Gísli secretly slays Thorgrím, the husband of his sister[1]. This sister eventually tells her second husband, Börk, Thorgrím's brother, that her brother Gísli was the slayer of his brother Thorgrím, and Gísli is outlawed. Twelve years pass, and Börk at last offers Eyjólf grái, who lives near Gísli's hiding-place, three 'hundreds' of silver (i.e. three whole wergilds) to slay Gísli. Now Eyjólf is first cousin to the slain Thorgrím[2], yet he took no action until bribed to do so. He does however kill Gísli, and then Gísli's sister, Börk's wife, wounds him in revenge for her brother. Börk offers him 'self-doom' for the wound, and he awards himself a full wergild, which Börk pays. They are first cousins[3]. The story ends (ch. 28) with the slaying of Thorkell, Gísli's brother, by Berg, Gísli's nephew, in revenge for his father Vésteinn's death, to which Thorkell had been a party. Whereupon Ari, another of Gísli's brothers, kills Berg.

North :

Vatsdæla Saga. Geirmund, son of the settler Sæmund, is bribed to give up his first cousin Hrolleif (ch. 25). In ch. 29 Már fights with his first cousins the sons of Ingimund.

Ljósvetninga Saga begins with a fight in which Thorgeirr goði is on one side and his son on the other: the son is wounded. In ch. 20 Guðmund ríki wants to burn a house with its inhabitants: he is not deterred by finding that his wife is in the house and refuses to come out, and he only abandons his intention when his son is also found to be within. In ch. 24, in a fight between Eyjólf Guðmundarson and Thorvarð Thorgeirsson, we find Starri is with Thorvarð, his first cousin once removed[4], although he is husband of Eyjólf's niece[5].

Víga-Glúms Saga hardly contains a fight which is not between relatives. Víga-Glúm begins by killing Sigmund, whose sister had married Víga-Glúm's brother (ch. 8). Thórarinn, brother of Sigmund's widow, sues Glúm for the slaying, though he is his second cousin[6] (ch. 9). The boy Arngrím kills his first cousin Steinólf (ch. 21). Víga-Glúm himself kills his second cousin Thorvald krók[7] (ch. 23) and is sued for the slaying by the chief Einarr Thveræing

---

[1] Ari   Thórdís   Thorkell   Gísli = Auð   Vésteinn
         m. (1) Thorgrím |
             (2) Börk   Berg.

[2] Thorgrím's mother Thóra is sister of Thórð gellir, Eyjólf's father.
[3] See 2. Thorgrím and Börk are brothers.
[4] Thorgeirr goði ⟨ Höskuld—Thorvarð
                    Tjörvi—Thorgerð—Starri.
[5] Herdís d. of Halldórr, Eyjólf's brother.
[6] Helgi magri ⟨ Ingjald—Eyjólf—Víga-Glúm.
                  Helga—Thórir—Thórarinn.
[7] Thorvald krók is Thórarinn's brother. See preceding note.

(ch. 25), who is second cousin once removed both to the slayer and to the slain[1]. Víga-Glúm's nephew wounds Guðmund ríki, his second cousin twice removed[2] (ch. 27). Landnáma (p. 252) adds one more to these slayings. Thorvald of Hagi murders Grím, his first cousin. Einarr Thveræing was plaintiff in the slaying-suit, which was defended by Víga-Glúm (Einarr's second cousin once removed[1]) and by his son Már, Thorvald's stepfather. Einarr had previously helped in the suit against Víga-Glúm on account of the slaying of Bárd by Glúm's son Vigfúss (ch. 19), and had been aided by Thórarinn Esphæling, Glúm's second cousin[3].

East:

The men of the East have sometimes been credited with being less quarrelsome than the rest of their countrymen, but their Sagas are by no means free from slayings and quarrels within the limits of the kindred:

Vápnfirðinga Saga. It seems that Geitir kills Broddhelgi (ch. 13, there is a lacuna in the Saga). Broddhelgi had married Geitir's sister, but had sent her away when she became ill. Bjarni, Broddhelgi's son, Geitir's nephew, first gets a wergild from Geitir, but finally kills him.

Droplaugarsona Saga. Grím is outlawed for the slaying of Helgi Ásbjarnarson. Grím's first cousin Thorkell spak takes money from Grím's enemies to betray his hiding-place (ch. 14).

Gunnars Saga Thiðrandabana. Thiðrandi, nephew of Ketill of Njarðvík, joins an expedition with one Thórir Englandsfari to declare a suit against a house-carle of Ketill's. As usual on such occasions, a fight ensues, in which Thórir, Thiðrandi's companion, kills Ketill, and Thiðrandi is killed by a guest of his uncle's. Helgi Ásbjarnarson keeps the slayer of Thiðrandi in hiding, and his wife, though first cousin of Thiðrandi, refuses to let her brother get at her husband's protégé.

South:

Njálssaga. In the great attack on Gunnarr of Hliðarendi (ch. 77) we find Eilíf auðgi on the side of the attackers. Gunnarr wounds him, but they are first cousins or first cousins once removed[4]. In ch. 130 Flosi talks of killing his niece's husband, Ingjald of Keldar, for refusing to join in the attack on Bergthórshváll. Flosi actually sends a spear at him across the river, and

---

[1] Helgi magri ⎰ Helga—Einarr—Eyjólf—Einarr Thveræing
⎱ Ingjald—Eyjólf—Víga-Glúm
⎰ Ingunn—Thórir—Thorvald krók.

[2] See preceding note. Guðmund ríki is Einarr Thveræing's brother.

[3] See note 6 on preceding page.

[4] Sighvat rauði ⎰ (Sigmund, Sigfús Nj.)—Rannveig—Gunnarr
⎱ Thorgerð—Eilíf auðgi.

The link Sigmund or Sigfúss is omitted in certain MSS. See Lehmann and Schnorr v. Carolsfeld, *Die Njálssage*, pp. 179—180.

Ingjald returns it, killing Thorsteinn Kolbeinsson, his wife's first cousin. The irony of the situation, though the Saga writer does not perceive it, lies in the fact that Flosi is actually more nearly connected with Ingjald than with the Höskuld whom he is avenging by his attack on Bergthórshvóll[1].

In all these cases it would seem impossible that the whole kindred, or even the greater part of it, should pay or receive wergild, and one would expect that a multitude of delicate questions would crop up, dealing with the right to wergild, or its forfeiture, among the near relatives of the opposing kinsmen, if indeed any custom approaching to that detailed in Baugatal was actually in force. Yet there is never a word of such a dispute. The ancient custom that there is no wergild and no vengeance for a slaying within the kindred[2] is obviously in entire abeyance.

We have already seen that in Baugatal the slayer is not expected to pay any share of the wergild, the assumption being that he was outlawed and therefore without property. But as a matter of fact it is seldom the case in Iceland that a man of any importance is really outlawed or his property really confiscated for a slaying[3]. The suit is seldom pushed to its legal termination, the settlement of differences being almost always finally adjusted outside the courts, and in such cases outlawry, or rather banishment for three years, is generally reserved for persons of minor importance. As regards the leader and instigator, the fines are his sole punishment. In this case it is natural that he should pay something of the wergild, but Baugatal hardly prepares us to find that he should pay it all. Yet this is frequently stated to be the case:

Eyrbyggja Saga, ch. 26, tells us that Snorri goði with six others kills Vigfúss of Drápuhlið. With great difficulty his widow induces her stepmother's brother to take up the suit: there is a settlement at the *Thing* with large fines, and "*Snorri paid up the money*[4]."

Laxdæla, ch. 67. Thorsteinn and Thorgils, the slayers of Helgi Harðbeinsson, pay the compensation for his slaying: Thorsteinn paid two-thirds

---

[1] Ingjald had married Thraslaug, daughter of Flosi's brother Egill. Höskuld Thráinsson had married Hildigunn, daughter of Flosi's *half*-brother Starkað.

[2] Cp. Seebohm, *Tribal Custom in A.S. Law*, pp. 63-4.

[3] See the cases adduced by Heusler, *Strafrecht der Isländersagas*, pp. 131 ff. He has not however distinguished between slayers of very different social standing.

[4] Ch. 27, "enn Snorri galt fé upp."

and Thorgils one-third[1]. The sole liability of slayers seems also to be suggested in ch. 71. Halldórr and his brothers have slain Bolli (ch. 55), and when Bolli's sons get older they claim compensation. Halldórr says : "I will agree, if that is the will of my brothers, to pay money for the slaying of Bolli"; but stipulates that there shall be no outlawry, and that he shall not have to give up his *goðorð* (chieftainship[2]). Money was paid at the Thórsnessthing. In ch. 75 Thorsteinn Kuggason wants to buy Hjarðarholt, Halldórr's farm, observing that Halldórr has little movable property (cattle and the like) "since *he paid bætr for their father to the sons of Bolli*[3]."

Hávarðar Saga. Thorbjörn Thjóðreksson has killed Óláf, son of Hávarð, on no provocation. Thorbjörn's brother-in-law, a just man, is shocked at the tale, and forces Thorbjörn to compensate Hávarð with three '*manngjöld*' (wergilds), observing that he could not award as much as Thorbjörn deserved "because thou hast not got it[4]"; so he says he will pay one of the three sums himself (ch. 7). Thorbjörn is to pay on the spot : he manages to produce one *manngjöld*, and declares it is all he has with him[5].

Grettissaga. In ch. 12 Flosi Eiríksson and his men fight the men of Kaldbak, a stranded whale affording not only the *casus* but also the *locus belli*, as well as many of the weapons. Flosi and his party are made *sekir* (banished for three years). Flosi "then became very short of money, because *he wished to pay the compensations himself alone*[6]"—i.e. for his men as well as for himself.

In ch. 43 Atli and Grím (the brother of Atli's brother-in-law) kill two sons of Thórir of Skarð. Peace is made, and "*Atli would alone pay the compensations*[7]" (i.e. without help from Grím).

In *Vallaljóts Saga* Hrólf kills Thorvarð. Money is paid. Björn, Thorvarð's brother, and his men kill Böðvarr, a brother of Hrólf, and three others, losing two men themselves. A settlement is made, and the slayings are equated, but in addition "*Björn shall pay a 'hundred,'* and be quit therewith[8]."

Ljósvetninga Saga. Guðmund ríki kills Thorkell hák (ch. 19). Thorkell's

---

[1] "Galt Þorsteinn tvá hluti bóta vígsins, enn Þorgils skyldi gjalda þriðjung, ok skyldi gjalda á þingi."

[2] "Þessu vil ek játta, ef Þat er vili bræðra minna, at gjalda fé fyrir víg Bolla, ...enn undan vil ek skilja sektir allar ok svá goðorð mitt, svá staðfestu; slíkt et sama Þær staðfestur, er bræðr mínir búa á."

[3] " 'hann hefir lítit lausafé, síðan hann galt þeim Bollasonum í föðurbætr....' "

[4] " 'Eigi kann ek, Þorbjörn, at gera svá mikit fé sem vært væri, fyrir því at þú hefir eigi til.' "

[5] "Þorbjörn gat goldit ein manngjöld, ok kvað þá lokit því er hann hefði til."

[6] "Varð Flosi sekr, ok margir þeir, er at höfðu verit með honum. *Varð honum þá féskylft mjök*, því at hann vildi *einn halda upp fébótum*."

[7] Ch. 44, "Atli vildi einn halda upp fébótum."

[8] Ch. 7, "Björn skal gjalda hundrað, ok vera þar með frjáls."

brothers meet him and his foster-son Einarr, and the latter says: "Guðmund will offer you '*bætr*' and a stiff wergild (manngjöld)." The brothers agree, and "afterwards *Guðmund paid up the money*, and they were ostensibly reconciled[1]."

Víga-Glúms Saga tells how Víga-Glúm paid Ketill, the son of Thorvald krók, whom he has slain, half his farm Thverárland "as compensation for his father": the other half he was made to sell, having to leave the district[2] (ch. 26).

Flóamanna Saga[3] (ch. 34). The aged Thorgils orrabeinsstjúp kills Helgi. Two years later his brothers come home from abroad, and Thorgils offers to pay full compensation for Helgi's death. He gives to one of the brothers a sword of value, and to the other five marks (40 aurar).

Njálssaga offers a sequence of slayings between dependents, each compensated for by the master, but as we have reason to cast doubt on their probability later on (p. 26) we will not adduce them here.

In any case the above instances are sufficient to produce a strong impression that the slayer usually paid the whole wergild. As however Baugatal says nothing at all about the slayer's liability, these instances of his sole responsibility, though totally contrary to ancient custom, cannot be said to prove that Baugatal was no longer used as a guide in other cases, though the fact that wergild was constantly received and paid within the family makes us wonder how much heed could be paid to its provisions.

But when we find that one or two individuals, *not the slayers*, are often credited in the Sagas with paying the whole wergild, we can hardly avoid the conclusion that Baugatal can only reflect a past age, not the period with which we are dealing. Instances are not far to seek:

Eyrbyggja Saga, ch. 29. After Björn has slain the two sons of Thórir viðlegg, Asbrand, Björn's *father*, "ratified the settlement on behalf of his son Björn, and *paid the compensation for the slayings*, but Björn was banished for three years[4]."

---

[1] "Guðmundr vill yðr bætr bjóða, ok stinn manngjöld...síðan greiddi Guðmundr fram féit; ok váru sáttir at kalla."
[2] "Glúmr galt Þverárland, hálft Katli, syni Þorvalds, í föðurbætr, enn seldi hálft við verði."
[3] Not a very good authority.
[4] "Ásbrandr gekk til handsala fyrir Björn son sinn, ok hélt upp fébotum fyrir vígin, en Björn var sekr gerr utan um þrjá vetr."

Ch. 32. The undesirable Thórólf bægifót persuades a poor man to attempt the life of one Úlfarr, and promises "I will pay the compensation for the slaying[1]."

Bjarnar Saga hítdælakappa. The rivals Björn and Thórð agree that anyone reciting (insulting) verses by either of them could be legally slain. Björn hears Thorkell, son of Dálk, reciting one of Thórð's verses, and kills him. Thórð considered himself to blame, and compensated Dálk (ch. 20). Later on in the Saga (ch. 28), Thorsteinn Kuggason suggests that Björn should pay a little compensation for each of the men he had slain in his feud with Thórð, and that he, Thorsteinn, should make up the difference between that and full compensation (though he is third cousin to Thórð and no relation to Björn).

Fóstbræðra Saga. The foster-brothers are egged on by their hostess to kill two evil-doers who are under the protection of the chief Vermund (ch. 5). When they have succeeded she gives Vermund three 'hundreds' of silver for his 'thingmen': the brothers pay nothing.

Vatsdæla Saga. Thorkell Krafla, who however is not fully recognized by his family, slays one Glæðir. Thorkell's great uncle Thórorm, and Thordís spákona (a woman who is no relation to Thorkell) "paid all the money" (one 'hundred' of silver)[2].

Grettissaga. Atli, Grettir's brother, is killed by Thorbjörn öxnamegin. Grettir kills Thorbjörn, and Thórodd drápustúf, Thorbjörn's brother, sues him; but as Grettir is an outlaw the case falls to the ground. But Atli's nephews sue Thórodd for the slaying of Atli by Thorbjörn. "Thórodd now had to pay compensation for the slaying of Atli[3]."

Svarfdæla Saga. Gríss, the fosterer of Klaufi, pays for a thrall that Klaufi has killed (ch. 15)[4].

Reykdæla Saga (ch. 19). Skúta kills two of the men who had been concerned in the slaying of his father. Thorsteinn, Skúta's brother, "paid compensation for them out of his money, as was laid down in the agreement between the brothers[5]." In ch. 25, Skúta kills another man, Thorgeirr Thórisson, at the *thing.* His father-in-law Víga-Glúm at once paid for him a 'hundred' of silver 'there at the *thing*[6],' but Skúta is not grateful, probably considering compensation unnecessary. In ch. 29 Thorgeirr goði lies in wait for Skúta, with the result that Skúta kills one of his men. Thorsteinn, Skúta's brother, and some other person (possibly Skúta himself) paid one 'hundred' of silver[7].

---

[1] "'ek skal bótum upp halda fyrir vígit....'"
[2] Vats. 44, "Guldu þau Þórormr ok Þórdis alt féit ok skildust sáttir."
[3] Gr. 51, "Varð Þóroddr nú at lúka bætr fyrir víg Atla; var þat tvenn hundruð silfrs."
[4] "Grísi bárust bætrnar, ok galt hann sex hundruð silfrs."
[5] "bætti Þorsteinn þá, bróðir Skútu, með sínu fé, sem rætt var í máldögum með þeim bræðrum."
[6] "Glúmr galt fyrir hann hundrað silfrs þar á þinginu."
[7] "Guldu þeir Þorsteinn hundrað silfrs fyrir víg Vestmanns."

Njálssaga (ch. 12). Thorvald Ósvífsson is killed, with his wife's connivance, by her kinsman. Ósvíf asks her father, Höskuld, for compensation for his son (*sonarbætr*). The award is two 'hundreds' of silver, to be paid at once. Höskuld produces it at once[1].

In all the above cases it is a near kinsman (father, brother, father-in-law, etc.) or the instigator of the crime, who pays the wergild, but there are a number of cases in which the chief (*goði*) pays for his *thingman's* misdeeds. It is not always the case that the chief is a relative of the slayer, and even if he is, Baugatal gives no indication that a chief should pay more than his share, far less the whole sum. To quote some examples:

Thorskfirðinga Saga (ch. 14). Two men kill Thórarinn ákafi, and go to the chief Gull-Thórir for protection. Gull-Thórir pays lands of his own in compensation for the slaying of Thórarinn[2].

Hávarðar Saga. In ch. 11 Hávarð kills the slayer of his son, and is protected by "Steinthórr" (probably meant for Steingrím Eyjólfsson), a great chief, but no relation. When it comes to settlement, one '*manngjöld*' is shown to be due from Hávarð's side. "Steinthórr pays also the 'hundred' of silver which had to be paid[3]."

Grettissaga (ch. 16). Thorkell Krafla, a great chief, pays the compensation for a house-carle of his, whom Grettir had killed while under his charge[4].

Reykdæla Saga (ch. 23). Eyjólf kills Bjarni, sister's son of Víga-Glúm, and appeals to his powerful first cousin Skúta for help. The result is that the wergild for Bjarni, a 'hundred' of silver, is docked from the dowry Víga-Glúm gives his daughter on her marriage with Skúta, so that though *Skúta* does not have to disburse anything it is he who pays the wergild[5].

Ch. 30. Ölvir spaki and the sons of Thórir flatnef kill Skúta. Thórodd, a chief, called 'kinsman' of the sons of Thórir flatnef, pays the compensation together with Ölvir spaki[6].

Droplaugarsona Saga (ch. 4). Thorkell Geitisson, a chief, and first-cousin of the sons of Droplaug, pays for their slaying of a freedman[7].

Surely these instances, taken from the length and breadth of the land, and from Sagas of all degrees of trustworthiness, go far

---

[1] "'Ok skal gjalda þegar...ok leysa vel af hendi.' Höskuldr gerði svá."
[2] Between 920 and 930.
[3] Háv. ch. 22, "Steinþórr geldr ok hundrað silfrs þat er gjalda átti."
[4] Grett. 16, "þorkell...hélt upp fébótum."
[5] "skal Skúta svá heima standa hundraðit, at Glúmr gyldi því minni heimanfylguna."
[6] "Enn þeir halda upp bótum fyrir ráðin ok tilförina, þóroddr goði ok Ölvir hinn spaki...."
[7] Ch. 4, "lauk þorkell fé firir."

to prove that Baugatal was a dead letter as far as the mass of the slayer's kindred were concerned, and that in fact either the slayer himself, or some near kinsman, or the slayer's chief, actually paid the wergild. But since, in countries where the wergild system prevails, it occasionally happens that while the *slayer's* kindred has freed itself of all liability to pay wergild, the kindred of the *slain* have by no means relinquished their claim to receive it, it is necessary for us to examine the evidence of the Sagas with regard to this point also. We should almost feel justified in a negative answer based only on the argument *ex silentio*. We have already seen what a vast number of slayings within the kindred are mentioned by the Sagas. Yet there is never a hint of any quarrel as to the distribution of wergild, even when it is paid by one first cousin to another, in which case there would be many delicate points to settle as to the relations who would be precluded from receiving it owing to their close kinship with the slayer or their participation in the slaying. But fortunately there is a good deal of more definite evidence available, and we shall see that practically all of it goes to prove that the wider kindred of the slain participated no more in the wergild than did the wider kindred of the slayer.

Thus we are told that Víga-Glúm pays Ketill, son of Thorvald krók, whom he has slain, half his farm Thverárland *as compensation for his father*[1], but there is no hint that Víga-Glúm paid anything more to other kinsmen of the slain.

Similarly in *Njálssaga* (ch. 12), when Hallgerð connives at the slaying of her husband, Thorvald Ósvífsson. His father asks Höskuld, her father, for 'compensation for his son[2]'—*sonarbætr*, and there is no mention of any other compensation.

In *Reykdæla Saga* Bjarni, Víga-Glúm's sister's son, is killed by Eyjólf, who seeks help from his first cousin Skúta. It is agreed that a 'hundred' of silver shall be paid for Bjarni, and that the money is to be handed over to his *mother*, Víga-Glúm's sister[3].

In *Grettissaga* (ch. 51), Thórodd pays compensation for the slaying of Atli. Atli's nephews receive the money—but evidently not for distribution

---

[1] *föðurbætr*. See above, p. 20.
[2] Ch. 12.
[3] Ch. 23, "Bjarna skal bæta hundraði silfrs; þat skal Glúmr láta koma í hendr Þorgerði systur sinni enn móður Bjarna."

among the kindred, nor yet for themselves, for the Saga adds "and took charge of it"—evidently for the outlawed Grettir, Atli's brother[1].

The evidence that does seem to suggest compensation to more than one or two near kinsmen must now be given. The case most frequently quoted by scholars seeking to illustrate the working of the laws from the Sagas—almost the only use, from a legal point of view, to which the Sagas have hitherto been put —is that of the compensation paid for Björn hitdælakappi in the Saga of that name. We will discuss the story in full.

Before Björn's death he and his friend Thorsteinn Kuggason agree that whichever of them survives the slaying of the other shall take '*sektir ok fébætr*'—outlawry (of the slayer) and compensation—for the other *as if they were brothers* (ch. 29). It is already quite clear that if Björn is killed it will be by Thórð, who is Thorsteinn's third cousin. In ch. 30 this Thórð agrees with all his companions that whichever of them actually slays Björn, all should be bound to pay up, if money compensation is taken for him; Thórð first, then Dálk and Kálf, the two other leaders. In ch. 32 they kill Björn. In ch. 34, Ásgrím, Björn's brother, who lives in the south, seeks out Thorsteinn, and they and Björn's friends prepare the suit for the Althing. Thórð secretly makes a settlement with Ásgrím, the plaintiff, giving him three 'hundreds.' When this is discovered, Thorsteinn is very wroth, and summons the 'Mýra-men,' i.e. Skúli Thorsteinsson, who was only Björn's second cousin by blood, but a foster-brother, Björn having been brought up at his home Borg. Thorsteinn tries to quash Ásgrím's settlement, in spite of his first cousin Thorkell's opposition. (Thorkell is only third cousin of Thórð, whom he supports against Thorsteinn.) Then Thorkell suggests that Thórð should not pay more, but that Thorsteinn should claim money from the other men at the slaying. Thorsteinn objects, and it is agreed that Thórð shall be further mulcted, as well as the others. Finally Thórð is to pay, besides the three 'hundreds' he had already paid to Ásgrím, another three 'hundreds' to save himself from exile, and a third three 'hundreds' to save Kálf from exile. Twelve marks (96 aurar) is to be paid to commute the punishment of the remaining twelve men to exile instead of outlawry. Thorkell got the kinsmen of the exiled men to contribute towards helping the exiles[2], and got them sent abroad. "The 'Mýra-men' also took much money from Thórð for granting him peace, those who were kinsmen of Björn. Björn's father, with much money which he received, went to live with Thorsteinn, and Ásgrím went back to the South with that money which he had got."

---

[1] "tóku þeir Gamli féit til sín, *ok varðveittu*."
[2] "lét frænda þeira leggja fé til hjálpar þeim þangat, ok kemr þeim utan um sumarit."

So the father, brother and foster-brother (second cousin) of the slain man each got a large share, and also presumably Thorsteinn Kuggason, the third cousin of the *slayer*, a foster-brother of the slain. We cannot claim that Skúli Thorsteinsson got his share in virtue of being second cousin to the slain, for it is obvious from Thorsteinn Kuggason's case that foster-brotherhood constituted the real claim. Thorsteinn Egilsson, Skúli's father, had fostered Björn. Those who look upon this story as a confirmation of Baugatal forget the important fact that Thórð evidently thinks he will get off with one payment to the slain man's brother, and that the Mýra-men take no part in the affair until summoned by Thorsteinn Kuggason, who is no relation of Björn's. As a matter of fact, Björn had plenty of nearer relatives who play no part in the suit at all. Thus we do not hear of his first cousin, Thorfinn Arnórsson thvara[1], nor of his second cousins Thórólf and Holm-göngu-Bersi, sons of Véleif gamli[2], nor of his seven first cousins once removed, the sons of Thorgeirr[3], or their descendants. Some of these must certainly have been living at the time. The whole story proves nothing more than that foster-brothers, if sufficiently energetic and well-supported, can obtain a share of wergild.

Another case in which 'kinsmen' are mentioned occurs in Vallaljóts Saga (ch. 2). Halli has been killed. His son Bersi asks the chief Guðmund ríki, his third cousin once removed, to take over the suit, and himself goes abroad. Ch. 4: "At the althing a 'hundred' of silver was paid for the slaying of Halli." Guðmund was not content with the way things turned out, but took charge of the money for the kinsmen of Halli[4]. The word 'kinsmen' is also mentioned in Ljósvetninga Saga (ch. 28): A certain Már, suspected of having done away with a kinsman, is finally induced to repent, and give half his goods to the poor, and half to the kinsmen of the man he had done away with. With regard to these two cases it is sufficient to point out that the word 'kinsman,' *frændi*, is constantly used of son or brother, so that its use here may refer to only a very narrow circle of kinsmen[5].

It will be noticed that so far we have not dealt with most of the wergilds in Njálssaga. It is because they seem to us somewhat suspicious. The early part of the Saga (Nj. 36—45) gives a series of slayings between the houses of Gunnarr and Njáll—

---

[1] Son of Björn's father's sister.

[2] Bálki — Bersi—Arngeirr—Björn hitdælakappi
        — Geirbjörg—Véleif gamli—Holmgöngu-Bersi and Thórólf.

[3] Thorhadd — Thorgeirr—Grím í Skarði and six other sons
            — Thordís—Arngeirr—Björn hitdælakappi.

[4] "varðveitti féð til handa frændum Halla." So far as we know, Bersi was the only kinsman for whom the money needed to be 'kept.'

[5] See supra, p. 6.

three on each side—beginning with servants, but finally reaching Gunnarr's kindred.

First Hallgerð, Gunnarr's wife, bids her servant Kol kill Svart[1], a house-carle of Njáll's. Gunnarr pays 12 aurar compensation. Then Njáll's wife sends her house-carle Atli to kill Kol. Njáll pays back the same 12 aurar. Then Hallgerð gets her kinsman Brynjólf to kill Atli. Gunnarr pays a 'hundred.' Then the son of a freedman of Njáll's, Thórð, kills Brynjólf. Njáll pays a 'hundred.' Then Sigmund, a cousin of Gunnarr's, kills Thórð. Gunnarr pays two 'hundreds.' Then the sons of Njall kill Sigmund. Njáll and his sons pay two 'hundreds.' There is something so very symmetrical about this that our suspicions are aroused. Why does not some kinsman of Brynjólf's appear on the scene after Brynjólf's slaying? And why does not some nearer kinsman of Sigmund's (they are all in the district) appear to receive wergild after Sigmund's slaying? Surely only because it would spoil the symmetrical interchange of wergilds, which pleases the Saga-writer. But to proceed.

In ch. 56 Gunnarr and his brother Kolskegg make a settlement at the Althing for having killed eight persons. The slayings were compensated for according to the estimate of the worth of the slain..."and Gunnarr's kinsmen produced money so that the slayings were all paid for there at the Thing[2]." What kinsmen we do not know. In ch. 61 Gunnarr kills a number of men who attacked him, and his brother Hjört falls. These men were compensated for by "half-compensations." (Ch. 64) Njáll had much money lent out to these attackers of Gunnarr, and he gave it all to Gunnarr towards these compensations. (Njáll and Gunnarr are friends, not kinsmen.) Gunnarr had so many 'friends' (vini) at the Thing that he paid up for all the slayings at once. According to ch. 69 he seems to have paid some land which had belonged, or did belong, to his mother.

Ch. 72. After Gunnarr's next slayings Njáll produces fourteen 'hundreds' of silver, plus interest, which he had taken from Gunnarr's enemies for an attack which he had foiled, and this was as much "as Gunnarr had to pay for himself[3]."

Nj. 77. Gunnarr, now an outlaw, is at last killed.

Ch. 79. Skarpheðinn, son of Njáll, and Högni, one of Gunnarr's sons, take a considerable revenge, and make one Mörð pay all the resulting compensations as the price of his own reconciliation with them for his part in the slaying of Gunnarr. (Gunnarr's other son takes no part in this vengeance.)

Nj. 92. Skarpheðinn, son of Njáll, kills Thráinn, whose brother Ketill is married to Skarpheðinn's sister. Ketill appeals to Njáll, who bids him

---

[1] The conjunction of the names Kolr (a proper name originally meaning 'black tom-cat,' from kol, 'coal') and Svartr 'black,' itself suggests a 'faked' story.

[2] "gáfu frændr Gunnars fjé til, at þegar váru bætt upp öll vígin þar á þinginu."

"átti að gjalda fyrir sik."

induce his brothers, who have to take 'baugar[1],' to accept an amicable settlement, and urges him to meet all those "who had to take payments[2]," and make peace with them. Ketill goes to see his brothers and made them all meet at Hliðarendi, where " manngjöld " was awarded for Thráinn's slaying : "they all received compensation as the laws provided[3]." Njáll paid the money. But (ch. 98) Lýting, husband of Thráinn's sister, kills one of the sons of Njáll (Höskuld) and defends himself by saying : "Everybody knows that I have received no compensation for my brother-in-law[4]."

The wergild cannot, then, have been paid according to the directions of Baugatal, and indeed it seems only to have been received by brothers of the slain and to have been paid by the father of the slayer. There is, moreover, a mistake in the use of the word 'baugar' in ch. 92. (1) The 'baugar' extended to first cousins (see p. 12 supra) and here only brothers are mentioned as receiving them ; (2) secondly, brothers should only receive one 'baug,' not 'baugar,' unless there are no other 'baug' relatives. In this case there are first cousins[5] (not mentioned here) who would have a claim to 'baug.' (3) Thirdly, this is the only passage in the whole range of Saga literature where wergild is called 'baug' as in Baugatal, and not merely 'compensation' (*bætr*) or *manngjöld*, so that its use here seems trebly suspicious. In order to explain these discrepancies, it has been suggested[6] that the outer circle of relatives and the *sakaukar* only received payment according to Baugatal if there were no baug recipients, a hypothesis which is hardly tenable in itself, and still fails to meet the objections (1) and (2) stated above.

Njála has been accused by Lehmann and Schnorr von Carolsfeld[7] of having drawn too freely and with too little discretion on a collection of laws, in order to fill in the details of litigation in the Saga, and though Prof. Finnur Jónsson's defence of the Saga[8] has vindicated it in several points, he has not quite cleared it. Surely we are justified in adding this use of the word 'baugar' to the indictments against it.

In ch. 99 the sons of Njáll kill Lýting's two brothers : there is a settlement, and Lýting is to pay full compensation (two 'hundreds' of silver) for Höskuld.

Ch. 106, in which Lýting tells the blind Ámundi, Höskuld's illegitimate son, that he has paid full compensation for Höskuld, and that Ámundi's grandfather and uncles (Njáll and his sons) received it, and that he will not

---

[1] Nj. 92, " bræðr þína þá er bauga eiga at taka."
[2] " er gjöld áttu at taka."
[3] " tóku þeir allir við bótum sem lög stóðu til."
[4] " þat vitu allir menn, at ek hafi við engum bótum tekit eftir þráinn mág minn."
[5] Sigmund kleykir, Eilíf auðgi (sons of Önund) and Mörð gígja. There are also nephews who would be entitled to ' baug.'
[6] Arnljótr Óláfsson, " Um lögaura og silfurgang fyrrum á Íslandi," in *Tímarit hins ísl. Bókmentafélags*, 1904.
[7] *Die Njalssage insbesondere in ihren juristischen Bestandtheilen*, Berlin, 1883.
[8] *Aarbøger for nord. Oldkyndighed*, 1904, pp. 115 ff.

pay any more, whereupon Ámundi kills him, is admitted by the staunchest supporters of the Saga to be an interpolation, so we need not discuss it.

In ch. 111 the sons of Njáll are induced by slanders to kill their foster-brother Höskuld, son of Thráinn. His widow makes Ketill, uncle of the slain, promise to avenge the deed, though he is brother-in-law of the slayers. The arbitrators award six 'hundreds' of silver, half of it they are to pay themselves, though some of them are relatives of the *slain*. Njáll pays one 'hundred': his sons and son-in-law Kári another 'hundred': all those present at the Thing are said to subscribe the rest. The settlement however is not concluded, and the money is laid by.

Ch. 130. Flosi, step-uncle of the slain Höskuld's widow[1], leads an expedition agains Bergthórshváll, the home of Njáll and his sons, and sets fire to the buildings. Njáll, his wife and his sons, all perish in the flames: only Kári, Njáll's son-in-law, escapes. Ch. 145: Kári joins with Thorgeirr Skorargeirr, Njáll's father's brother[2], Thorleif krák, Njáll's first cousin, and Thorgrím mikli, brother of Thorleif[3], and with Ásgrím Elliðagrímsson, father-in-law of one of Njáll's sons. There is a great fight at the Althing, and finally a settlement is made, which Kári and Thorgeirr Skorargeirr refuse to join. It is noteworthy that the great chief Hall of Síða renounces any compensation for his son, and a general subscription, amounting to four wergilds (eight 'hundreds' of silver), is made on his behalf. Ch. 146 : Kári and Thorgeirr kill five persons ; whereupon Hall of Síða urges Flosi to come to terms with Thorgeirr, at any rate. Thorgeirr will not pay for any of these slayings, but will take his third of compensation for Njáll and his sons. This seems to presuppose that Thorgrím mikli and Thorleif krák have each had a third of the *bætr*. But according to Baugatal Thorgeirr, Njáll's father's brother, should have more wergild than the other two, who are only first cousins. Moreover the Saga never regards the fact that Njáll has other relatives, as can be seen from the following table :

```
                         Thorgeirr
      ┌──────────────────────┼──────────────────┐
  Thorgerð           Njáll ·        Álöf              Thorgerð
  m. Ketill auðgi          m. Thorberg Kornamúli    m. Finn
  ┌─────┴─────┐                 ┌──────┴──────┐         Otkelsson
  Helgi    Ásgerð           Eysteinn      Hafthóra
                                     m. Eið Skeggjason
                                     ┌──────┴──────┐
                                    Eysteinn    Illugi[4]
```

Here as elsewhere Njála's evidence is halting and inconsistent, and it is moreover totally unsupported by the wergild-

---

[1] So Njálssaga.

[2] According to Landnáma Thorgeirr is Njáll's first cousin.

[3] According to Landnáma Thorgrím mikli is Njáll's step-uncle. But see Lehmann and Schnorr v. Carolsfeld, pp. 172–5.

[4] The sons of Eið Skeggjason were fighting men at this date, but lived in the West.

cases in the other Sagas. It is best explained on the hypothesis that the author had some slight acquaintance with a wergild law resembling Baugatal, but that he had not knowledge enough to fill in the details. From all other Saga literature we are forced to the conclusion that during this period Baugatal was a dead letter, and that the wergild customs actually in force show almost no traces of any solidarity of the kindred.

We will now consider the evidence for the 12th and 13th centuries, contained in the Sturlunga group of Sagas.

Inter-family feuds reach such a pitch that any arrangement of wergilds on Baugatal lines becomes almost unthinkable.

Thus we find Guðmund dýri joining with Kolbeinn Tumason to set fire to the house of Önund Thorkelsson. With Önund perishes his son Thorfinn, who is Guðmund dýri's son-in-law[1]. The long strife between the Sturlung brothers begins when Snorri takes sides with the men of Oddi against his brother Sighvat[2]. A few chapters further on we see Sæmund, the chief of the Oddi family, standing by helpless while Björn, who was the son of one of his nieces, and had married another niece, is killed by Lopt, Sæmund's nephew[3]; and later Sæmund is much blamed for not helping the latter. What part of the enormous wergild paid for Björn can Sæmund, his great-uncle, have had? Then Snorri sues his nephew Brand Jónsson to outlawry about an old money dispute which he had had with his sister Steinun, Brand's mother[4]. Brand must have been "small friends with the rest of his kin," as the Saga says later[5] of Sverting Thorleifsson, another nephew of Snorri's; and again later[6] of another kinsman of the Sturlungs, Loðinn Sigurðarson. Then we hear how Sturla Sighvatsson attempts to blind his first cousin Órækja[7], and later again Sturla fights with another cousin, Thórleif Thórðarson, and insists on his leaving the country[8]. The battle of Örlygsstað shows Kolbeinn ungi first wounding Sighvat, his aunt's husband, as Sighvat lies exhausted on the battle-field, and finally standing by to see Kolbeinn and Thórð, Sighvat's sons, and his first cousins, killed in cold blood[9].

The Saga of the first generation of Sturlungs ends with the expedition planned by Kolbeinn ungi, Gizurr, and Árni óreiða, all once sons-in-law of Snorri, to effect his death[10]. Klæng, Snorri's stepson, is on the expedition, and Böðvarr of Stað, Snorri's first cousin, meets the slayers and agrees to keep watch on Snorri's son Órækja for them. Later he and his brother intercede

---

[1] *Sturl.* I. p. 194. The edition quoted is that of Kr. Kålund, published by the Kgl. nord. Oldskrift Selskab, Copenhagen, 1906-11.
[2] I. p. 242.   [3] I. p. 345.   [4] I. p. 392.
[5] I. p. 408.   [6] II. p. 169.   [7] I. p. 485.
[8] I. pp. 497-8.   [9] I. pp. 527, 532. [10] I. pp. 552-3.

for the life of Klæng, one of Snorri's slayers. Matters do not improve in the second volume. Kolbeinn ungi captures his first cousin Tumi Sighvatsson, and has him slain[1]. On the arrival of Thórð kakali, Tumi's brother, even those of his relatives who have offered to support him draw back[2], and Einarr Vatsfirðing and his mother, who is Thórð's first cousin, send round to bid all their neighbours join his enemy Kolbeinn[3].

Svinfellinga Saga deals with the quarrel of Sæmund Ormsson with his aunt's husband Ögmund. Sæmund's first cousins, Thorvarð and Odd, the sons of Thórarinn, join Ögmund, their uncle, whereas Teit, their first cousin once removed, joins Sæmund's party. Finally Ögmund has Sæmund and his brother Guðmund killed in cold blood[4].

In the battle of Thverár-eyri between Eyjólf and Hrafn on the one side, and Sturla and Thorgils on the other, we find Auðunn Thómasson (and probably his brothers) on the side of his third cousin Hrafn against his first cousin Thorgils and his uncle Sturla[5]. Svarthöfði Dufgússon[6] is also on Hrafn's side, but he is married to Hrafn's sister and is only second cousin of Thorgils and Sturla. The latter win the day, and have Eyjólf put to death. He is the husband of Sturla's first cousin once removed[7].

Thorvarð Thórarinsson attacks and kills his second cousin Thorgils skarði[8].

Hrafnssaga ends with the slaying of Hrafn by his first cousin once removed, Thorvald vatsfirðing[9].

That these quarrels among kindred are not limited to the chiefs is clear from incidental remarks in Sturlunga:

We are told of one Glám who kills his mother's brother Geirr[10], and of Eyjólf Rögnvaldsson, who is with Einarr Ásgrímsson in his attack on Vigfúss of Breiðabólsstað, when it turns out that Eyjólf's father is in the house which they are burning. Eyjólf bids him come out, but he declines to do so unless Vigfúss may come out too. His son cries out with an oath, "Burn then, old man," and the father presumably perishes in the flames[11]. In several of the battles kinsmen of humble rank were fighting against each other, as can be seen from the account of Haugsnes: "Eyjólf Thorsteinsson was able to capture Einarr lang his kinsman, and gave him quarter....Several men were captured there to whom quarter was given by various kinsmen or friends[12]." And before the sea-fight in Flói, when Thorð kakali offers quarter to all Eyfirðings in his enemy's fleet, the other side hurriedly silence him, because they thought it not unlikely that some who had lost kinsmen, as yet

---

[1] II. pp. 55—56. [2] II. p. 60. [3] II. p. 81.
[4] II. p. 127. [5] II. pp. 268, 270. [6] II. p. 270.
[7] II. p. 269. [8] II. p. 297.
[9] *Sturl.* ed. G. Vigfússon, Oxford. Hrafns. S. ch. 20.
[10] I. p. 536. [11] II. p. 184.
[12] II. p. 97.

uncompensated, at the previous battle, might change their minds about following Thorð's enemy Kolbeinn[1].

We must now consider who paid and received wergild in the Sturlung period.

The power of the *goðar*, already on the increase in Saga times, is now at its height, and we find that humbler folk appeal to a chief if they want help in securing wergild.

Thus on Hneitir's death his widow and children apply to Thorgils Oddason, who gives them 12 'hundreds' (of ells of wadmal) on condition that he shall keep whatever he gets out of the chief Hafliði, with whom the slayer, Hafliði's nephew, has taken refuge. Thorgils claimed 30 'hundreds': "Hafliði paid the money to Thorgils as agreed, slaying-money after Hneitir[2]."

In *Sturlu Saga* Álf applies to Sturla after the wounding of his son Bárð. Sturla sued on Bárð's behalf and claimed 25 'hundreds' as compensation for him[3]. In *Guðmundar Saga Dýra*, Hákon, Guðmund's nephew, has killed Hrafn. Guðmund, who is now a *goði*, sends for Hrafn's brother, "who had to take the slaying-suit and money compensation after Hrafn," and induces him to accept 45 'hundreds.' Guðmund paid then at once every 'eyrir' of it—partly in land[4].

There is plenty of proof that individual chiefs paid for their own misdeeds without calling on their kindred for help.

After the burning of Önund and his son by Kolbeinn and Guðmund dýri the awards for compensation for life and property amount to vast sums, including one 'hundred' of ells for each man present on the attacking side, and "Kolbeinn was to pay half that money, and pay half the compensation for Önund[5]." After the Thing "Guðmund at once began to pay the money (his share), all that he could, out of his stock, both horses and other things of value as much as he could spare, all the summer through[6]." Guðmund and Kolbeinn are however dispensed from paying the whole amount, as Thorgrím alikarl, Önund's son-in-law, who had taken the chief part in the settlement, kills several of the burners, and so breaks the peace again. Finally Thorgrím attacks Guðmund and is defeated, so has to accept Guðmund's terms: "all the offences were then paid for, and then Thorgrím was penniless withal. And all the more important of those who had been present [at the attack] paid something[7]."

---

[1] II. p. 66.   [2] I. p. 16.   [3] I. p. 103.
[4] I. p. 169.   [5] I. p. 198.
[6] I. p. 198, "tok Guðmundr þegar til at giallda fé, alt þat er hann mátti ór búi sínu. Hann galt bæði ross oc aþra gripi allt þat svmar í gegnum, sva sem hann matti af miþla."
[7] I. p. 218.

Sighvat, son of Sturla Þórðarson, kills a man. Þórð, Sighvat's brother, paid the compensation[1]. (Sighvat had not yet received his paternal inheritance, see I. p. 238.)

Kálf Guthormsson kills Hall Kleppjárnsson. Hall's brother Klæng gets 'self-doom' from Kálf, and awards 240 'hundreds.' "Kálf paid all this money[2]."

Thorvald vatsfirðing slays Hrafn. Magnús Þórðarson, Hrafn's sister's son, sues, because Hrafn's sons were too young to do so. A sum of 120 'hundreds' is awarded, of which the plaintiff, Magnús Þórðarson, is to get 30 'hundreds,' so the rest presumably goes to Hrafn's sons[3]. The minor persons implicated evidently pay nothing.

Sturla makes an award against Þórð vatsfirðing for various slayings. "Þórð paid then 110 'hundreds.' He paid a ship's hull (?)[4], a farm, the right of flotsam on two stretches of fore-shore to the amount of 18 'hundreds,' and something in gold and silver[5]."

Sturla has the Vatsfirðings Þórð and Snorri slain. "Inheritance *and compensation* after them Einarr their (half-)brother had to take, but Illugi their (illegitimate) brother was plaintiff in the suit," Einarr being a child[6].

Kolbeinn ungi demands 50 'hundreds' for the slaying of his house-carle Þórálf. Brand, who has had Þórálf killed in revenge for the slaying of Kálf (see above), paid land, which his mother-in-law offered; she was the daughter of Kálf[7].

Þórhall asks Thorleif beiskaldi, his *goði*, and Einarr Thorgilsson, another *goði*, for help against Sturla, and they suggest that they will get rid of Sturla if he, Thorhall, will pay the wergild[8].

Víga-Hauk attempts to kill Thorvald vatsfirðing, but is foiled. Afterwards it appears that Lopt and Gísli, sons of Markús, were to have paid the compensation on Hauk's behalf, if he had been successful[9]. Under the circumstances they refuse to pay.

Kol auðgi (the wealthy) is declared by Orm Svínfelling to have promised him 120 'hundreds' if he killed Dagstygg Jónsson, but Kol denies it[10].

Tumi Sighvatsson's father and brothers have been killed at Örlygsstað. His uncle Snorri agrees to ride with him to the Thing to see about a settlement and compensation for his father for him[11]. It does not seem to occur

---

[1] I. pp. 237–38.
[2] I. p. 297, " Þetta fe gallt Kallfr alt sem giortt var...."
[3] I. p. 317.   [4] " skip-stvfinn."
[5] I. p. 420, "Gallt þorþr þa IX. tigi hvndraða. Hann greiddi skip-stvfinn, ok Inngvnnar-staði i Kroksfirði, XVIII. hvnðrat i reka aa Reykia-nesi ok i Skialldabiarnar-vik, ok i gvlli ok silfri nokkot. Mæltu menn, at feit uæri skoroliga af hendi greitt, ok þat munði mikit kosta. 'Vist er fe-gialld mikit,' sagði þórþr, 'en vel ann ek þeim, er uið tekr.'"
[6] I. p. 443.   [7] I. p. 540.
[8] I. p. 100.   [9] I. p. 299.   [10] I. p. 501.
[11] I. p. 548, " Snorri skyldi ríða til þings ok hafa Tuma með ser ok sea sǽttir ok *fauður-bœtr* honum til hannda."

even to Snorri, fond of money though he is, that he himself could claim as much compensation for Sighvat as Tumi, though that is the case according to Baugatal.

After the slaying of Snorri his illegitimate son Órækja claims, and eventually gets, compensation (240 'hundreds')[1]. There is no talk of Snorri's sister's son getting any compensation, though the slayers give him a share of Snorri's inheritance, in order to induce him not to claim more of it[2]. Órækja evidently pays the whole wergild of Klæng, whom he slew[3].

We find Ögmund paying 90 'hundreds' each for the slaying of his wife's nephews, Sæmund and Guðmund Ormssynir[4].

After the death of Thorgils skarði, Bishop Sigvarð claims 40 'hundreds' from Thorgils' brother Sighvat, which he says he paid on Thorgils' behalf for a slaying. Sighvat promises to pay[5].

A settlement is made with Thorvarð, the slayer of Thorgils. Thorvarð is to pay 150 'hundreds.' Of this sum he is to hand over 40 'hundreds' to the bishop, in settlement of his claim, mentioned above, 20 'hundreds' to another creditor of Thorgils, and 60 'hundreds' he is to pay to Thorgils' brother Sighvat[6]. Thorvarð also has to pay for two other slayings, 60 'hundreds' each. "All these compensations for slayings...Thorvarð paid well and handsomely[7]."

Lopt kills a follower of his half-brother Gísli. He is banished from the district and has to pay much money[8].

It seems however that *goðar* are able to levy contributions towards the compensations they are liable for, but they claim them from their *thingmen*, not from their relatives.

Thus when Thorgils Oddason has to pay the enormous indemnity of 28,000 ells, more for his warfare against Hafliði than for the original injury (cutting off one of Hafliði's fingers), he receives a third of the sum while still at the Thing "from his friends and kinsmen," and a great many people gave him handsome gifts on his way home; but finally money was craved all over the Vestfirðinga quarter[9].

In the quarrel between the chief Kolbeinn and Bishop Guðmund, the farmers pledge themselves to pay such money fines as the Bishop awards.

---

[1] I. p. 574. Órækja is to pay Gizurr 600 hdr. for an attack. Gizurr is to pay him 360 hdr. for an attack. The difference is to be Snorri's wergild, so neither disburse anything.

[2] I. pp. 553–4.

[3] I. p. 574. For Klæng's slaying 1½ hdr. is to be paid. "Þar skal gjalldaz Reykia-hollt haalft, Stafahollt haalft, Bersa-staðir haalfir (Snorri's properties which Órækja inherits) ok goð-orð þau er Snorri hafði haft."

[4] II. p. 130.   [5] II. p. 306.   [6] II. p. 307.

[7] "Vígsbætr allar, þær sem dæmdar váru fyrir víg Þorgils, greiddi Þorvarðr vel ok skǫruliga."

[8] I. p. 302.   [9] I. p. 46.

P.   3

The bishop claims 12 'hundreds': half the money was paid, but half not, because Kolbeinn wanted the Bishop to claim it from the farmers who had promised it, but the bishop wanted to claim it from Kolbeinn himself[1].

Áron goes into the West Firths, where he was chief, and "asked for money for the slaying-fines, and got some[2]."

We must now cite all the evidence that can be brought forward in support of a Baugatal division of wergild in Sturlunga, but it amounts to almost nothing.

Snorri, Sturla's brother, and Ingjald, Sturla's son-in-law, go bail (gengu til handsala) for Sturla when awards are made against him at the Thing. Sturla however considers the awards unjust, and has no intention of paying. He advises Ingjald not to pay either, and Snorri does not pay because he sees that it would be useless. This may only mean that Snorri and Ingjald were expected to pay if Sturla did not, but it may mean that they were to contribute something in any case[3].

In another case we hear of one Óláf Vífilsson who had 'gone bail' for his kinsman Thorsteinn at the Thing. "But nothing was paid," and so Thorsteinn remains an outlaw. The bishop, to whom he applies for help against the winter, advises him to apply to his surety Óláf, hoping that the latter would contribute towards Thorsteinn's support that sum which had not been paid towards freeing him from outlawry. However nothing can be got out of Óláf[4].

We cannot tell how much responsibility these 'bails' had. Hrafn, who is one of the bails in the award after the slaying of Markús, is a relative of the *slain* man (first cousin once removed)[5]. The slayer, however, is his *thingman.*

The disintegration of the kindred seems even more complete in the Sturlung period than in the preceding one. This circumstance opens the way to a criticism of the value of the evidence given in the earlier Sagas. No Saga, it may be urged, was committed to writing until the Sturlung age, and it is possible that the absence of any sense of the duties and privileges of kinship, which is so marked a feature of this period, may have been reflected into the earlier times by those who committed the earlier Sagas to writing. If the decline of the kindreds was progressive, it is possible that the earlier periods may have had

---

[1] I. p. 277.
[2] II. p. 185, "Fór Áróu þá vestr i fjǫrðu ok beiddi sér fjár til vígsbótanna, ok hann fekk nǫkkut."
[3] I. p. 86.   [4] I. p. 209.
[5] Hrafns. ch. 7 (Vigfússon's ed. of Sturlunga).

a stronger sense of the ties of kindred than actually appears in the Sagas as we have them now.

Fortunately we have in Landnáma a means of judging whether this was the case or not. If the settlement took place on a basis of kindreds, it seems probable that the Saga period would not be quite so individualistic as we find it represented in the Sagas. If, on the other hand, the settlement itself was individualistic, there is no reason to suppose that the ties of kindred would have very greatly and rapidly strengthened in the Saga period, and again become disintegrated in the Sturlung age.

Now there can be no doubt that there was no wholesale migration of kindreds from Norway to Iceland. In the list, in Landnáma, of the first settlements, the Norwegian place of origin of each settler is frequently mentioned, and it is clear that the immigrants who settle down side by side come from the most various parts of Norway. Evidently any local grouping of kindred must have been shattered in Iceland, even if it had existed in Norway. It may be thought, however, that each settler was accompanied by his kindred in the ship in which he came to Iceland. But that the settler seldom brought more of his kindred than his wife and children, if he had any, is clear both from the genealogies and from the Sagas dealing with this early period. Thus Egilssaga, which bears every mark of trustworthiness[1], goes into some detail as to the persons who accompanied Skallagrím and his father to Iceland. They are said to have had two vessels, each with a crew of thirty fighting men besides women and children. Amongst this crew we find all the dependents and neighbours, save one, who had previously accompanied Skallagrím on his dangerous errand to the king. Two are described as farmers, one as a freedman, one as a man who farmed his own land, two as the sons of a sorceress who lived close by, and so on[2]. There is never any question of kinship between the descendants of these persons and those of

---

[1] F. Jónsson's ed. *Fortale*, pp. lix ff.
[2] Ch. 25. We also find Grím of Hálogaland, presumably with his following: he is described as a life-long friend of Skallagrím and of his father, but neither he nor his descendants are ever said to be related to Skallagrím's family.

Skallagrím. His only kinsman in Iceland is his second cousin once removed, Ketill hæng, who however had settled in the south, while Skallagrím settled in the west.

Vatsdæla Saga, in this point corroborated by Landnáma, shows us the chief companions of the important settler Ingimund on arrival in Iceland: his wife and two young sons, the eldest perhaps three or four years old, his wife's brother, and two friends and followers of Ingimund, Eyvind sörkvir and Gaut.

But there is more striking evidence than this that settlers were almost completely independent of kindred:

The great Hámund heljarskinn, son of King Hjörr, settles in Eyjafjörð in the North of Iceland; his brother Geirmund settles in the inaccessible Western Firths[1].

Thorsteinn Sölmundarson settles in Kjós, in the South-West. His uncle Auðunn rotin comes to Iceland with Helgi magri, and is given land by him in the North[2].

Högni accompanies Hrómund and is given land by him on the north bank of the Hvitá, while his brother, Finn auðgi, comes out independently and settles in Hvalfjörd—a day's journey away[3].

Lýting settles in Vápnafjörð in the East, and becomes a great chief: his brother Thorbjörn settles at Statholtstunga in the West[4].

Sigmund Ketilsson settles in Snæfellsnes in the extreme West. His father Ketill Thistill is in Thistilsfjörð in the North-East[5].

Björn austræni settles in Snæfellsnes. His brother Helgi bjóla had settled in Kjalarnes (a little north of the modern Reykjavík)[6].

Thórólf mostrarskegg takes Thórsnes, on the south side of Breiðifjörð, but his son Hallsteinn goes to settle in Thorskafjörð in the North-West firths[7].

Hrólf digri, son of Eyvind eikikrók, takes land in the West: his brother Thórð illugi Fellsgoði is a chief in the South-East[8].

It must be admitted that the dispersion of kindred could hardly be carried to greater lengths.

The settlement of Iceland lasted from about 871 to 930 A.D. Now even taking the case of two brothers coming to Iceland at

---

[1] Ld. H. ch. 187, 87. (The edition quoted is that of Finnur Jónsson, Copenhagen, 1900. H. refers to Hauksbók; St. to Sturlubók; M. to Melabók.)
[2] Ld. H. ch. 19, 198.
[3] Ld. St. 46, 26.
[4] Ld. St. 50, 271.
[5] Ld. St. 75, 261.
[6] Ld. St. 84, 14.
[7] Ld. St. 85, 123.
[8] Ld. H. 61, 275.

the same time, about 880, each with children of ten years old, and allowing only 20 years to a generation, it would be at least 70 years before the descendants of either could have fourth cousins in Iceland, by which time surely the uses of a fourth cousin, as outlined in Baugatal, would have tended to become obsolete. But as the vast majority of settlers came merely with their wives and children, or alone, marrying after their arrival, and some of them did not arrive in Iceland till 920 or later, their grandsons' great-grandsons (for this is what it amounts to) would hardly be born until the year 1000 or after. Even if the original emigrants had been accustomed in Norway to the support of such distant relatives, their descendants in Iceland would have grown used to doing without them, and even to doing without nearer relatives, in the course of the first century in Iceland. It is this kinless condition of the vast majority of settlers which leaves a permanent impress on the Icelandic constitution. The bond between a chief (*goði*) and his *thingmen* or dependents is not that of kinship, but of neighbourhood, or rather, to speak more exactly, it is the bond between the priest and the congregation; and in the absence of kindreds this bond became the central fact in the Icelandic constitution. We have already seen how common it was for the *goði* to take over even the liability for wergild incurred by one of his *thingmen*. We constantly see *goðar* neglecting the claims even of close kinship: it is rare indeed for them to fail to champion their *thingmen*.

It seems then to be quite unthinkable that Baugatal was ever actually followed in Iceland. The groups of kindred do not pay or receive wergild in accordance with it, and the amounts of the wergild do not vary in accordance with it. Except for a vague reminiscence of its terminology in Njála, there is no reference to it in the Sagas, nor is its phraseology current in them. It is worth noting that Baugatal only finds a place in *one* of the three collections still extant of Icelandic law[1].

Is there then no legal ordering of the wergilds paid in Iceland? We believe there is, and that it is contained in the section Vígslóði, or "Consequences of Slaying," to which Baugatal

---

[1] There is what seems to be a reference to it in Staðarhólsbók (Grág. II. p. 333).

is merely an appendix. Certainly we find there a distribution of payment for slaying of which Baugatal knows nothing. The most important passage for our purpose runs thus:

"*All compensations for slaying suits belong to heirs* (arftöku menn), *whether men or women*, whosoever institutes the suit or is plaintiff (aðili)[1]...The mother has a third of the compensation for slaying as against the brothers of the slain by the same father[2]." And in the preceding section, after giving the order in which relatives are due to become plaintiffs, the paragraph on plaintiffs states: "If none of these men exist, then the [next] nearest freeborn...relative has the suit....The slaying-suit and *also the compensations* follow the branches of kinship in the same way as inheritance, even if there be only one man in one branch and several in another[3]." This evidently refers to a case in which there are no nearer relatives than cousins[4]. That the claim for compensation does not extend beyond the actual heirs is clear from another statement in this paragraph: brothers are all plaintiffs together[5], and divide the compensation equally among themselves[6].

It must be admitted that these clauses give a much more accurate picture of what actually takes place in the Sagas than Baugatal can be said to do.

---

[1] 'Whosoever' must mean 'no matter who,' or else this clause must date from a period preceding the year 994, when the new law was passed that women might no longer be plaintiffs in slaying-suits. The preceding paragraph on plaintiffs (Grág. I *a*, pp. 167–8) gives a statement of the order in which relatives must act as plaintiffs which is identical with the list of heirs in the section dealing with inheritance (Grág. I *a*, pp. 218 f.) save that it omits the females.

[2] Grág. I *a*, p. 171, "Bǿtr allar vm vigsacar eigo arftoco menn hvart sem þeir ero karlar eða konor huergi er söc söcir eða huergi sem aðile er...Moþir aþriðiung af vigs bótom eftir born sin scirborin við brǿðr samfeðra ens vegna." In Staðarhólsbók this reads: "as against the father and brothers by same father" (Grág. II. p. 354).

[3] p. 168, "Vig söc oc sva bǿtr hverfa sva ikne runna sem erfð þott . i . maðr se or avðrom enn fleire or oðrom knerunne."

[4] Cp. at the end of the list of relatives in the section on inheritance (p. 220), "Nv ero fleire menn iafn nánir þeir er taca eigo. þa scal iafnt skipta iknérunna alla." Outside the first degree all equally related persons inherit equally: thus there might be several sets of cousins with equal claims.

[5] pp. 167–8, "ef brǿðr ero fleire samfeðra....rett er at þeir bvi allir mal til oc þarf engi þeirra avðrom at selia."

[6] "eigo þeir allir iöfnom höndom þat er þeir á taka."

The order of succession, which these compensations for slaying are here stated to follow, runs thus[1]:

1. Son.
2. Daughter.
3. Father.
4. Brother by same father.
5. Mother.
6. Sister by same father.
7. Half-brother by same mother.
8. „ sister „ „
9. Illegitimate son.
10. „ daughter.
11. „ half-brother by same father.
12. „ „ sister „ „
13. „ „ brother „ mother.
14. „ „ sister „ „
15. Father's father.
16. Mother's „
17. Son's son.
18. Daughter's son.
19. Father's mother.
20. Mother's „
21. Son's daughter.
22. Daughter's daughter.
23. Father's brother.
24. Mother's „
25. Brother's son.
26. Sister's „
27. Father's sister.
28. Mother's „
29. Brother's daughter.
30. Sister's „
31. First cousins on both sides.

If we now compare the distribution of wergilds in the Sagas with these clauses in Vígslóði, we shall find nothing inconsistent or startling.

Thus the use of the word *föðurbætr*, compensation for the father, occasionally used in the Sagas for the *whole* wergild[2], is perfectly justified, for a son is his father's heir, and excludes all

---

[1] Grág. I *a*, pp. 218 ff.
[2] Lax. ch. 75, *föðurbætr* paid to the sons of Bolli (see above p. 19). Cp. Víga-Glúmss. ch. 26, wergild paid to Ketill, son of the slain Thorvald krók (p. 23 supra).

others in the matter of compensation for slaying. The passage in Sturlunga, on which we have already commented, where Snorri, the brother of the slain Sighvat, rides to the Thing with his nephew Tumi in order to secure *föðurbætr* for him[1], is perfectly clear if we follow Vígslóði : the son, as heir, excludes the brother. So also in the case of *sonarbætr*, used for wergild in two passages[2]: the compensation falls to the father in the absence of children to claim it.

In *Ljósvetninga Saga*, when Guðmund ríki gives wergild to the *brothers* of the slain Thorkell hák[3], it is presumably because he left no children and his father is dead, so that his brothers are his heirs. So also in the case of Klæng Klappjárnsson, brother of the slain Hall, in Sturlunga[4]. It is explicitly stated in the case of the Vatsfirðings, Þórð and Snorri. "Inheritance and compensation after them Einarr their (half-)brother had to take, but Illugi their (illegitimate) brother was plaintiff in the suit, Einarr being a child[5]." They had no children, their father is dead, and so their half-brother Einarr by the same father is heir and receives the wergild ; their next male relative on the list is No. 11, illegitimate half-brother by same father, which is Illugi's position.

In *Reykdæla Saga* we were surprised to find the *mother* of Bjarni receiving the whole wergild of a hundred of silver[6], instead of Víga-Glúm his uncle, but we now see that in the absence of children, of father or brothers, the mother had a claim far superior to Víga-Glúm, who only comes 24th on the list.

The curious case in Sturlunga, where the illegitimate son, Órækja, gets the whole wergild for his father Snorri[7], while the sister's son gets none of it, is also explained : Órækja, the nearest relative, comes 7th on the list, while Egill Sölmundarson, as sister's son, is 26th. According to Baugatal, Órækja the illegitimate son would have had no greater share in the wergild than the brothers-in-law and stepsons who were responsible for Snorri's death.

The only case which is inconsistent with the clauses in Vígslóði is that in *Bjarnar Saga hitdælakappi* (see p. 24 f. above), in which both the father and brother, as well as the foster-brothers, receive wergild. It is possible that what the brother received was really due to him as plaintiff[8], the father being too old to act in that capacity. With regard to one of the foster-

---

[1] Sturl. I. p. 548. In Sturl. I. p. 16, we find the widow and sons of Hneitir getting wergild—the widow probably acting on behalf of her sons.
[2] Bj. hit. ch. 20, to Dálk for his son (p. 21 supra). Nj. ch. 12 (p. 23 supra).
[3] Ljósv. ch. 19 (cp. also Flóam. ch. 34).   [4] Sturl. I. p. 297.
[5] Sturl. I. p 443.   [6] Reyk. ch. 23 (see supra, p. 23).   [7] Sturl. I. p. 574.
[8] Grág. II. (Staðarhólsbók), p. 354, § 324, "...nymæli. Þar er kona a at taka vigs bötr eða sa maðr er eigi a at søkia sakir sinar. Þa a aðili vigsakar þriðiung vigsbóta."

brothers, at least, the taking of wergild was due to an arrangement previously made, and it is likely that wergild was frequently extorted by foster-brothers —entirely without prejudice to the claims of the heirs, as is evident in the story of Bjarni.

The suggestion that the clauses of Vígslóði represent the true nature of the Icelandic wergild is thus borne out by all the evidence at our disposal; and they would probably have been recognized long ago as valid wergild clauses, but for the baffling presence of Baugatal, with which these passages had to be forcibly reconciled. This has been ingeniously accomplished. Finsen[1], the greatest authority on old Icelandic law, identifies the *vígsbætr*, 'compensation for slaying,' in Vígslóði, not with wergild, but with *réttr*, a fine (of 48 aurar) for various offences. Now *bætr*, *vígsbætr*, *vígsakarbætr*, compensations for slaying, or for slaying-suits, the words used in the above passages in Vígslóði, are also the words used for the whole wergild in the Sagas. It is therefore difficult to imagine that in the laws they only refer to *réttr*, a fine for various minor offences; which Finsen is forced to assume was also paid in slaying-suits in addition to the wergild proper. The assumption is made all the more difficult by the fact that wergild for Norwegians in Iceland is *exclusively* called *bætr*[2], or *vígsakarbætr*, in the laws; yet it is difficult to believe that Norwegians had no real wergild, only a *réttr* of 48 aurar. In the Sagas Norwegians have ordinary wergilds of a 'hundred' of silver.

It is true that one of the recensions of Icelandic laws (Staðarhólsbók) does know of *réttr* being paid in slaying-suits, but only as a sequel of outlawry:

[1] See *réttr* (*vígsakarbætr*, *vígsbætr*) in his Glossary: Grág. III. p. 661 f.

[2] Grág. I *b*, pp. 197-8, § 249, If an "Eastman" (Norwegian) without kin in the country is killed by a person who would inherit his goods, "that man who would have the [next] best right to inherit takes inheritance and *bætr*. If the *goði* who would inherit from him kills the stranger, the other *goðar* in his district take inheritance and *bætr*. If afterwards heirs of the Danish tongue come out, they shall take the inheritance and the *bætr* (if there are *bætr*) without interest. All such movable property as the heirs do not take [i.e. are not there to take], whether *vígsakabætr* or inheritance, let it be valued like the property of a pauper, and they [those who take it over temporarily] shall have the interest on it." Cp. also the use of the word vígsbætr in Staðarhólsbók (Grág. II.), p. 137, § 107, "Now if a man has supported a boy in his youth, and if that man (the boy) be slain afterwards, then the man shall take as much of the *vígsbætr* as he expended on him, without interest."

The plaintiff is to charge the slayer with the deed and to declare him outlawed, adding: "I claim that his property is all forfeited. I claim for myself or for that man who is plaintiff in the suit, *réttr* out of his property, 48 legal aurar. After that I claim for myself half what is left, but half for all those men of the quarter who have a right to forfeited property according to the laws[1]."

But this only establishes that the plaintiff has a kind of *praecipuum* on the outlaw's property: it by no means establishes the identity of *réttr* with *vígsbætr*, which is quite independent of outlawry.

The only other passage which might seem to suggest that these two terms, *réttr* and *vígsbætr*, could be synonymous, occurs in Baugatal, and runs as follows: "If a man breaks the [sworn] peace in a case where the *bætr*, compensations, of the suit are paid, then the *réttr* of every man who had paid compensation is increased by half for him [the peace-breaker], moreover no one may make a treaty in such suits without leave [from the Courts at the Althing][2]."

But this only seems to imply that the peace-breaker has to pay a fine, a *réttr* and a half, to all who paid compensation, as satisfaction to them for breaking the peace which they had paid for. And that this is the right interpretation is clearly seen in another passage in Baugatal: "It is old law in our land, that if a man is guilty of breaking truce [temporary truce, before the wergild is paid] those 12 men who are appointed to [be responsible for] the truce shall take *réttr* out of his property, 48 aurar[3]."

All other references to *réttr* refer to fines for blows[4], wounds[5], insults[6], or offences against women[7].

---

[1] Grág. II. p. 359 (§ 332).

[2] Grág. I a, p. 203, "Ef maðr ryfr trygðir þar er bøtt er sac bótum þa eycz þar rettr hvers manz hálfo. við þann þeirra er bøtto. enda scal a þav mál engi sættaz fyrir lof fram."

[3] p. 205, "þat ero forn lög a lanðe óro ef maðr verðr secr vm griða rof at þeir menn XII. er igrið ero nefndir eigo at taca rett ór fe hans VIII. aura ens fimtategar."

This passage goes on significantly for those who hold that Baugatal was in force in *Iceland*: "But that is law *in Norway* and wherever the Danish tongue runs that if a man does not keep truce that man is outlaw from one end of *Norway* to the other and forfeits both his lands and his movable property." Amira (*Germania* XXXII. p. 144) considers the fine Icelandic and the outlawry a mere reference to Norwegian custom, but such a reference is surely unparalleled in Icel. law.

[4] Grág. I a, p. 155.   [5] II. p. 364.   [6] III. p. 434.

[7] Grág. I b, p. 52. There are some references to *réttar fars sök*, suits for *réttr*, but there is nothing to indicate that these are slaying-suits. The term occurs in Vígslóði (which however deals with many non-slaying suits) as the sequel to a passage we have already quoted: "The mother has a third of the *vígsbætr* after her legitimate children, as against brothers of the slain by the same father, and so also she has the third of *réttr* suits about the daughters as against brothers of the same father. If another man than the [rightful] plaintiff sues in a *rétta fars* suit because he thinks he is the [rightful] plaintiff, and the rightful plaintiff pays no heed because he believes

There is thus no reason for supposing that *vígsbætr* means *réttr* in the laws any more than in the Sagas. It clearly refers to the whole wergild, and the whole wergild is therefore awarded to the heirs, and not to the kindred at large. In this matter of the wergild laws there may be said to be *no trace of the solidarity of the kindred.*

The individualistic settlement of Iceland has left other traces in the laws. The right of pre-emption of ancestral land by kinsmen, known in Norway as *odal right*, and persisting all over Northern Teutonic Europe (except in England) until after the Middle Ages, does not appear in the Icelandic laws at all, nor is there any trace of it in the Sagas. Except in the case of a man wishing to give his entire fortune away[1], only the heir has any hold over an owner of property, being able to prevent the owner from impairing his inheritance, or from giving the 'greater tithe' (a tenth of all his possessions) more than once in his life[2]. Again, not the kindred, but the *hreppr* or district, compensated a farmer for loss by fire or by disease among his beasts[3]. Only the law fixing the responsibility for paupers (infirm or young persons without means) shows the influence of the idea of kindred. A man was bound to maintain his parents, children, brothers and sisters if they were in want and unable to work, even if it involved going into debt-thraldom himself to the nearest kinsman who had means to support the paupers. He was further bound to maintain his more distant relatives, in the absence of any nearer kin, up to his fourth cousins, but only if he had a certain income increasing in proportion to the distance of the relationship[4].

---

the other to be rightful plaintiff, then the [real] rightful plaintiff shall have three-fourths of the [price of] peace, and that other who sued one-fourth etc." (Grág. I *a*, p. 171.) This means that just as the mother has a third of the slaying-fines for her *children* (i.e. sons or daughters), so she has a third of the damages in suits referring to her daughters' honour.

One text of Njálssaga (ed. F. Jónsson, Halle 1908) once uses *réttr* with reference to wergild (ch. 38), but if, as F. Jónsson thinks (p. 89, note 25), *réttr* here=*manngjöld*, it is clearly wrong in any case, or else a Norwegianism (cp. N. G. L. Glossar s.v. réttr, 3). *Fullum rétti* might however surely mean nothing more than 'in full measure.'

[1] Grágas I *a*, p. 249.   [2] I *a*, p. 246.
[3] Cp. V. Guðmundsson, Framfærsla og sveitastjórn á þjóðveldistímanum, Eimreiðin (Copenhagen), IV. (1898), pp. 97–8.
[4] Ómagabálkr, Grág. I *b*, p. 3 ff.

This, one may conjecture, was the old, pre-Icelandic law, modified, no doubt, in heathen times, by the permission to 'expose' infants, or in case of famine to put the aged and infirm to death. But it is surely going too far to say with Guðbrand Vigfússon and Norðström that this law is of entirely Christian (and Icelandic) origin, and that in heathen times there was no compulsion to do more for the penniless and infirm than to put an end to them. Maurer's view[1], that the system is old and came from Norway, is much more probable; in fact there are distinct traces of an early liability of the kindred in this respect, in certain provisions of the Norwegian laws regarding the responsibility of freedmen for their kinsmen.

Frostuthing's law, IX. 11, runs thus: "So shall the son of a freedman take [inheritance], and his son's son, and *his* son (great-grandson), and daughter and sister like son and brother, if there are none of these. *Each of these shall provide for the other*[2]." Gulathing's law (S. Norway) admits a responsibility of the master towards his pauper freedman, and we may assume that if the law did not allow him to divest himself of responsibility towards this class, by allowing them to die or putting them to death, still less would it have permitted him to put kinsmen of his own class to death. Yet the paragraph in Gulathing's law is too gruesomely restricted for us to attribute it to Christian influence: "If they [the freedman and his family] come to extreme want, they are 'grafgangsmen.' A grave shall be dug in the churchyard, and they shall be put into it and left to die there. The master shall take out the one who lives longest, and feed that one thereafter[3]." Such a provision bears marks of an extreme antiquity, and shows that the idea of enforced support of paupers dates from remote heathen times. The Icelandic Sagas, too, offer indirect evidence of some law with regard to paupers in heathen times. Twice[4], according to them, it was actually proposed in the stress of famine to give leave to kill off the old folk and expose the infants. In neither case was the proposal carried out, but the fact that it was mooted seems to show that the poor-law was older than Christianity, though no doubt the influence of Christianity was exerted to preserve it and enlarge its scope. As a matter of fact some provision for aged relatives is

---

[1] *Island*, pp. 316 ff.
[2] Fr. IX. 11 (transl. as in Seebohm, *Tribal Custom*), "Svá scal sunr leysingia taca oc sunarsunr oc þess sunr...oc svá dóttir oc systir sem sunr oc bróðir, ef þeir ero eigi til. Oc svá scal hvárt þeirra hyggia fyrir öðru."
[3] Gul. 63, "En ef þau verða at þrotom. þa ero þat grafgangs menn. Scal grava grof í kirkiugarðe. oc setia þau þar i. oc láta þau deyia. take skapdrottenn þat ór er lengst livir. oc fæðe þat siðan."
[4] Reyk. ch. 7 and Fornmanna Sögur, II. p. 222.

almost an integral part of any tribal society. It exists among the Southern Slavs of the Balkan peninsula[1], and is clearly traceable among the Greeks of Homeric times.

The point to note, however, is that in Iceland there is no *corporate* action, or liability, of the kin: the nearest relative, whoever he be, alone bears the brunt of maintaining his pauper relative.

But in Iceland, besides 'inheritance-paupers'—those who were supported by persons who would have been their heirs if they had had anything to bequeath—there are a number of classes of 'community-paupers,' whose support was a duty of the *hreppr* (parish), the *thing*-district, or the quarter (one of the four territorial divisions of Iceland). This, one would say, was an Icelandic development, and that to a certain extent it supplanted the older kinship-liability is evident from the paragraph 'On the children of outlaws[2],' which provides that the children and pauper relatives of an outlaw, or of a person banished for three years, should be supported by the '*quarter*' in which the outlaw's, or exile's, possessions had lain. The 'quarter' was partly indemnified, it is true, by receiving half the forfeited property in the case of an outlaw, but in any community where the solidarity of the kindred was a living principle, and where all the relatives really suffered for the misdeeds of one, it would seem a strange anomaly to cast all responsibility for the children of the outlaw and the exile, not on the kin, but on the district.

A candid examination of the sources may thus be fairly said to reveal that the much quoted solidarity of the kindred in Iceland really rests on Baugatal alone[3]. This is an extremely

---

[1] "In Montenegro...there was the closest union in war, revenge, funeral rites, marriage arrangements, *provision for the poor* and for those who stand in need of special help, as for instance in the case of fires, inundations, and the like." Prof. Vinogradoff, "Village Communities," *Encycl. Br.* vol. 28 (pp. 68—72). See also art. "Charity and Charities."

[2] Grág. I *b*, p. 23.

[3] The passion of the modern Icelanders for genealogical knowledge has often been taken as evidence for an earlier state based on the solidarity of the kindred. If so, we must place this earlier state before the settlement of Iceland. But in reality the genealogical interest of the Icelanders only illustrates their intense love of historical knowledge and local annals, together with a very justifiable pride in their descent.

insecure foundation[1], seeing that the laws supply another wergild code in which the wergild falls to the heir, and that all the evidence in the Sagas[2] corroborates the validity of this other wergild code. We have seen that the settlement was individualistic to a high degree, and that the constitution of the country was based on the bond between thingman and *goði*, and not in any sense on federated kindreds.

---

[1] The two appendices to Baugatal, on truce and peace, have been frankly admitted to be Norwegian, and many points in which Baugatal itself shows strong affinities to Norwegian law have been pointed out by Maurer (*Verwandtschafts- und Erbrecht*, p. 38) and by v. Amira, who goes so far as to speak of the "Widerspruch zwischen baugatal und sonstigem isländischem Recht" (*Germania*, XXXII. p. 133). The inclusion of the brother in the first baug, noted by v. Amira as a specifically Icelandic feature, may well be merely older Norwegian law: cp. the part played by the brother in Danish wergilds.

[2] The Icelandic Sagas are in the foregoing quoted in the small Reykjavík edition, with the exception of Egilssaga and Austfirðinga Sögur (ed. F. Jónsson and J. Jacobsen respectively), and of Njálssaga (ed. Copenhagen, 1875).

CHAPTER II

NORWAY

SAVE for the laws, there is very little evidence available for our purpose until the fourteenth and fifteenth centuries in Norway. The various Lives of the kings of Norway, whether of Norwegian or Icelandic authorship, do not deal with the general conditions of the people, and there is nothing to correspond to the Icelandic Sagas. A certain amount of pre-Icelandic genealogical lore can be gleaned, however, from one or two of the Icelandic sources, and sometimes the place of origin of Norwegian ancestors is mentioned. These insufficient sources give a glimpse of a progressive decline of the kindred, but they do not take us back far enough to see the beginning of the decline. Thus from the Icelandic genealogies it is possible to trace a tendency for earls and *hersar* (local chiefs) to intermarry, and so form an almost national Norwegian aristocracy. But as not more than one earl, and at most three or four *hersar*, lived in one district, a certain scattering of the kindred must have been a necessary consequence of such intermarriages. The following genealogy of persons living in the eighth and ninth centuries may serve as an illustration. It can be deduced from passages in Landnámabok:—

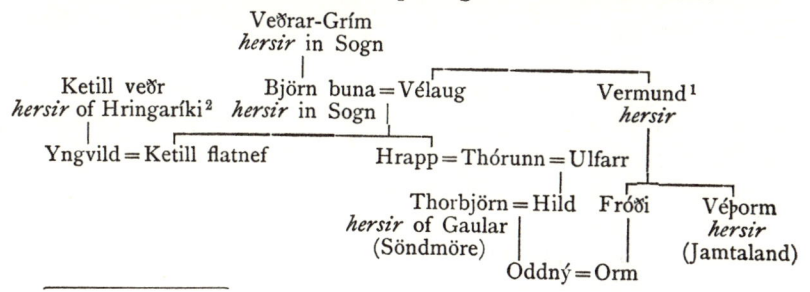

```
                    Veðrar-Grím
                    hersir in Sogn
                         |
       ┌─────────────────┼───────────────┐
   Ketill veðr      Björn buna=Vélaug    Vermund[1]
hersir of Hringaríki[2]  hersir in Sogn   hersir
       |                  |
  ┌────┴──────┐     ┌─────┴──────┐
Yngvild=Ketill flatnef   Hrapp=Thórunn=Ulfarr
                                |
                   ┌────────────┼──────┬──────────┐
              Thorbjörn=Hild   Fróði    Véþorm
              hersir of Gaular           hersir
              (Söndmöre)     |         (Jamtaland)
                          Oddný=Orm
```

---

[1] Ld. H. ch. 323.

[2] For the place names mentioned see the historical map of Norway in vol. I. of Magnússon and Morris' translation of the *Heimskringla* (Saga Library) or the map accompanying G. Storm's *Snorre Sturlassöns Historieskrivning*, Copenhagen, 1873. (In the former Hringaríki is translated *Ringrealm*, Söndmöre *Southmere*.)

Anyone with any experience of travelling in Norway, even in the epoch of railways, will readily realize that distance and natural barriers must have rendered any effective union of these kinsmen quite impossible.

Another interesting genealogy is found in Egilssaga :—

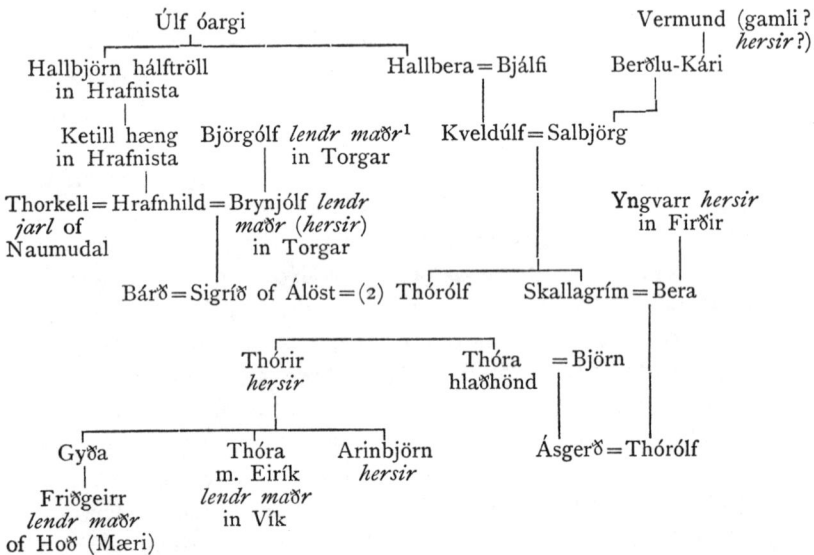

```
          Úlf óargi                                  Vermund (gamli?
   ┌─────────┴─────────┐                                 │  hersir?)
Hallbjörn hálftröll      Hallbera=Bjálfi           Berðlu-Kári
 in Hrafnista               │                           │
   │                        │                    ┌──────┴──────┐
Ketill hæng  Björgólf lendr maðr¹  Kveldúlf=Salbjörg
 in Hrafnista        in Torgar              │
   │                                  Yngvarr hersir
Thorkell=Hrafnhild=Brynjólf lendr        in Firðir
 jarl of           maðr (hersir)
 Naumudal          in Torgar
                        │
        Bárð=Sigríð of Álöst=(2) Thórólf    Skallagrím=Bera
                                    │              │
                        ┌───────────┴──┐     ┌─────┴─────┐
                     Thórir          Thóra  =Björn
                     hersir        hlaðhönd
   ┌──────┬──────────┐                      │
 Gyða   Thóra    Arinbjörn            Ásgerð=Thórólf
   │   m. Eirík    hersir
Friðgeirr lendr maðr
lendr maðr  in Vík
of Hoð (Mæri)
```

The districts of these kinsmen range from Hálogaland in the extremest north to the Christiania fjord. When it is recollected that the Norseman Ohthere told King Alfred[2] that it took more than a month to sail from his home in Hálogaland to the Christiania fjord, even with a favouring wind all the way, it will be obvious that these kinsfolk could not often call upon one another for help; and indeed according to the story Thórólf Kveldúlfsson never met his northern kinsmen until he went north with his second cousin Bárðr, whom he met at the king's court[3]. Moreover, if we are to believe Egilssaga (which is founded on family tradition and in this particular is likely to be correct), even in his own district Kveldúlf does not rely upon his kindred for support, but on neighbours (possibly dependents)

---

[1] *Lendr maðr* corresponds to *hersir*.
[2] In Alfred's translation of Orosius, ed. Bosworth, 1859. This passage is printed in Sweet's *Anglo-Saxon Reader*, 7th ed. (1894), p. 20. [3] Eg. VIII.

who are not kinsmen. Thus when Skallagrím goes to the king to ask for compensation for his brother Thórólf, whom the king has slain, he chooses as his companions men from among his housecarles and neighbours. We are given a number of particulars about these men[1], who afterwards accompanied Skallagrím and his father to Iceland, and there is never any question of kinship between their descendants and those of Skallagrím.

That the bond of kindred is considered less binding than that of loyalty to a chief to whom one has sworn fealty is clear from the behaviour of Thórólf's kinsmen after the king slays him. They are in the king's bodyguard, and neither claim wergild nor attempt revenge on those of their fellows who were concerned in the slaying.

From these fragmentary hints we can surmise that the decline of the kindred had already begun in Norway by the eighth century, though possibly chiefly among the aristocracy. For the following periods we must rely almost entirely on the laws. These are all compilations of the customs of various districts; and all show signs of having undergone revision and modification.

In the Frostuthing law, in force in the northern parts of Norway, the wergild law was only compiled in its present form under King Hákon Hákonsson (1217—1263). Fortunately we have a few fragments of an earlier law, which we will discuss later. King Hákon's law begins with a characteristic preface[2], in which the king deplores the frequent slayings, and declares that the most likely means of checking the abuse would be that the ordinance of St Olaf should stand, "though it has not been heeded hitherto on account of desire of money—that he who slays an innocent man should forfeit both property and peace and be outlaw." "St Olaf's law" of course only signifies 'old law,' St Olaf's name being used much as the Anglo-Saxon appealed to 'Alfred's law' or to the 'law of Edward the Confessor.' The "desire of money" presumably refers to the objections felt by the heirs to the total forfeiture of the outlaw's property. "Now if the slayer be out of Norway (fled), let his kinsmen pay

---
[1] Eg. XXV.
[2] Frost. VI. § 1 (in *Norges Gamle Love*, ed. Keyser etc.).

P. 4

one-fourth of the compensation, and he shall act who is most nearly related [to the slayer] of the paternal kinsmen, and also he who is most nearly related on the maternal side, and let them so pay to the [two corresponding] kinsmen of the slain. But if the slayer escapes in his outlawed state, then let his kinsmen pay half-payment according to the first ordinance *if his money does not suffice*[1]." If after this the king should make peace with the outlaw, the latter is to pay the remaining half of the compensation[2].

The reference to the earlier law by which the slayer was outlawed and his goods forfeited reminds us of Baugatal, where such is assumed to be the case. But the later clause, that the slayer's property should go towards wergild, is entirely alien from the spirit of Baugatal, and shows a very clear conception of the liability of the individual. The fact that only the two nearest kinsmen are responsible at all, and for half the wergild at the most—usually for only a quarter—is also significant.

The clauses which follow, however, are of a somewhat earlier date[3]. The wergild is thought of as a fixed sum, varying from 48 to 16 marks[4] according to the standing of the parties concerned. The following is the division of the largest wergild, 48 marks.

The payments (except I. i.) are made throughout to the corresponding kinsman on the other side (i.e. father of slayer to father of slain, and so on):—

I.		marks	aur.	ört.
i.	slayer (or his son) pays son of slain	5	0	0
ii.	father of slayer pays	5	0	0
iii.	brother	3	6	0
iv (*a*).	father's brother }	2	4	0
iv (*b*).	brother's sons }			
v (*a*).	agnatic first cousins }	1	5	1
v (*b*).	and second cousins, the latter taking ⅖ }			
	Total[5]	17	7	1

---
[1] Frost. VI. § 4.
[2] Ibid. § 5. These paragraphs date from 1260.
[3] Perhaps from c. 1244. Cp. Amira, in *Germania*, XXXII. pp. 162-3.
[4] 6 marks of gold to 2 marks of gold.
[5] Fr. makes this total 17. 7. 2. 0.

§ 5. II. *Sakaukar* or Increasers of Fines:

		marks	aur.	ört.	pen.
(a)	thrall-born son	2	1	0	0
(b)	half-brother by same mother	2	1	0	0
(c) (a) father's father }[1] (β) son's son	2	1	0	0
(d)	sons of[2] (a) and (b) 1. 3. 1. 0 (each?)	2	6	2	0
(e)	sons of (d), ⅓ less ... (approx.)	1	7	0	0
§ 6. (f)	father's half-brother through mother, and sons of (b)	1	3	1	0
	Total[3]	12	4	0	0

The compiler adds class (f) on his own account, observing that there is "great danger to the slayer" if they receive nothing.

For all this (I and II) the slayer is responsible in the last resort.

§ 7. III. *Mikla nefgildi* (to cognates):

(a)	mother's father } daughter's son	2	0	0	0
(b)	mother's brother } sister's son	1	4	0	0
(c)	first cousins (sons of father's sister or of mother's brother)	1	0	0	0
(d)	first cousins (sons of mother's sister)		5	1	0
	Total	5	1	1	0

§ 8. IV. 1. *Litla nefgildi* (to more distant cognates):

(a)	son's daughter's son	1	1	0	0
(b)	daughter's daughter's son		7	1	10
(c)	brother's „ „		6	0	0
(d)	sister's „ „		4	1	10
(e)	(?) second cousins[4] (cognatic): sons of (?) parents' female first cousins				
	(a) as cl. III. (c)		3	0	0
	(β) as cl. III. (d)		1	1	10[5]
	Total	3	7	1	10

---

[1] For the inclusion of these agnatic relatives among the 'increasers of fines,' cp. Maurer, *Verwandschafts- und Erbrecht nach altnord. Rechte*, p. 48.

[2] Sons of Sakaukar—presumably of (a) and (b). But cp. § 6 (f).

[3] Fr. makes this total 13. 3. 2. 0. (There are 20 penn. to the örtug: otherwise the reckoning is that given on p. 12, note 1, supra.)

[4] *Systkinadætrasynir* and *systradætrasynir*. I do not take these as first cousins once removed, as in that case no provision would be made for cognatic second cousins.

[5] These totals are given by Fr., but it requires a good many conjectural emendations in the text to attain to them.

§ 9. IV. 2. An extraordinary list of persons are here added, the writer confessing that they are not in the older Frostuthing's law. He seems to think that this omission was by inadvertence. The link with the kindred is through the mother only in each case, save (*e*).

		marks	aur.	ört.	pen.
§ 10. (*a*)	sons of father's half-brother and grandson of grandfather's half-brother	1	0	2	0
(*b*)	(a) mother's half-brother, (β) half-sister's son	1	0	0	0
(*c*)	sons of (a) and of father's half-sister		6	1	0
(*d*)	sons of mother's half-sister		3	1	10
(*e*)	thrall-born brother	1	7	0	0
	Total	5	1	1	10

§ 11. V. *Frændbætr* (kinsmen's compensations):

(i)	Bauggildi (payments to agnates). This is the sum of 1. 5. 1. 0, of which				
(*a*)	kinsmen of the fourth degree get ⅗	1	0	0	0
(*b*)	„ „ fifth degree get ⅗ of the remainder		3	0	12
(*c*)	kinsmen of sixth degree what is left		2	0	8
	Total	1	5	1	0

§ 12. (ii) Nefgildi (cognate's payments), 5. 1. 0 divided as above:

			aur.	ört.	pen.
(*a*)	fourth degree		3	0	12
(*b*)	fifth degree		1	0	16⅘
(*c*)	sixth degree		2		11⅕
	Total		5	1	0

The total, according to our computation, is rather less than the fixed amount, being 47 marks odd instead of 48[1].

There are some fragments of an earlier wergild law which are interesting as offering an indication that the Icelandic Baugatal is really an old North Norwegian wergild law. These fragments belong to Codex IV.[2], a single membrane torn down the middle, so that we only have half each line.

---

[1] For a different working out of Norwegian wergilds see C. Holmbœ, "Om Forholdet imellem Værdien af Guld og Sölv i Norge i Middelalderen," in *Samlinger til den norske Historie*, I. (Christiania, 1833), pp. 69—78.

[2] *N. G. L.* II. pp. 520—521.

As in Baugatal, there are 4 baugar. With regard to the fourth, we find the words: *Um fim dæillt fe*—"About money divided into fifths," which seems from its position to indicate that ⅗ of the sum goes to agnates and ⅖ to cognates, as in Baugatal. It is however possible that it may refer to a division between agnatic first cousins and second cousins as in the later Frostuthing's law.

The fragment has some traces of the careful reductions made in Baugatal in the case of the absence of certain relatives. Its third heading runs: "About the reduction of the chief baug...[1]," and its sixth heading deals in the same way with the third baug[2]. The fragment shows, it is true, the system of truce-buying, with which we are only acquainted in the earlier Gulathing's law (cp. p. 62, below). But the resemblance to Baugatal seems almost textually close in the two headings about a thrall and a freedman. The portion of these clauses is equally striking in both Baugatal and the fragment, since they are entirely unconnected with what precedes and what follows. The fragment has: "About the smallest baugar, which a thrall shall...[3]," while Baugatal has: "Now the smallest baugar shall be stated, which a thrall shall pay to a thrall[4]."

The fragment seems also to know of *baugthak*, so characteristic of Baugatal, for we read (l. 15, p. 521) ..."are 15 aurar and eyrir at baug...[5]," which can hardly be completed save by "-thak[6]."

That the earlier Norwegian law resembled Baugatal in assuming the outlawry of the slayer is clear from King Hákon's words quoted above (p. 49).

There is thus some definite evidence that the earlier Frostuthing's wergild law very closely resembled Baugatal. It will therefore be worth while to make a comparison between Baugatal and the *later* Frostuthing's law, with the object of noting the

---

[1] Um houuþ baug at skiærþæ i annat....
[2] Um þriðiu bauga skiærðing.
[3] Cod. IV. l. 16, "Um minztu bauga er þræll scal þ......."
[4] Grág. I a, p. 202, "Nv scal ina minnzto bavga segia er þræll scal þræli bǿta."
[5] ...ero atian aurar. oc æyrir at baug | (end of line).
[6] For the whole question of this fragment see von Amira, in *Germania*, XXXII. pp. 129 ff., where the text is skilfully restored.

modifications of the wergild idea in North Norway. Corroborative evidence will later be afforded by the similar tendencies observable in the South Norwegian wergild.

We will adopt the classification of Baugatal, and take the largest of Frostuthing's fixed sums—48 marks—as a basis of comparison. The proportion which Baugatal's maximum of 15 marks bears to this sum is as 5 : 16.

   I. (i) *Slayer* (Fr.). *Slayer's son, brother, father* (B.):
      Fr. 13. 6. 0. 0.
      B.   3. 6. 0. 0. ($\frac{5}{16}$ of Fr.'s sum would be 4. 2. 1. 2$\frac{1}{2}$.)

   (ii) *Grandfathers and grandsons* (Fr. II. *c* and III. *a*):
      Fr. 4. 1. 0. 0.
      B.   3. 0. 0. 0. ($\frac{5}{16}$ would be 1. 2. 0. 18$\frac{3}{4}$: i.e., Baugatal is more than double its proper proportion as compared with Fr.)

   I. (iii) *Uncles and nephews*:
      Fr. 4. 0. 0. 0.
      B. 2. 3. 0. 0.

Again Baugatal is nearly double its right proportion.

   (iv) *First cousins*:
      Fr. 2. 5. 1. 0.
      B. 1. 6. 0 0. ($\frac{5}{16}$ would be only 0. 6. 2. 0.)

   II. (i):
      Fr. This class is apparently not mentioned; the money (3. 3. 0. 0) being given to great-grandsons, etc. (IV. i. *a—d*), who are not likely to exist.
      B. 1. 0. 0. 0.

   (ii) *Second cousins*:
      Fr. 1. 1. 2. 10.
      B. 0. 5. 1. 0.

   (iii) *Second cousins once removed and third cousins* (*fourth degree*):
      Fr. 1. 3. 0. 12.
      B. 0. 5. 2. 5. ($\frac{5}{16}$ would only be 0. 3. 1. 10.)

   (iv) *Third cousins once removed and fourth cousins* (*fifth degree*):
      Fr. 0. 4. 1. 9.
      B. 0. 2. 1. 5. ($\frac{5}{16}$ would be 0. 1. 1. 4.)

   (v) (*Fifth cousins and fourth cousins once removed*):
      Fr. 0. 2. 2. 19.

III. *Sakaukar* (Increasers of Fines), (Fr. II. excluding (*c*)):

Fr. II.	10	3	1	0
Fr. IV (2).	5	1	1	0
	15	4	2	0
B.	1	4	0	5.

($\frac{5}{16}$ would be 4. 6. 2. 17½.)

We see then that Baugatal taxes the slayer himself not at all, and his brother and father somewhat less than Frostuthing's law. On the other hand the liability of grandfathers and grandsons, of uncles and nephews, and of first cousins is about twice as heavy, in proportion, as in Fr. In the third degree of relationship Baugatal apportions the liability to cousins, while Fr. gives it to great grandsons, etc.—an unlikely class. In the case of second, third and fourth cousins, again, Baugatal imposes nearly twice as heavy a fine, in proportion to the total amount. On the other hand, Baugatal's *sakaukar* class (relations by marriage, etc.) hardly pay more than a quarter of their due proportion according to Fr. *In Baugatal, then, the responsibility falls nearly twice as heavily on all the more distant kinsmen,* while the slayer's father and brother escape comparatively easily. That is to say that the conception of the corporate liability of kindred has been greatly weakened in Norway since the date of Baugatal's composition. There are some other features of the later wergild law which point to the same conclusion. Thus Baugatal (and the earlier fragment of Frostuthing's law) reduce the wergild in the absence of any set of kinsmen. The later law awards a fixed sum, and also apportions large sums to connections who are not likely to exist (Cl. IV. 2), which is significant in view of the fact that the slain man's two nearest kinsmen evidently keep the sums for which there is no proper recipient. The matter is entirely in the hands of these two kinsmen, but there is no legal machinery provided to force them to distribute the sum equitably. We may therefore safely assume that except in the case of kinsmen who were near neighbours, or very active in the suit, or very powerful, the distribution of wergild would frequently not take place at all, and the final result would be that the money would tend to remain in the hands of the two nearest kinsmen, i.e. the heirs, as in Iceland.

We will now consider the wergilds in South Norway. The earlier Gulathing law, in force in the southern parts of Norway, and compiled in its present form about 1200, contains three complete sets of wergild regulations. The first (*Gul.* §§ 218 seq.) is possibly the earliest. As some points in this first set of regulations have hardly received the attention they deserve, I make no apology for treating it somewhat fully. As in Baugatal, and in the early fragment of the Frostuthing law, the wergild is divided into two parts, the *baug*, and the *upnám* for the more distant kinsmen.

Gul. § 218 seq. I. Baug: Marks
  (i) Höfuðbaug (chief baug) paid by slayer to son, or son
     and father of the slain   10
  (ii) Brother's baug, paid by slayer's brother   5
  (iii) *Bræðrung's* baug (first cousin, agnate)   4
  (iv) Women's gifts: mother, daughter, sister, wife of slain
     each receive 2 aurar (paid by slayer?)[1]   1
                                                      Total   20

The slayer is in the last resort responsible for all these sums.

II. *Upnám* or *Saker*:   Aurar
  (i) Slayer pays to the slain man's
    (*a*) father's brother, brother's son, mother's father,
      daughter's son, each 8 aurar (4 persons)[2] ...   32
    (*b*) *bræðrung* (agnatic first cousin), mother's brother,
      brother's daughter's son, sister's son, father's
      sister's son[3] (5 persons), 6 aurar each   30
    (*c*) mother's sister's son, *bræðrung's* child, father's *bræ-
      ðrung*[4], mother's mother's brother, sister's daugh-
      ter's son (5 persons), each 4 aurar...   20
                                                     Total   82

It is to be noted that the *bræðrung* (agnatic first cousin) participates twice, in I. iii. and II. *b*.

---

[1] § 221, "Now if all the women are missing, then the *slayer* shall take that mark, and give it to the son of the dead."

[2] § 237 points out that by father's brother is meant all the father's brothers, so 'person' must be taken to mean 'person or group of persons.'

[3] systling.

[4] Elsewhere class (C) is counted as 4 persons, § 237.

NORWAY

II. (ii). *Cross-payments* or 'kinsmen's compensations' (frændbætr). The payments are made by classes II. (*a*), (*b*), and (*c*) to the relatives of the slain. A careful study of the text reveals that not only do each of the relatives in class (*a*) for example, pay to each of the relatives in the corresponding class on the slain man's side, but also to each of the relatives in the other classes. With regard to classes (*a*) and (*b*) this is indicated, but not made absolutely clear, by the wording[1], but in treating of the liabilities of class (*c*) the language used is unequivocal[2], and as it is impossible that class (*c*) should alone be thus liable, there is no alternative but to suppose that each relative in each class was actually bound to pay each relative in every one of the three classes.

§ 225. Each person in cl. (*a*) pays:	aur.	ört.	pen.
to the son of the slain 4 aur.[3] (× 4)	16	0	0
„ brother of the slain 8 ört. (× 4) ...	10	2	0
to each person in cl. (*a*) 5 ört. 3 pen. (× 16)	28	0	8
„ „ „ (*b*) 1 aur. 4⅔ p. (× 20)...	23	0	3⅓
„ „ „ (*c*) 2 ört. 4 pen.[4] (× 16)[5]	12	2	4
Total[6]	90	2	5⅓

---

[1] § 225. ...Now the father's brother of the slayer [cl. *a*] must pay the mother's brother [in cl. *b*] of the slain...So shall be paid the sister's son [cl. *b*] similarly, and the bræðrung and the brother's daughter's son and the systling [all in cl. *b*]. Now the father's brother shall pay...to the mother's sister's son [cl. *c*] of the dead, and so shall each of them in that upnám. So shall they pay the sister's daughter's son, and the bræðrung's child, and the mother's mother's brother [all cl. *c*] of the dead.

§ 226. ...Now the bræðrung of the slayer [cl. *b*] is to pay to the bræðrung of the dead [cl. *b*]. So [shall be paid] the brother's daughter's son of the dead likewise, and the mother's brother and sister's son, and the systling of the dead. Now the bræðrung [cl. *b*] of the slayer shall pay the mother's sister's son [cl. *c*] of the dead...So shall each of them in that upnám. So shall they pay the bræðrung's child, and his father's bræðrung, and his mother's mother's brother, and sister's daughter's son [all in cl. *c*].

[2] § 227. ...But to the father's brother of the dead [the mother's sister's son of the slayer must pay] three pennings less than an eyrir. The same to the brother's son of the dead and the mother's father and daughter's son. The same payment is due from the mother's sister's son of the slayer and the sister's daughter's son and the bræðrung's child, and the mother's mother's brother of the slayer. *Of these each shall pay* 18 *pennings to the mother's brother of the slain. The same shall be paid to the sister's son of the dead and similarly each of them* [*shall pay*] *the bræðrung of the dead.*

The earliest fragment C says : 12 pennings shall *each of them pay in the lowest upnám to each of those in the highest upnám* (p. 113).

[3] I.e. half what he would receive from the slayer. Cp. Maurer, op. cit. p. 54.

[4] § 233 has 1 aur. 5 pen.

[5] In this passage cl. (*c*) is counted as 4 persons.

[6] In these passages 10 pennings are reckoned to the örtug.

§ 226. Each person in cl. (*b*) pays :

	aur.	ört.	pen.
to the son of the slain 3 aur. (×5)	15	0	0
„ brother of the slain 5 ört. 3 pen. (×5)	8	2	5
to each person in cl. (*a*) 1 aur. 4⅔ pen. (×20)	23	0	3⅛
„ „ „ (*b*) 2 ört. 3 pen.[1] (×25)	19	0	5
„ „ „ (*c*) 1 ört. 8⅔ pen. (×25)[2]	15	1	6⅔
Total	81	2	0

§ 227. Each person in cl. (*c*) pays :

	aur.	ört.	pen.
to the son of the slain 2 aur. (×4)	8	0	0
„ brother of the slain 4 ört. (×4) ...	5	1	0
to each person in cl. (*a*) 2 ört. 7 pen. (×16)	14	1	2
„ „ „ (*b*) 18 pen. (×20) ...	12	0	0
„ „ „ (*c*) 12 pen. (×16)[3] ...	6	1	2
Total	46	0	4

§ 228. The brother of slayer pays :

	aur.	ört.	pen.
to each person in cl. (*a*) 5⅓ aur. (×4) ...	21	1	0
„ „ „ (*b*) 4 aur. (×5)	20	0	0
„ „ „ (*c*) 2⅔ aur. (×4) ...	10	2	0
Total	52	0	0

The total is something over 64 marks, of which the slayer and his brother pay more than half—32¾ marks (women's gifts included).

The slayer is not usually outlawed as a consequence of his act : § 218 observes that if the slayer is outlawed, the chief baug (I. (i)) is not paid. If however the slayer is dead, his heir is liable for it.

That there is no provision for father's father nor for son's son is to be explained on the principle that money received in other degrees in the direct agnatic line is considered to suffice. But a stranger omission is that of the *father's* mother's family, seeing that the *mother's* mother's brother gets wergild.

Cognates take practically one-third less than agnates.

But now we come to a series of paragraphs which tacitly conflict with the statements in the preceding paragraphs. Thus § 229 seems to mean that the slayer is to pay the fines devolving on his father's brother and his brother's son[4]. § 230 seems to conflict with the preceding clause as well as with

---

[1] § 234 says 1 ört. 7 pen.
[2] Here cl. (*c*) is said to contain 5 persons.
[3] Here cl. (*c*) is again counted as 4 persons.
[4] "Nu scal vigande hava med ser i sokum faður broðor oc broðor sun oc hallda upp sökum firi þa, þo at þeir væri alldrigi menn i heimi en sialver þeir firi sic ef þeir ero til."

earlier clauses :—"The brother's son shall be associated with the father's brother with regard to the fine. They both take one (fine) and so also pay (one fine), while the father's brother lives, but one third less when the father's brother is dead[1]." We have already seen above (p. 56, and note 2 same page) that they each take one whole share.

Then follows a clause giving to childless female relatives under forty years of age the shares which their sons would receive if they existed, and then we have three clauses (232—234) which at first sight merely seem to reiterate what was laid down in 226 ff. about cross-payments, but on examination prove to run counter to them. Thus § 232 states that the father's brother of the slayer pays a sum to the father's brother of the slain, and the brother's son to the brother's son, and so on : i.e., the payments of class (*a*) to the corresponding class (*a*) on the side of the slain are calculated as only between the corresponding kinsmen, not each to each as in § 225 ff. Clauses 233—234 provide for payments from one *upnám* into another, but there is no payment from (*c*) to (*a*), nor to (*c*) from (*a*) and (*b*), nor to (*b*) from (*a*). There are also one or two differences between these clauses and the preceding ones with regard to the sum paid. These may or may not be scribal errors, as suggested by the editors[2].

In view of this divergence we must suppose either (1) that these clauses are added by a later editor as glosses on the preceding statement—in which case it is clear that the later editor failed to grasp the preceding clauses, besides allowing his own statements in § 230, about uncles and nephews, to conflict not only with the preceding clauses, but also with his own explanation in § 231 ;—or (2) that they are a fragment, or rather two fragments (§§ 230—231 and 232—235) of another set of wergild regulations ; and this seems the more probable suggestion[3].

III. We now give the substance of § 235, which apportions wergild to twenty-six persons, beginning with the agnatic kinsmen nearest to class II. *a*.[4] Agnates in this list alternate with cognates, and the former apparently take one-third more than equally related cognates. Each person in the list takes one-third less than the preceding one. The sum to be taken by each person is given both in money and in ells. The ratio between these, in the first 4 cases, works out very accurately to 3 pennings to the ell (with negligible fractions such as $\frac{1}{53}$, $\frac{1}{69}$ and so on); till we get to the fourth agnate on

---

[1] "Broðor sunr scal fylgia faður brœðr til sakar. taka baðer eina. oc sva bœta meðan faður broðer livir. en siðan þriðiungi minna er faður broðer fellr i fra."

[2] *N. G. L.* I. p. 78, note 3.

[3] So Keyser, *Efterladte Skr.* I. p. 302, note 1; see however v. Amira, op. cit. p. 130.

[4] "sa maðr er nestr er at frendseme i karlsvift fra hinu œfsta upname." For speculations as to these kinsmen see Maurer, op. cit. p. 61. Note also the *talubót* of the fragment of Cod. IV. l. 24 (cp. v. Amira, op. cit. p. 151).

the list. There we find the ratio vary to about 3⅔ pennings[1] to the ell. The next degree receive little more than half the preceding sum, instead of two-thirds[2]. Then, startlingly enough, the ratio between pennings and ells jumps to 6½ : 1, and finally to 7½ : 1. The explanation of this can only be that the latter part of the money payments was calculated in a time when the penning had decreased in weight till it was only half its original value—i.e., in the twelfth century. The calculation was probably made by the scribe who committed the law to writing, and who amused himself by subtracting thirds until only fractions of a penning remained. That a gross error of this sort could then pass unnoticed shows clearly that these payments were entirely obsolete[3]. This is perhaps also indicated by the fact that the *payer* of these sums is never mentioned.

IV. Now come the *Sakaukar*, or Increasers of Fines. We have no means of knowing whether this passage belongs to the first group of clauses, which we will call A 1 ; or to the second, A 2 ; or to both.

§ 236. (1) The slayer pays to :   aur.
  (a) thrall-born brother, thrall-born son, half-brother by
      same mother, each 12 aur.   36

§ 237. (b) father's thrall-born brother, father's half-brother
      by same mother, each 6 aur.   12
  (c) mother's thrall-born brother and mother's half-brother
      by same mother, each 3 aur.   6

(2) The slayer's brother pays one-third less to each :
    to (a) 8 aur. each   24
       (b) 4 aur. each   8
       (c) 2 aur. each   4

(3) Slayer's father's brother pays one-third less again,
    i.e., a total of 24 aur.   24
                                                   ———
                                             Total 114

Then follows a paragraph entitled *misvígi*, dealing with offences that aggravate the crime of manslaughter. Then, § 239, we get the fines due to connections by marriage and others, payable by the slayer.

---

[1] 18⅔ pen = 5 ells : i.e. the ratio is as 3¹¹⁄₁₅ : 1.
[2] 9½ ells instead of 12⅔, the ratio of pennings to the ell has here decreased to 2¹²⁄₃ : 1.
[3] The omission of the 14th agnate in the list is probably merely due to inadvertence : cp. Maurer, op. cit. p. 28.

		aur.
V. son-in-law (or father-in-law)		12
brother-in-law		6
		18
stepfather		12
stepson		12
oath-brother		12
foster-brother		12
mother's mother's father (if of high birth[1])		12
	Total	78

All this is to be paid by the slayer.

The most noteworthy point about these payments in IV. and V. is the increasingly heavy burden on the slayer himself. If all the persons in the two groups existed,—an unlikely supposition, however,—the slayer would be mulcted of 132 aurar, in addition to his heavy baug and other payments. The greater part of these persons do not receive wergild in Baugatal, which we have seen reason to believe the earliest Norwegian wergild law extant, and this circumstance, combined with the fact that these sums are all payable by the slayer, leads us to imagine that these additional burdens were added at a late date, when the idea of the slayer's primary responsibility was becoming more prominent than it ever could have been while the solidarity of the kindreds remained unshaken.

We now pass to the second complete set of wergild payments, in Gulathing's law. It begins with paragraph 243; and we will call it B. It is called a *hauld's* wergild: *hauld* seems to be used in the same sense as *ódalborinn maðr* in § 218; and to refer to a landed aristocracy.

Its main features are as follows:

I. Baug. marks
  (i) *höfuðbaug* paid by slayer to son of slain ... 6
  (ii) *bróðurbaug* paid by brother to brother of slain ... 4
  (iii) *brœðrung's baug* paid by brœðrung to brœðrung[2] ... 2½
  (iv) *skógarkaup*, to redeem slayer from outlawry ... 3
  Total 15½

---

[1] If a *höldr*.
[2] § 249 however seems to declare that each baug-payer shall *pay* only ⅔ of what he would *receive*, which conflicts with the above.

II. Tryggva-kaup or Truce-Buying :   aur.[1] ört. pen.
    Slayer pays to (ii) and (iii) each 1⅕ aur.   ...   2   1   2
    Slayer's brother pays to (i) and (iii) each 1⅕ aur.   2   1   2
      ,,   bræðrung pays to (i) and (ii) each 1⅕ aur.   2   1   2
                                                    Total   7   0   6

"if all the kinsmen join in the peace at the same time."

III. Gifts :   aur. ört. pen.
   (*a*) Slayer, his mother, daughter, wife, each pay
       to wife, daughter, mother of slain one
       gift of 1⅕ aur. (× 12)   14   1   2
   (*b*) Slayer's sister pays ½ gift to sister, wife,
       daughter, mother of slain (2 gifts)   ...   2   1   2
   (*c*) Slayer, his mother, daughter, wife, each pay
       ½ gift to sister of slain (2 gifts)   ...   2   1   2
                                             Marks 2   3   0   6

Here a total is given, as if this were the whole wergild. This total is declared to be Mks 20. 2. 1. 2, whereas the actual total of the sums given is Mks 18. 6. 1. 2. Seebohm suggests that the difference may be due to the fact that 20 of the earlier Roman or Merovingian marks were equal to 18 of the later period. It would seem that these regulations cannot have been in full force at the time when the laws were committed to writing, or we should hardly have found an inconsistency about so large a sum.

   IV. The next clause is headed : "About *saker*"   aur.
    (i) (*a*) father's brother, brother's son, half-brother by same
         mother, thrall-born son, daughter's son, mother's
         father (6 persons) take 12 aur. each   72
      (*b*) mother's brother, sister's son, thrall-born brother, each
         9 aur.   27
      (*c*) first cousins 6 aur. (× 3)[2]   18
      (*d*) father's thrall-born brother (and son of thrall-born
         daughter if she married a freeman)   8
                                           Total   125

§ 249. All these receive from the slayer ⅔ (of the above sums or in addition to them?) and ⅓ from slayer's brother.

---

[1] The eyrir is here reckoned as equal to 12 ells : the previous regulations dealt with a 10-ell eyrir.

[2] *Systkinna synir* usually only means father's sister's sons and mother's brother's sons. As however no provision is made elsewhere for mother's sister's sons we assume them to be included here.

§§ 250—252. (ii) There are cross-payments between classes *a*, *b*, and *c* above, which would appear to amount to 31 aur. 1 ört. 5 pen., but may be more if they are from each to each in each class. There is no mention of any outer circle of kindred, so that the total wergild would be something over 38 marks.

The 'truce-buying,' of which we saw traces in the early Frostuthing fragment, seems here to aim at inducing all the nearer kindred to join in the peace at the same time.

The striking feature of the above regulations is the entire absence of any kindred more distant than first cousins. But Gulathing's law contains two regulations in which *baug* payments only are given. In § 179 we have the declaration: " But if both the hand and the foot be cut off the same man, he is worse living than dead, and shall be paid for *as if he were dead*. § 180. Now are stated the payments in Gula: a *hauld* shall be paid for with 18 marks of legal tender[1]." Eighteen marks is a baug payment only (see above, pp. 50, 56). Seebohm[2] suggests that the outer payments were not made because the man was wounded only, but this theory is directly contradicted by the preceding clause[3]. It seems we must allow that Gulathing's law contemplates a wergild of *baug* only, for we find again (§ 170): " If a man slays the *ármaðr* (official) of the King, he shall pay for him with 15 marks...at that rate of money as is current in Gula, aurar of 6 ells each[4]." If, as seems likely, these sums cover baug payments only, these two enactments would indicate that the claims of a wider kindred were not always considered.

The confusion of the above sets of regulations is so marked that we are not surprised to find a new law[5], added under the name of Bjarni Marðarson, who lived about 1223. He takes fixed sums,—the first is 6 marks of gold, i.e. 48 marks of silver, and shows how it is to be divided. He makes no clear distinction

---

[1] "Nu ero giolld told i Gula. giallda haulld XVIII. morcom logeyris."
[2] *Tribal Custom in A.S. Law*, p. 252.
[3] Cp. Grág. 1 *a*, 202.
[4] "Nu vigr maðr armann konongs. þa scal giallda hann. XV. morcom...at þvi aura lage scal giallda hann aptr sem mælt er i Gula. vi alna eyris."
[5] Gul. §§ 316—319. These clauses, though actually earlier than the Frostuthing wergild, are supposed to have been intended for the whole country (cp. Maurer, op. cit. p. 65).

between baug and outer payments[1], and he assumes that the son of the dead man receives the whole sum (from the slayer?) and distributes it himself to his kinsmen[2]. There is thus no longer any need for both sets of kinsmen to meet. It is to be observed that the son of the slain takes any share of the sum for which the proper recipient does not exist. A glance at the list of recipients[3] will show that the difference between the sum actually received, and the total of the payments to kinsmen, might be very large, so that the slain man's nearest relative would benefit largely. Moreover no means are suggested by which the recipient of the whole sum can be forced to distribute it among his relatives, so that more distant or less powerful relatives were very unlikely to obtain their share. As in the case of the later Frostuthing's law (see above, p. 55) we must surmise that these

---

[1] Maurer, op. cit. p. 66, observes that in these regulations "die Verwandtschaft zeigt sich somit ohne alle Gliederung in ihre Atome aufgelöst."

[2] Each kinsman of the slayer pays the same amount as the corresponding kinsman of the slain receives.

[3] I. (i) Son.
    (ii) Brother.
    (iii *a*) Father's brother and his sons (here follows in each case a complicated and not entirely consistent set of regulations providing for him if childless, for his illegitimate son, for possible daughter's sons, for his sons if he is dead).
    (iv) Father of slain.
    (v *a*) Half-brother by same mother.
    (v *b*) Father's half-brother.
    (vi *a*) Stepfather and stepson.
    (vi *b*) Brothers-in-law.

II. (*a*) Mother's father, and daughter's son.
    (*b*) Mother's brother, and sister's son.
    (*c*) *Bræðrung's* child; father's *bræðrungr*.
    (*d*) Father's sister's sons.
    (*e*) Mother's brother's sons.
    (*f*) Sons of sisters.
    (*g*) Brother's daughter's son.
    (*h*) Second cousins (agnatic).
    (*i*) Sons of female agnatic first cousins.
    (*j*) ,, ,, cognatic first cousins.
    (*k*, *l*) 4th agnates and 3rd cognates.
    (*m*, *n*) 5th ,, ,, 4th ,,
    (*o*, *p*) 6th ,, ,, 5th ,,
    (*q*) 6th cognates.

regulations were chiefly of use in order to establish what kinsmen had a right to wergild, if they chose, or were able, to claim it. Only thus, too, can we explain the ignorance and confused statements of the law-books. We must therefore beware of regarding these wergild-laws as conclusive evidence for the solidarity of the kindred in the 13th century.

King Magnus the Law-Mender (1263—1280) abolished all kinsmen's compensations both on the side of slayer and slain[1]. Only the nearest heir was to receive wergild. This new law was promulgated in 1271. In other countries, as we shall see later, constant and emphatic repealing of the old wergild laws was of little or no avail against deep-rooted custom. In Norway the participation of kindred must already have been rather half-hearted, for this one declaration seems to have sufficed to put an end to the custom, in so far as it may have still persisted up to that date. The entire absence of all mention of 'kinsmen' in Norwegian deeds of reconciliation, records of suits, etc. is very remarkable. In Sweden and Denmark the 'kinsmen' are included long after their legal right to wergild has been abolished, but the Norwegian legal documents show the heir or heirs briefly acknowledging that he has received so and so much from the slayer[2]. A deed of 1348 shows the slayer alone paying wergild to the brother of the slain, and though the nature of the reconciliation is fully stated there is no word of other kinsmen[3]. Sometimes a husband and wife give the receipt[4] or pay the money[5], sometimes a brother and sister[6], or the widow and her children[7], but more distant kinsmen are never mentioned. How

---

[1] Nyere Landslov, *N. G. L.* IV. § 12 (in 1271).

[2] *Dipl. Norw.* III. No. 258 (1348), I. No. 523 (1390), IX. No. 188 (1397), I. Nos. 608 (1406), 633 (1412), No. 637 (1413), XV. No. 75 (1449), XII. No. 213 (1447), XIV. No. 540 (1526), XV. No. 721 (1567).

[3] See Appendix II, No. 1 and *D. N.* I. Nos. 236 (1336), 513 (1389), XI. No. 249 (1482).

[4] *D. N.* I. No. 413 (1371). Helgi and his wife take wergild from Sölvi for the slaying of Amund. However, they hand over one quarter of the sum to another person; relationships not mentioned.

[5] *D. N.* I. No. 933 (1482). Thorkel and his wife pledge a farm to a widow and her children, Thorkel having caused the death of the husband.

[6] *D. N.* XIV. No. 794 (1542). Per Ulfsson and his sister Ingirid announce their reconciliation with Niels Engelbrektsson, who accidentally killed their father.

[7] *D. N.* I. No. 933 (1482), XV. No. 721 (1567).

completely the tribal idea of wergild has died out is seen in the fact that women receive the whole wergild[1], and in one case a woman pays the wergild due for a slaying committed by her late husband[2].

The later cases given in Norwegian Court Records of the sixteenth century, now published in the *Norske Herredags Dombøger*, show the same limitation of wergild to the heirs. An interesting case is given in Appendix II[3].

More striking still is the fact that in the letters of the kings of Denmark relating to slayings in Norway, the expression 'heirs[4]' is frequently used where in both the other Scandinavian kingdoms, with which the king was better acquainted, the words 'kinsmen and friends' is invariably employed. Only quite occasionally, and then, it would seem, by inadvertence, does the Danish king use the latter expression when referring to a Norwegian slaying-suit.

To sum up. There seems to have been a progressive decline of tribal solidarity in Norway. The earliest stages of this decline we are not able to trace, but we may suspect that it was already considerably advanced before the settlement of Iceland, at any rate among the aristocracy. As regards wergild, all responsibility of the kin in this matter is entirely at an end

---

[1] *D. N.* xv. No. 98 (1472). Gudrid Throndsdatter admits that she has received all that was due to her in fines for Thore Slampe. xv. No. 713 (1564). Ragnhild Björnsdatter declares that she has received the wergild for her son Gunleik, 11 marks of gold and 44 florins, besides a 'gift in friendship' of a spoon and a cow. This is a very large wergild. Cp. also ix. No. 183 (1390) and *Norske Rigsregistranter*, viii. p. 296.

[2] *D. N.* xv. No. 25 (1367). Sigrid paid land (which she had inherited from her brother), for the slaying of Baard Valthjófsson, whom her *first husband* had accidentally slain.

[3] No. 2. Cp. also N. H. D. iii. p. 33: two men and their co-heirs complain that the slayer does not keep to his agreement (1585); v. p. 321 f. (20 Aug. 1599): Peter Kieldsen is to pay 'fines to the dead man's heirs' (bøder til den dødis arffuinger); and vi. p. 34 f. (13 July 1604): Knud and Olaf go bail for their brother, who has slain a man, and declare that they have paid the wergild. Cp. also *Norske Rigsregistranter*, iii. p. 605 (1600): the slayer is to pay 200 florins to the slain man's *heirs*.

[4] *Norske Rigsregistranter*, iii. p. 689—90 (1586); iv. p. 42 (1604), p. 69. *Dipl. Norw.*, xi. No. 51 (1361), No. 58 (1369); xii. No. 211 (1446), No. 278 (1511), No. 599 (1541); xii. No. 21, 101, 167; xvi. No. 442; xv. No. 92, 147. *Kancelliets Brevbøger* (Copenhagen), ii. p. 284.

before the close of the thirteenth century, and possibly before that time.

Other signs of tribal custom also disappear early. The oath of twelve kinsmen does not appear even in the earliest laws, though in some cases the presence of one or two kinsmen of an oath-taker is required. The principle that there could be no feud and no wergild within the kindred, is already in the earliest laws restricted to the immediate family—parents and children[1].

It is only with regard to tenure of land that we can trace some of the ancient tribal principles. *Odal* land—land which had been inherited from grandfather's grandfather, could not be alienated unless first offered to the odal-sharers, i.e. those other kinsmen who had an inherited claim to it. In default of nearer kinsmen, these might be as distant as second cousins[2]. But before building up any theory involving solidarity of kindred on this institution it will be well to remember (1) that though originating in tribal ideas, its actual tribal significance is small, (2) that a similar institution existed all over the Teutonic part of the Continent until long after the Middle Ages[3], and (3) in Norway the institution was consciously strengthened by Magnus the Law-Mender, no doubt with a view to supporting the shattered aristocracy of Norway[4].

As in Iceland, it is the nearest heir who is liable for the support of pauper kinsmen, the burden being only shared when there are several heirs[5].

We may conclude our review of the evidence by asserting that in spite of the many survivals in the laws of a tribal mode of thinking, so ably pointed out by Seebohm, all organization of society based on the solidarity of the kindred was already on the wane in Norway in Viking times, and had completely broken down by the end of the thirteenth century.

---

[1] Gul. § 164. Frost. IV. 31.
[2] Cp. Boden, *Das norw. Stammgüterrecht*, Zs. der Sav. Stift. Bd. 22 (1901), pp. 109—154.
[3] *Retraktrecht, Vorkaufsrecht*, etc. Cp. the Fr. *retrait lignager*.
[4] Cp. O. Büchner, Anhang to Sering's *Vererbung in Schl. Holstein*.
[5] Gul. 115, 118. Cp. v. Amira, *Nordgerm. Obligationenrecht*, Bd. II. pp. 907 ff.

CHAPTER III

SWEDEN

To turn to the Swedish wergild laws after studying those of Norway is like emerging from a thicket into the open country. The latter have lost sight of every main principle in the multiplicity of detail, and darken counsel by heaping together all the wergild clauses or fragments of wergild regulations known to the compilers, who seem strangely regardless of inconsistencies. The earlier Swedish provincial laws show local divergence, it is true, but no inconsistency, and such obscurity as there is about them arises from the extreme conciseness with which they state the main principle of wergild distribution.

The contrast between the Norwegian and the Swedish wergild clauses is the more remarkable as some of the latter are first committed to writing considerably later than the Norwegian. This is the case with the Helsinge law, which was probably first written between 1310 and 1347. It was current not only in the modern province of Helsingeland but over the whole of Northern Sweden, extending its sphere as these regions were gradually settled.

Its wergild chapter runs as follows[1]:

"If a man kills another, and is legally proved guilty of (the) slaying: The plaintiff has the choice whether he will rather take vengeance or receive compensation. If he will receive compensation, he shall have 7 marks reckoned by weight. The king (shall have) 4 marks wergild. The aider and abettor shall each of them pay 15 marks[2] or deny (their complicity) with an oath of 14 men. Let the father or mother take for their son 16 öre: the brother 8 öre, the wife 12 öre. Let whoever is (next) nearest in kinship take 4 öre. A first cousin[3] 2 öre. A second cousin 1 öre. A third cousin half

---

[1] Helsingelagen, Manhæliæs B. XXXVIII. in vol. VI. of *Sveriges Gamla Lagar*, ed. Collin, Schlyter, etc. (1827—77).

[2] Possibly reckoned in minted money, not by weight.

[3] *Systlingi* should strictly be first cousins on the mother's side, but must here be taken to mean first cousins in general. Cp. Gloss. to vol. VI., *s.v.*

an öre[1]. Let each pay (compensation) in like manner as he receives it, up to the fourth man (third cousin). Once (only) shall kindred compensation (*ættæ boot*) be paid (on behalf of the same kinsman). Afterwards let each be himself responsible for his deeds."

Outside the first degree, each more distant degree of the kindred receives or pays half as much as the degree next nearest to the slayer or slain—a principle which runs all through Swedish and Danish wergild laws. Presumably the slayer himself pays the 7 marks received by the plaintiff. But there are other noticeable points in the regulations. (1) The plaintiff still has the actual right of vengeance acknowledged by the law—a very antique feature which is seldom so plainly alluded to in Teutonic law. (2) The claim, or liability, of the *mother*, possibly secondary to that of the father, but still definitely mentioned. (3) The very large share payable to the *widow* of the slain or by the wife of the slayer—another quite unique feature. (4) The absence of any distinction between agnates and cognates. (5) The father's and mother's kindred appear to share equally. (6) The restriction of liability for wergild-contribution on behalf of the same kinsman to one slaying. The kindred evidently aims at shaking off responsibility for a man who is too hasty with his weapons.

The older redaction of the Vestmanna Law, dating from early in the fourteenth century, has a very brief wergild clause which runs as follows[2]:

"Whoever slays a man, let him be liable himself if (his property) suffices. His brother, if he exists, divides with him (the liability to the extent of) half the compensation as against him (the slayer). Let him (the brother) pay with the kindred. Let them all pay half compensation. Let those brothers who are together (have a common household) pay all together for what one of them does amiss unless it be an *urbotarmal* (suit in which compensation cannot be taken) or (a case of) immorality."

---

[1] This adds up to 5 marks 3½ öre, but if we might reckon that the quota of the 2nd, 3rd and 4th degrees was really paid by each of the two sides of the family, paternal and maternal, and that the brothers paid their mark twice, once for each side, as in Skåne law, we should get a total of 7 marks 3 öre; i.e. approximately what the heir receives, as in the Vestergötland law (p. 72 below). If the father *and* mother each pay 16 öre, the total would then be 9 marks 3 öre.

[2] Vestmannalagen, *Sv. G. L.*, vol. v., 1. Manhælghis B. 10.

Though this is so briefly put as to be unintelligible without the analogy of the other Swedish wergild-regulations, it is fairly plain considered in conjunction with them. The slayer is presumably to pay, not the whole compensation, but a main part of it, if his property suffices: his brother pays half that amount, and each further degree half less.

That women share in wergild liability also in this law seems to follow from a paragraph in the marriage law:

" Now if a father marries his daughter to a foreigner (i.e. a man not of Vestmanna-land) or to another husband without the consent of kinsmen, then let the husband be himself responsible for his deeds as long as his goods and those of both of them suffice—unless they (the kinsmen) have previously received (a contribution towards) kindred-compensation from them[1]."

The above passage is also interesting as revealing that the father had not complete freedom to dispose of his daughter, but that his will was subject to the approval of the kindred.

Another interesting passage shows that slaying within the kindred was considered apart from other slayings, and that apparently no ordinary wergild could be paid for it:

§ 1. "If a father slays his son, or a son his father, that is 20 marks for the slaying. These are divided into three parts: let the king take one part, the bishop the second, and the third the *hundred* (district)....For the breach (of kinship) 40 marks: let the king take one part, the bishop the second, and the *hundred* the third.

§ 2. If a second or third cousin is killed, their slaying is 3 marks. For the breach (of kinship), 40 marks, let the compensation go as before[2]."

In the later redaction of the Vestmanna Law (also a private compilation), there is no mention of wergild-distribution.

The Upland Law, which we possess in an official revised version of 1296, has no reference to wergild-distribution, and the same is the case with the Södermanna Law, of which we possess an official edition from 1327. The Law of Östergötland, however, makes up for these deficiencies. It dates from about the end of the thirteenth century:

---

[1] Gipninga B. 3, § 2. Cp. Södermanna L. Gipn. B. 1.
[2] 1. Manhælghis B. 1.

"Now that kindred shall pay *oranbot* (feud-compensation) which attacked. That is 6½ marks and 4 örtughær (i.e. 6 marks 5⅓ öre). The father's kinsmen shall pay two-thirds, and one-third the kinsmen on the maternal side. If there is a full brother[1] he pays half for all (the paternal kinsmen), whether he is a legitimate or illegitimate son. Then let him who is next to him (in kinship) pay half for all [half the whole remainder]. Then all those who are within the kindred to the seventh man [6th degree], let each man pay (his share?) like every other[2]. *Oranbot* is received in the same manner as it is paid: the paternal kinsmen two parts and the maternal kinsmen a third: and so let him who is nearest on the paternal side receive half what is due to the paternal kinsmen, and he who is next to him half (the remainder). Now he who is nearest on the maternal side, he shall pay half of the third. So also he who is then nearest: he has to pay half of what is left of the third, or deny with a twelve-men's oath that he was so related to the slayer that he had to pay *oranbot* for him. § 2. Now the kinsmen of the slayer have to summon their kinsmen for *oranbot*: the paternal kinsmen the father's side, and the maternal kinsmen the mother's side. The kinsmen of him who was slain, they shall claim compensation on threat of feud[3], and shall make no summons. They have to demand from the paternal kinsmen (of the slayer), on threat of feud, that they should get two parts of the compensation, and the others (maternal kinsmen, similarly) from the maternal kinsmen (of the slayer) that they should get a third of the compensation[4]."

We note that the slayer appears to pay nothing, but analogy with the other laws would suggest that there is also an heir's compensation (*arvæbot*)[5] received by the heir in addition to the first share of the *oranbot*, and possibly paid by the slayer. Analogy may be our best guide in disposing of another problem. After the liability of the first two kinsmen (or rather classes of kinsmen) has been expounded, the þa gialde sua man sum man, "'let each man pay like every other," might be taken to mean that outside an inner circle of kinsmen the various degrees of kinship were treated alike, so that the sixth cousin would pay the same amount as the third. As we have no Scandinavian analogy for such an arrangement it is probably safer to supply some such phrase as " in each degree[6]," and to take the clause as

---

[1] *sambroþir*, but this seems contradicted by what immediately follows.
[2] þa gialde sua man sum man.
[3] *Ora æptir bot*. Schlyter (*Glossar*, *s.v.*) translates: "Vindictam minitando mulctam exigere."
[4] Östgötalagen. Drapa B. VII.
[5] Cp. Vestgöta law, p. 72 below.
[6] Cp. Vestgöta law, p. 72 below.

meaning that payment is reckoned *per stirpes* and not *per capita*. On this assumption the Östergötland *oranbot* would work out much as follows:

$6\frac{1}{2}$ marks $+ 4$ örtughær $= 160$ örtughær[1]. This would give $106\frac{2}{3}$ örtughær to the father's kindred, and $53\frac{1}{3}$ to the mother's kindred. The shares of the successive degrees of kinship would thus be:

Father's kindred.			Mother's kindred.		
Class (1)	...	$53\frac{1}{3}$ örtughær	Class (1)	...	$26\frac{2}{3}$ örtughær
,, (2)	...	$26\frac{2}{3}$,,	,, (2)	...	$13\frac{1}{3}$,,
,, (3)	...	$13\frac{1}{3}$,,	,, (3)	...	$6\frac{2}{3}$,,
,, (4)	...	$6\frac{2}{3}$,,	,, (4)	...	$3\frac{1}{3}$,,
,, (5)	...	$3\frac{1}{3}$,,	,, (5)	...	$1\frac{2}{3}$,,
,, (6)	...	$1\frac{2}{3}$,,	,, (6)	...	$\frac{5}{6}$,,
,, (7)	...	$\frac{5}{6}$,,	,, (7)	...	$\frac{5}{12}$,,
		$105\frac{5}{6}$			$52\frac{11}{12}$

On this method of computation the sum of these payments must of course fall short of the actual total ($106\frac{2}{3}$ marks, etc.) by the amount of the smallest contribution; but when we consider that the payment was probably partly in silver, partly in cattle and partly in wadmal, it is easy to see that the shortage of a fraction of an örtugh in the total amount was quite negligible.

We will now consider the earlier recension of the Vestergötland Law (the earliest Swedish law-book), which is also full:

§ 4. "If they[2] [the kinsmen of the slain] will receive compensation, there shall be paid 9 marks *arvæbot* (heir's compensation), and 12 marks *ættærbot* (kindred compensation). The heir[3] shall pay 6 marks (of the latter): 6 marks the kindred shall pay: 3 (marks) on the paternal side and 3 on the maternal. The most nearly related shall pay 12 öre. Then he who is next 6 öre: then he who is next 3 öre: he who is next $4\frac{1}{2}$ örtughær." § 5. So shall all pay and so shall all receive: each has less by half, to the sixth man. Compensation shall be shared as far as the sixth man. (Among) all equally related persons one branch[4] shall have as much as the other [i.e. the payment

---

[1] 3 örtughær 1 öre; 8 öre 1 mark.

[2] We note that the decision does not rest here, as in the Helsingland law, with the plaintiff alone, but with the kinsmen.

[3] i.e. the heir presumptive of the slayer.

[4] *Kolder*. Schlyter (*Glossar, s.v.*) regards the word in this context as meaning 'cognati paterni vel materni invicem oppositi.' The translation given above represents the view of Otman and of Beauchet; and seems preferable in view of the fact that the equality of the paternal and maternal kindreds is already twice stated in the passage.

shall be reckoned *per stirpes* and not *per capita*]. The heir shall have 6 marks of the *ættærbot* and the kindred shall have 6 marks: 3 on the paternal side and 3 on the maternal[1].

As in the Helsingland law, the contribution of the maternal and paternal kindreds is equal. The shares would work out as follows:

Each side receives 3 marks = 72 örtughær.

Class (1)	...	36 örtughær.
,, (2)	...	18 ,,
,, (3)	...	9 ,,
,, (4)	...	$4\frac{1}{2}$,,
,, (5)	...	$2\frac{1}{4}$,,
,, (6)	...	$1\frac{1}{8}$,,
		$70\frac{7}{8}$

In the later redaction of the Vestergötland Law there is a curious attempt to differentiate, not between paternal and maternal kinsmen, as in the Östergötland Law, but between agnates and cognates, though the amounts contributed by each are still equal. And here we find the first trace of inconsistency in the Swedish laws, for the passage begins by repeating the statement of the earlier recension, that *ættærbot* is 12 marks, of which the heir gets 6, and the kindred 6, and that this latter sum is divided equally between paternal and maternal kindred. But after repeating the whole of § 4 it goes on to say[2] that if brothers live apart *each* pays 12 öre, and so apparently with each degree. Such a method of contribution would of course greatly increase the total. But more than this, agnatic first cousins pay 6 öre, and cognatic first cousins also pay 6 öre, and so on. It is easy to see that a totally different method of wergild contribution has

---

[1] Vestg. I. Af mandrapi. I. § 4.
[2] Vestgötalag II. Dræpare Balkr. VII. Þre marker a fæþerne ok þre a möþerne. ok taki ingin ættærstuþi vtan en timæ. þo at han flere mæn dræpi æn en. þa skal þæn skilðaste bötæ tolf öræ....Bröþer saman sök til ættærbot allir firi eno garzliþi. böten allir tolf öræ. sökes huar þerræ sin staþ. böte huar þerræ tolf öræ. Bröþræ synir sökis huar sin staþ. botæ huar saman söktir. böte allir vi. öræ. æru at skilð böte huart þerræ æmmykit....Systræ syni saman. sökter. böte huar þerræ sæx öræ. atskylðir böte huar þerre æmmykit. Systrungæ börn saman sökt böte þre öræ, at skilð böte huar þerre æmmykit....
Similarly Vestgötal. III. 63 (Lydekini Excerpta et Adnotationes).

been sandwiched in between the provisions of the earlier law, for a distinction between agnates and cognates is incompatible with the statement that 3 marks are paid by the father's kindred and 3 by the mother's kindred. To meet this difficulty it might be suggested that 'mother's kindred' may really mean 'cognates,' 'persons related through their mother,' also in the earlier law. Such an interpretation, however, is impossible in view of the passage in the Ostergötland law which prescribes that the (near) paternal kinsmen summon the kindred on the father's side and the maternal kinsmen the kindred on the mother's side. This provision is even more definitely stated in the Skåne and Danish laws, and disposes of the theory that *möþerni*, 'mother's kindred,' might mean cognates, for it is obvious that the mother's uncle, for instance, could not be expected to summon the distant cognatic relatives on the father's side. We must therefore regard these particular clauses in the later Vestergötland law as an interpolation.

The Skåne law divides its wergild into three equal parts: one paid by the slayer, one by the paternal kindred and one by the maternal. As this scheme of division is also that of the other Danish laws, it will be more convenient to treat it in the following chapter.

Other manifestations of kindred solidarity are not far to seek. In oaths of compurgation it is never expressly stated that the oath-helpers are of the kin of the accused[1], but kinsmen's oaths play a considerable part in matters of inheritance and so forth. Thus in the Upland law the father's kinsmen and the mother's kinsmen divide the inheritance into shares for the children, and the latter draw lots which have been previously decided upon by the father's kinsmen. If disputes arise afterwards, eighteen first cousins present at the settlement declare what belongs to each disputant, or, in their absence the next nearest relatives[2]. In the

---

[1] Östg. Ærfþa B. XVII. Kære (han) lokan ælla spanan (that his servants have been lured away) : þa skal han dylia mæþ tolf manna eþe (the accused shall deny with a 12-men's oath). Cp. Hels. Manhæliæs B. XXXVIII: haldbani ok raaþbani...dyli mæþ XIIII. mannæ eþe.

[2] Upl. Ærfþ. XI. § 2. Nu aghu þer j flerum byum. þa skulu fæþærnis frændær ok möþærnis skiptæ hwarium sin lot...þær aghu möþærnis frændær lot skiæræ. ok

Östgöta law an heir accused by his brother or sister of not being legitimate (in a dispute over paternal inheritance) denies it with 15 (16?) kinsmen within the third degree : each must be over 15 years of age[1].

In the Småland (ecclesiastical) law a man or woman accused of having married within the forbidden degree of kinship can deny it with an oath of six paternal and six maternal kinsmen[2].

More interesting is the part played by the kinsmen in freeing a kinsman enslaved through debt or otherwise :

> When kinsmen have delivered their kinsman, by purchase, from a position of serfdom, "Now for all his deeds which he does his kinsmen shall answer after he is freed and not the (his) master. At Lionga *Thing* they shall proceed to a full oath of kinsmen : each in the third degree. Let him take so many of one family as he can get, of those who are 15 years old. So it shall be with all oaths of kinsmen as is now said. Two shall witness it and twelve thereafter that he is so near in kinship to them and so related in degree that they have to free him into the company of freemen. And thereupon another oath of 14 men (shall) so swear that 'we free him to kindred and kinsmen and not to the lot of a serf.' That is the legal (price of) freedom : three marks of wadmal, or six marks of minted coin, or four good beasts. And to swear a third oath so, that two shall declare : that this is kinsmen's property and not his property[3]."

---

fæþerni a skiöti haldæ. ok möþærnis frændær lot vp takæ. klandær þæt nokot syzkini siþæn fore andru. þa aghu þæt syzlungær ok brollungær vitæ atærtan þer sum boskiptis fastær waru. hwat a hwars þeræ lot kom. æru æi þer til. þa taki þöm niþum æru næstir. ok kyni kunnæstir...hawær son ællr dotter ærfft æptir faþur sin. þæt goþz. þa fyllin syzlungær ok bryllungær boskiptis eþ. at hwar ræþ fullum sinum lot. ok siþæn witi þa faþir fang. ok sun fæþærni mæþ atærtan mannæ eþe....

[1] Östg. Ærfþa B. VIII. Nu dela bröþær ælla systær um fæþrini sit annar kallar annan egh aþalkunu son uara : þa hauær han uitzs orþ uita mæþ enum at han mælte til þæt skula uara niþia hans innan þriþia knæ. annar giptæ maþrin (of the bride) : þriþi a fæþrinit ölbuþi uar til þæs öls (guest at his father's marriage feast) : fiarþi a möþrinit ölbuþi uar til þæs öls ok tolf æftir. man af kulle huarn i þriþia knæ : taki sua manga af enum kulle sum han kan fa þem sum fæmtan ara æru. So also § 1 :—þa skulu þæt uita fiughurtan mæn möþrinis frændær (in the case of a quarrel over maternal inheritance).

[2] Smål. Kristnu B, 13 § 8. giæti æ thet wizcustæ som hionælagh will haldæ. meth frændom sinom. oc kunnom mannom siæx aaf fæthringum oc siæx aaf möthringum. uiti thet aat ethe... etc.

[3] Östg. Ærfþa B. XVII.

Another clause provides that if such a man is afterwards accused of being a serf, he can prove the contrary by declaring with a kinsmen's oath of 14 men that he was freed "with money and the oath of kindred as was right and as the laws appointed[1]."

In the Vestgöta law one kinsman can free a serf if he declares with an oath of twice twelve that he is so nearly related to him as to have the right to free him[2].

The laws of central Sweden (Svearike) and the later national and town laws show that the duty of supporting a pauper relative fell on those who would be his heirs[3], as in Iceland.

The alienation of land is subject to similar restrictions as in other Teutonic countries[4]. We find Pope Innocent IV complaining in 1206 that no one in Sweden can give property to the Church " nisi presentibus et conscientibus heredibus[5]."

In the National Law of Magnus Eriksson (1347) the laws referring to kindred-compensation were finally abrogated, though the slayer could still purchase peace from the king and from the plaintiff[6]. Norwegian analogy would lead us to expect the total disappearance of all mention of kindred in wergild-treaties, and, still more, the absence of all contributions from kinsfolk towards wergild. Yet a whole series of deeds from the fifteenth century shows the kindreds still actively engaged in the negotiations for peace, and kinsmen also continue to pay wergild. The following example is fairly typical. It is dated at Linköping in 1413.

"This shall be known to all men, that we Marghit Joarsdottir of Askar, Magnus Niclisson and Hakon Niclisson, daughter's sons of the said Joar, Joan Joarsson of Gewinge and Staffan Joarsson, nearest kinsmen of the said Joar of Askum, declare with this our open letter that the honourable Ingolf

---

[1] Östg. Ærfþ. xxv. "þa uiti mæþ eþe fiughurtan manna mæþ niþiar eþe. at han uar löstær mæþ fæ ok frænda eþe sum atte ok lagh uara."
[2] Westg. II., Aruæ B. XXXI., and I. Arfþær B. 22.
[3] Upl. Jb. 21. Westm. II. Jordb. 17. Cp. v. Amira, *Nordgerm. Obligationenrecht* I. p. 750.
[4] Cp. Beauchet, *Hist. de la propriété foncière en Suède* (Paris 1904). A *retrait lignager* appears to exist in modern Swedish law. Beauchet, *op. cit.* p. 127.
[5] Liljegren, *Dipl. Suec.* No. 131.
[6] Magnus Erikssons Landslag. XIII.

SWEDEN

Toppir has made full compensation to us in (money-)compensation, masses and pilgrimages for the death of the said Joar of Askum, whom Klemet Ingolfsson, the said Ingolf's father, unfortunately slew..."[1]. They acknowledge their complete satisfaction and swear peace on behalf of Joar's and their own kinsmen and heirs[2].

In another case we find the mother and father's brother together with 'several others of our friends and kinsmen' making a complete reconciliation in the cathedral yard[3] of Linköping with the slayer Laurens Jensson, in consideration of pilgrimages, an *ærwe* (memorial mass?) with four and twenty priests and lights and torches, in this and the following year, a weekly mass throughout the year, and 140 marks to the nearest friends and kinsmen of the slain. For a hundred marks the slayer pledges a certain farm to the mother and father's brother of the slain. The 'friends and kinsmen' of both sides are invoked[4].

In 1419 Josse Svensson, Olaf, parish priest of Rogberga, Halvard, Brother Petersson, Arvid Smidh, Joar Arvidsson, and Ingegerd Arvidsdotter sign an *urfejde* (reconciliation deed) for Erik Gjörsson, who killed Sven Svensson. "We declare ourselves with this our open letter to have made, with the counsel of several of our friends and kinsmen, a reconciliation and a complete end with the honourable and well-born Erik Gjörsson for Sven Svensson's death, whom he slew," in consideration of a public apology (*sona*[5]) in Jonköping, to the brother, children, friends, and widow of the slain and her friends; besides masses, money and a piece of Persian cloth[6].

These and similar cases[7] stand in strong contrast with the purely individual nature of the Norwegian reconciliation-deeds. Unfortunately the publication of the Swedish Diplomatarium has not yet proceeded beyond the middle of the fifteenth century, so that we are not in a position to draw conclusions as to the

---

[1] Silfverstolpe, *Svensk Diplomatarium*, II. No. 1783.
[2] " For^da Joars ok wara frænda oc arfwa...."
[3] These reconciliations seem commonly to take place in the precincts of churches. Cp. *Sv. D.* I. No. 30 (Scriptum apud ecclesiam Wi antedictam).
[4] Ib. I. 1, No. 200. 1 July, 1402. Linköping.
[5] In one case a hundred knights are to be present at a '*sona*.'
[6] Ib. III. No. 2683. 1419.
[7] Cp. ib. II. No. 1600 (1412, Nyköping), III. 2664 (1419: effter myna frender och wener raadh oc samthøkke, folbordh ok godhueliæ).

length of time that this form of kin-solidarity persisted, unless we assume that four persons who go bail for a wergild in 1608 in Uppland are related to the slayer[1]. Until more records of local courts are published, however, it must remain uncertain how long kinsmen continued to contribute to wergild in Sweden.

---

[1] G. O. Berg, *Huru rätt skipades i Sverige för trehundra år sedan*. Utdrag ur uppländska Domböcker för år 1608 (Uppsala 1908), p. 20 : "Thessa effter[ne] haffua utfest mandzbooth för Önde smedh, som slagen bleff i thet förledne åhr 1607 : Matz Person i Bäkenberga i Bromma sochn peninger 25 daler, Jöran skomaker i Bromma 25 daler, Hans underfougde på Drotningholm 25 daler, Mårten Hendrichson i Bromma 12 daler... "

CHAPTER IV

DENMARK

FOR Denmark, as for Sweden, the evidence for the solidarity of the kindred in early times depends chiefly on the wergild clauses in the laws of the various provinces (Skåne, Sjælland and the smaller islands, and Jutland with Fyen). These laws date in their present form from the first half of the 13th century. Like the Swedish laws, they content themselves with stating the principle on which wergild is to be distributed, and even this they do so briefly as to leave us in some doubt as to details. As the separate study of each law would involve us in confusing repetitions, we will here content ourselves with summarizing their statements.

Wergild is paid in three equal sums or instalments, the first by the slayer himself, the second by his paternal kinsmen, the third by his kinsmen on his mother's side[1]. There is no differentiation between agnates and cognates[2]. The paternal kindred are summoned to a meeting to discuss the amount due from each of them: "are they many," says the second Sjælland law, "then each of them pays so much the less; are they few, so much the more." So also with the maternal kindred. Each degree of relationship pays one-half less than the degree nearer. The kindred is limited in the Jutland law by the 'fourth man' (third cousin), in the other laws by the minimum payment of one örtug. The

---

[1] A slightly different arrangement in E. Sj. L. 3, 36, but the proportions remain the same.
[2] Thorsen, E. Sjæll. Lov. 3, 26: "If compensation is to be taken, the son is the nearest to receive it after his father, if there is a son, if there is not a son nor *a daughter's son nor a son's son*" the heir comes next.

limit would probably be the same[1]. No provision is made for connections by marriage or for illegitimate sons, as in the Icelandic and Norwegian laws. On the recipient's side, the heir of the slain man takes one-third of the whole sum, together with an additional gift (*gjörsum*)[2]: the paternal and maternal kindred each take one of the two remaining thirds. Women neither pay nor receive wergild, except in the case that a woman is nearest heir to the slain, without brothers, when the Jutish law awards her the heir's share and *gjörsum*.

In Skåne, Sjælland, etc., the wergild was originally 15 marks of silver, reckoned by weight. In Jutland it was 18 marks of silver, and this sum finally became the standard wergild all over the kingdom.

All the laws contain provisions which show acquaintance with the actual working of the distribution of wergild. Thus they incorporate an edict issued by Knud VI. for Skåne, that the slayer may not receive the contributions from his kindred until the very day and hour when he is to hand them over, lest—so the Skåne Law adds—he should dissipate the money and his kindred be forced to pay twice over[3]. The law makes the slayer take an oath with eleven others of his kindred

---

[1] The Skåne law (5, § 9) seems to suggest that the brother pays half the 5 marks due from either side: in this case we should get payments much as follows on either paternal or maternal side:

	mks.	aur.	ört.
Brother	2	4	0
First cousin (brother's son, Sk. L. 5, 9)	1	2	0
First cousin once removed		5	0
Second cousin		2	$1\frac{1}{2}$
Second cousin once removed		1	$0\frac{3}{4}$
Third cousin			$1\frac{7}{8}$

[2] In the town of Schleswig *gjörsum* was generally a mark of gold: Slesv. Stadr. § 3: Flensb. Stadsret § 3. An 18th century translator of the Jutish Law (Eichenberg, 1717) adds a note to the word: "Gjörsum is an addition to the wergild to be made by the slayer's kinsmen on account of fear of revenge, and the greater the fear, the higher the Gjörsum." Eichenberg, J. L. Bk. III. xxi. § 3.

[3] Sk. L. 5, 1. Tha sæli the hanum ær man drap aldrigh en pænning før æn thæn sama dagh oc the samma stund ær han scal bøta...thættæ hauir kunung fore thy swa skipat, at hin ær man hauir dræpit sculu æi taka ættæ bøtær af frændum sinum oc fore hæghtha oc frændær nøthæs atær sithæn til at bøta annat sinni mæth hanum. Cp. E. Sj. L. 3, 26. Cp. Andr. Sun. Lex. Scan. 45 (Thorsen, p. 126).

DENMARK

(presumably five from the paternal and six from his maternal kin), that he would be content with the same compensation as he is paying, had his been the injured kindred[1]. It further provides that if any kinsman denies his liability he must either pay or point out a nearer kinsman with an oath of 12 men of his kin[2]. In the case of a refusal to pay on the part of any of the kindred, the Jutland law allows the slayer to distrain goods from him by force to the extent of his liability. The Jutland and Sjælland laws empower the slayer to take twice the amount by force, but only after he has obtained the consent of the kindred, and demanded payment in vain at three *Things*[3]. The Skåne law, in accordance with the edict of Knud VI. mentioned above, expressly forbids all distraint, but allows the other kinsmen to sue the defaulter[4].

In case of the flight, death or outlawry of the slayer, his kinsmen are still bound to pay their share of the wergild.

In all the laws the brother of the slayer plays an important part. In Skåne the brother not only pays most, but, as equally related to the slayer both on the paternal and maternal sides, contributes equally to the paternal and maternal payments[5]. In Jutland law the father or son is said to be nearest to the slayer on the paternal side, and the brother on the maternal, but if there are two brothers, financially independent, one is the first of the paternal and the other the first of the maternal kindred.

In Jutland law it is emphatically stated that the King cannot allow a slayer to purchase peace from him until he has been reconciled to the kindred of the slain[6].

All the points mentioned above indicate that, as in Sweden, the wergild laws were actually in force in Denmark at the time they were committed to writing. It is interesting to note that the liability of the kindred for wergild was annulled by royal edict earlier on Danish territory than in any other Scandinavian country. According to the contemporary legal historian

---

[1] Sk. L. 5, 29, foræ...iafnaþæ eþ mæþ tolf næfndom mannum i kyni sinu.
[2] J. L. 2, 25. Cp. E. Sj. L. 3, 26.   [3] J. L. 2, 28, E. Sj. L. 3, 26.   [4] Sk. L. 5, 1.
[5] It does not seem quite clear whether he contributes *half the whole* 5 *marks* paid by each side, or only half the whole payment due from him.
[6] J. L. 2, 22, "ok æi å kunung frith køp af hanum at takæ, fyrræ han ær såt vith hins døthæ kyn."

P.

Archbishop Andreas Sünesøn, the edict of Knud VI. for Skåne was found unavailing to check the frequent cases of manslaughter, and Valdemar II. (1202-41) issued a more definite ordinance:

"If a man slays another man, let him pay compensation for him entirely out of his own property, unless another kinsman will of his good will give him something towards it." If the slayer does not offer compensation at the first three *things* after the slaying, he becomes an outlaw, but while he is in the country revenge may not be taken on any one else. If he flees, the nearest kinsmen on the paternal and maternal sides must offer compensation—two parts of the wergild—"and take two parts of the truce, while the slayer flees with the third [of the truce], and let him never come again into the country until he gets the goodwill of both the King and the kindred [of the slain[1]]." But though the compensation is all to be paid by the slayer, it is still to be distributed to all the kindred of the slain, as before. This ordinance was revived by King Erik Menved in 1304.

We cannot tell what effect these edicts had at the time, but that they had no permanent effect is clear from an ordinance dated three centuries later than Valdemar's. Thus in 1537[2] King Christian III. complains:

"It is a general plague in the kingdom that the one seeks the life of the other on trivial grounds, and the only cause is that money is taken for manslaughter, and the slayer's innocent kindred and friends (connections by marriage?), yea the very babe[3] that lies in the cradle, must collect money and help to compensate for the dead, whereon many rely, and commit such deeds, which they would not do if they knew that a death-punishment awaited them in their turn." He therefore ordains that if any farmer or townsman commit manslaughter, except in self-defence or by accident, life should be paid for life, and limb for limb[4].

In these last words, with their echo of the Mosaic Law, we trace the influence of the force which did more towards the

---

[1] Sk. L., Valdemar II.'s Forordning om Drab (Thorsen, p. 244).

[2] King Christian II. had previously ordained that all who commit manslaughter are to pay life for life, except in a case of accidental slaying, when the slayer is to pay all compensation himself (Chr. II. geistl. Lov, § 57, 62). But his laws were all repealed in 1523, after his banishment.

[3] Eriks sjællandske Lov (3, 26) states, that if one of the slayer's female relatives on the paternal side bears a son before the wergild payment is due the infant has to pay his share.

[4] Reces, 1537 § 7. (Quoted by Matzen, *Forelæsninger over den danske Retshistorie*, Bd III. p. 35.)

disintegration of the kindred than all the opposition of the kings—Protestantism. Not only did the Mosaic Law, and such texts as Matth. xxvi. 52, afford kings and clerics good warranty for inveighing against the practice of blood-money, but the Protestant insistence on the doctrine of individual responsibility militated against the ancient traditions of kinship.

In his 'Kolding Recess' of 1558 Christian III. works out his penalties:

"If any townsman or farmer commits a manslaughter, and it does not occur by misadventure or in self-defence, and the slayer is seized, let him pay life for life, and his share in the farm (hovedlod) be forfeited, half to the dead man's nearest heir and half to his lord, and let the slayer's kindred be therewith quit and free of all further feud, and not be burdened with any further compensation... But if the slayer quits the place and flees, so that he cannot be heard of or seized, and is sworn an outlaw, then let his relatives pay rightful wergild to the kinsmen of the slain according to the law, and therewith be free of feud, and let his share in the farm be forfeited to his lord. But if the slaying is found and proved to have been committed by misadventure and in self-defence, and the slayer is sentenced to pay compensation and remains in the place, then let 3 times 18 marks of minted money (= 18 marks of silver reckoned by weight) be paid, and not more, and let each pay in compensation what he undertakes to pay, and the slayer and his kindred be therewith without feud, and the King's sheriff shall be bound to declare that he is in the King's peace at the *Thing*. But if the slain man's kindred venture to attack or let others attack the slayer or his kin after this, each of those who act so shall pay 15 marks of minted money to the King's exchequer and shall have forfeited the fines due to them[1]."

It seems as if the threat of a death-penalty had at first the opposite effect to that which was intended. Previously the law-suit instituted by the kindred of the slain man had been certain to result in the receipt of wergild, in which all the kin participated. Now it might result in a death-sentence, in which case only the heir of the slain man reaped any financial advantage. The consequence was that there was a strong tendency to avoid bringing slaying-suits into the courts at all. The kindred of the slayer, or such of them as were on the spot, use every effort to make a hurried private treaty with the

---

[1] V. A. Secher, *Corp. Const. Dan.*, *Forordninger, Recesser og andre Kgl. Breve* (Cop. 1887—1903) Bd I. p. 19: Chr. III.'s Kolding Reces 1558, 13 Dec. § 13. *Hvorledis holdis skal, nar manddrab skier.*

kindred of the slain, before the seven days had elapsed in which the representative of the latter must declare the suit. The frequency of such treaties can be deduced from the 'open letters' which the next King, Frederick II., found it necessary to send to all the sheriffs in the various provinces:

"It has come to our knowledge," he writes to the authorities of Helsingborg, "how many slayers live in Helsingborg province without any fear, when they for a small sum of money have satisfied the slain man's kindred and friends"; and in a similar letter addressed to all sheriffs he says that he learns "that when a manslaughter has occurred, such matters are secretly settled and hushed up between the plaintiff and the slayer's kindred, with the approval and knowledge of the lords of the parties concerned; and that such slayers have sought and demanded of the judges, and to some extent have actually obtained, through their lord's intervention and permission, that they should be declared at the *Thing* to be in the King's peace (liuset Fred over dennom til Tinge), although sentence has not been given by *sandemend* or *nefn* (doomsmen) according to the edict[1]."

This practice is now strictly forbidden, but the books of the King's Chancery are full of references to slayings which have been "hushed up" by the interested parties, and though so many cases came to the King's ears[2], we may be sure that there were many others which did not. The King could not even be sure of the loyal support of his officials, for as late as 1630 we find the chief judge of Skåne reversing a sentence of death passed on a slayer, and adducing, as the reason for his action, a "home-made deed of reconciliation, called a *trygge*[3]" (pledge of peace, the

---

[1] Secher, *Forordninger*, Bd II. p. 414 (No. 415) and p. 540 (No. 510). In the Jutish Law the fine to the King was four-fold if a treaty had been made before a verdict had been given; but these secret treaties are concluded without any reference to the King at all.

[2] *Kancelliets Brevbøger i Uddrag*, udg. af Rigsarkivet. (Cop. 1885—1910, 10 vols.) x. p. 95 (593); p. 228, 250, 342, 371 (1594), p. 635 (1596). For later times see the various *Tegnelser* in the Rigsarkiv; esp. *Jyske Tegnelser*: 1613, fol. 13, 18, 225; 1614, f. 24; 1630, f. 147 (bis), 225, 253; 1632, fol. 334, etc.

[3] *Herredags Dombog*, Anno 1630 (in the Rigsarkiv). No. 33, 19 June, f. 263-6. Cp. also the case published in Secher's *Rettertingsdomme*, II. p. 507 (1613). E. Kruse, chief judge in N. Jutland, aids the slayer to hush up his deed by intimidating the wife and mother of the slain into accepting terms while the brothers are abroad. The deed they were induced to sign does not specify the nature of the injury done them, and no doubt some such subterfuge was often practised.

word used in the ancient laws). And in 1615, when the noble Hans Lindenov is tried by the King's Court for having killed one Peder Danmark in Bornholm, the defence is put forward that his father, who was actually Governor of the island at the time, had made a private treaty with the deceased's wife, daughter, wife's father and nearest kinsmen[1]. As late as 1679, the plea is put forward by the defence that the slayer had made a private treaty with the mother, brothers and sisters of the slain man[2].

Indirectly, however, this same haste to come to terms worked for the disintegration of the kindred. Slaying-suits had to be declared by the nearest kinsmen of the deceased within seven days of the slaying, and the urgent need of coming to terms with the slain man's representatives before this period was over left no time for the formal agreement of the whole kindred on either side. In such cases, though the relatives who sign the agreement expressly declare that they do so " on behalf of their whole kindred " they possess no deed empowering them to act on behalf of those not present, an essential formality if the inclusion of the absent kinsmen is to be legally binding[3]. Thus

---

[1] *Herredags Dombog*; 1615 fol. 100 ff. Printed in: J. R. Hubertz, *Akstykker til Bornholms Hist.*, 1327—1621 (Cop. 1852). No. 414.

[2] *Sjællands Landsting* 1679, 9 April (in the Provindsarkiv for Sjælland). (For this reference I am indebted to Professor Paul Jörgensen.) In some cases the King appears to have been satisfied with such a private treaty even after the slayer had been sentenced to death or (in his absence, which was more usual) to outlawry. See *Kanc. Brev.* II. p. 268 (Mogens Lauritzen); 305 (Povel Kock) in 1559, 381-2 (Peter Jostsen) in 1560, III. p. 41 (Peder Lauritzen); VI. p. 378 (Lauritz Friis) in 1578, etc. The most remarkable case is from 1630: Hans Jensen, a skinner's apprentice, killed Lambert Laursen, a shoemaker's apprentice: Hans was outlawed, but he succeeded in making a treaty with the kindred of the dead man and securing an *orfejde*, after which he obtained the King's pardon. *Saml. Jysk. Hist.* VI.; Kinch, *Af Ribe Bys Tingbøger*, p. 168.

[3] Cp. the foll. case: "And the aforesaid Morthen Persen (brother-in-law of the slain) declared himself to be legally empowered (fulldmechtig) on behalf of all other common kinsmen and relatives, to give such an undertaking of peace, which he proved with a sealed deed of witness drawn up at Löding Herreds *Thing*, and which is now to be found in the deed-box of the town. Similarly he said that the signature and seal of the nearest paternal and maternal kinsmen had been entrusted to him, that he might seal [the document] therewith in their absence." (P. V. Jakobsen, *Uddrag af Helsingørs Kammerregnskaber og Thingbøger i det* 16 *Aarh.* p. 246. Ny Kgl. Saml. No. 697 f. 4to.)

we have such cases as that recorded for the Supreme Court in 1632 :

Niels Bundesen killed Niels Aagesen. The slayer, his father and mother, and his brother, Aage, together with Niels Aagesen (nephew of the slayer?) and his wife, and Jens Nielssen (son or uncle of the slayer?) and one Sven Budmansen, probably a connection by marriage, all repair to the slain man's house, where they find the widow and her six sons. A reconciliation is made, and the slayer's father, Bunde, pays 6 florins to each of these boys. But Oluf Aagesen, the slain man's brother, not being present at the reconciliation, evidently does not consider himself bound by the treaty, and becomes the plaintiff in the suit[1].

The King could at least assert his authority in the case of such secret treaties, if once they came to his ears. But where the payment of wergild was still lawful, as when the slaying had been committed by accident or in self-defence (and these pleas were often successfully urged in the most surprising circumstances), the royal will was actually subject to that of the injured kindred. The King could not admit to peace any slayer, no matter how accidental the slaying, unless the kindred of the slain man was willing to come to terms with him. In none of the royal letters of pardon in such cases does the King forget to state that the slayer has satisfied the slain man's kindred and friends (*Slægt og Venner*) or, if this is not yet accomplished, to add the proviso that it is to be done before the pardon can be valid[2]. Occasionally, and when dealing with common folk, the King can take a fairly high hand, as in the case of Christiern Matzen, who was sentenced to pay compensation for a slaying, but is perpetually threatened by the slain man's brothers, kindred and friends. The King shortly orders all who wish to complain about him to sue him properly at the *Thing*. But in the case of nobles the King is sometimes reduced to vain pleading. Thus when Erich Bilde has slain Jörgen Rud the King asks that Jörgen's brothers should give Erich a safe-conduct, so that he and his kindred may discuss negotiations for a

---

[1] *Herredags Dombog*, 1632. 5 June, fol. 172 ff.
[2] *Kanc. Brev.* I. p. 258 (1553), p. 407 (1555); II. p. 268 (1559), p. 396 (1560); III. p. 5, p. 38, p. 66–7 (1561), p. 277 (1563), 382 (1564), p. 435; V. p. 48, 83 (1571), p. 234, 239–40 (1573), p. 425 (1574); VI. p. 141, 148, 378, 481–2, 584 (1577); VII. p. 4 (1580), p. 250, 338 (1585), p. 790 (1587), etc., etc.

reconciliation. But it is more than a year before the Ruds yield to the King's repeated solicitations[1].

If it appears that all the kindred of the slain are not included in the reconciliation the King at once withdraws his pardon.

Peter Jostsen, of the Aarhus district in Jutland, has slain Lauritz Chrestensen, and is sentenced to outlawry. He succeeds, however, in coming to terms with some of the slain man's paternal kinsmen, and gets a deed of reconciliation from them, and with this he secures the King's pardon. It presently turns out that he has not satisfied the rightful plaintiff (in this case the mother's brother of the slain), nor the maternal kindred in general. The King states that as his pardon was only valid if the slain man's kindred and friends were satisfied, the matter is to be dealt with by the sheriff[2].

In another case the King pardons Hans Mule, a citizen of Odense (but with some pretensions to nobility) and renounces the fine due to him, as Hans has placated the slain man's kindred and friends. Subsequently, however, the widow complains that she and her children have received no compensation. The slayer is ordered to satisfy them at once, or he will be liable to another slaying-suit[3].

The fact that the slayer could shift some of his responsibility on to his innocent kindred was, as we have seen, particularly repugnant to Protestant ideas, and consequently it was the liability of the slayer's kindred which tended to disappear first. This can be guessed from the cautious reference to it in the edict of Christian III. quoted above: "let each pay in compensation what he undertakes to pay, and the slayer and his kindred be therewith without feud."

Several cases indicate that contributions could now only be extracted from the kindred if they had been definitely promised[4]. Thus we have a royal letter from 1552, dealing with a suit by

---

[1] *Kanc. Brev.* VIII. p. 250 (1585), p. 564, 573 (1586). Cp. also III. p. 46, 58 (1561); VII. p. 638 (1583); IX. p. 679 (1591).

[2] Ib. II. p. 581-2 (1560).

[3] Ib. III. pp. 46, 58 (1561). In the matter of women's participation in wergilds almost all other evidence is at variance with the laws.

[4] In *Danmarks Rigens Ret*, a private collection of laws dating from 1592, and partly founded on precedents from the Supreme Court, we read (§ 20): "But if any man is sued for having pledged himself for the payment of wergild, he shall be sued for wergild first at the district *Thing* and then at the provincial *Thing* (Landsting), as for any other debt" (*Danske Magazin*, III. R. Bd I. p. 177 ff.). (The persons who pledged themselves for wergild were, however, not always relatives: their function was more that of bails.) Weylle, *Gloss. Jur. Dan.* (Copenhagen 1652), has the following remarks under *Bod* (p. 101): "This wergild can be required and secured by

the slayer against his kindred and friends, because they will not help him to compensate for the slaying, although they undertook to do so in a duly-sealed deed[1]. In Helsingör we find the kindred of the slain man maintaining in court that they are not bound to share the wergild with one of their number, Iver Jörgensen, because when a kinsman of theirs had committed a slaying in Jutland, and they had applied to Iver for help towards the wergild, he had always rejected their plea, and would not pay any of the wergild with them[2]. This seems to suggest that after the Reformation, the other relatives were powerless to secure the co-operation of any recalcitrant member of the kindred, unless he had given a definite promise.

In some cases it would appear that the wider kindred is not even appealed to, or so we must deduce from the entertaining letters of Dorthe Bølle, wife of Knud Rud, on the occasion when she represents her husband and son at a meeting with the Skram family to settle wergild. Erik Rud, her son, had killed Niels Skram. She accepts the offer of financial help from her friends present at the negotiations, but insists on regarding it as a loan,

---

distraint, if it is withheld, which, however, seems strange and as if contrary to the law, yet *ex beneplacito statuentis*, employed both in Jutland and elsewhere here in Denmark, and is practised according to the directions of the text..."

[1] *Kanc. Brev.* I. p. 143 (1553): Royal letter to certain officials, requesting " at de skulle hjælpe Hans Korsen til hans Ret ... i Anledning af, at hans Slægt og Venner, som have lovet at hjælpe ham til en Bod for en Karl, han slog ihjel, og givet deres Brev og Segl derpaa, nu ikke vil opfylde deres Löfte."

More usually it is the kindred of the slain who sue, but the same question of promises crops up. Thus in 1545 Anders Crestensen sues four persons on account of a promise they gave him for wergild (Tegnelser over alle Lande fra 1545; in *Danske Magazin*, R. IV. Bd I, p. 168). A case of the year 1549 records that one Jesper Nielsen, acting for the father of the slain, sues two persons for 20 marks, a black garment of Leiden fashion (?), and four florins, which had been promised by them and two others—presumably relatives of the slayer—as compensation for the slain man (Kolderup-Rosenvinge, *Gamle danske Domme*, I. No. 56, p. 112 ff.). The case of Anders Crestensen, in Tegnelser over alle Lande fra 1545 (*Danske Magazin*, R. IV. Bd I. p. 168) seems to be similar.

[2] "Item Morthen perssen och lass Gieldssenn gaffue tilkende, att Saadan wlocke er tilfornn hendt theris slechtinge wdi Julland, och the haffue ladit besögtt for[ne] Iffuer Jörgennssen om hiellp til boid alt bekomme, tha haffuer hand alltiid Slagid sig ther frann, och Inngen boid wiille wdgiffue mett thennom..." Iver Jörgensen has a representative in court, but we do not hear the upshot. (P. V. Jacobsen's *Uddrag af Helsingøers Thingbøger*: Ny Kgl. Saml. No. 697 f. 4to p. 246 ff.)

and there is no hint that the Rud family intend to appeal to their kinsmen[1]. This was in 1543, but that it was an exception is clear from many later cases. Thus a law-suit of 1559 describes how, after the slaying of Oluf Rytter by Niels Kaas, "Niel's father, Mogens Kaas, Jens Spend of Skammergaard, together with several of the aforesaid Niels Kaas' kindred, offered gold, silver and moneys *on their own behalf* and on that of the aforesaid Niels Kaas[2]." This case, like the following, deals with nobles.

In one of the earlier deeds, dated 1513, after the slaying of Niels Hak by Anders Bille, the sum to be paid is promised by eight persons:

"We whose names follow, Steen Bille of Lynsgaard, Niels Høg of Eskjær, Tyge Krabbe of Brustorp, Axel Brahe of Krogholm, knights, Hans Bille of Egede, Knud Bille, High Sheriff, of Gladfaxe, Johan Oxe of Nielstrup and Holger Gregersen of Torup, squires of noble birth (armigeri), make known to all with this our open letter, that we have promised and pledged, and with this our open letter do promise and pledge to the nobly-born men, Her Henrich Krummedige, Knud Gøye and Anders Hak, on behalf of the nobly-born man Anders Bille, this compensation, damages and additional gift for the death of the honourable and nobly-born man, Niels Hak, whom the aforesaid Anders Bilde unfortunately slew: (viz.) to pay one thousand marks at Lund before this next St Martin's Day; farm lands taxed at three loads of corn and certain to produce this, to be paid in Skåne, Sjælland and Laaland before this next Easter; one thousand marks to be paid on the following St Michael's Day, at Lund, and further one-and-a-half thousand marks, also to be paid at Lund on the St Michael's Day next following, and therewith one jewel [to be chosen] according to the pronouncement of six kinsmen on each side. To this we pledge ourselves and our heirs, to pay and discharge to the aforesaid Henrich Krummedige, Knud Gøye, and Anders Hak, to them or their heirs, on behalf of the aforesaid Niels Hak's children, the aforesaid amount of money and goods before the aforesaid dates, as is written above, without any repudiation or excuse of any kind[3]."

---

[1] The letters are quoted at full length by Vedel Simonsen, *Efterretninger om de danske Ruders* (Odense 1845).

[2] *Gamle danske Domme*, I. No 130, "for^ne Niels Kaasis Fader, Mogenns Kaaes, Jens Spend thill Skammergaard, med flere aff for^ne Niells Kaasis Kiönn, och först tilböd paa for^ne Niels Kaasis och dieris egenn Vegnne Guld, Sölff och Pendinge."

[3] See Appendix II. No. 3 for original.

It is to be noted that the slaying was in 1508, so that five years elapsed before the reconciliation, and still longer before the payment was complete.

Fortunately it is possible, with the help of the admirable *Danske Adels Aarbøger*, to discover with some fair degree of accuracy the exact relationship to the slayer of most of the signatories. We find them to be:

His brother Hans Bille[1] of Egede.

His first cousins: Johann Oxe, Knud Bille, Holger Gregersen Ulfstand[2].

His uncle Steen Bille[3].

His wife's uncle Niels Høg[4].

The presence of Axel Brahe and Tyge Krabbe is more difficult to account for on the score of relationship, unless a dictum of Professor Vinogradoff's, in his *Geschlecht und Verwandtschaft im altnordischen Rechte*, is borne in mind : " Aus den Erzählungen von den Fehden...ist auch so viel zu ersehen, dass es keineswegs auf die Verwandtschaftsnähe ankam, wenn es galt, einen einflussreichen Vertreter irgend einer Forderung zu finden[5]."

Both Axel Brahe and Tyge Krabbe were among the most distinguished men of their time, and the slightest connection with them would be seized upon eagerly. So far as the present writer can discover, there was no nearer connection at this date between the Bille family and Axel Brahe, than that after her death Else Bille's husband, Gregers Ulfstand, married Axel's sister. Else is Anders Bille's aunt. With Tyge Krabbe the connection seems to be of an even flimsier sort, but it is possible in both cases that some unrecorded marriage connected both much more closely than we can now guess with the Bille family.

On the other side, Anders Hak is probably the son of the slain man[6]; Knud Gøye is his son-in-law[7]. Henrich Krum-

---

[1] Hans and Anders are both sons of Bent Bille.

[2] Bent Bille's sister Inger m. Johan Oxe, the father of the above. Knud Bille (High Sheriff 1505—1543), of Gladsaxe, was son of Peder Bille, uncle of Anders. Holger Gregersen Ulfstand was son of Else Bille, aunt of Anders.

[3] This Steen Bille, of Allinde and Lyngsgaard, is brother of Bent Bille.

[4] Anders second wife was Anne Lykke, whose mother was Kirsten Høg, sister of Niels Høg, of Eskjær.

[5] *Zs. f. Social- und Wirthschaftsgesch.* Bd VII. pp. 1—43.

[6] See No. 19 in *Sv. Riges Registranter*, No. 51 (Rigsarkiv, Copenhagen).

[7] He marrried Lene, Niels Hak's daughter (*D. A. A.* 1896, pp. 47—49).

medige can hardly be nearer than second cousin, or even second cousin once removed[1], of the slain man.

All this reveals a considerable degree of solidarity among the kindred, and the later deeds show little falling off in this respect. In a deed of 1542[2] six persons sign on behalf of the slayer, Peder Stygge Rosenkrands, and they prove to be his brother[3], two first cousins once removed (cognatic)[4], the husband of a first cousin, and his brother[5], a second cousin[6], and a second cousin once removed[7]. The difficulty of tracing the genealogy of the family of the slain prevents our discovering the relationship of the three persons of the slain man's kindred who sign the deed, but it is fairly certain that one of them[8] can only be related through the slain man's grandmother.

The *orfejde*, or deed of reconciliation, was equally common among all classes, but for obvious reasons those of the nobles have most often survived the changes and chances of the centuries. For obvious reasons, also, those of the poor are much more brief[9]. We have to return to court records to find a full

---

[1] *D. A. A.* 1900, p. 236.
[2] See Appendix II. No. 4.
[3] Christoffer (Stygge) Rosenkrands and Peder, the slayer, are both sons of Eiler Rosenkrands.
[4] Christoffer and Anders Johansen, sons of Berete, d. of Erik, Eiler Rosenkrand's brother.
[5] Eiler Hardenberg, who married Karen, sister of the above-mentioned Berete. Also his brother, Jacob Hardenberg.
[6] Hartvig Tammesen, great grandson of Niels Jensen, Peter Stygge's great-grandfather.
[7] Christoffer Rosenkrands of Skjern, great-great-grandson of the above Niels Jensen.
[8] Oluf Glob. Both Niels Mogenssen's grandmothers were of the Glob family.
[9] See O. Nielsen, *Gamle Jydske Tingsvidner* (Cop. 1882), p. 99, where nine persons, one of them a fisherman, swear *orfejde* at the *Thing*, in 1459. Another such deed is preserved in the Rigsarkiv: five persons, one a goldsmith, acknowledge payment of wergild at Roskilde *Thing* in 1493, and swear peace (see *Fortegnelse over nogle Diplomer*, No. 12, *Drabssager*, 69 Danmark Bd I., in Rigsarkiv). Another, between the inhabitants of Kjerteminde and an Odense family in 1512, is given in *Aktstykker udg. af Fyens litt. Selskab*, pp. 154-5. See also Hubertz, *Aktstykker vedkommende Aarhus* (Cop. 1845), I. p. 85 (1497). (The exclusively early dates of these deeds are only due to the fact that later on they were written on easily destructible paper, while the early ones are on parchment.) Even a *hovkarl*, a labourer bound to the soil, has to satisfy the slain man's kindred and friends after a slaying, before the King will grant him pardon. *Kanc. Brev.* II. p. 268 (1559).

account of a reconciliation between non-noble kindreds. In the *Thing*-books of Ribe a case of 1586 is recorded in which one Mads Bertelsen was accidentally killed in an attempt to separate two combatants.

Peder Madsen, the slayer, was allowed to purchase peace, seeing that the slaying was accidental. The two Provosts (*Fogder*), two Councillors and the Town Clerk, together with eight other persons "witnessed that Bertel Sörensen (the father of the slain), of Hjordker in Skadtsherred, stood here to-day before the *Thing*-Court with his nearest kinsmen both on the paternal and maternal side : to wit, on the paternal side first Hans Terkelsen of Terreborg, Niels Bertelsen of the above-mentioned Hjordker, the aforesaid Bertel Sörensen's son, Kristen Laurtsen of Tranebjerg, Thames Laurtsen of Snepsager and Nis Hansen of the above-mentioned Terreborg; similarly, on the maternal side Jep Madsen of Holdsted, Peder Jenvoldsen, citizen of this town of Ribe, Thames Jepsen of the above-mentioned Holdsted, Peder Jepsen of Tvilde, Oluf Nielsen of Nørre-Vejrup and Niels Povelsen of the same place; and audibly, both with hand and voice [*lit.* mouth], granted and gave to Mattis Madsen of the above-mentioned Vejrup a full and faithful *orfejde* and friendship for born and unborn, according to the law, for his son Peder Madsen, [who] (alas !) had the misfortune to kill the aforesaid Bertel Sörensen's son, to wit Mads Bertelsen ; so that henceforth from this day this affair shall be finally and completely settled, finished with, and clearly decided; this matter shall never henceforward or in future be brought up again or discussed, nor shall the aforesaid Bertel Sörensen, or anyone belonging to him, at any time either trouble or persecute, or allow anyone else to persecute, the aforesaid Peder Madsen himself, his father aforesaid, or anyone belonging to him, either on the paternal or maternal side, with word or deed for this cause in any manner whatsoever, on a penalty of (loss of) honour and of a suit in which fines will not be received. Thereupon, at the same *Thing*, Mattis Madsen paid over the legal compensation—out of his own property, or so he said—on behalf of his son, to Bertel Sörensen, who himself received it in the presence of the Court and of his kinsmen[1]."

We note that with the slayer's father six of the paternal and six of the maternal kindred of the slain take the oath of reconciliation—i.e. it is the full *trygde-ed* of twelve kinsmen.

Owing to the energy and determination of the Kings, such public and official reconciliations as this were possible to non-nobles only if the slaying could reasonably be called accidental. But we can find later cases still among the nobles, who were very

---

[1] *Af Ribe Bys Tingbøger,* af J. Kinch. In *Samlinger til Jydsk Hist. og Topografi,* Række I. Bd III. p. 166–9.

powerful at this period, and could bring pressure to bear on the King. In the following case the King's consent is almost taken for granted.

Christoffer Lunge, in 1601, killed David van der Osten, another young nobleman, in an encounter which had some of the characteristics of a duel. The deed, which is in German and very long, begins with a full history of the quarrel and the duel, and observes that Christoffer Lunge disappeared immediately afterwards. But on hearing that the most distinguished member of the slain man's kindred, Heinrich Fleming, mother's brother of the slain, together with certain others of his kinsmen, 'happened' to be in Copenhagen, Christoffer Lunge's relatives begged for peace, and offered to do all that could fitly and reasonably be demanded of them, and anything else which might show " friendship, love, honour and service" to the kinsmen of the deceased. The matter is settled, on consultation with the deceased's father, brothers and "all other blood-related friends," on the Lunge party undertaking that the slayer shall give a thousand florins *ad pias causas* ; and that he with seven or eight of his nearest kinsmen shall sue the pardon of the kindred of the slain, in the presence of the King[1]. On the van Osten side three persons sign. These all belong to the German Holstein nobility, and I have not been able to discover their relationship with the deceased. On the other side sign :—

Holger Ulfstand (brother-in-law of the slayer)[2].

Axel Brahe of Elved (second cousin once removed of slayer)[3].

Vloss (Oluf ?) Rosensparre[4].

Erich Lunge (slayer's father's brother).

Otto and Georg Skeel (Axel Brahe's great nephews, the slayer's second cousins three times removed)[5].

Jens Bille and his father Steen Bille. (The Billes, Ulfstands and Lunges are closely connected for generations, but the exact relationship here evades me.)

---

[1] For a fuller description of this ceremony see the Brockdorf-Ranzow document, Appendix II. In an earlier *orfejde* from Helsingborg the affair is on a more impressive scale : " On Feb. 24, 1405, King Erik of Pomerania is witness that Her Jens Nielsen [Lowenbalk] was summoned before him in the presence of Queen Margaret," various high ecclesiastics, and twenty-seven knights and seven noble-born squires, and " the kindred and friends on the paternal and maternal sides, and swore peace to the father, sons and all kinsmen and friends of the slain Jens Jensen " [Brok]—" consensu et voluntate consanguineorum, cognatorum, propinquiorum et amicorum tam paternorum quam maternorum partis utriusque natorum et nascendorum." K. Barner, *Fam. Rosenkrantz Hist.* (Cop. 1874) Dipl. pp. 47–8.

[2] Married (in 1600) Karen, the sister of the slayer.

[3] Christoffer Lunge's great-uncle, Tyge Lunge, was Axel Brahe's great-grandfather.

[4] His grandmother was Birgitte Bille, d. of the Steen Basse Bille from whom Steen Bille and his son Jens Bille (see below) are descended.

[5] Axel's brother Otte married Beate Bille. Jørgen (Georg) and Otte Skeel are the grandchildren of this couple.

Claus Düring. (Presumably a member of the Danish branch of the Bremen family. I cannot trace his relationship to the Lunges[1].)

Another 'orfejde' for a slaying in the same year (1601) offers several points of interest. Albret Skeel has killed Niels Juel at Aalborg:

We, whose names follow, Ove Juel[2] of Meilgaard on my own behalf and on that of my deceased brother's children, whose legal guardian I am, and also on that of my sisters, whose legal guardian I am; Iver Juel of Villestrup, Mouritz Stygge of Holbekgaard, the legal guardian of Fru Anne Stygge, widow of the deceased Niels Juel of Kongeslevlund, Christoffer Mitelsen of Lundbek, Hertvig Kaas of Hørupgaard, make known to all and declare with this our open letter, that whereas the honourable and high-born man, Albret Skeel of Jungergaardt, has (unfortunately) killed and slain our dear husband, brother, brother-in-law and blood-relation, the honourable and high-born man Niels Juel of Kongeslevlund; for the which he was summoned before the Council of His Royal Majesty and of the kingdom in general; and whereas, since his kindred, stock and blood-relations, brother-in-law and friends have both now and frequently before pleaded with us on his behalf, that for the sake of his wife and children, who are also of our kindred, stock and blood-relations[3], we would renounce what accusation and suit we might have against him for the aforesaid cause; and whereas, yielding to their constantly-urged request and negotiations, and for their sake and for that of his wife and children, and that of their kindred and friends, we have renounced the aforesaid summons and accusation...; we have therefore, on the contrary, granted security to the above mentioned Albret Skeel, on behalf of the aforesaid relict of Niels Juel, her children and heirs, as also on our own behalf, for ourselves and for our kindred and stock, on the paternal and maternal side, for both born and unborn; and we have granted him, and now with this our open letter do grant him and his children, kindred and stock, both on the paternal and maternal side, both born and unborn, a faithful, true, steadfast, irrevocable reconciliation and *orfejde*....

As the further proof thereof...we, with the above-mentioned wife of Niels Juel, have attached our seals here below, and signed with our own hands, and kindly request to seal and sign with us the honourable and high-born men: Christen Holch of Høygaard, High Sheriff of Hald, Niels Stygge of Søgaard, Thomes Malthesen of Tonderup, Eric Høg of Klarupgaard, Erich Lunge of

---

[1] It is of course not suggested that any of these deeds show the participation of the complete kindred, but it cannot be denied that, for such scattered clans as those of the Danish nobility, the meeting seems usually to be fairly representative.

[2] This family later spelt its name Juul, and is not to be confounded with the Juels. See *D. A. A.*

[3] I have not been able to make out any relationship between the Skeels and Anne Stygge.

Skovgaard and Frantz Juel of Palstrup. *Actum*, Viborg the 20th day of February, 1602[1].

This document may be considered complementary to the preceding ones in a certain sense; in this the kindred of the slain alone appear, whereas the others were written more from the standpoint of the kindred of the slayer.

The persons mentioned in it may be classed as follows[2]:
Ove Juel, brother of the slain.
Frands Juel, his son, nephew of the slain.
Iver Juel, another brother of the slain.
Mouritz Stygge, brother of the slain man's wife[3].
Hertvig Kaas, brother-in-law of the slain[4].
Niels Stygge, second cousin once removed of the widow[5].
Thomes Malthesen, great uncle of slain man through his mother[6].
Erich Høg, first cousin once removed of the widow[7].
Erich Lunge, great uncle of slain man.

There is an interesting sequel to this 'orfejde.' We know that the slayer or his family had to pay 2000 florins to secure peace. By good fortune a deed has been preserved, dated 20 January 1604, in which Ove Juel, on his own behalf and that of Niels' five children, his widow, Anne Stygge, and her guardian Mouritz Stygge, Iver Juel, Hartvig Kaas, Dorte Juel of Østergaard, Elize Juel of Herup and Kirsten Juel of Kærsholm, make known that "in order that God's stern wrath and punishment for such a reconciliation for slaying, which is threatened in many passages of the Holy Scriptures, may to some extent be moderated and turned away, they had set up the 2000 florins as an endowment for the Aalborg and Viborg schools." The Juels were to administer the legacy[8].

---

[1] For original see Appendix II. No. 5.

[2] I have not been able to place Christen Holch and Christoffer Mitelsen (Tornekrands).

[3] Barner, *Familien Rosenkrantz Hist. i det 16 Aarh.*, p. 236 makes Mouritz the brother of Niels (Hansen) Stygge, but this seems impossible, as Mouritz is here called Niels Juels *Svoger*. [4] Married Anne Juel (Hofman, *Fundationer*, I. 157).

[5] Anne Stygge is the great-granddaughter of Enevold; Niels is the grandson of Mouritz, Enevold's brother.

[6] Niels Juel's mother's mother, Anne, was sister to Thomes Malthesen (*D. A. A.* 1911, pp. 499–50).

[7] Anne Stygge's great-grandfather, Enevold, was Erich Høg's grandfather.

[8] See *Saml. til Jydsk Hist.* 2 R. Bd IV., p. 540; Skeel, *Optegnelser om Familien Skeel*, pp. 114–118, and 372–3; also Hofman, *Fundationer*, III. pp. 281–3.

The number of names in the deed of gift is a clear proof that the proceeds of a slaying were still usually distributed among the relatives, but the reference to the Divine wrath shows how it came to be thought impious to participate in the wergild. It is no doubt this motive which induces two kinsmen in the Helsingör case cited above to declare in court that they will not receive any of the wergild paid for their kinsman's death, and that their shares are to be divided among the other relatives[1]. In cases where the widow and children are left in poverty we can easily understand how the other kinsmen would hesitate to claim their share in the face of public opinion, and would willingly concur in the general view that such money could only be fitly accepted if it went to alleviate the poverty of the widow and children[2]. Still this new view only made very gradual progress against the deep-rooted traditions of solidarity among the kindred, and it was not until 1666, under Christian V., that the wergild was limited by law to the heirs of the slain man[3]. That this limitation was not an absolute matter of course, even then, transpires from the fact that in the first draft of the new legislation we still find the old provision, that if a slayer escapes his kinsmen shall pay two parts of the wergild[4]. Still, this was cut out of the law in its final form, so that for us Christian V. marks the end of the old wergild system, which had really received its death-blow at the Reformation, though it was long in dying[5].

Before leaving the subject of wergild it might be interesting to note the discrepancies between the wergild-payments as actually made and recorded

---

[1] " Frandz Perssenn och Christoffer Jörgennssen fremkomme huer epter annden, berette att aff then boidtt, Som gaffues for for[ne] Jenns Pederssen, wiille the alldelis intid opbere eller anname wtaff ij nogen mode, Menn then motte deelis mellem anndre Slechtninge, som ther aff wiille haffue, the wiille were then fraslagenn."

[2] Thus Erich Lykke, in 1641, appears only to pay wergild to the widow and heirs. *Sjællandske Tegnelser*, Act. pub. 1639–48, B. (2) 4 (Rigsarkiv).

[3] *Kong Christian den Femtes Danske Lov*, ed. Secher. Bog VI. Cap. XI. § 1: Dræber mand anden af Vaade...bøde fyrretyve Lod sølv til den Dræbtis *Arvinger alleene* og dermed være angerløs.

[4] Secher and Støchel, *Forarbejderne til Chr. V.'s Danske Lov*, Bd II. Første Projekt, 5 Bog, 6 Cap. § 9—12.

[5] The principle of wergild, given to the heirs, was not abolished in Danish law until 1866, in the new Penal Law, §§ 308,309.

in law-suits and *orfejde*-deeds, and the wergild-payments as set forth in the laws. Two points strike us at once. Firstly, the sum paid is seldom the 18 marks of silver enjoined in the laws, in spite of repeated injunctions that it shall not exceed that sum. If it were only the wergilds of the nobles that were too high, we should suppose that the laws had omitted to mention the sums to be paid by this class. As in Sweden, there are no class-distinctions in the wergild clauses of the laws[1]. But plebeians also receive larger wergilds than their due[2].

The other point in which nearly all the cases are at variance with the laws is in the matter of the participation of women. All the laws exclude women, but a great number of the cases of which we have documentary evidence admit them to the wergild.

Thus we find the widow included in more than one case[3]. In 1537 a widow sues the brother of her slain husband, for having kept the wergild paid for his brother, so that neither she nor her son had received their rightful shares[4]. He is ordered to give her and her son a considerable sum. In another case, of 1567, the slayer promises the widow 34 florins and a suit of clothes[5]. Again in a law-suit of 1611 the widow is especially mentioned as included in the wergild[6].

In 1537 the daughter sues a male kinsman (her brother?) for having kept the first instalment (arfsal) of wergild, together with the additional gift, which he had received for her father's slaying. He is ordered to give it up[7].

In a Helsingör case of 1566 the *mother* is to have "five good Jochum-florins and a suit of clothes[8]." The mother shared the wergild in the case of 1613 mentioned above (p. 84, note 3).

The *sisters* receive wergild in a case of 1552, but here it seems that their shares were given to them by other kinsmen[9]. However, a letter of the

---

[1] Unless in the *gjörsum* or additional gift.

[2] Anders Sørensen killed a man at Ribe in 1573. The family of the slain demanded 1000 florins and two pieces of English cloth, but this was considered excessive and they did not get it (Kinch, *Ribe Bys Hist.* p. 221).

[3] See case of Hans Mule, p. 87 supra, and the Lunge *orfejde*, p. 93. In 1641 Erich Lykke is pardoned on having satisfied the "wife and heirs" of the slain. *Sj. Tegn.* Acta pub. 1639-48 B. (2) 4.

[4] "at for^{ne} Tomes Nielssenn hagde opbaarett Bodt oc Bedring for samme Mandödt oc ey hun eller hindes Börnn fangett theraff hues hende hörte med Rette." Kolderup-Rosenvinge, *Gamle danske Domme*, II. No. 22, p. 32 ff.

[5] Helsingör Byting: 7 Ap. (For this reference I am indebted to Prof. Jörgensen.)

[6] Secher, *Rettertingsdomme*, II. 29, "høstrue slegt og venner."

[7] Kolderup-Rosenvinge, *Gl. d. D.* II. Fortale No. 20. Elline Christiernsdatter *c.* Jens Christiernsen.

[8] 1566, 25 July (Frands Persen, etc.), P. V. Jacobsen, *Uddrag*, p. 246.

[9] *Gl. d. D.* I. No. 83, p. 172 f. After the slaying of Niels Mogenssen the paternal kinsmen present the whole of their shares and the full third taken by the paternal side to their cousins, the sisters of Niels Mogenssen, minus a fourth part

king's to the Rud family in 1593 seems to show that he regarded the sisters of the slain man as having some share in granting terms to the slayer, for he observes that the proffered terms were rejected by the brothers and *sisters* of the slain[1]. We have already seen that the sisters of Niels Juul obtained wergild in 1602. It is however to be noted that all these female relatives were *near* relatives of the slain. We never hear of a female cousin receiving or claiming wergild.

The only evidence that objection was ever taken to the women's share appears in a case of 1599, when Karine Matsdatter sues one Jörgen Jull for wergild for the slaying of her son, and then it is perhaps characteristic that it is a lawyer, engaged on Jörgen Jull's side, who pleads that "since the law declares that women-folk neither pay nor receive wergild, he presumes that Karine Matsdatter cannot claim it legally." Jörgen has already satisfied the 'kindred' of the slain, who have given him an *orfejde*. Unfortunately the judgment does not decide the question of Karine's claims[2].

The position of women is more prominent than the laws would lead us to expect in one other point. The laws do not apportion any share of wergild to connections by marriage. Yet we find Frantz Persen entitled to a share of wergild in the Helsingör case[3], though he is only married to the slain man's sister. So also Holger Ulfstand, in the van Osten *orfejde*[4], and Hertvig Kaas, in the Juel *orfejde*[5]. Knud Gøye appears to receive wergild for Niels Hak, though he is only his son-in-law[6]. In this connection it is perhaps worth noting that the kindred of the wife seem to play a considerable part in deeds of reconciliation[7]. After the death of Councillor Anders Sörensen Klyn at the hands of Søren Jensen Bramming, at Ribe in 1598, which they give to their own sister, who is in a nunnery. But finally they decide to present the whole wergild (1500 marks) to hospitals and schools, as it seemed to them too small for them to receive with dignity. Frantz Dyre, who has married one of Niels Mogenssen's sisters, then claimed his wife's share.

[1] *Kanc. Brev.* x. p. 115, 'södskende.'
[2] Secher, *Rettertingsdomme*, I. 298, 20 Oct. 1599. There is another case turning on the right of women to be *plaintiffs* (*eptermålsmænd*) in slaying-suits (*Gl. d. D.* II. 505, 1597). We may note several cases where a woman was plaintiff in slaying-suits: thus the widow, in 1611 (Secher, II. p. 375); the widow and sister's son, Helsingör Byting, 1579, 26 Oct.; the widow, ibid. 1587, 9 Jan.; Rettertingsdom, 1615, 7 March (fol. 94): ib. 1647, 5 May, fol. 146: the stepmother, ib. 16 Aug., 1672 (Sylow, p. 43). In all these cases it is probable that the plaintiff received wergild, if it was paid.
[3] "Frandz Perssenn och Christoffer Jörgennssen fremkomme huer epter annden, berette att aff then boidtt, Som gaffues for for^ne Jenns Pederssen, wiille the alldelis intid opbere," etc.
[4] p. 93 supra.   [5] pp. 94, 95 supra.   [6] p. 89 supra.
[7] Thus, in the Bilde *orfejde*, Niels Høg is the wife's uncle (p. 90 supra): Niels Stygge, in the Juel *orfejde* (p. 95), is an even more distant relation of the wife: Erich Høg is her first cousin.

the terms of peace (in 1603) were that the slayer should produce 400 florins to be spent in charitable purposes in Ribe, at the discretion of the widow and *her* kindred and friends[1].

The history of the oath of compurgation is more difficult to trace. We have seen that the Jutish law demands an oath from six of the paternal and six of the maternal kindred of the slayer when a treaty is being concluded, and we find a reference to this as late as 1586[2]. (We may note the "pronouncement of six kinsmen of either party" stipulated for in the Bille *orfejde* (p. 89 supra).)

The oath of twelve kinsmen is a common method of proof in all the laws. A person accused of manslaughter, for instance, can clear himself by taking an oath of innocence, together with eleven of his kinsmen chosen by the other side[3]. Such an oath, the *kyns næfnd* in older Danish, later *kiøns næfn*, serves to establish the right of inheritance of an infant, etc.[4] A somewhat similar *næfn* serves the purposes of an arbitration court. Brothers and sisters cannot go to law with each other about landed property; if they are discontented with their shares they must summon "twelve of their best kinsmen," who will redistribute the lots if necessary[5]. This is called the *samfrænder ed*, 'oath of common kinsmen.'

The oath of compurgation was peculiarly repugnant to Protestants as favouring perjury, and the *kjøns nævn* finally became degraded, any stranger who could be persuaded to swear being bribed to do so. In 1615 Christian IV. complains: "Similarly among the common folk also a great abuse is common, namely that when any farmer is required to give his *kjønsed*, it is their way to seek these far away and fetch them, sometimes from outside the province, sometimes from outside the district, such as will allow themselves to be persuaded to swear their oath[6]." But he does not restrict the oath-takers to

---

[1] Kinch, *Ribe*, II. p. 218. [2] p. 92 supra.
[3] J. L. 2, 9. Cp. also 2, 113, 115.
[4] J. L. I. 4. Sk. L. I. 2.
[5] Eriks sj. L. I., VIII. For cases of *kiøns næfn*, see Heise, *Dipl. Vibergense* p. 128.
[6] Reces, 31 Mar. § 42. Secher, *Forord*. III. p. 449.

kinsmen, only to persons within the same district, and in 1642 Weylle only describes the oath thus : "*Kiøns Eed*, so the oath is termed which is taken within the *kiøn*, i.e. nearest kindred and relatives within the fifth degree (*in old days*)[1]."

But the *samfrænder* remained a flourishing institution very much longer, as it did not come into collision with Protestant prejudices. Christian V.'s new law still ordains arbitration by them in cases of disagreement between brothers and sisters with regard to inheritance[2], and in settling disputes within the family as to profits of a farm[3]. It is only when we come to Baden's *Danish Law Dictionary* of 1822 that we find that the *samfrænder* need no longer be connected with the disputing parties[4].

In law-suits of the end of the 16th and first part of the 17th century, references to *samfrænder* occur fairly frequently. Thus in a case of 1595 one Neils Olsen states that twelve *samfrænder* have been at the farm to decide on the amount of his share[5]. In the same year a Fru Anne Tidemandsdatter, a widow, sues Anders Malthesen for not carrying out a 'judgment of the *samfrænder*' to hand over her dowry, etc.[6]

As in Norway and Sweden, the alienation of inherited land was restricted by customs of an originally tribal nature. In Denmark such land might not be sold until it had been offered to the prospective heirs at three *Things*[7]. We have however already pointed out that the survival of such a right of pre-emption on the part of the heirs is of no value in estimating the degree of solidarity in the kindred at any given period.

The evidence we have just surveyed is far from complete, for it is probable that the local archives stored in Viborg would yield much information if searched. But we have seen enough to justify us in concluding that in Denmark the kindred was capable of acting as a corporate body for nearly a century

---

[1] Weylle, Glossarium, s. v. *Kjøns eed*. Italics mine.
[2] Chr. V.'s Danske Lov, v. c. 2 § 68.
[3] Ib. III. c. 12 § 1—3.
[4] s. v. *samfrænder eed, samfrænderskifte*.
[5] Secher, *Rtd.* p. 33.
[6] Ib. p. 35. Cp. also p. 109 (1596), p. 452 (1603), p. 555 (1604), p. 606 (1604).
[7] See Baden, *Dansk Juridisk Ordbog*, 1822, s.v. *Lovbydelse*.

after the Reformation. The attacks of Knud the Great, of Valdemar II., of Erik Glipping, renewed by Christian II. and Christian III., shook, but could not shatter a solidarity which was rooted in we know not how many hundred years of popular custom; and the energy with which Christian IV. set himself to enforce the edicts of his predecessors would hardly have succeeded, we may surmise, but for his mighty ally, the Protestant Church.

CHAPTER V

NORTH GERMANY AND HOLLAND

I. *Schleswig-Holstein*

FROM no point of view can the modern province of Schleswig-Holstein be regarded as homogeneous.

Ethnologically[1], the main distinction is of course between Danes (or perhaps we should rather say Jutes) in the greater part of Schleswig, and Saxons in Holstein. But a dividing line cannot be definitely drawn along the boundary between the two, for Schleswig is not entirely Jutish. The inhabitants of the islands Sylt, Föhr and Amrum seem to be akin to the invaders of Britain, and there is probably still Anglian, or more properly English, blood in Angeln. Besides this original substratum, there is a considerable colony of a Frisian type, which was already settled on the west coast north of Ditmarschen, in the district known as North Friesland, by about 850 A.D. Moreover most of the Schleswig noble families are of Holstein extraction.

But if the population of Schleswig is not homogeneous, that of Holstein is still less so.

The bulk of its population is Saxon, but these Saxons appear to be of a mixed origin, a people with affinities apparently English rather than German having descended on another people of more definitely German type, the result being that the latter absorbed them. The inhabitants of Ditmarschen are supposed to be Saxon, with a leaven of Frisian blood.

---

[1] A survey of the evidence is given by Sering, *Erbrecht und Agrarverfassung in Schl.-H.* (1908), pp. 19 ff.

Wagrien, the eastern part of Holstein, left desolate by migration, or so it is said, was given over to the Wends by Karl the Great, and only won back in the 12th century. Lauenburg seems to have been originally Slavic, but the Slavs were gradually ousted by Saxon colonists in the 12th century. That there was a large subject population of Wends in most Saxon districts is revealed by the 13th century *Sachsenspiegel.*

Nor was there any political homogeneity in early times. Until the fifteenth century Schleswig was often under Danish rule, while Holstein was a Saxon possession. In the fifteenth century, however, they were united under their own Dukes, but Ditmarschen, which had broken free after the battle of Bornhoved in 1227, remained an independent republic, under the nominal suzerainty of the archbishops of Bremen, until 1559.

In 1326 the islands Föhr, Sylt and Amrum were apportioned to Denmark, together with part of North Friesland, while the marsh-land and moor districts of North Friesland fell to the Dukedom. In 1426 and 1435 Sylt and Amrum were joined to the Dukedom. On the other side of the peninsula the Dukes of Sönderburg remained practically independent[1].

Under these circumstances it is not wonderful that the legislative system of Schleswig-Holstein is somewhat complex. In most parts of Schleswig the Jutish law was in force. North Friesland, however, had two laws of its own: the *Siebenhardenbeliebung* of 1426, superseded in 1572 by the *Nordstrander Landrecht*; and the *Eiderstedtische Krone der rechten Warheit*, of 1426, superseded by the *Eiderstedter Landrecht* of 1591. In the east, the Sonderburg Dukes exercised independent legislative powers; and after 1683 Christian V.'s Danish Code was in force on the islands of Als and Arröe.

In Holstein, the *Neumünster Kirchspielsgebräuche* and the *Bordesholmer Amtsgebräuche* seem to have been committed to writing in the 12th century, and were in force over a large part, if not the whole, of Holstein (except for Ditmarschen). Like the Jutish law in parts of Schleswig, they were not officially superseded until the end of the 19th century. The *Sachsenspiegel*, however, seems to have played a subsidiary part in some districts of Holstein[2].

---

[1] For the practical difficulties and evasion of justice made possible under this system, see a letter of the Amtmann of Steinburg to Christian III. (pub. in *Neues Staatsb. Mag.* IV. pp. 250 ff.). A slayer had sent 3 of his kinsmen to the Amtmann, "um mit des Toten Freunden zu verhandeln, so den Doden wolden tho gelden nehmen," but the noble Jürgen von Ahlefeld took the slayer and all his goods to Krummendiek, whereby he escaped the jurisdiction of the Amtmann, " Iuw. Kön. Matt. Gerichte und Hoheit vnd des Doden Frünt nicht tho ein geringen vorkleinerunge." Also quoted by D. Detlefsen, *Gesch. der holsteinischen Elbmarschen*, II. p. 191 (Glückstadt 1892).

[2] Sering, *Erbrecht und Agrarverfassung in Schl.-Holst.* p. 31. Cp. G. W. Dittmer, *Das Sassen- und Holstein-Recht in practischer Anwendung auf einige im 16de Jhdt.*

The island of Fehmarn had its own laws, and so of course had Ditmarschen. Most of the towns had their own laws, but Burg in Fehmarn, and Tondern in Schleswig, had adopted Lübeck law, which was considerably influenced by Hamburg and even Westphalian law. In the marsh districts there were also various local marsh- and dyke-laws, some customary, one conferred by the Danish King Christian III. in 1552 or 1557.

The wergild laws not unnaturally reflect more clearly the original racial cleavage between Schleswig and Holstein than their late political unity. For this reason it will be easier to treat of their development separately.

A. Schleswig.

For a discussion of the Jutish law we need only refer to the preceding chapter. As in Denmark, wergild (in place of the death-penalty) was restricted in 1558 to cases of manslaughter in self-defence or by misadventure; for though theoretically the Kolding Recess of that date had no validity in Schleswig, as a matter of fact the German annotators of the Jutish law insert its clauses against wergild into their editions[1].

The Siebenharde charter of 1426 deals almost entirely with inheritance; the only clause of interest to us is § 7. "Whatever man shall slay another dishonourably, or after a reconciliation and payment, that man shall be dishonoured and have no peace in the 7 *harde* (districts), and the kinsmen shall pay for the slain man 24 English pounds" (a complete wergild)[2].

For the five districts (fünfharde), which came to compose the Nordstrand territory, the following account, by Johannes Petreus, of the legislation of 1518 gives sufficient information:—

"Anno 1518 the Five Districts assembled again at the order of the Lord of the country, Duke Friedrich,...to consider the law of the land and previous

---

vorgekommene Civil- und Criminal-fälle (Lübeck, 1843), p. 95, "Sassisch Noet- unde Vhaer-Recht" (1579). But p. 180: a reference to the 6 weeks within which wergild must be paid must refer to the Schlesische Landrecht (cap. 110) or to a town law, rather than to Sachsenspiegel (which has 12 weeks); see Gaupp, *Das Schles. Landrecht*.

[1] That these clauses of the Kolding Recess were in force in Schleswig before the passing of the Act in 1636 (see p. 108 below) is proved by a case published by Stemann (*Schl. Recht- und Gerichtsverfassung*, Schleswig und Flensborg, 1855), p. 211, Wies Harde No. 5) for 1631–2, where the local court condemns the slayer to death although he has come to terms with the kinsmen of the slain.

[2] Richthofen, *Friesische Rechtsquellen*, p. 579. Cp. p. 570: Judgment of 1439, 2.

ordinances, and to explain better certain Articles, whereupon especially the ancient devilish and godless custom and blood-rule: 'whoso has fists may smite and whoso has money and goods shall pay'—was partially expunged and deleted. For when a slaying was committed here, the blood-relations who are nearest related to the slayer used to be considered just as guilty as the actual culprit, and were attacked in their houses and beds, before they were aware of what had befallen, by the kinsmen and blood-relations of the slain; often killed, or brought into imprisonment, bound or set in irons, until they had paid up the established compensation, 90 gulden, and so had made peace with the kinsmen (of the slain). Such a godless custom and evil tradition was to some extent annulled at this assembly, and the following article substituted for it:

'If anyone commits a slaying, howsoever and wheresoever it shall happen, it shall be at the stake of his own neck and property, and the kinsmen shall be wholly and entirely clear of the slaying[1].'

At such new articles, and at others which were somewhat bettered, the common folk and especially the fire-brands[2] and mad-caps were very ill-pleased, and have often severely censured and abused the Five-District Councillors, and reproached them as traitors to the Fatherland, and as infringers and destroyers of the good old traditional privileges and rights; and such persons desired none the less to proceed and continue in their old ways; until His Majesty Christian III. was forced on several occasions, as in Anno 1534 and 1540, to fortify and confirm by public mandates the Five-Districts' amendment of the law[3]."

The above restrictions do not, however, prevent the Nordstranders from adding, in the same amended edition of their laws, various clauses regulating the receipt of wergild[4], and we shall see that wergild was still paid by kinsmen long after 1518.

In the Eiderstedt district of North Friesland the "Krone der rechten Warheit" of 1426 divides the wergild into two parts, one called *boyne-bothe* paid by the slayer to the *barne bloet*, the heirs; and the other for the kindred at large[5]. The latter sum is

---

[1] "van dem dodtschlage fry sin." In 1558 this is expressed as follows: "de frunde scholen gantz und gar darvon sin"—"the kinsmen shall be wholly and entirely dissociated from it."

[2] "isenfreter."

[3] Petreus, *Beschriving Nordstrands*, in *Quellen-Sammlung der Gesellsch. f. Schles.-Holst. Gesch.*, v. (Kiel 1901), pp. 121–2.

[4] Nordstrander Landrecht (1572), §§ 11, 27.

[5] Theoretically the first-mentioned is called *boyne-bothe* (*slayer's bothe*) or *bothe*, and the latter is the *thale*. But the whole wergild is frequently called *bothe* in this law, and in the Beliebung of 1444, § 1, the *boyne bothe* [or the whole wergild (?)] is obviously called *thale*, since it has to go to the *barne bloet*. *Fr. Rq.* pp. 571 f.

18 "grote Mark." On the strength of a charter of 1466 (see below p. 108), we may perhaps assume that in this law, as in other Frisian laws[1], the *boyne-bothe* was twice this amount[2], in which case the total would be 54 " grote Mark[3]." The distribution of the wergild would seem to be as follows[4]:—

		grote Mark
A. (*boyne bothe*) paid by slayer to sons (and sons of daughters, § 18)		36 (?) —
B. 1. *enhizkes bothe* ('household' bothe) to brothers: of this the sons of [? deceased][5] brothers and of sisters take ⅓ (§ 19)		6
2. [descendants of grandparents exclusive of father and mother]:		
(uncles and first cousins)	*a.* paternal *fedriethom* and *fedethom*[6],	3
	b. maternal, *omesthom* and *medderthom*[7].	3
3. The four *Kluffte* [descendants of four pairs of great-grandparents exclusive of cl. 2 above]:		
(parents' great uncles, 1st cousins 2nd cousins sons of 2nd cousins once removed)	*a.* paternal (α) and (β)	1½
	b. maternal (α) and (β)	1½
4. The 8 *Fechte* [descendants of 8 pairs of great-great-grandparents exclusive of cl. 3]:		
(grandparents' 1st cousins parents' 2nd cousins 3rd cousins)	*a.* paternal (α—δ)	1½
	b. maternal (α—δ)	1½
		18

The mother's kindred thus benefits equally with the father's kindred.

---

[1] See infra under Friesland.

[2] But cp. the earlier charter of 1446 (p. 108, note 1, infra) where it says that if the slayer fled the kinsmen are to pay two-thirds of the wergild. It is conceivable that this might be their original share, in which case the proportions would be as in Danish and not as in Frisian laws.

[3] The Danish wergild is 54 marks (18 marks by weight = 54 marks of minted money).

[4] Richthofen, *Friesische Rechtsquellen*, pp. 563 ff., §§ 15—23. Cp. v. Amira, *Erbenfolge und Verwandtschaftsgliederung nach altniederdeutschen Rechten*, pp. 162 ff.

[5] This seems to me to follow from § 19: hebben*se* [the brothers] brodersons edder süstersons, so bört enen dat drudde deel to nemende: otherwise it would have been simpler to say hebbense *söne*.

[6] These terms might be reproduced in German as 'Vaterbruderthum' and 'Vaterschwesterthum.'

[7] 'Mutterbruderthum' and 'Mutterschwesterthum.'

NORTH GERMANY AND HOLLAND 107

The four *Kluffte* share equally, each receiving 18 "olde torneye[1]" (evidently = ¾ mark). Within each *Kluffte* each class—great-uncle, first cousins or second cousins—appears to take an equal amount[2]; and on the slayer's side the *Kluffte* seems similarly subdivided[3]. So also, no doubt, in the case of the *Fecht*[4]. Each *Fecht* takes 9 "olde torneye."

In 1446 Duke Adolph issued an edict for Eiderstedt, imposing a death-penalty except in cases of self-defence. If the slayer fled, the paternal and maternal kinsmen were to pay two-

---

[1] Large silver pennies of Tournai. In 1356 32 "olde grote tornosen" = 1 mark (not a grote mark). Cp. Schiller-Lübben, *Mnd. Wb.* s.v. *tornose*.

[2] Or so I understand § 22: "Dat is de erste kluffte vp des vaders side, de oldevader sin broder de nimpt de XVIII. olde torneye mit sinem brodersone vnde mit sinem süstersone, vnd mit sinem brodersones sone vnd mit sinem süstersones sone. Des geliken de oldemoder vp des vaders siden, ere broder de nimpt ock XVIII. olde torneye mit siner süster thom vnd broderthom, vnd de fadrye vnd de oem de nemen den andern del, vnd de süsterson vnd de broderson nemen den drüdden del." I take this to mean that if there is a great uncle living (we will call him *A*), he takes ⅓ of the whole, and his sons or sons' sons nothing: if one of his brothers, deceased (*B*) has left a son (*Bb*) (1st cousin once removed of the slain) he (*Bb*) takes ⅓ as against his uncle: then (regarding this son *Bb* as the uncle (*fadrye* or *oem*) of *Ccc*, the descendant of a third great-uncle, *C*) *C* and *Cc* both being dead (or *Cc* being a woman) *Ccc* (2nd cousin of the slain) would take the remaining third. Of course there might be many more than one in any class.

[3] The above system would apply to the slayer's kindred also, and does seem to be indicated by the puzzling § 15, which appears to mean that on the slayer's side kinship is recognized by the number of degrees between the *slayer* and the common ancestor, not between the common ancestor and the contributing kinsman. Thus we should avoid the difficulty noticed by Brunner (*Zs. der Sav. Stift.* III. 'Sippe und Wergild,' pp. 22–3) of a difference between the method of reckoning liability for wergild and that of participation in wergild. The hypothesis receives support also from § 18 (for the *boyne bothe*). "Of the daughter's sons' boyne both, when the sons take the both...." But see Brunner, pp. 22–3, and v. Amira, *Erbenfolge und Verwandtschaftsgliederung*, p. 163.

[4] In this case it would be *Aa* (grandfather's 1st cousin), *Bbb* (father's 2nd cousin) and *Cccc* (slayer's third cousin) who would share equally (each 3 olde torneye). Perhaps a diagram would make this clear:—The supposed recipients have asterisks; the persons supposed to be living are underlined. f. = female.

Fecht a (α):

				gtgtgrandfather
D	*C*	*B*	*A*	gtgrandfather
Dd	*Cc*	*Bb*	*Aa**	grandfather
Ddd f.	*Ccc*	**Bbb*	*Aaa*	father
*Dddd	**Cccc*			slain.

thirds of the wergild[1]. In another charter, of 1466, the Duke is conservative in apportioning the relative responsibility of the kinsmen :—

"Of every wergild the kinsmen shall have the third part as *tale*. The father's kinsmen and the mother's kinsmen shall divide it among themselves, and they shall divide it among themselves when the payment for the man is made[2]."

In 1522 manslaughter, blinding and maiming were all recognized as *Fründeschaden*—injuries involving the participation of the kindred. In the Landrecht of 1591 the slayer is not to be liable to pay wergild, if he can prove that he committed the slaying in self-defence. But if he has in any way overstepped the limits of pure self-defence he is liable to pay wergild to the kinsmen of the slain[3]. There is perhaps an attempt to limit the field of recipients in the following :—

Art. 50 § 1. "If a man, for the above mentioned reasons, is not punished in his life and person, then the wergild...is due to the slain man's nearest blood-relations and *heirs*, and those who are not connected with the heirs are not entitled to such wergild[4]."

In 1607 secret treaties between the two kindreds are declared invalid[5].

In the Danish parts of Schleswig, then, the first serious check on the practice of wergild occurred in 1558, with the publication of the Kolding Recess. In 1636, however, an Act was passed by the Schleswig Landtag[6], in the names of the Danish King and of the Duke, lamenting the revival of the highly penalized 'fist

---

[1] *Fr. Rq.* p. 574 : "Wert de handdadige ock landflüchtig, so schölen des vaders vnd moders fründe betalen twee saale." Saal is the word in use in the Jutish law for wergild instalments.

[2] *Fr. Rq.* p. 576 (§ 8) : "van eyner iewelken manbote scholen de vründe dat drüdde deel to tale hebben. De vadervründe vnd de modervründe scholen de under zyk delen, vnde dat scholenze vnder zyk delen wan de man betalt werd."

[3] This had evidently become a necessary stipulation, cp. *Fr. Rq.* p. 571 (1444), § 1 : "de nam do de bothe vmme vnd scheffte de thaale nicht eher he starf."

[4] *Das Eyderstedtische Landrecht*...von B. Grauer (Tondern 1737), p. 141 : "sind diejenigen, so des Entleibten Erben unbefugt, solcher Mann-Busse nicht fähig."

[5] Stemann, *Gesch.* pp. 229 ff.

[6] Landgerichtsordnung, Glückstadt 1637. Constitutio de Anno 1636...betreffend die *Ecclesiastica* und *Criminalia* : p. 103, "mit wieder einführung des hoch verbottenen Faustrechts."

law'..."which has resulted in recent years in the slaying of many men, not only nobles, but also persons of humbler rank being miserably put to death, without any kind of punishment, wherefore the whole country is as it were flooded in spilt blood, which cries to God in Heaven for vengeance"...

It is said that "hitherto, either the kinsmen of the slain have not wished to prosecute at all, or allowed the slayer to buy off the suit after suing for pardon or for a certain sum of money: but such '*transactiones*' do not wash away the innocent blood from the land in which it is shed, nay, far from it, and do obstruct and hinder the just and legitimate use of the sword, placed by God in the hands of the legitimate authorities. Consequently all such and similar treaties will not be heeded in future, but the slayer will have to clear himself in the eyes of the Government notwithstanding[1]."

It is further ordained that the kinsmen of the slain are to prosecute either in the High Court (Landgericht) or in the seignorial courts[2]. This last is a blow aimed at the little local *Things* of each district, but the records collected by Stemann, some of which will presently be quoted, show us that slaying-suits continued to be prosecuted in the latter until the beginning of the 18th century.

The complaint made in the Act as to the 'revival' of feuds (and therefore probably of wergild) is probably justified. In the first fervour of the Reformation we find the kindred of the slain occasionally renouncing their right to a composition, and urging the execution of the slayer on religious grounds. This tendency is particularly noticeable in the Flensborg records.

In the "Red Book, wherein are all evil deeds which have been brought before the Court at Flensborg since the year 1560[3]," we find the injured

---

[1] Ib. p. 109, "Vnd weil des Entleibeten Freunde biss anhero | entweder gantz nicht klagen wollen | oder auch der (?den) Thäter | der anklage | nach geschehener Abbitte | oder vmb gewisses Geld erlassen | solche *Transactiones* aber | dass vnschüldige Blut von dem Lande | worinne es vergossen | nicht abwaschen | viel weiniger | der ordentlichen Obrigkeit das Schwerdt | welches ihr von Gott in die Handt gegeben | vnd desselben ordentlichen rechtmässigen Gebrauch | hindert vnd beniemet | Als sollen solche vnd dergleichen Verträge | ins Kunfftig nicht *attendiret* werden | sondern nichts destoweniger | der Thäter sich selbst *ad purgandum* bey der Regierung schuldig seyn."

[2] Ib., p. 107.

[3] Schleswig, *Staats-Archiv*, Acta C. XIX. 1. No. 30, "Rodeboeck darinne alle oueldeder so sedder Anno 1560 tho Flensborch...vorclageth."

kindred repudiating the offer of terms made in the Court by the slayer's kinsmen, while either they or the 'doomsmen' enunciate such sentiments as the following: "Since the Lord God has ordained, that every man who fights with the sword shall also fall by the sword[1]." "We do not condemn thee, but thine own deeds, and the holy law[2]."

Occasionally we note an attitude of apology at receiving wergild. Thus in 1589 Johan Boye was killed by Dr Berendt Schwering. At the Schleswig court the brother of the slain, Boetius Boye, a Protestant minister, forgives the slayer on his own behalf, that of his wife, and his heirs, born and unborn. "*In order that this treaty may be kept the more firmly and steadily*, a hundred gulden are to be paid up for the said reconciliation...[3]"

In other cases the relatives declare themselves willing to forego their shares in favour of the widow and children of the deceased.

Thus in 1627 Niss Anderson, a bricklayer in Flensborg, has been killed by Peter Meyer, a furrier. The 'brother, relatives and kindred' enter into a treaty, by which Peter Meyer is to pay 176 marks for the use and support of the deceased's young children, and to give the widow a good mantle worth 6 marks. He is therewith to be quit of all liability for further wergild[4].

---

[1] Ib., p. 14—17, 1562 (North Friesland). "Dewile Gode de here gesprakenn, dat Je Jemen de mit deme swerde fechtenn mith deme swerde ock vmmekamen schollen."

[2] Ib., pp. 64 f. (1566), "So vorordelen wy dy nicht, sundern dine eigene daet, vnnd dat hillige Recht."

Cp. also p. 147, "Die freundtshafft des Entliueden L. P. hefft sich tho keinem Handell oder affdrage wollen vermoegen lathen, sondern alleine vmb ordeill vnd Recht Instendig gebeden" (1581); and p. 174: Bernt Magnussen killed Nickels Tadessen. Four of the latter's relatives demand 'life for life,' though the other side offer the enormous wergild of 1500 marks.

[3] *Schles. Arch.* Acta A. xx. No. 364. 24 May 1589, "Darmit ock disse vordrach desto vaster vnnd krefftiger mochte geholdenn werden : | tho solcher uthsonung, hundert guldenn, allhir by vnns thoerleggen." The Boyesens are a Ditmarschen family, and the case was first tried there (24 Ap.), but the slain man seems to have lived at Eckernförde. Hence perhaps the appeal to (the town of) Schleswig.

[4] *Schl. Arch.* Acta C. xii. 1, 94. Niss Andersen of Flensborg. "Peter Meyer zu behueff vnd Vnterhalt ihrer kleinen kinderlein, eines für alle 176 mk. Lub. zuentrichten vnd abzutragen solle schuldig seyn...vnd anstat 6 mk. einen gueten frawen Peltz auch eingelifert werden...Vnd da etwas Vber verhaffend wegen ihres Sehl. Ehemanss vnd respective Vattern, eine manbote ins kunfftig ihnen auch solte zuerkandt werden, dessen wollen sie sich hiemit begeben haben, vnd solle selbiges mit ingemelter Summa...eingerechnet vorbleiben."

In another case, in 1625, the guardians of the slain man's child, a girl of about two years old, intimate that they only accept the offer of wergild for the sake of their ward, because she inherits absolutely no property from her parents[1].

From the language of the Act of 1636, however, we can gather that there were dangers in thus inducing the kindred of the slain to forego wergild, for it was likely to occur to them that it would be more satisfactory to carry out the death-penalty on the slayer themselves. Hence, perhaps, the recrudescence of feuds which the Act deplores[2]; and hence the re-appearance of the view which the Roman Church had always upheld, that as it is Christian to forgive, it must therefore be Christian to accept a reconciliation. This older tradition gradually gains ground on the more uncompromising Protestant attitude.

Thus in 1625 a deed of reconciliation (unfortunately not final) begins "In the name of the Holy Trinity a Christian meeting was held...on account of a slaying[3]," and in 1651 a treaty between Sylt and Hamburg families respectively is called a "Christian reconciliation[4]."

If the Protestant spirit among the people themselves could

---

[1] *Schl. Arch.* Acta A. xx. No. 364. (Document beginning: "Wir vntenbenamte Vormunderen des Sehligen mans Claus.")

[2] Thus in 1600 the brother and kinsmen of Hans Bade, whom Heinrich Lass and Heinrich Brammert slay, publicly declare that if the slayers put so much as a foot on the territory of Wulf von Alefeldt, on which the Bades live, they will never return alive to their own house. And one of the slain man's kinsmen, who lives, like the slayers, on ducal territory, goes about with a gun, trying to shoot Heinrich Lass. Acta A. xx. No. 364, 2 Jan. and 9 June.

[3] *Schles. Arch.* Acta C. xii. 1, No. 94. The father, mother, mother's brother and father's brother's sons of the slain man will, after due consideration, accept reconciliation, if it should prove that the slayer, Jacob Schmidt, is sufficiently well-to-do to produce and pay 75 Lübeck marks. The reference to the Trinity was probably pre-Protestant and traditional: it also occurs in a similar document in 1634 (*Schl. Arch.* Acta A. xx. No. 364: a reconciliation between persons from Apenrade, Sönderborg and elsewhere).

[4] *Schl. Arch.* Acta A. xx. No. 737. But it is only in consideration of the expenses (unkosten) that the kindred of the slain consent to the 'Christlichen Reconciliation.'

In a case from 1632 the kindred of the slain declare that they have forgiven the slayer his deed "out of Christian pity." *Schl. Arch.* Acta A. xx. No. 393. 12 Dec. 1632.

do no more than this, it is not to be expected that the wergild custom would yield rapidly to legislation imposed from above. The Recess of 1558 prescribed a death-penalty for all slayings except those committed in self-defence. The enormous number of deaths by violence that occurred in the next century and a half can hardly all come under this head, and indeed very often there is scarcely any attempt to plead self-defence. The efforts of the slayer's kin are all directed towards negotiations with the kindred of the slain man, and if these are satisfactory they can face the authorities with comparative equanimity. Thus in 1615 a wife pleads to the Duke for pardon for her husband "in gracious consideration of the fact that it will not be impugned by the kinsmen of the deceased[1]." In another case the treaty with the kindred of the slain is conditional on the Duke's approval. Nis Matzen has killed a man. The two families conclude a treaty, in which Nis Matzen and his whole kindred are to give the brother and kinsmen of the slain 160 Lübeck marks; in exchange for which the latter are to give the slayer "a sure safe-conduct in and out of our territory...always supposing that His Grace the Duke will give pardon and safe-conduct. And if however the said Nis Matzen should obtain no safe-conduct from the Duke, all this treaty shall be quite void and invalid[2]."

In another case the slayer pleads for pardon from the Duke "in gracious consideration of the fact that the kinsmen of the slain man have offered that as soon as I have gained peace from Your Grace, they will allow me to meet them and will be reconciled with me[3]."

---

[1] *Schl. Arch.* Acta A. xx. 364. Anna Jans Weberen zur Oldenswort pleads: "In gnediger betrachtung dasselbe von des entleibten freunden nicht wird angefochten werden."

[2] *Schl. Arch.* Acta A. xx. No. 364. 1634, 6 Oct. See also another document in same collection: Peter Bennck the District Sheriff witnesses a reconciliation pardoning the slayer, Jes Iverssen, on condition that the Duke will also pardon him—so ferne dat F. G....vorgeuen will.

[3] Ib., 13 Ap. 1635 (Schluxharde): Assmus Kallissen has slain Peter Höck. "In gnädigen erwegungh, dass sich dess entleibten freunde erboten, dass sobalt ich mit E. F. G. gnädig versöhnet, sie sich auch finden lassen, vnd mitt mihr verdragen wollen."

It is curious to find the Duke himself demanding to see the reconciliation-deed before he will pardon a slayer. Thus in 1635 he orders enquiries to be made among all the relatives and friends of the slain Jacob Ströh, as to whether the slayer Hans Schnor has come to terms with them[1]. In reply the Duke receives two documents, one from the slain man's brother, Joachim Ströh, which declares that he and his relatives are satisfied[2], and the other the *orfejde*-deed or "schein" required by the Duke :—

14 Dec. "We...the brothers, relatives and friends of the slain Jacob Ströh, herewith publicly acknowledge that : Because we have seen, that the slayer Hans Schnor regretted from the bottom of his heart the deed he committed, we, on our own behalf and that of our heirs, friends and relatives, none excepted, have concluded, thoroughly and entirely and satisfactorily, a friendly and well-meaning reconciliation with him....In proof whereof we brothers and friends, in default of writing, have signed this with our inherited marks : Jochim Ströhe jun. the brother of the slain. Jochim Ströhe sen. the father's brother of the slain. Jacob Ströhe the father's brother of the slain. Heinrich Ströhe the father's[3] brother. Marx Ströhe the brother of the slain. Heinrich Steffens the brother-in-law of the slain. Jürgen Ströhe the father's brother of the slain[4]." Here the only excuse of the slayer appears to be that he repents his deed.

Even the Act passed by the Schleswig *Landtag* in 1636, refusing all validity to inter-family treaties (except where the slaying had been committed in self-defence), does not seem to

---

[1] Ib., 14 Dec. 1635.   [2] Ib., 27 Nov.   [3] Veters (?).
[4] Ib., 14 Dec. "Wir...des entleibten Jacob Ströhen Brüdere, Anverwanten vnd Freunde bekennen hiemit offentlich : weil wir gesehen, das dem Todtschläger Hanss Schnoren seine begangene thatt von grundt seines hertzen Leidt gewesen, dass wir vns mit Ihme vor Vnss, Vnsere Erben, Freunden vnd Verwanten niemandt ausgenommen gantz vnd gahr zum grunde freundtl. guthl. vnd wohl Vortragen...Vhrkundlich haben wir Broeder vnd Freunde in manglung des schreibens, dieses mit Vnsern angebornen mercke vnterzeichnet...J. Jochim Ströhe des Entleibten Brueder. Ol. Jochim Ströhe des Entleibten Vaters Brueder. Jacob Strohe des Entleibten Vaters Brueder, Heinrich Strohe des Entleibten Veters (?) Brueder Marx Ströhe des Entleibten Brueder Heinrich Steffens den (!) Entleibten Schweger, Jurgen Ströhe des Entl. Vaters Brueder."

In 1632 the Duke receives an answer to a similar query he has made with regard to another slayer, Hans Harder, and the "schein," signed by 9 relatives, is forwarded to him. *Schl. Arch.* Acta A. xx. No. 393, Dec. 12 and 13, 1632 (letter from Steffen Henningck). Here also the case is not one of self-defence, the only plea put forward is that the slaying was committed in a brawl, not deliberately.

have convinced the Schleswigers of the justice of a death-punishment except at the wish of the kinsmen of the slain; for in 1646 a slayer seeking pardon pleads extenuating circumstances to the Duke :—" All this the slain man's parents and friends have been well aware of, and for that reason have gladly come to terms with me and accepted wergild from me, and wished to grant me peace, and therefore have themselves pleaded with your gracious Highness[1]."

In 1651 a treaty is made between two kindreds from the island of Sylt and Hamburg respectively, in which the injured kindred promises to apply for pardon for the slayer from the Duke[2]. We find instances of such treaties up to 1700[3].

If the kindreds could make such a good fight against adverse influences from without, it is not surprising that we find them far less disintegrated in the 17th century than was the case in Denmark a century earlier.

On the slayer's side as well as on that of the slain, we sometimes find evidence of a considerable solidarity. In Flensborg in 1581 the "kinsmen, brothers-in-law, brothers and entire kindred " offer wergild[4]. The "entire kindred" may not mean much, but some very much more definite evidence for wergild-solidarity is forthcoming. In a case of manslaughter, and subsequent wergild, which came before the local court of

---

[1] *Sch. Arch.* A. xx. No. 604 (Wilhelm Berckmans, May 24): "Solches alles haben des Todten Eltern vnd freunde woll gewest, derohalben sich gern mit mir Verglichen die buese genommen mir den frieden gunnen wollen, vnd desswegen selbsten bey E. hochfurstl. G. fur mir gebetten."

[2] *Schles. Arch.* Acta A. xx. No. 737. 17 May (Poul Steveken and Marten Jenssen).

[3] In 1665 we find the mother of a slayer pleading to the Duke for his pardon, showing that she has made a friendly treaty with the kinsmen of the slain (*Schl. Arch.* Acta A. xx. No. 364, H. Priez and J. Selmer). Even in 1692, though the family of the slain man does not venture to conclude a treaty before the case is judged, a signed deed is produced in Court in which they declare that they are *inclined* for a reconciliation with the slayer, for the consideration of 200 marks. In this case the public prosecutor sues (Acta C. vi. 1, No. 102 *c*). So also in 1700, a slayer is condemned to death in the local court of Hvidding Herred, unless he can obtain grace from the Duke. He appeals to the Duke, and at the same time offers to seek a reconciliation with the kinsmen of the slain (Stemann, op. cit. p. 125, No. 152).

[4] *Schl. Arch.* Roedeboeck, Acta C. xix. 1, No. 30, p. 147. (Vorwandtte, Schwegere, Broedere vnnd gantze Frundtschop.)

Hvidding Herred in 1635, a deed of witness, drawn up at the *Thing*, declares "that Laures Perss of Bircheleff first cousin, Poul Bertels og Hans Jess of Gansager in the third degree of relationship, Anders Lauesen of Normsted in the third degree, Hans Pers of Bircheleff as of the fourth degree, stood here to-day before the *Thing*-Court and consented and agreed to pay compensation with Lass Trøgelsen in the wergild and additional gift which he is to pay for the unfortunate manslaying he fell guilty of; first cousin 1 Rixdollar, 'Third man' 4 mk. (?), 'Fourth man' 12 skillings[1]."

In another case, of 1669, from Nørre Rangstrup Herred, we find Iver Jensen acknowledging that he had promised and pledged 50 marks on behalf of Niels Michelsen to Niss Bundsen, as satisfaction (*Feyring*) for the slaying of Niss Bundsen's brother, because he was related to Niels Michelsen, the slayer, in the third degree[2].

In another case, of 1679, one Matz Hakke appears on behalf of the slayer, and produces a deed signed by five other kinsmen, empowering him to act on their behalf. He declares that "he stands before the Court in the name of all Jürgen Jürgensen Arnkiel's (the slayer's) friends and blood-relations, and offers to give an honourable and reputable wergild to the widow, children and friends of the deceased[3]."

But it is not only the actual wergild which the kinsmen help

---

[1] Stemann, *Schl. Rechts- und Gerichtsverfassung im* 17de *Jhdt* (1855), p. 64. Hvidding Herred No. 1, 19 Jan. 1635: "At Lauress Perss i Bircheleff Sødschindbarn, Poul Bertelss og Hans Jess i Gansager Tridie Mand, Anders Lauesen i Normsted Tridie Mand, Hans Perss i Bircheleff som Fierde Mand de stod her idag for Tingsdohm og bevilget og samtete at bøde med Lass Trøgelsen i den Bod og Minde som hand schall udgiffue for den uløkkelig manddrab hand paakom, Sødschindbarn 1 Rixdr. Tridie man 4 [Mk.?] Fjerde mand 12 szl." (For the third man Stemann has 4 Rixdr., which is impossible. Possibly the original had 24 szl.—skillings.)

[2] The pronouns are somewhat obscure in the original, but the above must give the sense: "Iffuer Jensen ved sin sed bekiende, at han haffde loffuett og godsagt for Niels Michelsen til Niss Bundsen for 50 Mk. som de schulle hafve paa Sal. Tiellof Pedersens Brøders vegne for den Dødslag, Niels Michelsen paa deres S. Broder haffuer beganget, og blef samme Penge udlofuet til en Feyring, efterdi at hand og Iffuer Jensen i tredie Led med huer andre er beslegtitt." (The wergild was 400 mk.) Stemann, op. cit. p. 136.

[3] *Schl. Arch.* Acta C. XIX. 5, No. 5. Haderslebem Gerichtsprotokoll 2 Aug. 1679: "so stehet er hier für gerichte im Nahmen Jürgen Jürgensen arnkiels sämbtliche freunden vnd blutsverwandten und erbiehtet sich gegen des Sehl. Mannes Wittwenn kindern vnnd freunden ein Ehrlich vnnd reputirlich boet...zu geben." So also, in 1630, Jyss Nissen's "brothers and kinsmen" offer to pay wergild for him. Stemann, p. 210 (Wies Harde).

to pay, but also the fine to the public authorities. In one case the slayer has been sentenced to pay a fine of 50 Rixdollars: it is observed that "the slayer himself would perhaps find a difficulty in producing it, unless, according to the usual custom in these parts, his blood-relations came to his help both with this and with the other sum which he has to pay as additional gift, besides the wergild." A note at the end of the letter observes: "The slayer's father has freely offered to give 40 Rixdollars[1]."

A curious instance of the solidarity of the slayer's kindred is preserved in a case from Nørre Rangstrup Herred in 1670.

J. T. (one of the slain man's kinsmen) complains in court of the expenses he has been put to in having the slayer executed. His kinsmen declare that they will do him the justice of each paying their share. The question is brought up again some months later, and a recalcitrant kinsman declares that if all the other relatives gave something towards the expense, he would also contribute. The slain man's nearest kinsmen have each promised their share, their liability being apportioned according to their degree of relationship[2].

Perhaps we can now understand why it needs such a number of kinsmen to urge the public authorities to execute justice, since the cost of the execution will fall upon them[3]. The kindred

---

[1] *Schl. Arch.* Acta A. No. 364 (Jep Petersen—Matz Persen): "Welche vielleicht der Thater selber beschwerlich vermöchte zu entrichten, Wan Ihm seine Bluetfreunde, beide in diesem, vnd anderm, so er zur feirunch oder Giorsum, Item der manbuesse, erlegen muess, vblichem gebräuche nach an dieser orten, nicht zu Hulffe kemen... P.S. 40 R. Thaler, hatt des Thaters Vater sich guetwillich erbotten zu geben."

It is probable that the contributions of the kindred were by this time entirely voluntary. Eckenberger, in his *Klein Kort Tractätlein van Prozessen*, observes: "Konde averst ein Nothwehr od wadis gierning dat de Doetslag unwarings beschehen were, beviset werden. So betere he (the slayer) 3 mahl 18 Penninge oder Mk. und mehr nicht, wortho jeder Fründt geldet, und tholegt, so vele alse he uthgelavet hefft...." (*Staatsbürg. Mag.* VI. p. 624.)

[2] Stemann, pp. 136—7. (Stemann unfortunately omits the names of the kinsmen who agree to pay in the first instance, nor does he even mention their number. It was not possible to consult his original.) "1 March 1670, Eftersom J. T. tiltaler nogen for den Omkostning, hand haffuer giort paa S. A. Ch. at lade rette, da erklærede...at de ville gjøre Ligtighed med ham, enhver deris Anpart at betale.— 14. juni. Ch. P. Suarede, dersom alle de andre Slægtninge gaff noget til Omkost, da ville hand og giffue sin Anpart dertil. N.T.'s neste Frender haffue lovet enhver sin Anpart, som de efter Slagt og Byrd kunde tilkomme."

[3] In one of the 16th century cases in the Red Book of Flensborg, mentioned above (p. 110), the appeal to Holy Writ is made by the brothers of the slain, Paye Folquartsen

appear also to share the costs of the law-suit with the actual plaintiff, to judge by a plea sent in by the "frunde" (kinsmen) of Sivert Leuessen in 1605, urging that they should not be liable for the expenses of a (new?) law-suit against the brothers Veddersen, who slew their "kinsman and uncle" seventeen years previously[1].

The *orfejde*-deeds afford similar evidence with regard to the participation of the slain man's kindred. The following deed, from 1610, is one of the most complete[2] :—

"Hans Chrestensen, working for Hans Simonsen of Ausgaard, has to-day received in all 107 Lübeck marks on account of his slain brother Peter Karstensen of Rohrkeer. And it is to be known that the whole sum is 120 marks, for which a sealed deed has been given. Whereof however the deceased's wife has received 10 marks as a consolatory gift[3], and the District Sheriff 3 marks : i.e. one mark for each third [of the wergild], according to the custom of the district. The brother has therefore received 107 Lübeck marks, in the presence of the deceased's kinsmen, Peter Jepsen of Schonby, Jürgen Thomsen, Niss Hansen, Rasmus Nissen, Niss Jessen of Weibull, all of whom have sworn, clasping hands before the Court, that they pledge house and farm as a guarantee that they will satisfy and content their *blood-relations, to whom the wergild rightfully belongs*[4], in such fashion that Hans Iversen [the slayer] and his wife shall never be reproached nor blamed

and Janne Folquartsen, together with their entire kindred, to wit, Jens Feddersen, Jens Poensen, Paye Poensen, Broder Paysen, Rickert Taders, Tercke Hunsen, all domiciled in the Marsh at Dagebüll in Bokingeharde, who prosecute the slayer and demand his execution. Similarly in the second case, where the slayer, Peder Nalle of Flensborg, offered compensation. "However the kindred of the deceased would not consent thereto, but Poppe Ludtsen his father's brother, Nis Nissen, Hans Nissen, Boye Rekerssen his (the deceased Andreas Nansen's) half-brothers, together with Jacob Shoemaker his wife's brother..., sued the said Peter Nalle before the court and complained that he had slain their cousin (*fedder*), brother, and brother-in-law [respectively]." They demand his execution. So also in the third case (quoted in note 1, p. 110). The slain man's father, Peter Tunen of Hoge "together with his connections by marriage [*schwegere*, sons- and brothers-in-law] and kinsmen, earnestly pray for nothing more than law and judgement."

Cp. also in a case of 1620 : Grosse Gösche Odenfeyde kills Jacob Wulf's youngest son with a bread-knife. Jacob Wulf pleads with his "gantze Freundschafft" for the slayer's execution. *Schl. Arch.* Acta A. xx. No. 364.

[1] *Schl. Arch.* Acta A. xx. No. 364 (28 Feb. 1605).
[2] Printed in Stemann, p. 188 (Slux Harde, 1 Dec. 1610), but without the names of the other kinsmen, which are however given in *Statsbürgerliche Magazin*, p. 249.
[3] "tho en Linrung."
[4] "dat se ere Blotfrönden, so de Bote mit Recht gehöret, contenteren und befriedigen willen, by Verpfändung ere Huss und Hoff."

on account of the past slaying, wergild or additional gift; but on the contrary receive thanks for full payment...."

It appears from the above that the wergild is still divided into the third for the heir, the third for the maternal kinsmen, and the third for the paternal kinsmen. That this is the case is evidenced by the following brief notice in the Court records:

"Peter Laurensen of Steenild has to-day acknowledged, that Rasmus Paulsen of Thingeleff has paid him 18 marks for the wergild due to the spear side on account of his deceased brother Michell Laurensen[1]."

Another document, from 1632, is signed by nine relatives :—

"Since an unexpected quarrel and brawl took place between Claus Hesche of Tugendorp and Hans Harders, so that he, Hans Harders, was killed by the said Claus Hesche in the said brawl (but accidentally and without deliberation); and therefore, as a result of prosecution, [Claus] was banished from his property and from the land, in which banishment...he wanders to the present date ; we, all the under-mentioned kinsmen, hereby acknowledge openly and make declaration to all, that we have received sufficient satisfaction from the above-mentioned Claus Hesche, the slayer, on account of the slaying criminally committed on our kinsman, and have forgiven him the deed out of Christian pity, and have come to a thoroughly good understanding with him...." They sign 'with names and one mark': Detleff Bulcke, Hans Delvess, Jochim Harder, Grete Harders, sister, Kla Bulken, Jochim Bulcke, Harder Delvess, Heinrich Wisen, Harteich Weitorp; with the Provost of the Parish, Johann Gotte, as a witness[2].

Another document, of 1652[3], describes how Marten Jensen of the island Sylt was killed in the previous year by a citizen of Hamburg, Paul Steveke, whereupon Marten Jensen's wife, children and kindred 'not unnaturally made

---

[1] Stemann, p. 188–9 (Slux Harde, No. 6), June 12, 1616.

[2] *Schl. Arch.* Acta A. xx. No. 393 (enclosed with a letter of Steffen Henninck to the Duke), 12 Dec. 1632: "Demnach zwischen Clauss Heschen zu Tuugendorp vndt Hanss Harderss ein vnvermutlicher Zannk vnndt schlegerey entstanden, dass er Hanss Harderss von gemeltem Claus Heschen |: Jedoch vnvermuthlicher weise vnndt ohne vorsatz :| in solchem Tumult entleibet worden, Vndt Dahero Auff Angestelleter Clage, seiner guter vndt des landess verwiesen, in welcher verwiesung er...bis dato herumb schwebet, Wir samptliche vntergenante freunde Aber, bekennen hirmidt offentlih vnnd thun kundt Jedermenichlih, dass wir von obberuhrten Clauss Heschen theters, wegen dess am vnsern Anvorwanten freuentlich begangenen niederschlagess, gnuchhafft befriediget, Ihme die that auss christlichem midtleiden vergeben, vndt vns midt ein Ander zugrunde vortragen haben....

Johann Gotte kirchspelsvogt Detleff Bulcke Hanss deluess Jochim Harder Grete Harderz. swester kla Bulken. jochim bulcke, harder deluess Hinrich Wisen, Harteich Weitorp."

[3] *Schl. Arch.* Acta A. xx. No. 737, 1652, den 17 May.

claims and demands on him' (the slayer), but finally, all and sundry make a 'Christian reconciliation,' though without prejudice to the Duke's prerogatives[1]. Peter Tacken is to sign on behalf of the widow, his sister-in-law, because she cannot write, and one of the sons on behalf of his brothers and sisters, together with all the kinsmen present, and in the name of all the absent kindred. Five persons sign besides Peter Tacken, who is the Sheriff (Landvogt) of Sylt. The reconciliation seems to have taken place at Eiderstedt[1].

That the constant reference to "the entire kindred" was not a mere empty formality can be deduced from the care with which the letters of attorney, entitling representatives to act for the kindred, were scanned by the opposing party. A case of manslaughter which came before the Hadersleben court in 1679 gives the following details:—

"Jürgen Nielsen Kellöt appears, in accordance with the deed of attorney he has with him, as representative of the widow and kinsmen of the deceased Friedrich Nielsen of Andrup.... The deed is read out and *Productu* written thereon[2]." The representative of the other side, Matz Hakke, then produces his deed of attorney, from the brothers of the slayer (Jürgen Jürgensen Arnkiel) and the other kinsmen and brothers-in-law, to wit, Jens Petersen, Peter Jepsen and Jess Hansen of Brandsöe. Jürgen Nielsen asks for a copy of the deed, which is granted to him. At the next sitting of the Court, on August 9, an objection is made to Jürgen Nielsen's deed of attorney. "Jürgen Nielsen Kellöt answers that...since the deed was drawn up by the Town Clerk himself, in the presence of the near friends and kinsmen...he supposes that the same will continue to be valid[3]."

But the most startling evidence of the participation of the slain man's kindred is furnished by one of the latest cases of wergild which has as yet come to light. Thanks to the lucky accident that in the year 1693 the town clerk of Hadersleben,

---

[1] "obbesagte Marten Jensenss frauwe kinder undt gesampte Siepschafft sampt vndt sonderss für sich vndt Ihre Erben vndt männiglich an Eyderstat mit Handt vndt Mundt versprochen diese beschehene Verzeihungh nimmer zu bestreiten...Jedoch in dem allem der hochfurstl. Obrikeit Herlikeit...hiemit ohnvergriefenn vndt ohne Intragh...."

[2] *Sch'. Arch.* Acta C. XIX. No. 5. Hadersleben Gerichts Protocoll. 2 Aug. 1679. "Jürgen Nielsen Kellot erscheinet laut habender vollmacht *nomine* sehl. friedrich Nielsen in andrup Wittwe v. freünden....Die vollmacht is verlesen v. Productu druff geschrieben....Matz hakke erscheinet *nomine* Jürgen Jürgensen auss Tollstede brüdere, Crihstoffer arnkiehl, Rasmus Jürgensen arnkiehl und der anderen befreündten vnd Schwäger alss Jenss Petersen, Peter Jepsen vnnd Jiss hansen von Brandsöe produciert Vollmacht. Jürgen Nielsen begehret copiam der vollmacht so ihm indulgieret."

[3] 9 Aug. "Jurgen Nielsen Kellot antwortet weil...die Vollmacht von dem...Stadt Secretario selbst in gegenwart der nahe(n) freunde v. verwandten vffgesetzet...so meinet er dass dieselbe bey macht...verbleiben werde."

who reported the cases, had a marked interest in the affairs of his neighbours, and in financial questions (an interest which is shown almost on every page as long as his handwriting continues) —the following detailed account of the various shares of wergild has come down to us[1] :

"28 Jan., 1693, Niss Iferssen of Friedtstedt appeared as attorney for Fru Magdalen Classen and her son Hans Classen and produces a treaty with the surviving friends of the deceased Marren Oluf on account of the wergild, which sum, in accordance with the said treaty, amounts to 154 mk. And the kinsmen have declared once more that they will abide by the treaty, with the exception of Sören Sörensen of Falstrup, who asks for a copy of the verdict pronounced by the doomsmen (*Sandmänner*), but will not participate in these moneys. Niss Ifersen has however deposited the moneys, sealed, in court, and the day for the distribution of the moneys is fixed for the 18th of Feb. in this year, on which date those who are stated to be kinsmen, who have once again declared in Court [that they intend] to abide by this contract, and make no further claims, and who are also in agreement with each other as to the degrees of relationship, shall receive the moneys without further citation.

Specification of those who are declared to be kinsmen of the deceased Marren Oluf, and in which degree each is concerned, as follows :

Of the 154 mark agreed upon 4 are subtracted for costs— there remain 150 mark.

Thereof 4 persons in the 2nd degree receive each 8 M. = 32 M.
    „ 20 „   „ 3rd „   „   „ 4 M. = 80 M.
    „ 19 „   „ 4th „   „   „ 2 M. = 38 M.
                                                                    150 M.

	Gradus.		
	2	3	4
Bertel Hansen of Hjemdrup has 3 sons:	2		
Laue		3	
Andreas		3	
Sören		3	

---

[1] For a transcript of the original see Appendix II. No. 6.

	Gradus		
	2	3	4
Sören Bertelsen's son, by name Bertelt ...			4
David Kusser of Sommerstedt has 4 sons:	2		
the first		3	
the second		3	
the third		3	
the fourth		3	
Three sons' children:			
first			4
second			4
third			4 "

And so it goes on until it has reckoned up 44 persons who are to receive their due share of wergild. The entry: " Trouelss Jensen...has two sons, who participate on account of their mother " is interesting as showing that cognatic relatives shared equally in the wergild, as prescribed in the Jutish law. Such of the places mentioned as are easily identifiable[1] lie within a radius of about ten miles round Hadersleben, but some of them are at a considerably greater distance from each other.

It is not to be supposed that the relatives invariably participated to such an extent at the end of the seventeenth century: in fact, as we have already seen[2], cases are extant where only the widow and children benefit, and there is an interesting case from 1669 in which the widow, six brothers, and the son of the slain each receive 50 marks, the total of the wergild being 400 marks—which leaves nothing for other relatives. A dispute having arisen in this case, the arbitrators award the son 125 marks, plus interest for 15 years, 133 marks 5 skillings in all[3]. We must suppose that the brothers took more than their share while their nephew was an infant, and that he eventually claimed his rightful third, as heir, and was awarded the interest of it as well. But evidently no one more distant than the brothers

---

[1] Friedtstede, Falstrup, Sommerstedt, Tystrup, Stepping, Faurwra, Jarup, Seggelund.
[2] Supra, pp. 110 f.
[3] Stemann, p. 136. Nørre Rangstrup Herred, No. 10. 1669, 30 Nov. "4 Mend med Herritzfogden lignet og beregnet den Mandbod efter S. Tiellof Pedersen, da tilkommer Peder Tiellosen af berørte Boed, som var 400 mk., deraf 133 mk. 5 sk. og deraf resterende Rente udi 15 Aar. 8 mk. 5 sk. ialt 125 mk."

participated in this case. We note that the large share taken by the widow appears to be unquestioned by the arbitrators, and in fact, as in Denmark, we find mothers and sisters also participating in the wergild[1].

In the matter of the amount of wergild, though the sum varies very much[2], the actual wergild laid down in the Jutish law, 3 times 18 marks of coined money, is more often paid than in Denmark, and it is frequently referred to as being the legal wergild[3]. We also find the 90 Gulden which was the legal wergild for Nordstrand being paid in that district[4].

It may be observed that we have made no mention of the nobles in the foregoing. The reason is that the nobility of Schleswig cannot be treated separately from the Holstein nobility (from whom in fact they sprang)[5], their properties and families being scattered over both duchies.

Falck, in commenting upon Blüting's "Observatio 10 : von mancherlei Todtschlägen im Jütschen Lov" notes with surprise

---

[1] See above, p. 118, Claus Hesche and Hans Harders case; and cp. also *Schl. Arch.* Acta C. XII. 1, No. 94, Gotschalk von Ahlefeldt's letter requesting the authorities of Flensborg to see that the *mother* and relatives of Christian Jensen, who was killed by the son of the Pastor at Bredstede, receive satisfaction : "das des Entleibten Mutter und Vorwanten Befridigett werden" (1599). Cp. also the curious case in *Schl. Arch.* Acta C. XIII. No. 61. Claus, Jürgen Peter and Johann Ratken prosecute the two brothers Royen for killing Hans Ratken. Hans was over 70 years of age, and his body showed no signs of violent treatment. The *Sandleute* observe that the only witnesses of the alleged slaying are Hans' uncles, son, *daughter*, step-son of the daughter and brother's son : i.e. all persons who are pecuniarily interested in proving it to be a slaying, as participating in wergild (Vnd die Manbuesse nach Lohebuchs Rechtt mittgewertich), and dismiss the suit (Arensharde, 1626–27).

[2] The largest that I have noted among non-nobles appears to be 900 mk., *Schl. Arch.* Acta A. xx. No. 364: 1636, Mar. 15. "gedachte Hans Jacobsen [the slayer] schall des entliweden Fruwen, kinderen, Bröderen Vnd Samplichen Bloedefreunden, Eins vor alle, vtegen feyringh Bloedwiede vnde manbotte geuen, Negenn hundert marck Lubisch." But this seems to include fines (blodwide). In Eckernförde in 1647 the legal wergild is declared to be 60 Lübeck marks (Stemann, op. cit. p. 245).

[3] *Schl. Arch.* Acta A. xx. No. 364 (14 June 1601) Pawell Jürgensen has killed Peter Hennings. The latter's kinsmen demand 'ein Übermessiges' but are to content themselves, 'vermüge Lohebuchs Recht,' with thrice 18 marks. Cp. also Acta C. XIX. 5, No. 5, Hadersleben Court, 1679, 6 Sept. and Stemann, pp. 179, 193, 220, 228.

[4] *Schl. Arch.* Acta A. xx. No. 364, 1626, June 26 : Jans Hansen "zue ausszahlungh 90 gulden gewohnlichen Manbuess" (in Nordstrand).

[5] Cp. Sering : *Erbrecht und Agrarverfassung in Schl. H.* (1908), pp. 344–5.

that his author speaks of the Jutish law as still perfectly valid in criminal cases. Blüting was born in 1570, but his annotations to the Jutish law were probably written about 1643. Falck observes that it is known that the penal sections of the Jutish law had ceased to be valid in the towns of Schleswig by the end of the 16th century, and he demands, full of doubt: " Sollte denn die Praxis in den Hardesgerichten von der städtischen Praxis so ganz verschieden seyn[1]?" Stemann, in his selection from the Court records of the various rural districts (*Hardesgerichte*), has produced much evidence for the persistence of wergild customs in the rural districts until the end of the 17th century; and the case just quoted from Hadersleben gives good reason for supposing that wergild, and its distribution among the kindred of the slain, lasted quite as long in some Schleswig towns as in the country. The town of Schleswig itself, or rather its Cathedral Chapter, seems to yield as late as 1692 to the prevailing custom of the country in considering that the existence of a treaty with the injured kindred made it awkward to condemn a slayer to death[2].

The oath of compurgation with oath-helpers of the kindred is known in Schleswig, but appears to last longest in the districts of North Friesland. In this locality it appears in the charter of 1466[3], and in actual cases from 1439[4] to the first part of the 17th century. Thus in 1601 the plaintiff in a case of slander is to swear to the truth of his accusation with eleven of his blood-relations[5]. In Slux Harde, also, we come across a case of this oath as late as 1618: "Peter Hansen has sworn his *Kjøns Eedt*—with his blood-relations, at the proper time of day, himself and eleven others[6]." In the town of Schleswig, however, this form

---

[1] N. Falck: *Neues Staatsbürgerliches Magazin*, III. p. 212.
[2] *Schl. Arch.* Acta C. VI. 1, No. 102ᶜ (an answer of Christian V. to the Schles. Domkapitel).
[3] Richthofen, *Fr. Rq.* p. 576, § 10. In 1558 we find mention of an oath of 8 kinsmen, *Verclaringe des Landrechtes*, § 64, Petreus, p. 158.
[4] *Fr. Rq.* p. 570, No. 2.   [5] Stemann, *Geschichte*, Theil II. p. 324, No. 213.
[6] Stemann, *Schl. Rechts- und Gerichtsverfassung*, p. 189 (No. 7): "Peter Hansen sinen Kiøns-Eedt...mit sinen Blotfruenden tho rechter Tidt Dages sülf 12 nha Landesrechte hefft geleistet."

of oath was no longer in use in the 17th century, for in 1605, in replying to a question asked by the authorities of North Friesland with regard to a certain case, the magistracy of Schleswig reply that a 12-men's oath is not customary in that town[1]. In 1609 we are told that the opposing party refuse to accept the sole oath of their opponent, but demand a twelve-men's oath. The mayor and council of Schleswig thereupon declare that this form of oath was "abrogated many years ago by their forefathers[2]"—probably at the time of the Reformation.

An interesting case of the arbitration of common kinsmen (*samfrænder*) is given by Stemann in his account of the Andersen family in Karr Harde.

The disputing parties are Mette Andersen and Anders Momsen. The twelve kinsmen should be related to both parties, but their efforts at arbitration result in a majority report, for only eight sign and "the other 4 of Anders Momsen's *samptfründe* have separated themselves from us[3]."

In another lawsuit about inheritance, in 1593, when Christoph von Alefeldt sues the heirs of his wife in the High Court of Schleswig, he is ordered to produce 6 *Samfreunde*[4].

The kindred in Schleswig was thus able to offer a passive but effective resistance to the enactments of 1558 and 1636, which should have limited wergild to so few cases that the custom would soon have become obsolete. We have seen how the people evaded, and popular opinion forced the Duke to override, the new clause forbidding treaties between the kindreds, and how the slayer did not always even take the trouble to keep up the legal fiction that his act was committed in self-defence. It seems safe to say that up to 1700 relatives as distant as third cousins frequently though not habitually participated both in the liability for wergild and in the receipt of it. It was a more insidious enemy than officially promulgated edicts to which the

---

[1] Stemann, *Geschichte*, Th. II. p. 333, No. 221.   [2] Ib. p. 335, No. 223.
[3] V. Stemann: Die Familie Andersen in der Karrharde, *Slesvigske Provindsial-efterretninger*. Ny Række. C. Juel og F. Knudsen, Haderslev. Bd III (1862), p. 280 (Urk. 13).
[4] Brinkmann, *Aus dem deutschen Rechtsleben* (Kiel, 1862), p. 258. Other references to samptfründe: *Schl. Arch.* Acta C. XII. 1, No. 94...Über Hans Trötzen zu Husum... verübte Gewaltat, 1563-90.

old customs finally yielded. At no time were the penal clauses of the German code known as the Caroline imposed by Duke or Parliament on the country. Gradually, however, its ideas permeated the lawyer and official classes, and the old Jutish penal law was gradually forgotten and superseded, though theoretically, except for the limitations imposed by the Act of 1636, it remained valid in many parts of Schleswig, until the first of January, 1900. It would be difficult to find a better example than Schleswig of the dangers of trusting to the laws technically in force for a picture of the conditions of any given period.

B. HOLSTEIN.

We have now covered the specifically Scandinavian territory, which was to be our main task, and are faced with the extraordinarily complex conditions of North Germany. For the cogent reasons indicated in the Introduction, it is impossible for us to give more than a series of very superficial sketches of these conditions in general. We have however treated Ditmarschen more fully, as offering, in the *Slachte*, an interesting example of agnatic organization, unique on Teutonic territory.

§ 1. *Ditmarschen.*

The history of Ditmarschen is so sharply divided from that of Holstein, with which, as with its other neighbours, the little republic was usually on bad terms, that it would be necessary for that reason alone to treat it apart from the rest of the Duchy, though from an ethnological point of view it is very similar, the population being of Saxon origin, though perhaps with a Frisian admixture[1]. But the peculiar constitution of Ditmarschen would in any case render it advisable to treat it separately.

The solidarity of the kindred has left its mark on every sphere of Ditmarschen life. It was the kindreds, or *Slachte*[2], which in the 10th and 11th centuries built the great dykes to prevent the sea flooding the marsh land, and so gained some of the richest lands in the peninsula. It was the *Slachte* which governed Ditmarschen until 1447, when a supreme authority, the College of the Forty-Eight, was established. The *slachte* could enter

---

[1] Sering, op. cit. p. 22.   [2] Also written slaht, schlachte, etc.

upon commercial enterprises[1], and could not only form alliances among themselves, but conclude treaties with their foreign enemies[2]. Such clearly defined groups must obviously have been organized on an agnatic basis, and this certainly seems to have been the case[3]. It is in this point that the clans of Ditmarschen are so unlike the shifting kindreds which we find elsewhere on Teutonic territory. There are however other differences. Thus a Ditmarschen *slachte* resembles other agnatic clans in the fact that the bond of kindred was extended almost indefinitely, instead of terminating with fourth cousins, as in Denmark. A powerful *slachte* was often a confederation of a number of minor groups of kindred. Besides this, artificial relationship was resorted to, and strangers were admitted as 'cousins.' The best description of the internal organization of the *slachte* is given by the chronicler Neocorus, although he wrote when their day was over. Neocorus, who became a pastor in 1590, says:

"There are in every parish (*Carspel*, Kirchspiel) splendid old kindreds (Geschlechter) of unimaginable antiquity; adorned because of their uprightness and noble deeds with magnificent blazons and coats-of-arms, which are divided among themselves into special *brodertembte* or *klufte*, and have had great alliances among themselves, that no member should forsake the other, even the meanest and poorest, if any one wished to encroach upon him or treat him unjustly. Now in case any one from foreign lands desired to settle down in a parish and to be connected with and enter a *Geschlecht*, if such a one brought with him honest and blameless witness of his honourable birth, origin, and habits of life...they would adopt him as a 'cousin' of the *Geschlecht*, and regard him not less than their nearest-born kin,...and all fighting men of the whole *Geschlecht* would on his account have risked life and limb or gone to war[4]."

---

[1] Ldrecht, II. xcii: "Vortmer so mach en islik slachte, kluft edder brodortemede offte gilde ere pandinge hebben...." (A. L. J. Michelsen, *Sammlung altdithmarscher Rechtsquellen*, Altona 1842. Cp. pp. 263-4: a law-suit between a village and the Boldersmannen.)

[2] See Michelsen's *Urkundenbuch* (Altona 1834), pp. 18 (1316), 28-9 (1384), etc.

[3] Being agnatic, the Ditmarschen *slachte* cannot have been in the least analogous to the North German *Fechte, Fange* or *achtendeele* (the 8 branches of descendants of great-great-grandparents), as has sometimes been assumed. These latter are based on the equal recognition of agnates and cognates, of father's kindred and mother's kindred.

[4] *Neocorus, Chronik*, ed. Dahlmann (Kiel, 1827), pp. 206 f.: "It sin in Idern Carspelen herliche olde Geschlechte, so van undenklichen Jahren hero, umme ehrer Uprichticheit unnd ehrlichen Daden willen, mit herlichen schonen Herteken unnd Wapen geziret, de under sich in sonderliche Brodertembte edder kluffte gedelet unde

It was indeed a very closely-knit community which the stranger was thus privileged to enter. If he had a quarrel with a member of another *slachte*, he could not compose it except with the consent of his whole *slachte*, with all its *klufte*[1]. The laws suggest that the interests of the *slachte*, the corporate kindred, were paramount, and the independence of the individual very much subordinated to them. Even the wergild laws show traces of this tendency. Thus it appears in the earlier law (of 1447) that the individual is primarily responsible for wergild, if he has committed a slaying, and if he has insufficient means to meet the demand, it is not the *slachte* which becomes responsible, but only his immediate kinsmen[2]. Yet if a member of a *slachte* is slain, part of the wergild falls to the kindred[3]. In the later law of 1539,—i.e. after the supreme authority had been taken from the hands of the *slachte* for nearly a hundred years,—the *slachte* may become liable for wergild if the slayer cannot pay; but it still has the choice of repudiating the culprit if he cannot pay the fine to the authorities[4]. The dis-

---

under sick grote Vorbuntnisse gehatt, de eine dem anderen, ock den Allergeringsten unde Armesten nicht tho vorlaten, so ehn Jemant vorunrechten unde belastigen wolde. Im Falle nun einer uth frombden Landen sich in einem Carspel neddergelaten unnd in ein Geschlechte sich tho begeven unde to befrunden begeret, wen desulve ehrliche, underdelhaffte Tuchnisse siner ehrlichen Gebort, Herkamendes, Handels unde Wandelss gebracht,...hebben se densulven vor einen Vedderen dess Geschlechtes angehamen, ock nicht geringer geachtet, alss ehren negesten angebarnen Frundt,... und alle wehrhaffte Manschop des ganzen Geschlechtes wol hedden sinethalven sich in gefahr Livess unnd Levendes gestoken unnd tho Felde getagen."

[1] The Reformers enacted that the individual should be free to compose differences with members of another *slachte*, but still forbid him to appeal to public authority in a dispute with a member of his own *slachte*. In the latter case the matter is to be submitted to the arbitration of four members of the *slachte*. A. Viethen, *Beschreibung und Gesch. des Landes Dithmarschen* (Hamburg, 1733), p. 160.

[2] Ldrecht, I. § 72: "Item eft dar en man enen man dale sloghe, vnde he dat gud nicht en hedde, dar he ene mede betalen konde, so schullen sine *neghesten* to tasten vnde betalen den man...."

[3] Ldrecht, I. § 79: "Vortmer efft dar eyn man geslaghen worde, so schal de bane bliuen by de swert siden, vnde dat andere manghelt dar id van rechte bliuen schal." Cp. Brunner, *Sippe und Wergeld* (Zs. der Sav. Stift. III.), p. 24.

[4] II. xxx. "Vortmer offt dar en man enen dale sloghe vnde he so vele nicht en hadde, dat he sin antal holden konde, so schal *dat slachte* allike wol den man betalen, vnde den hantdadigen moghen se ouergeuen vor den vrede."...(In this event the culprit is executed, see II. xxxi.)

tribution of wergild is thus described : " Further, if a man be slain, the *bane* remains [among the immediate kindred?] on the agnatic side, and the other wergild shall be divided according to the law of the *slachte*[1]."

Moreover if debts are to be taken out of the wergild of a slain man, the *bane*, the share of the near relatives, is first sacrificed, and only secondarily the rest of the wergild, if the *bane* should not suffice[2].

The laws evidently regard the details of wergild distribution as a matter for the *slachte* concerned, and vouchsafe no further direct information beyond the statement that the usual wergild was 100 marks[3]. We can, however, deduce from the following clause that the wergild was divided between the *slachte, kluft* and *brodortemede* :

"If a man die, and it is claimed that he had received wergild due to his *slachte, kluft*, or *brodertemede*, and if he leaves a son, the son shall pay those goods to his *slachte, kluft* or *temede*. If the goods should have fallen to the wife's kindred (after the division of the property) the *slachte, kluft* or *brodertemede* must each claim the part due to them with a *nemede* (oath of 9 men)[4]."

Another matter in which the bond of kindred must have frequently been somewhat irksome is the system of corporate oath-taking, which was carried to great lengths. The ordinary 'nemede' consisted of nine persons of the oath-taker's *slachte*, besides himself. They were chosen by the opponent, and the oath-taker could reject five of them[5]. A 'full oath' consisted of twelve persons. The law of 1447 provided that anyone accusing another of manslaughter must produce a *nemede* (9 oath-helpers) from his own *slachte* for the first oath, and six

---

[1] II. xli. "Vortmer efft dar en man geslagen worde, so schal de bane bliuen by der swertsiden, vnde dat ander mangheld schollen se delen na eres slachtes rechticheit."

[2] Ldrecht II. xl. "Vortmer efft dar en man geslagen worde vnde so vele schuldich were, dat me de schult nicht betalen konde van sinen acker vnde gude, so schalme de schult betalen van der bane, offt me dar nicht mede betalen konde, so schalme dat nemen vt dem ganzen manghelde." The earlier law only prescribes that the debt shall be paid out of the wergild—'van sineme bitteren dode.' (Ldrecht I. § 88.)

[3] Ldrecht I. § 70.

[4] I. § 163. "Vortmer efft en man wech storue vnde worde beschuldiget, dat he scholde uppe nomen hebben sines slahtes manghelt effte kluft effte broder themede," etc. Cp. II. c. clxxx.

[5] I. § 113.

out of the twelve in twenty-nine supplementary 'full oaths' (with 12 oath-helpers). All these should be different persons if the *slachte* has sufficient, if not, the same persons can act in several 'full oaths[1].' The remaining six persons of each 'full oath' are taken from *slachte* which are not concerned in the matter.

That one *slachte* could be expected to produce as many as 174 males of an age to act in this capacity may seem surprising until we read in Neocorus' Chronicle that the clan of the Woldersmen, counting some minor branches, used to be able to bring 509 men into the field[2].

The obligation to commit perjury in this way, and on so large a scale, was the chief objection made by the Protestants against the whole clan system, and must have been an intolerable tyranny[3].

In general, the tendency of the *slachte* seems to have been on the one hand to encroach more and more on the rights of the individual or family—though this tendency was to a certain extent checked by the efforts of the Forty-Eight[4], and on the other, to repudiate the responsibility of any acts of the individual that might be inconvenient. For example, in 1323, in the treaty of Ditmarschen with Gerhard the Great, it is agreed that the kin shall pay for any theft committed by one of their number who then evades capture[5]. But in the later law we find the clause: "Henceforth a thief may not steal the property of his kinsmen[6]" —i.e. the kindred was not to be liable to indemnify the person whose goods were stolen.

It was not until their acceptance of Protestantism that the Ditmarschers began to conceive of individual responsibility.

---

[1] I. §§ 74, 76: see note, p. 287.   [2] Neocorus, ed. Dahlmann, I. p. 244.

[3] The model 'Bundbrief' composed by the Reformers (cp. Bolten, *Ditmarsische Geschichte*, Flensborg and Leipsic 1781–88, Theil IV. p. 85 note), after forbidding the practice of taking oaths in matters of which the oath-helpers are entirely ignorant, observes that such oaths are false witness and perjury, and are against the commandments of God (formula in Viethen, op. cit. pp. 161 ff.). The actual institution of oath-helpers persisted after the Reformation, but the function was to be exercised by fellow-parishioners, not kinsmen. (Cp. Nitsch, *Das alte Dithmarschen*, pp. 22 f. and Dahlmann, *Neocorus*, II. pp. 573 ff.)

[4] K. W. Nitsch, *Das alte Dithmarschen* (Kiel, 1862), p. 22.
[5] Michelsen, p. 329.   [6] II. clxxxiv. § 5.

The Protestant pastors thundered against the oaths of compurgation and against the deeds of alliance between *slachte* or their dependent groups. We may perhaps venture to guess that their crusade would not have been so successful if the people themselves had not begun to chafe at the tyranny of the old organizations. In any case, the effect of the Protestant tirades was quickly visible. In 1538 an Act was promulgated which gives clear expression to the new views:—"God be praised and magnified, the country has been so instructed and so taught in the word of God by our superintendents and preachers, that all the evil alliances of all *slachte* of old throughout the whole land of Ditmarschen have been dissolved, annulled and loosed[1]."

The second triumph of the Protestant pastors comes in 1554:

"Whoever slays his fellow-Christian, whom God redeemed through Christ, who for that cause shed His precious blood on the gallows of the Cross, be he poor or rich, of high or low estate, he shall, without any help from proofs of having acted in self-defence, in his turn die and be punished with the sword, according to the commandment of God and the holy Bible[2]."

But the autonomy of the Ditmarschers was nearly at an end. In 1559 they were conquered by the combined Danish and German forces, and henceforth formed part of Holstein. The new law of 1567 again expressly abolishes the oaths of compurgation[3]; but tempers the severity of the previous edict

---

[1] Ldrecht II. ccxlv. "Wat vor recht me in de stede slachtes nemede geuen schal.... Indeme, Godt gepryset vnde gelouet, dat Land dorch öre Superattendaten vnde Predicanten mit deme worde godes so vnderrichtet vnde geleret, dat alle de vordömelike vorbüntenisse aller Slachte vormals, dörch dat gantze landt tho Dithmerschen, vpgelöset, vornichtiget vnd fry gemaket...."

[2] III. 2. "Wer auerst sinen euen Christen minschen, so Godt dorch Christum erlösset vnd darauer he am galgen des Crüces sin dürbar bloth vorgaten hefft, dodtsleith, he sie arm edder rick, hoges edder nidriges standes, de schal sunder jennige behelp van Notwertüchnisse edder anders, na Godes geboden vnd der hilligen Bibel, wedderumme steruen vnd mit dem Swerde gestraffet werden."

As a matter of fact the Protestant pastors were against the death-penalty being meted out to those who had acted in self-defence, but possibly the Ditmarschers intended to avoid the evasion of a death-sentence through specious pleas of self-defence or accident, which were so common in the neighbouring districts.

[3] Dithmarsische Land Recht (Glückstadt, 1667), Art. 13, § 1: "...Darumme heven Wy hiermit up und casseren allent wat in dem olden Dithmarschen Land Rechte van den schlachtnehmenden, klufftnehmenden karcknehmenden und den anderen Eeden...bruklyk gewesen."

as to manslaughter by making an exception for slayings committed in self-defence[1]. As a matter of fact the Duke seems seldom to have insisted on the infliction of the death-penalty, but to have contented himself with extracting heavy fines[2]. But he struck a more effective blow at the Ditmarschen clans by enacting (1559) that female heirs were to share equally with male heirs in landed property as well as in movables, or at least (1567) were to be bought out. The confusion resulting from these laws imposed on an agnatically organized society did no doubt tend towards the disintegration of the clans; especially as the lawyers ruled that in cases where there were no children to inherit, the *mother* came before the brothers of the deceased[3]. Curiously enough, we find women—not only widows of the slain, but also sisters[4], partaking of the wergild or taking part in treaties, as well as brothers-in-law[5] and even a wife's step-father[6]. These cases, though mostly occurring very soon after the promulgation of the new law, may be due to the confusion caused by it, or they may possibly indicate that the agnatic principle was not so strictly carried out in wergild matters as the law would lead us to suppose.

Except for the constant expression "and his whole kindred" occurring in pleas to the Duke, whether for the pardon or for the execution of a slayer; and sometimes in treaties with the kindred

---

[1] Art. 118, § 10. "Werd de Nohtwehr also bewyset so schall he dem heren de Broke geuen." § 11, "Und des Doden halven mit synen negsten Fründen sick uhtsohnen und verdragen." In 1607 the Duke forbids private treaties, Michelsen, *Urkundenbuch zur Gesch. Dithm.* (Altona 1834), No. CLXX. pp. 388–9.

[2] In one case 3000 Mk: *Gemeinsch. Arch.* (Copenhagen, Rigsarkiv) XXI. 72 (Henning Clawessen).

[3] Michelsen, *Urkundenbuch zur Gesch. Dithm.*, Altona 1834, pp. 233 f. (quoted by Sering, op. cit., p. 142).

[4] Copenhagen Rigsarkiv: *Gemeinsch. Arch.* XXI. 72 (*Hansborg*). Junge Suells Johan pleads to the Duke that he has "des entlyuedenn broder vnd Schwester... gefrediget...vnd dermathen gestillet, dat she my...christlich vorgeuen hebben," 1574. See also XXI. 72 *b*, the treaty: "Im Namen seiner Soesteren Vedderenn vnnd Verwantten."

[5] ib. XXI. 72 *b*. An appeal to the Fürst and Räthe: "...ihm namen vnd von wegen ihrer Principalen vnd ahngeborne freundt öhme, shone vnd *schwegerer*." So also *Schl. Arch.* Acta A. XX. No. 737, 9 Aug. 1634 (Jeronimus Bartelt).

[6] ib. XXI. 72 *c*, case of Heinrich Carstens Heinrich, one of the signatories is Claus Jurgen (G. Johan's *fruuwen Steffader*).

of the slain[1], there is very little extant evidence for the persistence of the *slachte* in Ditmarschen for the century following the Reformation. But the *klüfte*, at any rate, had not been entirely broken up, for documents are extant from the 17th and 18th centuries which show that they survived in a modified form. These are the so-called *kluftbücher*, containing provisions for mutual help, etc. among the members of the *kluft*. There is frequently some mention of their rules being submitted to the official of the district for approval, without which formality such associations were illegal. Thus the '*kluftbuch* of the Mengermann's kindred[2]' has the following preface:

[1] Rigsarkiv (Copenhagen), *Gemeinsch. Arch.* XXI. 66, Reinholt Rodens "frundschafft vnd vorwandten" (1563); XXI. 55 (Vertecknuss der Totschleger Im Sunderdeel Dithmarschen wnnd ihrer gueder): for slaying a foreigner: "Nhun hebben ehme sÿne frůnde geholpen, dat he dess entlÿueten Eruen gestellet"; XXI. 72, "Wy hinrich Vagdes grote Johans nachgelassen brodre vnnd wy andere mit In nhamen der gantzen frundschop" (29 Nov. 1575); XXI. 72 *b*, "Seligen Claus Vogdts vnnd Heinrich Vogds Grosse Johanns nachgelassene Brudere Vettere vnd freunde" (1575), ib., Peter Denkers "ahngeborne freundt, öhme, shone, vnd schwegerer"; ib. "wy auerst vann des *dedernn* Frundtschop...thom oftermale dath menn idt tho enem vordrage kamen laten muchte, angelanget...wy...ock des entliuedenn Andern Veddern vnnd frunden"; ib. "olde Kruuss Per Clawess, syne fruntschop vnnd vedderenn...ick ock vann vegenn mynes entliueden söns dar suluige peter Krussen und seine Vedderen vnnd der gantzenn fruntschop" (1573); ib. "Stellanus Sestedenn Gantzenn freundschafft" (12 Nov. 1573); ib. "der beiden deder fruntschop" (in a letter of Henning Boie to the Duke). Cp. (ib., in a wergild treaty) "Dass sie die obbenante des entleibtn (*sic*) Vatter vnd Vatters bruder fur sich vnd alle Ihre angehörige Verwandte freundtschafft mit den obbenante des Carsten Lowerhofs freundten solche todtschlags...halben sich vorgeliechen."

[2] Kieler, Univ. Bibl. Cod. MS. H. 195 D.D.D. 4to. "Wir die sämmtliche Klufts Vettern des Menger-Manns Geschlechts alhier auff Büsum, Uhrkunden und bekennen hiemit vor Uns und unsern Erben. Demnach bereits von langen Jahren her unsere Vorfahren unter sich eine Vetter- und Brüderschafft auffgerichtet, und gestifftet, krafft welcher ein Kluffts Vetter dem Andern wie ein Bruder in allen Nöthen hatt Hülffe und Beystand leisten müssen: Wir auch so viel Uns möglich gewesen, Solches in Observance behalten. Es aber jtzo das Ansehen fast gewinnen will, als wenn ein oder ander Articul, so unsere Vorfahren vorhin wohl bedächtlich gemachet, jtziger Zeit nicht recht nachgelebet wird, wie es bereits die Erfahrung gegeben, weil die Mehresten nicht deutlich genug exprimiret, noch die Confirmation gehörig darüber gesuchet worden. So haben Wir, mit reiffen Vorbedacht bey Uns beschlossen, diese unsere alte Articulen von unserm Kirchspielschreiber durchsehen, und verbessern zu lassen; nicht zweiflende, ein hochpreyssliches Gericht werde solche nachgesetzte Articulen Nahmens Ihro Königl. Hoheit gütigst zu confirmiren geruhen."

"We, all the 'Klufts Vetter' of the Mengermann's kindred here in Büsum, make known and declare herewith for ourselves and our heirs: Whereas already long years ago our ancestors founded and established a *Vetterschaft* and brotherhood amongst themselves, by virtue of which one *Klufts Vetter* must help and succour the other, like a brother, in all difficulties; and we also, so far as lay in our power, have kept the same in observance: but now the view seems to gain ground, that perhaps one or another article, which our forefathers made of old no doubt with due consideration, cannot be followed rightly at the present day, as experience has already shown, because the most of them are not clearly enough expressed, nor has confirmation of them been duly sought. Therefore, after full consideration, we have decided amongst ourselves to have these our old articles looked through by our parish clerk, and corrected, not doubting that the worshipful Court will deign to confirm such articles as follow in the name of His Royal Grace."

The articles, briefly stated, are as follows:

1. Each to help the other.
2. The *kluft* to clear any member who is slandered, if it is notorious that he is innocent.
3. To tend the sick at night in turns. In the case of contagious disease to pay for a nurse.
4. Men and women to appear at any member's funeral 'in ihren besten Trauer Habitt.'
5. If any member is ill at harvest-time, each *Vetter* to give a day's work free of charge, if required.
6. If a *Vetter* dies without issue, his heirs to pay the *Kluft* 6 mk.
7. Any *Vetter* leading a dissolute life, or making a 'despicable' marriage, to be ejected from the *Vetterschaft*.
8. Any *Vetter* making mock of these articles, or *leading the Vetterschaft into a law-suit with outsiders*, pays 6 marks to the Kluft and 6 marks to the Ducal Chancery, and will be ejected from the *Vetterschaft* if he offends in this way twice.
9. Two 'Älter Leute' to be chosen every year.
10. The *Älter Leute* to have charge of the great drinking horn, mounted in silver, and the funeral pall. The horn can be lent to members of the *Kluft*.
11. A yearly meeting on the Monday following Rogation Sunday, in order to discuss whether or no a tun of beer shall be drunk.
12. A feast the Monday after Whitsunday; all members over 18 years of age to attend it.
13. No strangers allowed at the feast.
14. Cursing and swearing forbidden at the feast, penalty of 3 mk to the *Kluft* and 3 to the Ducal Chancery.
15. Quarrels and blows forbidden at the feast, penalty 6 marks to the *Kluft* and the same to the Ducal Chancery.
16. If the *Kluft* has need of more money, every male member of the *Kluft* to contribute equally.

17. Arrangement of the pews in church belonging to the *Kluft*. On the death of occupier the nearest relative takes the pew. No one outside the *Kluft* may lease them.

18. Women of the *Kluft* to help each other.

On the 18th August, 1737, 37 persons sign the above (mostly with marks). The document is 'approved by the authorities on Dec. 11, 1737'—on condition that all insults and quarrels are announced to the Chancery. The book is handsomely bound.

Another '*kluftbuch*,' dated 1671[1], is of interest as re-confirming an alliance between the ' very ancient Dickboleman schlacht' and the Hackens men. This book contains 55 names; and notes the payment of fines, admission of new members, etc. The last entry in it is dated 1811. In another *kluftbuch*, written in 1717, that of the Hersens, there are 58 names, but only the three surnames Dyrsen, Kroeger, and Sieverts occur[2]—conclusive evidence that these gilds are really based on kinship, even if they occasionally admit persons who are not kinsmen to their associations. That they fulfilled real functions is vouched for by Pastor Harm, who observes that until about 1760 no workhouses were needed in Ditmarschen, nor fire insurance societies[3]. As regards the latter, indeed, gilds still exist in Ditmarschen, more especially in Büsum, which fulfil these functions, and are a shadowy survival of the ancient and powerful *slachte*[4]. According to Sering[5], two '*klüfte*' still own landed property in common; shares in it are still inherited according to the ancient agnatic principles of the commonwealth.

---

[1] Kiel. Univ. Bibl. S. H. 195 D. Heckens *Kluftbuch*.

[2] Printed in A. Niemann's *Miscellaneen*, II. 2 Stück. Altona and Leipsic 1800, pp. 132 ff. Cp. also the Mollersen *Kluftbuch* (Kieler Univ. Bibl. Cod. MS. S.H. 195 D.D.) which declares that it was founded in 1588 "aus keinen andern Grund, alss dass Einer dem andern in Noth und Tod wie Vettern und Bruder beystehen... sollen," and it was reconstituted in 1735. It has 25 signatories (the last two were admitted in 1777), all with one exception surnamed Hübber, Hannssen or Matthiessen. (This is also a very handsomely bound book.)

[3] C. Harm's *Vermischte Aufsätze*, Kiel, 1853, p. 77, and p. 75 : "Wo noch am längsten sich eine Geschlechtsverbindung erhalten hat, freilich ohne Schlachtbrief, bis auf unsere Zeit (i.e. middle of 18th century) da gab es reiche Leute bis auf unsre Zeit und nun nicht mehr—in St Annen."

[4] Sering, op. cit., p. 129.

[5] Op. cit., p. 127.

§ 2. *Holstein exclusive of Ditmarschen.*

The understanding of the Holstein laws is rendered much easier by our previous study of the Ditmarschen law, for in the rest of Holstein we find the same tendencies, though not so strongly marked. It will be best to begin with two edicts from the 15th and 16th centuries respectively. The first is written at the order of the Danish king Christian I. to the nobility of Schleswig-Holstein, in 1480:

"His Grace had also heard of certain *Schlechten* which have allied themselves to one another, the which his Grace had no intention of permitting: since his Grace is a prince of the country, his Grace considered himself capable of settling any quarrel and dissension arising in his dominion, so that his Grace will suffer no alliances, neither among the common folk, nor, in especial, among you[1]...."

The next is addressed to Bordesholm monastery by Duke Johan, in 1556[2]:

"And whereas it has come to our notice, and is in fact notorious, that in the domain of our monastery Bordesholm, many manslaughters and evil

---

[1] Printed in N. Falck, *Sammlung zur nähern Kunde des Vaterlandes* (Altona, 1819-25), Bd III. p. 356: "Syner Gnaden were ock bygekamen van etlichen *Schlechten*, de sick malck ander verbunden, welck syner Gnade nenerley Wiese dechte tho lidende, dewiele siene Gnade ein Fürst der Lande were, dachte siene Gnade Unwillen und Misshelligkeit in synen Landen riesende wohl tho scheidende, so dat syne Gnade nenen Vorbund noch in dat Gemene, noch in besonderheit dechte edder will hebben, und wo sine Gnade darentgegen wes befunde, denket und will syne Gnade straffen, so sick dat behört."

[2] Rigsarkiv, Copenhagen: *Gemeinsch. Arch.* (*Hansborg*), XXV. 9: "...Vnnd alss wy yn erfarung kamen, vnnd egenthlig berycht werden dath ynn vnsses Closters Bordesholm gebede, vele todtslege vnnd bosse daden gheoueth vnnd begaen werden, vnnd eyn tydt lanck her de ghebruck vnnd ghewanheith ghewessen, dath vor ersth, des enthlyueden frunde szolchs myth der fusth rechnen wyllen, vnnd szyck de deder, szo ethwes befrundet vnnd vormogens szynn myth ghelde vthwercken vnnd darmyth der lyffstraffe gheoueryth vnnd entf(ry)eth szynn...Demnach meynen vnnd wyllenn, ghebeden vnnd beuelenn wy vth furstlicher macht gnedig vnnd gansz ernstlig dar szyck henfürder (der)ggelicke todtslege thodrügen, Gy wylleth de vorbrekunge nicht myth ghelde wo beth her gescheen, affkopenn lathenn, szundern ahm lyue strafenn vnnd vngeacht eyniger ghewonheith, hals vor hals nhemen wo denn byllig vnnd szolchs ock yn ghemeynem beschreuenn Rechten vorordenth. Des scholen szyck ock de frunde an ghelyck vnnd recht szedigen vnnd benughenn lathenn, vnnd daedtliche vorhandlung an des deders frunden by vormydunghe lyues straffe vthernn vnnd entholden...Actum Flenszburg 20te octobris anno clvj (1556)." (Printed in Westphalen, *Mon. ined.* II. 539-40.)

deeds are practised and committed, and that for a while the custom and usage has existed here, that, to begin with, the kinsmen of the slain man will avenge such deed with the fist, and that the slayers, if they be fairly provided with kinsmen and goods, can redeem themselves with money, and thereby override and escape the death-punishment...we consequently graciously and very earnestly desire and wish, order and command with our princely authority, that when henceforth such slayings occur, ye will not suffer the crime to be bought off with money as has happened heretofore, but punish it by death ; and, in despite of a certain degree of custom, take neck for neck, as indeed is fitting, and is laid down in the common written law. The kinsmen shall moreover allow themselves to be satisfied and content with justice and equity, and shall refrain and withhold themselves, on pain of death, from violent dealings with the kinsmen of the slayer."

In some part of Holstein, then, the formation of alliances among the kindreds was already marked enough to cause alarm to its ruler. In the districts where the Sachsenspiegel was in force, we have no further knowledge of such *schlachte*, but in the eastern part of Holstein the laws, as we shall see, make mention of *vetterschaften* which must surely resemble the Ditmarschen *klüfte*.

Unfortunately the only manuscripts extant of the Bordesholmer Amtsgebräuche and the (almost identical) Neumünster Kirchspiels Gebräuche are very late, from *c.* 1690 and 1712 respectively, though the custumal itself dates from the 12th or 13th century[1]. It is thus natural that they restrict the wergild to cases of self-defence[2]:

In such cases the slayer shall pay a fine to the lord, and come to terms with the kinsmen of the deceased. "In this matter the custom is to be

---

[1] Seestern-Pauly, *Die Neumünster'schen Kirchspiels- und die Bordersholmerschen Amts-Gebräuche* (Schleswig 1824), pp. 19 f., 114 ff.

[2] Ib. pp. 114 ff., *Neumünster Kirchspiels Gebräuche*, Art. LXII.: "Hierbey ist der Gebrauch (so des Todtschlägers Freunde bey Erlegung des Aussöhn-Geldes, oder des entleibten Freunde bey Empfangung des Söhne- oder Vortrag-Geldes, halten) in acht zu nehmen, die Vetterschaft wird also gehalten, wenn einer ihres Mittels der Vettern einen Todtschlag begehet ; so müssen die gesammte Vettern zu ihrem Theil erlegen 40 Mk., die übrigen 20 Mk. aber der Thäter. Begiebt sichs auch, dass eine in der Vätterschaft wurde entleibet, und die Entleibung also beschaffen wäre, dass der Thäter zum Aussöhne gelassen werden kőnte, auf solchen Event ziehen die Vettern 40 Mk., die übrigen 20 Mk. empfahen die nächsten Erben, und theilen selbige unter sich ; Hierbey ist sonderl. zu merken, liess der Entleibte eine Wittwe, nebst einem Sohne und Tochter, hinter ihm, so nimmt der Sohn die 20 Mk. und schleust Mutter und Töchter aus: Ursachlich, dass dis Werk das Geschlecht oder

heeded (which the kinsmen of the slayer observe when they pay the reconciliation-money, or the kinsmen of the slain on receiving the peace- or treaty-money): the *Vätterschaft* is similarly bound, when one of its group of 'cousins' commits a slaying: the whole body of 'cousins' must pay 40 marks as their share, but the slayer the remaining 20 marks. If it should further chance, that one of the *Vätterschaft* is slain, and the slaying was done in such wise, that the slayer might be admitted to reconciliation, in such an event the 'cousins' receive 40 mks; the remaining 20 marks are received by the nearest heirs, who divide the same among themselves. Hereby it is specially to be noted, that if the slain man left a widow, besides a son and daughter, the son takes the 20 marks and excludes mother and daughters. The reason is, that this work concerns the kindred or the stock (Stamm), and those born into it belong to the father's and not the mother's kindred: on this account this peace-money goes to the son as the [descendant of the] stock, and does not extend to reckoning the *Vätterschaft* on the women's side: therefore the latter cannot or may not be included. If however no sons exist, such 20 marks go to the mother and daughters, who divide the same among themselves."

The passage in the Bordesholm text ends: "annulled, Dec. 2, 1619[1]," but the Neumünster text, otherwise identical, has no word of the repeal of the law.

It appears from the above that the *vetterschaft*, or *schlecht* as the earlier edict has it, is an association of kindred, on an agnatic basis, like the Ditmarschen *kluft*. On the other hand, it must be noted that the law evidently considers the possibility that the slayer, or slain, is not a member of such an association at all, for it bases the payment to the *vetterschaft* on the analogy of payments to the kinsmen in general.

The little island of Fehmarn, near Lübeck, is generally supposed to have been populated by Ditmarschers after the devastation of the island in 1419 by Erik of Pomerania[2]. In

---

den Stamm angehet, und die so gebohren werden, folgen nach des Vaters und nicht der Mutter Geschlecht, derowegen dies Sohngeld dem Sohne als dem Stamme folget, und erstrecket sich nicht zu rechnen die Vatterschaft auf die Frauens Bilde, die den dahero nicht können oder mögen dazu gezogen werden. Seind aber keine Söhne vorhanden, fallen solche 20 Mk. auf Mutter und Töchter, und theilen selbige unter sich."

[1] "abgesprochen d. 2 Xbris ao. 1619."
[2] So Sering, p. 32, and others. But cp. Sarauw, " Nachtrag zum Versuche einer gesch. Darstellung des polit. Verhältnisses der Insel Fehmarn," *Neues Statsbürgerliches Magazin*, IV. pp. 499–504.

any case the organization is very similar to that of Ditmarschen, though the groups of kindred are termed '*vetterschaft*' as in East Holstein. With regard to wergild, the statutes of the Witte-Mackeprang *vetterschaft*, of 1611, ordain that if one of its members kills a man, the *vetterschaft* shall aid him to the extent of 60 marks. But if one of their members is the victim, the slayer shall have no peace without the consent of the whole *vetterschaft*[1].

As late as 1822 a Danish observer found two *vetterschaften* in existence at Burg, and had an opportunity of examining the *vetternbuch* of one of them. He found that the old articles of 1563 had been confirmed in 1656 by the mayor and Council of Burg, and had been translated in 1776 into High German. The rules, which closely resemble those of a Ditmarschen *kluftbuch*, were still in force in 1822[2].

Since the customary law known as the *Sachsenspiegel* was in force in the remaining districts of Holstein, at any rate where it did not conflict with local custom, it may be well to discuss it here, though its validity extended over a much larger area. It dates from the first quarter of the 13th century. Unfortunately its wergild clauses are so brief and so obscure that we can only glean the information that wergild can be paid in cases of self-defence, and the law seems also to contemplate it in other cases[3]. All free classes seem to have approximately the same wergild[4], a feature in which Sachsenspiegel resembles the Jutish laws. But the wergilds, mostly in kind, of various inferior classes are also given. Wergild is paid to the kinsmen,—'magen,' but we are not told who these are[5]. One passage seems distinctly to suggest that kinsmen sometimes helped to pay the wergild:

---

[1] Brunner, *Sippe und Wergeld*, p. 13. Cp. *Schles. Arch.* Acta C. XIX. 4, No. 4 (18 Sept. 1605) "...Wan nhun...zwischen Beklagten als des Theters Vatter vnnd des entleibetes *Vetteren*, Brueder vnnd Freunden ein Vertrag...auffgerichttett...."

[2] *Statsb. Magazin*, IV. p. 250: "Vetterschaften auf Fehmarn." MS. copies of the Rauert's *Vetternbuch* (made by Michelsen?) are in the Kiel Univ. Bibl., Cod. MSS. H. 503, O., 4to., and ib. 503, P., 4to.

[3] J. Weiske, *Sachsenspiegel*, Leipsic 1895, Buch II. Art. 14, § 1.

[4] *Sachsenspiegel*, III. 45, § 1. "...Vürsten, vrîe herren, schephenbâre lûte, die sint glîch in bûze und in weregelde...." Cp. Ph. Heck, *Die Gemeinfreien*.

[5] II. 14, § 1. "den magen ir weregeld."

"Where more people than one promise together a wergild or other payment, they are all bound to produce (it), as long as it is unpaid; and not any one of them the whole; for each shall pay as much as is fitting for him, so far as he can be forced thereto by the court, (by him) to whom the sum was promised, or by him with whom he promised, if he (the latter) has already paid it[1]."

But it is to be noted that the law apparently only forces them to pay if they have promised to do so.

A clause ordaining that every man is bound to give security for his lord or for his *swertmac*[2], agnatic kinsman, in cases of slaying or wounding, seems to indicate a tendency towards an agnatic system of kinship, but of this there is little other trace; and in the 16th century in Steinburg, which was presumably under Saxon law at that date, we find a case in which the '*mother's* brother and his kinsmen' attempt to avenge the death of a nephew[3].

There is good reason for supposing that kinsmen (possibly only near relatives) took part in reconciliations, and even paid and received wergild, until the beginning of the 17th century. Thus at a reconciliation which took place at Oldeslohe in 1607 two brothers pay 120 marks to the 'kindred' (freundschafft) of the man whom they slew[4]. In a case of 1579 the Court

---

[1] III. 85, § 1. "Swar mêr lûte den ein zu samene geloben ein weregelt oder ein ander gelt, alle sint sie phlichtic zu leistene, die wîle ez unvergulden ist, und nicht ir ieclich al; den ieclich sal gelden als vil als ime gebüret, und alsô verne als man in dâr getwingen mag von gerichtes halben, der deme ez dâ gelobet ist, oder der ez mit ime gelobete, ob erz vor in vergulden hât."

[2] *Ssp.* II. § 1. "Gewere sal iewelk man dun umme dot slach unde umme lemesle unde wunde, vor sinen herren, dem he bestat unde vor sine svertmage." H. Rosin, *Der Begriff der Schwertmagen* (Breslau 1877), thinks this means: a man who is himself wounded shall pledge himself that no claim be made by his *Swertmag* against the offender.

[3] Copenhagen Rigsarkiv: Indkomne Sager 1530–50, T.K. (I.A.), I. No. 24. The "getruwenn rede vnnd landtsathen der fürstendome" plead for their "ffrunt vnnd landtman" Heinrich Blome (of Steinburg): "Wo her peter schramme de der frantz Iuersenn moder broder Is myt syner fruntschop schole dar na trachtenn und stann dat he...eme na halse en liff vnd gude stann vnd handele eme vnde syner fruntschop tho keyner geringenn vorkleninge...."

[4] *Schl. Arch.* Acta A. XX. 364, 7 July 1607, the 'Vertrags Briff': "die gebrüdere Bartellt vnd Dithmar Dithmarsen Einhundertt vnd zwantzigk margk leubisch, nebens allen angewendeten Unkostungen vnd schaden, obberůrten vnseren Mitburgern Claus Kraegens *wegen der anderen freundschafft* vulderlich erlechtt vnd zugestellet...," and Copenhagen Rigsarkiv, loc. cit. (1548), "Rathlouenn Veddern vnd fruntschup."

sentences the slayer of a fisher-boy to death, unless within four weeks he can come to terms with the kinsmen of the deceased, and his lord[1].

An interesting case from 1669 shows that in the matter of support of needy kinsmen a corporate responsibility of the kindred lasted in Holstein until a very late period. In 1669 one Adam Trutenberg, plaintiff on behalf of Anne Wilde, sues Johann Hasse for alimentation. The Court decides:

"If the accused can prove by oath within 17 days that he is not related to the plaintiff within the third degree (second cousin), he is to be absolved from the suit: in default of the oath, however, he will be liable to contribute pro quota to the cost of alimentation[2]."

This verdict was given in the Wilstermarsch; and the liability of the kinsmen might be considered to be a custom of that district, which has its own customary Marshland law, but that a Holstein lawyer, writing of a similar case in 1738, observes:

"Relatives who are related to the needy person within the third degree, canonical computation, are liable to contribute pro quota to his support, in such fashion that, if the children of brothers and sisters contribute 1 Rixdollar, the grandchildren of brothers and sisters give 24 sk....Therefore it seems to me right and necessary that Mr N. should first in a friendly manner desire of all his relatives who possess means and are related to him within the third degree, that they would give him something annually to help him. If this does not avail, he must have them prosecuted on this plea before the worshipful government (as the same is *forum ob connexitatem causae*, since the relatives live under divers jurisdictions) and I hope that, when they see that he is in earnest, they will soon meet him (in the matter)[3]."

---

[1] G. W. Dittmer, *Das Sassen- und Holstein Recht...im 16de Jhdt*. Lübeck 1843, p. 95, No. XIX. Cp. also p. 180 (1609).

[2] Falck, *Samml. der wichtigsten Abh. zur Erläuterung der vaterländ. Gesch.* (Tondern 1821), Bd I. p. 89: "In Sachen Adam Trutenberg nomine Annen Wilden Klägerin, wider Johann Hassen Beklagten, gesuchter Alimentorum: Erkennen die 16 Gerichts-Personen hiemit für Recht: Wird Beklagter heute über 17 Tage eydlich erhalten, dass er der Klägerin im 3ten Grade nicht verwandt, ist er von angestellter Klage zu absolviren: in Ermangelung des Eydes aber zu den Alimentations-Kosten pro quota mit zuzuschiessen gehalten. Wilster 10 Nov. 1669."

[3] Falck, *Samml. der wichtigsten Abh.* Bd I. p. 89. Cp. also p. 507, where Falck observes that it would be a good plan to revive the rule, but that in that case the rights of the kindred over the inherited lands, done away with in 1798, would have to come into force again.

This liability for maintenance must thus have been in force in the whole of Holstein, for the case could else hardly have been brought up before the High Court. It is extremely interesting from two points of view. In the Icelandic law the duty of maintenance only fell on the nearest kinsman; here, the kindred is regarded as corporate: all relatives within the prescribed degree are liable for a contribution, as in wergild.

The second point to note is that this liability extends to cognates as well as to agnates: the children of brothers and *sisters* contribute the same amount. We must beware then of regarding the possibly agnatic *vetterschaften* of East Holstein as indicative of a society organized on an agnatic basis, as in Ditmarschen. The following cases seem to furnish further evidence to the contrary, at least for the nobles and the towns. In the 'Solemn Apology' of 36 noble persons, on account of the slaying of Gerhard Ranzow by Friderich Brockdorf[1], dated 1558, we not only find women taking part in the public plea for pardon, but the various surnames of the male relatives, Brockdorf, von Qualen, Ahlefeldt and von der Wisch, can only indicate that they were not all agnatically related to the slayer. The same thing is shown in a plea to the king from the relatives of Friderich von Ahlefeldt, signed by a von Bockwolt, a Sehested, a von der Wisch, a Bülow, two Ranzow brothers and a Pentze, who call themselves 'cousins, brothers-in-law and kinsmen of the slayer[2].'

So also in the towns of Kiel and Lübeck[3]. Here however the kindreds certainly lost their solidarity earlier than in the rural districts, so that we must take our examples from an earlier time. The following deed of reconciliation of 1423, in Lübeck, shows the participation of nine kinsmen of the slain, who, to judge by their surnames, can hardly all be agnatically connected with him:

---

[1] See Appendix II.
[2] Rigsarkiv (Copenhagen): Indkomne Sager 1530–50: T.K. (I.A.) I. No. 24.
[3] Cp. Pauli, "Über das Lübeckische Mangeld," *Zs. des Vereins f. Lüb. Gesch.* Bd III. (1876), p. 298, H. Luppe, *Beiträge zum Todtschlagsrechte Lübecks im MA.* Kiel 1896, also *Mitth. der Ges. f. Kieler Stadtgesch.* Heft 17, No. 55 (1541).

"Marquardus vam Sande, Wennekinus Brassche, Nicolaus Brassche, Hinricus Gutendorp, Nicolaus Gutendorp, Detlevus Svartekop, Hinricus Morssel, Tydekinus Morssel, Nicolaus Wulff, propinquiores heredes et consanguinei et amici et nomine omnium aliorum heredum seu amicorum dicti Hennekini Lubberdes coram consilio et hoc libro recognoverunt, se conjuncta manu ad suffienciam sublevasse et percipisse a Johanne Olrikes XL. marcas lub. den. in satisfacionem seu emendam interfeccionis seu occisionis dicti Hennekini Lubberdes[1]."

The evidence of the following case (Lübeck 1441) is less clear:

"Scylye, the widow of Peter Senneken of blessed memory, Henneke Senneken, Michael Stolte, Byke, Bernd Nyendorp and Tydele of Hameln, by birth kinsmen of the aforesaid Peter Senneke, on behalf of the said Scylye's children and all heirs, relatives and kinsmen...of the said Peter Senneken, have acknowledged in the presence of the Council and on the book, that for the slaying and compensation...they have taken over and received to their satisfaction 40 marks of Lübeck money[2]."

There is however more definite evidence than this that wergild was not restricted to agnates in Lübeck law, for we find the *filius sororis patris* taking wergild[3], and in another case the *filius sororis*[4]. In yet another case, also of the middle of the 15th century, we find the brother and *sister* receiving wergild[5]. In 1461 the half-brothers of the slain swear the oath of reconciliation on behalf of themselves, their heirs, and those who are connected with them on the *spindle* side[6]. On the other hand,

---

[1] Pauli, op. cit. p. 298 (Niederstadtbuch of Lübeck).

[2] Pauli, p. 308. Niederstadtbuch, No. XXXVIII. "Scylye, wedewe Peter Senneken seliger dachtnisse, Henneke Senneken, Michael Stolte, Byke Bernd Nyendorp vnde Tydele van Hameln, angeborne vrunde des erbenomeden Peter Senneken, van der erbenomeden Scylyen erer kindere unde van wegen aller erwen, mage, unde vrunde...des erbenomeden Peters Senneken vor dem rade unde vor dem boke hebben bekant, dat se Clawese Wildeshufen von den dotslach unde beteringe...to ere genoge upboret unde entfangen hebben vertych mark lub. pen." Up to 1500 we occasionally find kinsmen helping to pay the wergild: Lüb. Urk. B. VI. 735, VIII. 269, Pauli, No. LVII., LIX., XCIX. (1500): "sodane gelt van dem manslachtigen manne *unde sinen vrunden* entfangen hefft."

[3] Pauli, op. cit. No. XXX.

[4] Ib. No. XXXI.

[5] Ib. No. XL.

[6] Cod. Dipl. Lüb. Bd X. lvi. "...also dat Hans vnde Gereke Plate noch ere eruen noch alle de ghenne, de ze van der spille syde mechtich zint...nicht manen

in 1457 Herman Vischer sues two brothers for wergild for Hinrik Rekeman, his wife's father; but the council decided that wergild went to the spear side, and not to the spindle side[1].

The older Lübeck law also knows of the oath of compurgation by 12 kinsmen, but contemplates the possibility that such kinsmen are not available[2].

It is curious to find an official edition of the statutes of Lübeck, published in 1728, still containing the following clause: "With regard to slayings and woundings the guilty party may not come to terms with the kindred of the slain or wounded man, nor they with him, without the previous knowledge of the Court[3]."

II. *Hamburg and Environs.*

Before we cross the Elbe, a glance at the Court records of districts under the jurisdiction of Hamburg will not be out of place. These give a highly instructive account of a case in 1609, in which the Public Prosecutor appears. The counsel of the accused pleads that 'the step-father, father's brother, brothers and brothers-in-law of the deceased' had while he was still alive, and with his consent, made a treaty with his principal[4]. This document, signed by both parties, he appears to have read aloud in Court, after which he urged pardon in consideration of the

---

edder zaken schal." This case is interesting because it contains a clause disavowing the half-brothers' responsibility for peace if it should happen that the son of the slain should wish to make trouble.

[1] Pauli, No. LXVI. "...Darup de erscr. rad...delede unde affsede vor recht : dat id ervede in de swertsyde, unde nicht in de spillenzyde... (i.e., not to females)."

[2] J. F. Hach, *Das alte Lübische Recht*, Cod. I. xci : "Habebit autem ad expurgandum se uiros XI. comprobatos, se ipso XII. existente. Si uero parentum uel amicorum carentiam habuerit, in quotcumque ei deficit. tot iuramenta iurabit. Jurare autem hoc debet quod parentes non habeat nec amicos qui ei astare possint. & in hoc perficiens erit in omnia."

[3] Statutes of 1728, Art. 1. Tit. 8, Lib. IV. (quoted by Luppe, p. 53).

[4] *Archiv der freien und Hansestadt Hamburg*: Stadt Archiv Cl. VII. Litr. Md. No. 5, Vol. 4, a. 2 (1607-10), 15 March 1609: "Dat Recht contra Hans Möller. Alss hedde sich des entliueden Steiff Vader, Vadernbroder, Fulbrodere und Schwegere mit Consent und vorweten dess Vorwundeten sich mit seinem Principaln...vorgelicken vnd vordragen."

fact that the kinsmen of the deceased were not prosecuting[1]. The Public Prosecutor retorts that: 'as far as the treaty was concerned the deceased kinsmen were over-persuaded to it, being poor simple folk,' and that there are still five brother's children who will not be content to leave matters as they are[2]. The counsel for the defence then declares that if any one wishes to prosecute, the kinsmen who have made the treaty must settle with him[3]. But the verdict is that the accused is to die by the sword[4].

In another case of the following year, the father of the slain, knowing that his son had given great cause of offence to the slayer, refused wergild and forgave the slayer[5]. The accused is acquitted. In the same year a 'treaty with the deceased's wife and nearest kinsmen' is pleaded, but the Public Prosecutor dismisses the treaty as invalid and worthless[6].

It is interesting to see that treaties with the injured party could still serve in Court as pleas for mercy[7]. From the point of view of the solidarity of the kindred the evidence they furnish is not convincing: the kindred of the slayer does not appear, even in the treaties, and the kindred of the slain appears to be limited

---

[1] "Vnd wolde demnha Im nhamen dess armen gefangen diewile desz entliueden Frunde nicht Clageden lutter vmb Gottes willen gebeden hebben seinen Principaln van der angestelten Pinlichen Clagen tho *absoluiren*...."

[2] "Wat dem vorlesenen vordrage anlangede wehren dess entliueden Frunde alse zympeln entfoldige lude dartho vorleidet...Diewile...noch 5 broderkinder Im leuende welche solches alles nicht wollen gudt sin laten."

[3] "woferne noch Jemandt vorhanden so Clagen wolden so mugten die Frunde so den vordrach vnderschreuen solches affdragen vnd darup geschlaten."

[4] "der Angeclagter...mit dem schwerde ahm leuende gestraffet werden soll." Cp. (for Bergedorf) Hans Kellinghausen in *Zs. f. Hamb. Gesch.* XIII. p. 311; and *Arch. des Amtes Bergedorf* (Hamburg Archiv), Pars I. 1, vol. 1, Fasc. 2 (Criminalakten der vormaligen Landgerichte), 1595, 21 Dec. (Michael Kilm), and 1611, 29 Jan. (Harman Wobbe).

[5] "Vnd dan ock des entliueden Vader nhademe er erfahren...dat sin sohne nicht alleine ein Anfenger sunder ehr ock tho solchem nedderschlage grote orsacke gegeuen kein blodtgeldt begeret sunderlich mit seinem Principaln vorgelicken vnd vordragen."

[6] Datt Rechtt contra Matthias Krabbenhouet. "Vndt wehre die vorlesene Vordragh Krafftlos und von keinem Verden."

[7] For cases (up to 1600) in which self-defence is successfully pleaded, and the slayer merely sentenced to pay wergild, see G. Trummer, *Vorträge über Tortur, etc., in der Hamburgischen Rechtsgesch.* (Hamburg 1844), Bd I. pp. 340, 341, Anm. 2.

to very close relatives; but it is highly probable that earlier documents would show larger groups of kindred. The neighbouring districts show more signs of the solidarity of the kinsmen in these matters. In 1567 the Council of Hamburg made an effort to persuade the two parishes Altenwalde and Groden to introduce the death-penalty for manslaughter. The inhabitants however object, on the ground that they are related to their neighbours of Hadeln, and that the law and usage in Hadeln is that the slain man can be paid for with money, and they have no more intention than the Hadeln folk of giving up this custom[1]. As a matter of fact the Archbishop of Bremen had eleven years before this (1556) issued a charge to Bremen, Verden and Hadeln, making death the penalty for manslaughter when committed by non-nobles, and forbidding the abuse that the kinsmen of the dead should be satisfied with money, and that the *slayer's kinsmen*, as well as the slayer himself, should be obliged to redeem him by the same method[2]. Since the people of Hadeln apparently succeeded in evading this new law, it is possible that the customs mentioned in their law of 1439 were still adhered to: "If it should be the case that the slayer is refractory and will not pay for the dead when he is prosecuted before the lord, then, firstly, he may be attacked in his life and goods, and thereafter his nearest cousins as far as the 4th degree, all those, who would benefit by or atone for the slayer (i.e. would receive wergild for him if slain, or contribute to one for which he had become liable): these shall be attacked in their property, arson excepted[3]."

---

[1] H. Joachim, *Die Begründung der Doser Kirche und des Doser Kirchspiels* (Zs. des Vereins f. Hamburgische Gesch. XIII. 1908), p. 19, quotes: "Datsulvige konnen se nicht ingaen und wylligen, dewyle se sick myt ohren naberen den Hadeleren befrundet, und de gebruck und id recht im lande tho Hadelen is, dat men den doden myt gelde kann betalen; dat wyllen se na older gewaenheit och so geholden hebben."

[2] W. Wittpenning, *Mittheilungen zum älteren Criminalrechte*, p. 385, in *Archiv des Vereins f. Gesch. und Alterthümer der Herzogthümer Bremen und Verden und des Landes Hadeln*, Bd IV. (1871).

[3] Grimm, *Weisthümer* (Göttingen 1840–69), Bd IV. pp. 703 ff., Rechte von Altenbruch, Ludingwort und Nordleda (1439), § 2.

In the districts under Hamburg control we find references to treaties with the 'entire kindred' well into the 17th century, but we suspect that this phrase has no longer the comprehensive significance of an earlier date.

Thus, at the *Göding* of Bergedorf Amt, the plaintiff in a slaying-suit prosecutes "in the name and on behalf of all the kindred of the deceased there present[1]."—Unfortunately their names are not given. In another case, of 1611, one Joachim Jürgen has been fatally wounded, but makes peace with his opponent before he dies. The Court asks "whether any of the deceased's kinsmen were also present at the reconciliation, whereto is answered yes, that the mother, Hans Lutken and Vicke Brulle were present, and that Harman Wobbe (the slayer) promised Joachim Jürgen a certain sum of money...which Joachim Jürgen received." After Joachim's death, nevertheless, the 'kinsmen' prosecute him. The decision is that "since Harme Wobbe had come to terms with the deceased Joachim Jürgen and his kinsmen, he could not be condemned to outlawry on that count[2]."

We see that a treaty with the kinsmen is still considered to preclude judicial action against the slayer, but on the other hand, in a community where the kindred still had their full rights in such matters, the hasty and informal treaty with the dying man would not be held binding on the whole kindred[3]. It is not till 1649 that the religious objections to these treaties are stated:

"Since then, not only in the common written imperial laws, and in the Ordinances for the Criminal Court, Caroli 5, art. 137, but also especially in God's Holy Words, it is very earnestly ordered and commanded that every slayer should forfeit his life, and that whosoever sheds blood, his blood shall be shed in turn[4]...."

---

[1] *Archiv der freien und Hansestadt Hamburg*: Arch. des Amtes Bergedorf, Pars I. Vol. I, Fasc. 2, 21 Dec. 1595: "Im nhamen vnd von wegen der gantzen vmbstehenden entlyuden frundtschafft."

[2] Ib. 1611, 29 Jan. The Landleute ask: "efft ock von des verstoruenen frunde etliche mitt by dem vordrage gewesen darup geanttwordett Ja, datt de modur hans Lutken vnd Vicke Brulle darmitt by gewesen Alss der vordrach geschehen...vnd datt der Harman Wobbe dem Joachim Jurgen ein gewisse geldt tho geuende thogesecht... welche Joachim Jurgen enttfengen....De landtlude sagen...dewile der Harme Wobbe sich mit den vorsteruenen Joachim Jurgen vndt sine frunden vordragen, datt he des wegen nicht konde fredeloss gelegtt werden."

[3] See Denmark, pp. 85 f., supra. (The inhabitants of Bergedorf, as of all the 'Vierlande' district, are of Dutch origin, so perhaps much importance should not be ascribed to their customs in this context.)

[4] *Hamb. Archiv*, as above, 1649, 14 July.

III. *Friesland.*

In Friesland we find the kindreds highly cohesive, and active in a variety of ways, to which the customary laws testify. In the eastern district, which later fell under the Counts of Oldenburg, a legal text of the 13th century gives us the following curious information:

> "This is also Frisian law: if the poor man raises a hat (=banner) aloft, and cries: 'Ethelings follow me, have I not enough wealthy kinsmen?' all those who follow him and fight, thereby risk their own property, because the poor man is the least of all men; he can involve the property of all his kinsfolk, but cannot push matters as far as to an *ofledene*[1]."

A 14th century source tells us that the leader of an attack (he who carries the 'hat') pays all fines arising out of the fray, to his last penny, when his companions are called on to contribute, but that if his 'kin' had previously proceeded to an *ofledene* with him in court, and the judge could testify to the fact, the kin of the leader were also liable[2]. Whatever the meaning of *ofledene*[3], it would seem that kinsfolk were able to repudiate responsibility for a member of the kindred who led non-kinsmen (?) into a battle, unless he was notoriously poor, in which case they had to contribute; and further that it was customary for the kindred to declare in public their intention to bear the expenses of a feud collectively—surely an invitation to non-kinsmen to join in it[4]?

---

[1] Rüstringer Rechtssatzungen, Richthofen, *Fr. Rq.*, pp. 121–2: "Thet is ac friseck riucht: sa hwer sa thi blata enne hod stekth and sprekth: ethelinga folgiath mi; nebbe ik allera rikera frionda enoch? Alle tha ther him folgiath and fiuchtath, thet stont op hiara eina haua, thruch thet thi blata is lethast allra nata; hi mi allera sinera frinda god ouir fiuchta, hi ne mi hit thach to nenere ofledene skiata."

[2] *Fr. Rq.* (Recht der Rüstr. aus einer hs. von 1327), p. 540, § 37: "Alle thet ma fiucht domliachta di and bi skinandere sunna under up haldene hode, thet skil thi beta ther thene hod dreith, alsa longhe sa hi enigene pannig heth. Ac ne mi thi hodere ther nawet al beta, sa skilma thene fiuchtere seka, and thi skil mithi beta, hit ne se thet ken anda liodwarue mith him to there ofledene gengen se, and thi redieua thet hlia dure, sa skil thet ken mith him beta."

[3] See His, *Strafrecht der Friesen*, pp. 62 ff.

[4] These laws seem to have remained in force until the end of the 16th century, in spite of the protests of the Counts of Oldenburg. Cp. C. Borchling, *Die älteren Rq. Ostfrieslands*, Aurich 1906, p. 32. It appears from a law of Brokmannaland (also in East Friesland) that the judge could refuse to sanction an *ofledene* (*Fr. Rq.* Brokmerbrief, p. 157, § 46).

It is in the same districts that we find a clear enunciation of the old tribal principle, that there can be no litigation within the kindred. A dispute between father and son, between brothers, between father's brother's son and mother's sister's son, mother's brother's son and father's sister's son, cannot be decided in court in the ordinary course of justice, for "all the common kinsmen shall settle it, or it shall be decided with oaths[1]" (i.e. of kinsmen[2]). It is to be noted that the first cousins mentioned are not blood-relatives, are in fact not related to each other at all: a common relationship suffices to bring them within the kindred.

There are many references to wergild in the Frisian laws, all of which are complicated by our uncertainty as to the coinage referred to[3]. However, by concentrating our attention on the actual distribution of the wergilds and not on their relation to each other, we can avoid most of the highly disputable questions. In most cases the liability of the kinsmen for wergild is declared to be only secondary, being conditional on the slayer's poverty. But, as von Amira[4] points out, the emphasis laid on this point allows us to conclude the prevalence of the contrary practice.

In East Friesland the clearest wergild regulations are contained in the Low German Butjadinger Küren of 1479:

"§ 5. Every man who was not present at the quarrel and fight, shall pay *machtal* (kindred compensation), as is hereinafter written: this the first, that the brother shall redeem and free his property with 20 white marks.

§ 6. If it should be the case, that someone slew a man on the ale bench or in the inn,...the 'brother's child' (? i.e., first cousin) shall compensate for

---

[1] Rüstr. Rechtssätzungen, *Fr. Rq.* p. 123: "Thit is ak frisesk riucht, theter ne mi twisk thene fader and twisk thene sunu, twisk thene brother and twisk thene otherne, twisk thene fidiran sunu and twisk thene modiran sunu, twisk thene emes sunu and twisk thene fethan sunu,—ther ne mi nen stef tha nen strid twisk risa, nen asyga dom tha nen aldirmonnes lhiene, buta thet skilun alle tha mena friond skifta, ieftha thet skilma al mith ethon riuchta." Cp. p. 540, § 31.

[2] Cp. the Danish *samfrænder ed*, p. 99 supra.

[3] Cp. H. Jaeckel, *Zs. der Sav. Stift.* Bde 27, 28; Ph. Heck, *Die altfr. Gerichts-verfassung* (1894) and *Die gemeinfreien der Karolingischen Volksrechte* (1900). Also His, *Strafrecht der Friesen im MA.* (Leipsic 1901) and in *Zs. der Sav. St.*, Bd 28, pp. 439 ff.

[4] *Erbenfolge und Verwandtschaftsgliederung nach den altniederdeutschen Rechten* (Munich 1874), p. 155.

him with 15 white marks, the 'right third' [third cousin] with 5 white marks, the fourth (fourth cousin) shall be quit[1]."

Unfortunately, as the second case is different from the first, it would be rash to make certain that the payments in all cases were:

1. Brother   20 white marks.
2. First cousin   15   „
3. [Second cousin 10]   „
4. Third cousin   5   „

but we can be fairly certain at any rate of the contributions of the last three classes.

Only in West Friesland do we find any full regulations for the distribution or payment of wergild among the kin. Here also the money-reckoning is fairly simple. The regulations are contained in the *Allgemeine Gesetze des westerlauwerschen Frieslandes*, and may be summarized as follows:

The liability of the slayer's kindred is primary.

There appears to be an initial payment of 2 pounds[2], but it seems as if this was paid by the injured party, as a pledge of good faith.

The wergild is divided into two parts: (*a*) 8 pounds (pond) 10 ounces (enze) and $13\frac{1}{3}$ pence (penning), due to the heirs of the slain man (and payable by the slayer and his father?); and (*b*) 4 pounds 5 ounces and $6\frac{2}{3}$ pence[3], collected among the kindred of the slayer and paid to the kindred of the slain. This latter part is called *menteel* or *meitel*. The proportions between the two (2 : 1) appear to be the same all over Friesland[4]. The *menteel* is divided as follows:

		pond	enze	pen.
1. [*male descendants of father*] i.e. brother	...	1	0	0
2. [*male descendants of grandparents on both sides (exclusive of father)*]:				
a. father's brother (fedria)	... ...		9	0
b. mother's brother (eem)	... ...		6	0[5]

---

[1] Richthofen, *Fr. Rq.* p. 545. Cp. His, op. cit. pp. 223–254.

[2] p. 410, § 1. "Dat is riucht, al deer di frya Fresa ene oderne to dada slacht ende dat hine ielda schil, soe aegh hi him to biedane twa pond to iaen, dat hy riuchta ielda ontfaen wil." Richthofen takes *iaen* as *ievane*, to give, but it seems to be more consistent with the sense, if I understand it rightly, to read it as from *ia*, to acknowledge.

[3] There are 20 pennings to the ounce, and 12 ounces to the pound. The total is thus $13\frac{1}{3}$ pounds.

[4] See, however, Jaeckel, *Zs. der Sav. Stift.* 1906, p. 280.

[5] *een hael pond.* Brunner, p. 25 (owing to a misprint?) says 4 ounces.

			pond	enze	pen.

3. [*male descendants of* 4 *pairs of great-grand-parents* (exclusive of grandparents)] (i.e. great-uncle, first cousins once removed, and second cousins):

   a. paternal
      (α) descendants of father's father's brothers and sisters   3   8
      (β) descendants of father's mother's brothers and sisters   3   8
   b. maternal
      (α) descendants of mother's father's brothers and sisters   2   5
      (β) descendants of mother's mother's brothers and sisters   2   5

4. [*male descendants of* 8 *pairs of great-great-grand-parents*[1] (exclusive of great-grandparents)] (i.e. first cousins twice removed, second cousins once removed, and third cousins):

   a. the 4 *fangen* on father's side, descendants of
      (α) father's father's father's brothers and sisters   1   18
      (β)   „   „   mother's   „   „   1   18
      (γ)   „   mother's father's „   „   1   18
      (δ)   „   „   mother's   „   „   1   18
   b. on maternal side
      (α) mother's father's father's brothers and sisters   1   17
      (β)   „   „   mother's   „   „   1   17
      (γ)   „   mother's father's „   „   1   17
      (δ)   „   „   mother's „   „   1   17

                                                                 4   5   6

We notice that it is a singularly clear and consistent statement, having strong affinities to the North Frisian wergild-division. As in the latter, there are 15 classes of recipients, counting all subdivisions[2].

---

[1] Richthofen (Wb. s.v. *mentel*) does not appear to include the 8 fangen in his reckoning, but the words of the text are quite clear, p. 411: "nu aghen oen der fadersyda dae fyouwer fanghen elker lyck xxxviii penningen....Nu sinter tredlingan fyower fangen fan synre moder syda, nu agen da fangen elker lyck xxxvii. penningen etc." It thus appears that a tredling, thredkniling etc. is a person related in the *fourth* degree, not, as Richthofen says (Wb. s.v. thredkniling, thredknia, thredling) in the third degree. See Brunner, *Wergild und Sippe*, p. 26.

[2] v. Amira, *Erbenfolge*, p. 162.

If there is no brother living[1], his son or a sister's son takes his share; and so with the uncles. If none of these recipients exist, the share falls to the heir, but whoever actually receives it has to swear the oath of peace. Whoever receives a share (for distribution) and does not share it with those equally related must give back twice the amount and pay a further fine of 2 pounds. The sum should be paid in three equal instalments, 21 nights between each (and apparently the *mentele* last?), but it would seem that the whole sum may be paid on the 63rd night. Before that time the slayer shall warn the kinsmen liable for contributions, each in his own home, in the presence of two witnesses, who can be appealed to in case of a dispute, which can come before the magistrate (*frana*). After this the final reconciliation takes place, at which apparently a representative of each class kisses the slayer on swearing the oath of peace, thereby wiping out the feud. These representatives appear to receive a premium of 4 pence out of the sum destined for their class of recipients[2].

As in the Swedish and Danish laws, the problems connected with the distribution and collection of the wergild are thus fully dealt with, an indication that the custom had not fallen into desuetude at the time when the law was committed to writing.

The only other sets of regulations which throw much light on our problem are those contained in the Hunsingoer Küren of 1252[3], and in the Fivelingoer and Oldampster custumal, of which the extant MS. dates from the 14th century[4].

We will consider the Hunsingo text first[5]. It begins (§ 40) by attributing a wergild law to Our Lord, which is interesting as indicating that the Frisian Church was not hostile to the institution[6], and goes on to say that wergild was later fixed at 40 marks, to which 6 were added for the *friunden*—kinsmen. It has been pointed out by von Amira that in Old Saxon and Old Frisian law the word *friund*, kinsman, does not usually include

---

[1] Richthofen (s.v. *mentele*) assumes that only the eldest brother receives or pays this share, but the analogy of the Scand. and North Frisian laws would lead us to suppose that brother stands for 'brothers,' 'uncle' for uncles, and so on.

[2] "Nu aghen da eeftersusterbern oen der moeder moeder syda fyf penningen twae eynsa etc. Nu agen dae deer dyne ferdeed swared, dyne fyaerda penning off toe nimen, hit ne se dat him syn ewenknee kestighia ende gwe: tzies du hor du swerre, ende lethe wessa al euendeel. Nu sinta ieta to swaren acht freededen...."

[3] *Rq.* p. 336, §§ 40 ff.

[4] Ed. by M. de Haan Hettema, *Het Fivelingöer en Oldampster Landregt* (1843).

[5] Huns. Busstaxen, §§ 40 ff., *Fr. Rq.* p. 336.

[6] Cp. the part played by the priest in the deed of 1443, p. 157, infra.

the relatives of the first degree[1], and the context shows that in this case it must be taken as meaning 'kinsmen of the second and more distant degrees.' The payments seem to be as follows:

			marks	blud	fiardeng
A.	1.	Father (or brother[2] and sister) ...	10		
B.	1.	Father's brother ...	2		
	2.	Mother's brother ...	$1\frac{1}{2}$		
	3.	*Forma bernig* (first cousins (and nephews?))[3] ...	1		
C.	1.	Second cousins (*other susterbern*) ...	$\frac{1}{2}$		
	2.	*Thredda halua knileg*, second cousins once removed ...		6	
	3.	Thredda [knileg], third cousins ...			1
			15	6	1

i.e. approximately a third of the whole wergild of 46 marks[4].

The absence of a class of first cousins once removed, to correspond to class C 2, can be best explained on the theory that wergild shares are not given to males whose fathers participate[5]—i.e. not to the sons of uncles—and that the *forma bernig* refer to the sons of *aunts*, while the second cousins once removed refer to the sons of female second cousins only. In this case the table would be perfectly symmetrical[6].

---

[1] *Erbenfolge*, p. 145.

[2] Apparently a brother is not liable to pay wergild until a second slaying, § 42, but cp. v. Amira, op. cit. p. 157.   [3] But cp. v. Amira, op. cit. p. 159.

[4] v. Amira reckons the 6 blud 1 fiardeng as $\frac{1}{3}$ mk, but his method of reckoning seems to have the difficulty that class C 2 pay more than class C 3 ($\frac{2}{15}$ as against $\frac{1}{6}$). It seems that 5 fiardengs go to the *white* mark, of which 16=20 marks, Jaeckel, *Zs. der Sav. Stift.* xxx. p. 98. In this case 1 fiardeng would be equal to $\frac{4}{25}$ of a mark. The contributions of classes B and C cannot amount to more than $5\frac{1}{2}$ marks, instead of the 6 marks of the previous paragraph. Brunner (p. 29 Anm. 1) suggests that the missing half mark may be paid by classes B 3 and C 1—3 on the mother's side, but is it not also possible that the historical § 40 is not meant to apply exactly to actual conditions as portrayed in § 41? Cp. the other inconsistency re uncles, p. 153 infra.

[5] The secondary nature of the brother's liability, if the father pays, seems to confirm this view.

[6] It could be tabulated on the same lines as the Westerlauw. wergild:
  1. Father and his descendants, i.e. brother.
  2. Male descendants of grandparents (exclusive of 1), i.e. uncles, and first cousins (sons of aunts).
  3. Male descendants of great-grandparents (exclusive of 2), i.e. great-uncles, first cousins once removed, second cousins, and sons of female second cousins.
  4. Male descendants of great-great-grandparents (exclusive of 3), i.e. great-great-uncles, first cousins twice removed, second cousins once removed, and third cousins.

NORTH GERMANY AND HOLLAND

It will be seen that the share of the father's brother stands to that of the mother's brother in a ratio of 4 : 3, though in § 40 the paternal kindred are said to contribute twice as much as the maternal. Possibly, as we have already suggested on the previous page (note 4), the historical § 40 is not meant to apply exactly. We are told that the sister's son (of the slain) may act as plaintiff in the slaying-suit, in which case he receives the sum of $10\tfrac{2}{3}$ *blud*[1], a piece of information which would be useful if we could establish the value of a *blud*. The liability of the sister is also to be noted[2].

We now pass to the Fivelgo clauses[3]. The provisions of the first paragraph may be tabulated as follows:

		pond	enze	pen.
1.	Brother	3	0	0
2.	first *swira* (uncles and first cousins?)		11	4
3.	second *swira* (great-uncles and their descendants?)		5	12[4]
4.	third *swira* (great-great-uncles and their descendants?)		2	16
		4[5]	1	12

The total wergild in this case would therefore probably be 12 pond 4 enz. 16 pen.

The paragraph adds that half the *meitele* is paid for the maiming of 6 limbs, and full *meitele* for outrages on women[6]. Half-brothers, etc. pay their full share of *meitele*. A man can escape liability for his share of *meitele* by one oath, unless relationship can be proved against him[7]. Widows and children under age, priests[8] and *nobles* (walberan, Low G. text welgeboren) pay no *meitele*.

The next paragraph I would regard as independent of the preceding, for it proves on examination to be practically identical with the second Hunsingo clause, though somewhat less condensed; it omits the paragraph offering

---

[1] § 41. [2] § 42, "alsa stor sa thiu suster ac tha brothere."

[3] Ed. by M. de Haan Hettema, *Het Fivelingoër en Oldampster Landregt*, pp. 112 ff.

[4] The third sum is given as 5 enze 1 scilling. From the analogy of the Hunsingo regulations we might assume that this sum was half the preceding; and if we take the scilling as equal to 12 pen. (one of its many possible values, see Richthofen, Wb. s.v. *enze*) we obtain this result, and the next sum, stated in enze and pen., works out at half 5. 12. There seem therefore sufficient grounds to justify the adoption of this reckoning.

[5] The *pond* is here stated to contain 18 *enze*.

[6] § 5 : "sex lithe rekat half meytel. Tho tha nedmonda herder ful meytele."

[7] I am in doubt about the meaning of "Thredkingis meitele is ma niar to betiugane dan to vnswerane," but I presume it might signify that one man's oath *for* the existence of kinship between a supposed relative and the slayer weighs more than one oath against it; cp. Richthofen, Wb. s.v. *ni* (7).   [8] But cp. *Rq.* p. 320 (§ 2).

a historical review of wergild, but otherwise the 10 marks paid by the father, the distinction between father's and mother's brother, etc. all reappear, and it repeats, more emphatically, the statement as to the sister's liability, which we may compare with the following passage in the Hunsingoer Busstaxen:

§ 43. "When the outlaw slays a man, wergild shall be paid for him, then each 'knee' (of kindred) shall stand by the other, the *niece* with the nephew, if she have borne no warrior (son): this wergild is called a *ield-stopa*. § 44. When the mother is a widow, and the daughter an orphan, the poor defenceless orphan needs not to give any *meitele*[1]."

This, with the Swedish law of Helsingland, is almost the only mention of the primary liability of women (other than heirs) to wergild, though we have seen reason to suspect that their actual participation was more frequent than the laws allow.

In the case of slayers too poor to pay their whole liability in wergild we find various regulations in force. In the West, such a slayer is bound to produce one-third of the wergild, on pain, apparently, of outlawry, and also for the fine for breach of peace, while the kinsmen "as their custom has been" give the other two-thirds, i.e. twice their normal contribution[2]. In the East the slayer is bound to produce the *wrield*[3], whatever that may mean, while the kinsmen pay 20 marks.

In two of the laws we find the interesting provision that an outlaw cannot be between two 'lands': but that the relatives living in the 'land' where he is accused shall pay the fine for him[4].

The oath-helpers of the kindred appear frequently in Frisian law, but are most explicitly alluded to in the Western districts.

A man can produce twelve oath-helpers of his kindred to clear himself of accusations of stealing[5], of complicity in crime[6], of sheltering an outlaw[7],

---

[1] *Fr. Rq.* p. 336.

[2] Huns. Küren of 1252 (*Fr. Rq.* p. 329), § 9: "Umbe thene blata, gef hi enne mon sle, thet thrimene geld, and thi frethe lidzie uppa sine halse; thet twede geld geue sine friund, as er syde was." So also in 1448, *Fr. Rq.* p. 322 (§§ 19, 21).

[3] *Rq.* p. 116 (Rüstr. Küren). Richthofen translates *wrield* 'zugabe zum wergeld,' but there is no evidence for an 'additional gift' in the Frisian laws. Possibly it refers to the *forma ield.*

[4] Ems. Pf. schuldb. § 24 (*Rq.* p. 200) and Brokmerbrief, § 132 (*Rq.* p. 169): "Hir ne skel nen freta wesa tuisca londum; falt thi tichtega oppa thene freta, sa felle tha holda ther fore."

[5] *Fr. Rq.* (Huns. Küren of 1252), pp. 329–30, § 19.

[6] Ib. p. 328, § 5.   [7] Ib. § 9.

of falsely accusing (?) a judge[1]. But besides oath-helpers, Frisian law knows of witnesses (*orkenen*) of the kindred, and a man suspected of secret manslaughter has to clear himself with his four 'fachten'—descendants of his great-great-grandparents—and with 72 witnesses within his kin[2]. To repudiate an accusation of having come to fisticuffs in church also needs the support of 72 kinsmen of the four 'fachten[3].'

Guardianship. Another point in which the earlier Frisian laws show considerable solidarity of the kindred is in the matter of guardianship of orphans. Before he can alienate his ward's property the guardian must have the consent of 'all the kinsmen[4].' He himself is related to his ward on the paternal side, but when taking over his charge he must pledge 'green land' to the mother's kinsmen for the movable inheritance of the ward[5].

In East Friesland Count Edzard's Landrecht, from the beginning of the 15th century, still shows many traces of the solidarity of the kindred, though great efforts have evidently been made to bring the law into accordance with the spirit of the times. The following passage from Wicht's 18th century edition of the Landrecht (which was still technically valid at the date of issue) may serve as typical:

"Although it be a custom that a man shall and may redeem his neck with money, when he has slain a man, as is said before; yet such statutes from which one can know beforehand how one can pay for the life of a man are of small value...for everywhere there are presumptuous folk who heed not the money if it be their wish to slay a man. For that reason the laws are much better arranged, if one does not know from them, with how much money one may redeem one's neck, but if it is left undecided, when a man is slain, whether and how the slayer may secure peace from the ruler of the country or the relatives. If the ruler of the country or the relatives will not allow themselves to come to terms for the wergild, the slayer must die[6]."

However in ch. 24 it seems to be indicated that only the heir receives the wergild:—"The slaying may be paid for or compensated for in three instalments: The first in money, the second in cattle, the third in cloth. The nearest of the persons 'fully' related to the slain takes the wergild. If

---

[1] Ib. § 16.
[2] *Rq.* p. 426 (Allgemeine Küren des Westerlauwerschen Frieslands, § 5): "soe schillet hiase sikria mit hiara haudpapa ende mit tuam frya foegheden, ende mit hiara fiower fachtum, ende mit twa ende sauntige orkenen binna hiare kinne."
[3] *Rq.* p. 407 (Allg. Gesetze des Westerlauwerschen Friesl.), § 5.
[4] Ems. Pfenningschuldbuch, §§ 6—7, *Fr. Rq.* pp. 196–7.   [5] Ib. § 8.
[6] v. Wicht, *Das ostfriesische Landrecht* (Aurich n. d.), p. 677, Lib. III. cap. 22.

however such a one does not exist, then the nearest of those half related takes it[1]." The law adds that the kinsmen of the slayer used to be obliged to help in the payment[2].

For West Friesland the Groningen *Landregten van Stad en Lande*, of 1448, still state:

"When a man is slain, the kinsmen shall not be liable for more than the two-thirds of a wergild, and for the third part the slayer's neck shall be at stake[3]."

In 1467 it is decided at Groningen that when peace is sworn between two parties, it shall include the father, brothers, children, and first cousins, and the husbands of any of these persons. If any more distant kinsman wishes to be included, he must be mentioned by name in the deed of reconciliation[4]. This indicates a considerable solidarity, in spite of the restriction of the bounds of the kindred.

In 1596 we still find the son appearing before the court with his brothers and sisters, together with the 'whole kindred,' as plaintiffs in a case of manslaughter[5]. It was not till 1679 that these districts finally seem to have adopted a death-punishment for manslaughter[6]. In a case of self-defence the slayer is to be free of all liability.

---

[1] Ib. pp. 679–80, cap. 24: "Der nechste von denen voll-besippeten empfängt das Geld. Ist aber keiner derselben vorhanden, so nimmt es der nechste von denen halb-besippeten."

[2] Ib. p. 114.

[3] *Groningen Archief*, H.S. in fol. no. 16, p. 17 : "Wanneer ein mensche is dootgeslagen, so sullen de ffrunde niet hoger beswaret wesen, dan de twedeel van ein man gelt, vnd dat dardedeel sol staen op den dootslagers hals."

[4] *Warfsconstitution en Oordeelen, tot en met het Jaar* 1601, bijeenverzameld door Mr H. O. Feith, Groningen, 1863, p. 104: "Item so waer ene bevredinge genomen wort tusschen twen parten, den vrede sullen holden vader, broders ende kinderen, vorenbaren ende zwagers, de so nae sint. Ende wolde yemant vorder van den vrenden bevredet wesen, den salmen by name jnden vredebreeff mede setten ende scriuen laten."

[5] op. cit. 1596, 24 May (p. 196): "Inder scheelinge tusschen den Erbaren Walco Itens vnde siner broederen vnde susteren, sambt gantser bloetuerwandtschap clegeren ther Ener, vnde den ock Erbaren Tydde Frocme beclegeden anderdiels." Cp. *Groningen Archief*, Rechterlijke Archieven N[r] III. i. i. 2 fol. 8, where as late as 1618 the 'father and kinsmen' of a slain man declare the slaying in Court: (17 Aug.) "Opt' versoock van den vader vnde vrunden van hindrick harmens nedergeslagen van Albrordtt Cordes...moordt geroepen sal worden."

[6] *Landrecht van Hunsingo, Fybelingo...op eenen gemeynen Land-dagh van den Staten der Stadt Groningen ende omlanden geanesteret*, Groningen 1679, p. 123, Bk VII. 1. It is interesting to note that a legal text-book of 1778 still prescribes wergild in cases of accidental slaying, *Aanleiding tot de eerste Beginselen der Groninger Regtskennis*, pp. 357 f.

A remarkable piece of evidence for the solidarity of a slain man's kindred has been preserved in a deed from East Friesland, dated 1443. It is a declaration that the widow and 28 male persons, the 'common kinsmen' of Enno Abekena, standing round his open grave[1], had each promised a contribution of money or land to any one who should kill Ippo, Enno's slayer. That such a public and united incitement to manslaughter on the part of the slain man's kindred was not regarded as anything shocking or unusual is evidenced by the fact that a priest writes the deed, and that the nuns of Dichusen acted as witnesses[2].

An entry in a register of fines kept by the town of Emden in the 15th century reveals some interesting facts:

1467. "Geltat Nonnena...must prove...that there is no relationship nor kinship, nor ever has been, between him and Siwet's father of Twixlum: if he cannot accomplish this, then Siwet's 'kinsmen's deed,' to which Bold Hacken and Onneko of Lockwart witness, shall take effect[3]."

We must suppose that Geltat Nonnena has refused to share some burden, such as the payment of wergild. The 'kinsmen's deed' (*vrunde breff*) is probably a contract binding the kindred to reciprocal help, like the *slachtes breve* of the Dithmarschers.

---

[1] In Denmark, too, it was usual to enter into wergild negotiations with representatives of the slayer at the grave-side.

[2] See Appendix II. No. 8. Such an instance of solidarity encourages us to place some weight on the frequent inclusion of 'kinsmen' in treaties: cp. E. Friedlaender, *Ostfr. Urkundenbuch*, II. pp. 711 ff. No. 1753 (1409): "twisschen Kenen, Hisken unde Ennen vnd *eren vrunden*"; 2: "Item alse Kene...claghet uppe Hyszken van Emeden, uppe...Ennen van Norden und uppe *ere vrund*," "Kene...sete mit eme und synen vrunden in ener geswornen sone"; p. 713: "item dat syne vrund den Emederen affgheslaghen hebben 6 man...Kene antwordet dat de gheschen sin in opener veyde"; p. 714: "so schall he den doden dorch Gode und den vrunden beteren," Bd I. p. 415, No. 455 (1436): "vor [uns] is gekomen Frederik Plump mid sineme sone Martinse unde anderen sinen sonen unde frunden..."; No. 336, p. 299 ff. (1426). Cp. also A. Driessen, *Monumenta Groningana*, pp. 193 ff. No. LV. etc., and Ehrentraut in *Friesisches Archiv* (Oldenburg), I. pp. 126 f., 145, 509–11.

[3] "Eine Brüchteregister des Amtes Emden," hrsg. von G. Liebe, *Jahrbuch der Ges. f....Altertümer zu Emden* VII. (1886), p. 82. (The transcribing of the names does not always seem above suspicion), 1467: "Geltat Nonnena...schall bewisen...dat daer nene maechscap offte sibbe sy edder gewesen hebbe twischen eme und Siwets fader to Twixlum; offte he des nycht doen mach, so schall Siwetes *vrunde breff*, dar Bold Hacken und Onneko Ukena to Lockwart inne tugen, vortgangh haben."

Several other entries show that kindreds were on occasion bound over to keep peace with one another, as thus : " At Lopsum, Baelda and his kinsmen are to keep the peace with Her Haryngh and his kinsmen[1]."

For the 16th century the East Frisian Court records show that the slayer usually paid the wergild unaided, and that occasionally, at any rate, only the nearest kinsmen of the slain received wergild. Thus in 1530:

"Wyppe Heren has paid the third and last instalment on account of the slaying of the deceased Eylart of Wenningermoer, Cordt's brother, in such fashion that Cordt thanks him and forgives all which happened[2]."

But the following case may be equally characteristic:

Hewe of Erklum has been killed by Balter of Leer. Egerick Beninga, the *Drost* or Provost, is chosen arbitrator by both sides. The wergild is to be 110 florins, to be paid in three instalments, the first in money, the second in linen, and the third in cattle. " That the slaying has not been compensated for so highly as has previously been the case in that kindred the kinsmen of the deceased Hewe have kindly overlooked in Balter by the request of the above-named arbitrators[3]." This case has a sequel in 1532, when the brother of the slain appears in court together with the other kinsmen and the guardians of the children, and declares that he has been paid in full[4].

The chroniclers, of course, only deal with the noble families, but their evidence is all in favour of cohesive kindreds. In the Chronicle of Abbot Emo (d. 1237) of Witte-Wierum in West Friesland, we are told that because a man was slain in an attack on the monastery of Schildwolde, the relatives of the slain began burning down the houses of the *relatives* of the Prior of the monastery[5].

---

[1] Ib. p. 86, see also pp. 27, 31, 72, 77.
[2] Aurich, *Staatsarchiv*, Msc. A. 24, fol. 153 (a). "Altera Cantate hefft wyppe heren bytaelt den derden und latesten termyn van wegen des nedderslags szalig Eylarts vp wenyngermoer Cordes broder, also dat Cordt one bydancket vnd doeyt vorlatung alles wes daer geschen ys...."
[3] Ib. A⁰. xxxj. (fol. 152). "Dat nhu de Nedderslach szo hoech nicht als In vortzden vth dem geslechte geschen gulden ys worden, hebben szaligen hewen frunde, dorch bede, der vorschrenenen dedingesluede, Balthe tho guede gelathen."
[4] Ib. fol. 135. "Am achten dage nae pinxteren synt erschenen de broder Meloff(?) to Eskulum een broder saligen Howen mit sampt der anderen vrunden unnd vormunderen der kynder vnt hebben bekandt dat de summa als de doetslach yn frundtschop ys begelacht dat se synt van den borgen to vreden gestalt den Ersten pennick mit den lesten Yn bywesent Eggerich beningha droste to Lerort," etc.
[5] Mon. Germ. S. S. 23, p. 507.

Menko's chronicle describes how in 1270 Rodbernus of Farmsum, a noble, fought successfully, *solus cum sua parentela*, against the three neighbouring districts of Oldampt, Emsigerland and Reiderland, whose warriors retreated *confusi et erubescentes*; and how only the fear that himself *and* his parentela would be completely impoverished by the compensation for damages demanded by his own neighbours led him to yield by leaving his stone house to be destroyed[1]. Another story shows Egbert and his brother fighting, calling to their aid their *fratrueles* Rodulf of 'Niurech' and Menzo of 'Amnem' and their *patrueles* in a complicated and very destructive feud with the Gelekonidae and Papelingi[2].

The continuation of this chronicle (1276—1280) constantly speaks of frays in which each side fights *cum omnibus consanguineis et amicis*[3]. In 1295 we find the kindred (*parentela*) of the Menalda at Hellum carrying on feuds with four other kindreds, the Tadema, the Rondage, the Hagginga and Snelguere, and with the Merethia[4]. Two centuries later, in 1486, a West Frisian charter shows the kindred of the Haringsma carrying on a feud on behalf of the monastery of St Odulf at Staveren[5].

IV. *Drenthe*[6], *and Non-Frisian Holland.*

The term 'non-Frisian Holland' is something of a misnomer, for it is generally agreed that there is a leaven of Frisian blood all through the Northern Netherlands. The description must therefore be taken to mean nothing more than those parts of the country where Saxons or Franks, or both together, finally predominated, i.e. in Western and Southern Holland. There can be no doubt that a very great mingling of peoples must have taken place, especially in South Holland, along the banks of the Rhine.

The question of wergilds in mediaeval Holland has been so fully dealt with by Brunner[7] that it will not be necessary for us

---

[1] M.G. S.S. 23, p. 559.
[2] Ib. pp. 523–61.
[3] M.G. 23, pp. 561–72. Cp. p. 569.
[4] Ib. pp. 568 f.
[5] Quoted by His, *Strafrecht*, p. 67.
[6] Drenthe, as being under the Count of Holland, is included in this section.
[7] "Sippe und Wergeld nach altniederdeutschen Rechten," in *Zs. der Sav. Stift.* Bd III.

to go into details. In the counties of North and South Holland and Zeeland, owing to the fact that the whole of the slayer's property fell to the Count of Holland, the kindred were liable for the whole wergild. There was no fixed wergild maximum. The contribution of each kinsman was proportionate to the amount of wergild, and that it could be a very heavy burden may be deduced from the number of 'privileges' granted by the Count in the 14th century, in which the maximum contribution for the outer limits of the kindred was fixed. Nothing could be better evidence of the actual survival, in practice, of the liability of the wider circles of kindred than these 'privileges.' Incidentally, they afford some evidence as to the proportions in which wergild was divided. The Count limits the contributions of the cousins as follows[1]:

1. (a)	each first cousin (*moeyensoen*)	10 schellingen
(b)	„ first cousin once removed (*ouder moeyensoen*)	10 „
2. (a)	„ second cousin (*aftersusterkynt*)	5 „
(b)	„ „ „ once removed (*aftersusterkynt in eenen halven ledena*)	5 „
3. (a)	third cousin (*eerste lit*)[2]	3 „
(b)	„ „ once removed (*vyfde lit*)[2]	3 „

It will be seen that the above does not deal with the contributions of the nearer relatives. Brunner holds that these also would be reduced in proportion, but since we find wergilds of varying amounts even after these 'privileges,' it seems that the nearer kinsmen must have had to meet the difference, whatever it was, between the sum of the above contributions and the total amount of the wergild[3].

But the best evidence for the actual distribution of liability or

---

[1] Mieris, *Groot Charterboek*, II. p. 30 a, 9 June 1303: cp. II. p. 271 a, etc., and Keurb. v. Haarlem, 45. In other charters the third cousins receive 2½ sch.; so at Dordrecht (S. Holland) P. H. van de Wall, *Handvesten...der stad Dordrecht* (1 deel, 1770), p. 118 (1303), and Haag (1377), Kennemerland (1404–5), and Waterland, cp. Brunner, p. 81.

[2] For explanation of these terms see Brunner, op. cit. pp. 82–3.

[3] In Utrecht, any citizen who received larger contributions was to be expelled till he made restitution (1366); Müller, *Rb. der stad Utrecht*, p. 79.

claim for wergild is afforded by the custumal of the town of Briel[1] in Zeeland, compiled by Jan Matthijssen early in the 15th century.

Four second cousins, one from each of the four *vierendeele*[2] of the kindred, represent the kindred in the public declaration of the slaying, and in the negotiations for peace. The wergild, as is usual in this province as well as in those of North and South Holland and Drenthe, is divided into three equal parts: *moetzoen*[3], for the plaintiffs (the four second cousins above-mentioned), *erfzoen*, for the heirs, whether male or female, and *maechzoen*, for the kindred in general. This *maechzoen* is divided into four equal parts, of which one is handed over to each of the four second cousins above-mentioned, who subdivides it among his own group of kindred, according to their number. The kindred is further subdivided into *achtendeele*—i.e. it includes third cousins. As in all Dutch law, the mother's kindred and the father's kindred participate equally. The principle on which the wergild is divided is somewhat complex, but shows a complete comprehension of the parentelic method of reckoning kinship. The minimum share, that of the third cousin, is taken as the norm. If we call this share x, the brother gets $8x$, the first cousin $4x$, the second cousin $2x$, and the third cousin[4] x. But the brother does not simply take his share out of the whole amount: he takes two shares out of the amount due to each *vierendeel*; the first cousin takes two shares out of each of two *vierendeele*, the second cousin two shares out of one *vierendeel*, the third cousin one out of one. The significance of this arrangement is obviously that the brother is equally related to all four *vierendeele*: the first cousin only to two *vierendeele* whether on the paternal or on the maternal side, and so on[5].

---

[1] *Het Rechtsboek van den Briel*, uitg. door J. A. Fruin en M. S. Pols, 's Gravenhage, 1880, pp. 219 ff. (5th Tractaet, caps. 5–8).

[2] A *vierendeel* is the group of kindred descended from one of the four pairs of great-grandparents, i.e. it includes second cousins.

[3] Also called montzoen. The voorzoene of S. Holland custumals (Leiden, Dordrecht, etc.) is probably the same thing, cp. Brunner, p. 75: see Verwejs en Verdam, *Middelnederlandsch Wb.*, s.v. The Zeeland keuren (Mieris, I, 305 a, c. 41, and I, 515 a, c. 43) divide wergild into ⅔ hoeftgeld (Hauptgeld, cp. Baugatal's höfuðbaug, p. 12 supra) and ⅓ maechsoene, i.e. the proportions are as in Friesland and not Frankish, as Brunner points out (pp. 79–80).

[4] Brunner, op. cit. pp. 83 ff. In Enkhuizen (N. Holland) the brother only pays one share in each *vierendeel*: "ende elcke broeders te gelden in elck vierendeel een afterskint maechgelt ende niet meer," *N. Bidr. v. Rechtsgel. en Wetg.* Dl. IV. (1878), 19, 91. Zierikzee (Zeeland) reckons on this principle also (in 1509), but the number of shares of the brother (6) seems open to suspicion: *Rechtsbronnen van Zierikzee*, uitg. d. W. Bezemer, 's Gravenhage, 1908 (O. Vaderl. Rb.), p. 473.

[5] This is more explicitly stated in the Westfriesche Dingtalen (*N. Bidr. v. R. en W. N. Reeks* VI.) 15: "Een oude vader, dat is een vierendeel, een afterskynt gelt. Item een vader, dat is een sijd twee vierendeel, dat is twee afterskynderen. Item een

The slayer's kinsmen, as we know, are responsible for the whole wergild, and the representatives of this side are also the four second cousins, one out of each *vierendeel*[1], each of whom pledges a quarter of the wergild[2]. No one, poor or rich, shall omit to pay his share, "unless he cut himself off from all his kinsmen. For the matter is not the burden of the culprit alone, but of all those who are related to him." In case he has failed to pay up by the appointed day, the kinship must be formally proved to the authorities of the town, who must then distrain on his goods to the amount of his liability, and hand the proceeds over to the kinsmen[3]. A wergild debt takes precedence of all other debts. All the kinsmen seem bound to appear at the *voetval* or public plea for pardon in church.

In Waterland the penalty for a breach of a wergild-reconciliation is reckoned according to the degree of kinship: it is £10 if committed by a third cousin of either of the principals, £20 for a second cousin, while a first cousin forfeits his life and property[4].

The laws thus offer us ample evidence of strongly cohesive kindreds. We might indeed be at a loss to know how long they survived, but as far as the counties of Holland, Zeeland and Drenthe are concerned, the charters of the Counts of Holland leave us in no doubt, at any rate as to persons of some social standing[5]. Among these it became the custom to submit disputes

---

rechte broeder, dat is vier vierendeelen, elcke vierendeel een afterskynt ghelt. Item een halve broeder twee vierendeel, elcke vierendeel een afterskynt," etc.

[1] Briel, p. 219: "vier achtersusterkinderen uut des misdadighen vier virendeelen, die malcander niet en bestaen"—are not related to each other.

[2] In Graf Willem's charter to Oudgiessen, it is stipulated that no one can be forced to act as pledge for wergild, though he must pay his share (Mieris, II. p. 271 *a* in 1322). In Kennemerland and West Friesland the slain man's kin choose six out of the slayer's kindred, each of whom acts as surety for one-seventh of the whole sum, the slayer being also responsible for one-seventh. Cp. Th. van Riemsdijk, Het Zevendeel leggen na Doodslag, in *Versl. en Meded. der Kon. Ak. Wet., Afd. Lett.* IV. R, I. D (1897), pp. 341–441, and R. Fruin, Over den aanbreng van doodslag, ib. IV. R, II. D (1898).

[3] Briel, p. 222. So also the officials of the Count, Brunner, p. 85: 1380, 1415: and for Leiden (1346).

[4] So Handveste for Waterland, 1415: Brunner, p. 82; Oude Keuren van Enkhuizen (*N. Bidr. voor Rechtsgel. en Wetg.* Dl. IV. (1878)), 17, 84, awards death to the actual pledger of peace (soo wie vreede name ende geve), £20 penalty to the 1st cousin, and £10 to the 2nd cousin. Cp. also Dingtalen van Delft (*N. Bidr. voor R. en Wetg.* N. Reeks, V., 1879), 62, and Oude Keuren v. Dordrecht, 9, 2.

[5] For the lower classes in West Friesland and Kennemerland much evidence has been collected for the latter half of the 14th century by Th. van Riemsdijk, op. cit.

arising out of slaying-suits to the arbitration of the Count, and thus we are provided for almost a century with a series of documents whose evidence is of the greatest value. These awards[1] date from 1316 to 1413[2]; and they show all the features of the wergilds and treaties with which the laws have made us familiar, including representatives of the four *vierendeele*. Frequently, besides the orthodox wergild, the Count provides that an extra sum shall be paid, to be distributed among the kinsmen, perhaps especially among relatives of illegitimate birth.

In the following case, as Brunner points out, Gheryt van Assendelf and Willem van Adrichem are representatives of two *vierendeele*, and they are to choose one other out of each of the remaining *vierendeele*:

"Also for the death of Heynrik van Overcroft six hundred pounds of good money are to be paid: of this the kinsmen of Gheryt Moen's son are to pay the one half; and the kinsmen of Dirc Boudyn's son, and the kinsmen of Willem of Gheervliet are to pay the other half, each the half of it; and Gheryt of Assendelf, and William of Adrichem...shall distribute this compensation [among the kindred], and they shall associate themselves with two men out of the other two *vierendeele*, who are not related to them[3]." This is at Haarlem, in 1380.

An award of 1396-7 deals with the death of Floris van Rysoort, who was killed by order of the Count, apparently by Willem Herman's son and Willem Heyne's son. Heer Jacob van Rysoort applies for compensation with

---

For Leiden (same period), see Appendix II. No. 9, infra, and P. J. Blok, Leidsche Rechtsbronnen, 1894, in the *Zoenboek*, passim, esp. pp. 27-8, 41-2. For Dordrecht (1456), see J. A. Fruin, *De oudste Rechten der stad Dordrecht*, Vol. II. No. 171 (pp. 132-3), and No. 66 (pp. 49-50).

[1] Uitspraak ter verzoeninge, Zoening, Zoenbrief, etc.

[2] Brunner refers to 15 deeds, many of which deal with several cases.

[3] Mieris, III. 365. "Item van Heynrix doet van Overcroft salmen ghelden zes hondert pont goets ghelts, des zullen Gheryt, Moens zoens maghe, ghelden die een helft, ende die ander helft Dirc, Boudyns zoens maghe, ende Willems maghe van Gheervliet, gheliken half ende half, ende dese zoene sullen smaeldeelen Gheryt van Assendelf, ende Willem van Adrichem, Bertout Hoenen broeder, ende sullen bi hem nemen twe manne uten anderen twe vierendeel, die hem niet en bestaen." Cp. also Mieris, III. 501: for the death of Gheryt Colens 679 pounds 6 groschen are to be paid: the 79 pounds 6 groschen are a *praecipuum* which goes to nearer kinsmen: of the remaining 600 pounds 150 pounds are to be paid: (1) into the vierendeel to which Willem van Driemilen belongs: (2) into the vierendeel to which Haerbaeren Aernt's sons belong: (3) into the vierendeel to which Meeus Snac belongs: (4) into the Cuystinger vierendeel. (Quoted by Brunner, p. 56.) These would seem to be non-nobles.

27 of his father's kindred and 18 of his mother's, all named in the award. The two Willems with their kinsmen are to pay 400 and 200 Dordrecht gulden respectively. The amount is to be paid in three instalments, as usual, but the actual sum is to be divided into four parts: *erfzoen*, of which Floris' mother is to have half, *voorzoen*, *maechzoen*, and a fourth part for *bewysing*, wherewith Heer Jacob shall at his discretion satisfy his bastard kinsmen[1]. We may assume that neither of the two sums was paid over, for in 1415 the Count has to make another award, dealing not only with the slaying of Floris, but also with that of Willem Heyne's son. This time, for added security, kinsmen are made to act as sureties:

Willem Herman's son and his kinsmen are to produce a thousand 'gouden Vrancryksche (French) cronen.' There are five sureties on the side of Willem's mother's kindred, to act jointly for 'one whole side,' presumably both maternal *vierendeele*; four on the side of his father's father, and four on the side of his father's mother[2]. A number of second cousins of the deceased Willem Heyne's son are to undertake various pilgrimages (one is to go to Jerusalem), and all his kinsmen are to subscribe together to meet the cost of these expeditions[3].

As late as 1455, Duke Philip of Burgundy complains that whenever there is a feud in his lands of Holland, from which slayings, etc., arise, the kinsmen of both parties who were *not* concerned are yet equally involved in the feud[4].

His ordinance prohibiting kinsmen's contributions to wergild dates from 1462[5], so we must presume that the practice persisted until that date. In Drenthe we have evidence of it for nearly a century longer, though Bishop Rudolf of Utrecht had put an end

---

[1] Mieris, III. 652.

[2] Mieris, IV. 325–6 (at Leyden). "Item so sullen borgen wesen dit voirsz. gelt van der zoenen te borde te bringen van Willem, Hermans zoons moeders wegen...(5 names) gesamender hant van een heel zyde. Item van Willem, Hermans zoons oude vaders wegen...(4 names) gesamenderhant voir een vierendel. Item van Willem, Hermans zoons Vader moeder wegen, sullen borgen wesen...(4 names)...."

[3] Ib. "Item, des so sullen Willem, Heynric soens, magen gemeenlic den personen voirnoemt, die dese voirsz. bedevairden doen sullen, also veel geven te hulpen horen cost opter reysen mede te doen, als redelic, ende besceydelic sal wesen."

[4] Costumen und Rechten von Kennemerland: "Dat so wanneer in onsen Landen Holland enigh Vechtelik geschiet, daar Doetschlagen, Lemte, of Quetsinge uf komen, dat die Maghen van beide Parthyen, die niet med im Raede noch im velde gewest, niet hebben na der Vechtelik ehrer Magen, de gerechtet hebben, einen Freden" (quoted by Dreyer, *Nebenstunden*).

[5] M. S. Pols, De middeleeuwsche Rechtspleging in zake van Doodslag, in *Verslagen en Meded. der Kon. Ak. v. Wet.*, Afd. *Letterkunde*, III. R, II. D (1885), p. 223.

to its legality in 1447[1]. Exactly one hundred years after the publication of his law a "Report on abuses which prevail in criminal cases in Drenthe" demonstrates the futility of his enactment, which prevented official regulation of kinsmen's contributions without apparently scotching the custom:

"In Drenthe...many wicked persons are tempted and drawn into committing slayings lightly, because they find therein an easy way of getting money. For, when the slaying is committed, they hold a friendly meeting, to which are summoned a great number of persons, and these, each according to his means, come to his (the slayer's) aid (with contributions) towards the fine and the compensation to the kinsmen of him who is slain, and he gets thus a tenth or twentieth part over and above the amount of the compensation, amends or reparation, or usually more, according to the quality of the evildoer and the numbers present[2]."

There can be no doubt that these contributors are mainly kinsmen.

Drenthe was very conservative owing to the isolation caused by the barren nature of the country, and we actually find a judgment of the 16th century ordering three *vierendeele* of a slayer to pay the whole *maechtaele*, in the absence of the fourth *vierendeel*[3]. A secondary liability of the six nearest kinsmen for fines to the lord is found in the Drenther Landrecht of 1412[4] and actually lasted until 1557–8[5].

---

[1] S. Gratama, *Drentsche Rechtsbronnen* (O. Vaderl. Rb.), 1894, p. 38, § 5, "...die doetslager sall den doetslach...den heren ende vrienden beteren mit sijns selves goede, ende die mage en sullen hem van rechtswegen geen hulpe doen."

[2] Ib. p. 77, VI. "In Drenthe baven tselve voirhen verhaelt der kleynicheyt der broecken angaende, worden noch mannige boesen gehelden unde getoegen, omme dootslaeghen lichtlick tdoene; want sij daerdurch eine manyer vinden omme geldt te krijgen. Toe weeten, als de nedderslach gedaen is, holden sie fruntelijke daeghen, daer tho geroepen wordt eine groote mannichte van volcke, diewelke hem, elck naer vermoeghen, to hulpen koemen totter broecken unde soeninghe der frunden, die doot geslaegen is, ende bekompt dan den thyndenn ofte twintichstenn penninck gemeenlick meer, nae qualiteytt der misdaediger oeck na advenant der ankoemelinge, dan die boete, amende off soene bedraegett, woewell bij bisscop Roloffs tijden heurin ander mit ordinantie verseen is."

[3] *Ordelboek van den Etstoel van Drenthe*, uitg. d. H. O. Feith, p. 48. Usually the quarter of the wergild due from a missing vierendeel simply lapses, cp. Fruin, *Over den aanbreng van doodslag*, etc., p. 65.

[4] Richthofen, *Fr. Rq.* p. 528, § 31 (cp. § 33).

[5] Brunner, pp. 86–7.

An interesting side-light on the strength of kinship-solidarity, and one which we have not met with before, is the provision found in the customs of Dordrecht that not more than a certain very limited number of kinsmen may serve together as officials of the town. In the court of justice there are never to be more than two persons who are nearer related even by marriage than second cousins[1]. On the *heemrad* or rural Council two persons related to each other within the third degree are never to serve at the same time[2]. At Utrecht no two kinsmen within that degree, or persons married to kinswomen within that degree, can serve as *borgermesters* at the same time[3]. The 15th century was thus already warring against the first beginnings of that jealously exclusive caste of civic authorities, all connected by kinship, which exercised a paramount influence on Dutch history until the end of the 18th century[4].

We find the institution of oath-helpers of the kindred persisting even into the 16th century, though as a rule not more than six kinsmen are required for the oath[5], which is called *custinghe* or *custeet*. Most cases of *custinghe* appear to be from Zeeland, but we learn that the institution was not abolished in Amsterdam until after 1523[6].

---

[1] van der Wall, *Handvesten...der stad Dordrecht* (Dl. I., 1770), p. 521: "Dat namaels tot ghenen tyden niet meer dan twee personen en sullen te samen in den gherecht sitten off wesen die naerre malcanderen sijn van maegscappen *off van zwagherscappen* dan aftersusterkint" (in 1432). (Also printed in Fruin, *Oudste Rechten der stad Dordrecht*, I. pp. 107–8.) In 1455 two persons are ejected for this reason, Fruin, p. 123, van der Wall, p. 593.

[2] van der Wall, p. 542 (1442).

[3] *Rechtsbronnen des stad Utrecht*, uitg. Muller (Oude Vaderl. Rb. 1881), p. 19.

[4] Cp. H. van Loon, *The Fall of the Dutch Republic* (1913), pp. 29, 43, 93; and G. W. Vreede, *Familieregeering*.

[5] Brieler Rb. Tr. III. c. 6, p. 164, "die clagher sal nemen by hem vive sijnre maghen dit mit hem die custeede doen zullen." In a judgment of the Count over a fray in Zeeland, persons accused are to clear themselves with an oath of five kinsmen from the accusation that they were concerned in the 'perlamente' (1342), Brunner, p. 80.

[6] Fockema Andreae, *Het oude-Nederlansch Burgerlijk Recht* (Haarlem, 1906), p. 209. Cp. for Overijssel: "Weert sake dat yemant enigen man off vrouwe aensprake dat die hem hoerde te rechte, so sal hy den man off frouwe wynnen mit twee gueden knapen, die hem sijn achtersusterkynder ende niet veerre en sijn, die van der selver side zijn daer hy den van aenspreket." *Overijs. Stads Dijk. en Markerechten* (uitg.

There are also distinct traces that the four *vierendeele* exercised a combined guardianship over minors even up to the 18th century[1]. Further, it appears that in S. and N. Holland parents could not legally marry a daughter under age without the consent of kinsmen from all four *vierendeele*[2]. At Haarlem, in 1422, a couple who had given their daughter (under age) in marriage "without leave or consent of the child's kinsmen of her four *vierendeele*," pay a fine to the Count of Holland[3].

The only districts in what is now Holland in the laws of which little or no trace of the solidarity of the kindred have come to light are Geldern and Loon, on the right and left bank of the Rhine respectively. The Geldern Landrecht of 1619[4] knows nothing of *maechzoene*: the whole wergild goes to the heirs. So also in the Landrecht of Loon[5]. Brunner aptly points out that these districts lie within old Ripuarian territory, and reminds us that the Lex Ribuaria already shows a remarkable absence of kin-solidarity. The laws in question are late, but on the whole their testimony is borne out by other sources. For instance, an award by arbitrators in 1460 shows the slayer paying the wergild by himself, and, still more significant, performing the *voetval*, or plea for pardon, alone. On the other hand, four kinsmen, besides the son and brother of the slain, have made the appeal to the arbitrators[6].

But for these exceptions, we may fairly say that there is evidence for the existence of remarkably cohesive kindreds in

---

d. d. Vereeniging ter bevord. van Overijss. Regt en Gesch.), I[1]. p. 104. For arbitrators of the kin, see *Ordelen van den Etstoel van Drenthe* (uit. Joosting), p. 98 (1530), where the disputants are ordered to choose each two kinsmen and an impartial 'averman,' who are to make peace in a friendly way on pain of a fine of 100 olde schijlde (olde schild = 24 sch.).

[1] Brunner, p. 51. A board of guardians representing all the relatives was suggested for the minority of William V. (1753).

[2] *Handfeste f. Wieringerland*, 1382, Mieris, III. 386. So also at Leiden, 1406, Brunner, p. 50.

[3] Mieris, IV. 660 a, 1422 (quoted by Brunner, loc. cit.).

[4] Brunner, pp. 68–9. [5] Ib. p. 4, pp. 68–9.

[6] J. A. Nijhoff, *Gedenkwaardigheden uit de Geschiedenis van Gelderland*, IV. Deel (Arnhem, 847), pp. 314–6, No. 356.

practically all the towns[1] of the various provinces comprised in modern Holland, and among the upper classes, until the end of the 14th century, and even, in some parts, until the middle of the 16th century.

V. *Hanover, Münster, Hesse.*

It is only possible for us to glance at the more central and southern districts of Germany. It will be most convenient to retrace our steps and begin again in the east.

There is ground for believing that in Hanover the kindreds had become somewhat disintegrated by the middle of the 16th century. By that date the slayer appears to be responsible for the whole wergild[2]. On the other hand, we find the father of a slain man asking the Duke if he may fitly prosecute the slayer, "with the help of my kinsmen and relations." The slayer happens to be the official executioner[3]. In another case of 1572 three brothers, together with their 'whole kindred,' demand justice against a slayer[4]. However it would seem that only the near family actually received the wergild[5].

In the Celle district of Hanover wergild continued to be paid until 1751, but the amounts were absurdly small, and the payment was evidently made by the slayer to the heirs[6]. The same observation may be made with regard to the Osnabrück

---

[1] For rural districts direct evidence is less plentiful, except for Kennemerland and Drenthe.

[2] *Staatsarchiv*, Hannover, *Cal. Br. Arch. Des.* 23. x. d. No. 2, 1559, 7, 23, 26 Ap. A servant of Jost von Adelebsen kills a man while accompanying his master; Jost tells him he is to remain at the place until he has satisfied the kindred of the slain.

[3] Ib. 13 Dec. 1564: "ob woll derselb theter...von mir, mit Zutadt meiner verwandten Lund freunde pillich verfolgt worden sein solte."

[4] Ib. 12 May, 1572: "Tileke, Jacob und Berendt gebrudere...sampt der gantz freundschafft."

[5] Ib. 1574, 26 and 29 Nov. The paternity of the slain man being doubtful, there is a dispute between the half-brother on the mother's side and the *nearest heirs* on the father's side (1st cousins), as to which is to take the wergild. The assumption seems to be that the plaintiff receives the wergild.

[6] F. von Bülow and Th. Hagemann, *Practische Erörterungen...mit Urtheils-Sprüchen des Zelleschen Tribunals*, II. (Hannover, 1799), p. 260.

wergilds of the 16th century. In a Register of Amt Fürstenau[1] we find such entries as the following:—

1532. "For a slaying, as compensation 10 Mark.
For a slaying 10 Mark,"

and sometimes as little as 6 or 7 Marks is paid. The fines to the public authority usually exceed the sums paid as wergild.

For Münster a wergild treaty of 1596 from Warendorf is worth quoting:

"Whereas about 16 years ago Evert Schröder of Westkerken wounded Berndt Grundtmann of Lynen in such wise that he received his death thereby: on the 11th of June of this 96th year, in presence of good folk, also relatives and friends, the proper reconciliation therefore took place in the following fashion: that the said slayer Evert Schröder shall for the deed he committed, firstly, give to the poor six bushels of rye, of which three shall be expended on the poor at the place where the slayer is domiciled, and the other three at the place where the deed took place.... He has besides promised and pledged himself to give to the relatives as reconciliation-money, 25 Rixdollars, which he shall and will gratefully produce and pay in the three following instalments....On the other hand, Peter Versmel called Grundmann, and Johann Menneman called Wandtmacher, of Glandorp, have promised *sub hypotheca bonorum*, that the said reconciliation shall be adhered to[2]."

For districts further south it is useless to search in such late records even for faint traces of kin-solidarity, but from the last quarter of the 13th century two wergild-treaties are extant from Wetzlar and Worms[3], in Hessian territory, both showing traces of the participation of the kin. In the first, of the year 1285, both parties declare themselves to be "cives Wetslarienses."

For the slaying of Ludowicus three persons, Heinricus de Nuveren senior, Wernherus the son-in-law of Gerhard de Nuveren, and Craftho "filius Sanne," make reparation to Wigandus called Dytheren, Heinricus de Catzenfurt, and Conradus the son of Heinricus de Dridorf, kinsmen

---

[1] J. Möser, *Patriotische Phantasien*, II. Th. No. LXXI. pp. 313-4 (Berlin, 1778).

[2] Printed in F. Philippi, *Landrechte des Münsterlandes*, Münster i. W. 1907, p. xxxiv. The author observes: "Andererseits haben sich aber in keinem Teile Westfalens die Landgerichte so lange und mit so geringen Modifikationen den Character des Volksgerichts bewahrt, wie im Münsterlande."

[3] Or its immediate neighbourhood.

(*consanguineis*) of the slain. Peace is made on behalf of both parties and their heirs and 'friends' (*amicis*).

The second deed, dated 1288, is drawn up under the auspices of the King of the Romans and his brother the Archbishop of Mainz.

It is a contract between the Count of Leiningen on the one hand and the Wilschüssel brothers with their kinsmen and friends on the other, the Count having killed Heinricus, the nephew (*filius sororis*) of the four Wilschüssel brothers. Besides making these a money payment, or its equivalent in land, the Count is to send a man on a crusade or pilgrimage, pay for masses, etc., and also provide for four kinswomen of the deceased in Cistercian convents. He is further to do his utmost to secure for the sister of the slain the fief about which the quarrel had originally arisen, and if he fails in this he is to pay her a sum of money. Ten persons (relatives of the Count?) stand surety for him[1].

In Worms, the *Leges et Statuta familiae S. Petri*, manorial customs of about 1024, give half the wergild to the *amici* of the slain man, but soon after this date the Abbot claims the whole[2].

A law from Metternich, in the principality of Trèves, still recognises treaties with the kindred as late as 1563, if they are accompanied by the pardon of the authorities[3].

Note. From the analogy of Silesia, whence Frauenstädt has collected a number of cases of reconciliations between kindreds[4], it seems possible that the town records (Stadtbücher) of Central and Southern Germany might furnish some similar evidence for kinship-solidarity in the Middle Ages, but this is a line of research which I have not been able to pursue. In country districts in South Germany it appears that reconciliations between the slayer and the slain man's 'kinsmen' persisted to a late date, but we have no reason to suppose that these 'kinsmen' included any but near relatives. Thus at Nuremberg in 1485 we find the slayer reconciled with the widow only[5]. In Appenzell, in Switzerland, wergild is said

---

[1] These two documents are printed in *Zeitschrift für deutsches Alterthum*, VI. (1848), pp. 21 ff.

[2] Markgraf, *Das moselländische Volk in seinen Weistümern* (Gotha, 1907), pp. 203–4.

[3] H. Loersch, *Die Weistümer der Rheinprovinz*, Abt. I. p. 291, Weistum, 102, § 2. "So magh er ainsoechen ain unsers gnedigen hern schultheiss vmb geleidt 3 tag und 6 wochen, wanne aber die 3 tag und 6 wochen umb seint und mit der oberkeit und fruntschaft nit zufreden kan werden."

[4] Frauenstädt, *Blutrache und Todtschlagssühne im deutschen MA* (Leipsic, 1881).

H. Knapp, *Das alte Nürnberger Kriminalrecht* (Berlin, 1896), p. 174: "mit

in 1555 to go to the heirs[1], but we find the 'kinsmen' of the slayer, as well as of the slain, included automatically in the peace enforced by the town after a slaying[2]. Occasionally we find the slayer forbidden to come into the presence of kinsmen of the slain, but the prohibition extends only to the second degree of kinship[3]. In Augsburg those who can get a slayer outlawed are only the immediate family, the uncles and aunts and first cousins. Here however the custumal of 1276 appears to permit the right of feud to any agnatic relative of the slayer within the seventh degree[4]. Kinsmen through women are debarred altogether from participating in the feud[5]. In the cantons of Glarus and Schwyz, in Switzerland, it appears that plaintiffs are invariably women, and the reason given is that their judicial action does not preclude the men of the family from taking vengeance[6].

Switzerland yields one document of 1257 which establishes quite a degree of kindred-solidarity. Count Rudolf of Habsburg is called in to settle a quarrel between two kindreds, "the people called Itzelinge and their kindred on the one side and the people called of Gruba and their kindred on the other." The injured party receive 60 marks. "Peace (*sone*) is established in such fashion that in each kindred twenty men have sworn peace: in the kindred which is called Itzelinge these have sworn: Itzeli and Ulrich...." "These 40 have sworn the peace...[7]."

It would seem that the 'Itzelings' are only a family whose father is a man called Itzeli, but the participation of twenty kinsmen on each side indicates a very considerable degree of solidarity.

In Austria the practice of making treaties with the kindred of the slain is

---

des erslagen weib gütlich vertragen." In these districts it was still a question in the 17th century whether the authorities could proceed against a slayer who had made peace with the kinsmen of the slain, p. 175.

[1] Blumer-Heer, *Staats- und Rechtsgesch.* (1850–9), II. 2, p. 3.
[2] E. Osenbrüggen, *Das alemannische Strafrecht im deutschen MA* (Schaffhausen, 1860), p. 30.
[3] Blumer-Heer, op. cit. p. 3, Osenbrüggen, op. cit. p. 29 (in 1660). Cp. Knapp, op. cit. p. 151 (1611).
[4] Osenbrüggen, p. 31.
[5] "Es enmag auch kein wibes friunt vint gesin umbe den totslach."
[6] Osenbrüggen, p. 26.
[7] Tschudi, *Chronicon Helveticum*, ed. J. R. Iselin (Basel, 1734), Th. I. p. 155: "die Misshellende und Tod = Gefẽchte (blood-feud) die da was under den Lŭten die man da heizzet Itzelinge | und Ir Geschlãchte einhalb | und dien Lŭten | die man da heizzet von Gruba und Ir Geschlãchte | anderthalb | ...dieselbe Sone ist also gesetzet | dass in jedwederem Geschlãchte 20 mann die Sone gesworen hand in deme Geschlechte | dass man heizzet Itzelinge | so het gesworen Itzeli und Ulrich sin Etero. Chuno des Gottzhãss Ammann von Wettingen etc....Dise 40 hand die Sone gesworen...."

opposed by the authorities from 1499 onwards[1]: it is forbidden by the *Landtag* at Innsbrück in 1518[2], and again, for Lower Austria, in the ordinances of 1540[3]. In southern Tirol, indeed, the law permitting 'pace-suchen' with the kinsmen of the slayer is only abrogated in 1773[4], but the only evidence afforded by this survival is that these extra-judicial reconciliations had once been common.

Such indications of solidarity as are afforded by blood-feuds are plentiful all over Germany, as a reference to Frauenstädt's pages will show, but a considerable proportion of these illustrate feudalism rather than kin-solidarity, and are therefore of no value for our purpose.

---

[1] W. E. Wahlberg, *Gesammelte kleine Schriften...über Strafrecht* (Vienna, 1877), II. p. 123.
[2] Ib. pp. 91, 101.   [3] Ib. p. 123.
[4] Ib. p. 91, and p. 123 note.

CHAPTER VI

BELGIUM AND NORTHERN FRANCE

I. *Belgium*

FOR Belgium, as for Holland, the chief difficulty in our task is the multiplicity of sources and of provinces with distinct and characteristic customs. On the other hand, Belgian historians have been fully alive to the part played by the kindreds in the fourteenth and fifteenth centuries, and a considerable number of works dealing with the subject have appeared in recent years, notably Petit-Dutaillis' *Documents Nouveaux sur les Mœurs populaires dans les Pays-Bas au* XV. *siècle*[1]. As regards wergilds Brunner's *Sippe und Wergild* remains, and is likely to remain, the best exposition of the subject as a whole. For this reason any attempt at an exhaustive treatment of the subject is unnecessary in this work, and we shall content ourselves with picking out a few salient features.

Flanders furnishes the fullest information with regard to the distribution of wergild, for the laws of Ghent, Bruges, Alost and Oudenarde all enter into great detail. Of these we will take the *Keure* of Oudenarde first. They date from 1300[2]:

Of the wergild, *mondzoene* goes to the eldest brother of the slain as plaintiff and is one-third of the whole sum. The rest is divided into four

---

[1] Paris, 1908. It contains a bibliography, to which add: Benary, "Zwei altfranzösische Friedensregister der Stadt Tournai," in *Romanische Forschungen*, XXV. (1908), pp. 1–196.
[2] Printed in Warnkönig, *Flandrische Staats- und Rechtsgeschichte bis zum Jahr* 1305, II. 2, pp. 156 ff.

equal parts, and all the brothers together take a quarter from each of these. So that what falls to the share of the other kinsmen is after all only half of the total wergild, as in the ancient Salic law, which these provisions closely resemble[1]. The next class (first cousins) takes two-thirds of this remaining half, the next (second cousins) two-thirds of what remains, and the last class (third cousins) receive the remainder. Fortunately our source goes on to give an example of the division of a wergild of 100 pond, which can be tabulated as follows[2]:

		pond	sol	den
1. (a) Eldest brother (*Mondzoene*)	... ...	33	6	8
(b) All the brothers	... ...	16	13	4
2. *Rechtzweers* (first cousins[3])				
(a) On father's side	... ...	16	13	4
(b) „ mother's side	... ...	16	13	4
3. *Anderzweers* (second cousins)				
(a) On father's side	... ...	5	11	2[4]
(b) „ mother's side	... ...	5	11	2
4. *Derdelingen* (third cousins)				
(a) On father's side	... ...	2	15	6
(b) „ mother's side	... ...	2	15	6
		100	0	0

In Denmark we have also seen the *brother*, as related to the slain on both sides, preferred before the son as recipient of the largest share of wergild[5]. It is to be noted that the sons of the slain receive nothing according to our present text, and this is corroborated by a much later wergild statement, from the Custumal of Alost[6], which follows a scheme similar to the foregoing, and gives the *mondzoene* to the nearest relative on the father's side. It informs us that the wergild of a free man is 36 *pond*, and adds the interesting provision that the kinsmen are bound to pay the costs (of the suit) unless the *mondzoendere*, the plaintiff, consents to bear the expenses with them[7]. The Customs of Ghent give us fuller details[8]:

---

[1] Cp. Brunner, pp. 35 f.
[2] Warnkönig, op. cit. III. 1, pp. 187 f., 192 f.
[3] Verwijs en Verdam, *Mn. Wb.*, s.v. *rechtzweers*, make this word mean nephews, but all analogy, as also the use of anderzweers and derdelingen, is in favour of the translation I have given above.
[4] Cp. Brunner, p. 36. 1 pond = 20 sol, 1 sol = 12 den.
[5] And in East Friesland?, see p. 156, note 1, supra.
[6] Warnkönig, op. cit. III. 2, pp. 112-4. It is later than 1437.
[7] Gheldolf, *Coutumes de Gand*, I. pp. 515 ff.
[8] Ib., I. p. 517.

The wergild of a freeman is 36 pounds. One-third of this—i.e. 12 pounds—is *mondzoene*, and falls to the nearest kinsman on the paternal side. The wergild is then divided into four equal parts (six pounds each) and of each of these shares the plaintiff takes one quarter, i.e. six pounds in all. Thus he receives half the wergild (18 pounds). But if he will pay all costs he can claim two-thirds of the total wergild. The further contributions are as follows:

		s.
1.	The brother takes 20 s. out of each of the four parts	80
2.	First cousins take half less, 10 s. out of each of two parts. (*a*) paternal	20
	(*b*) maternal	20
3.	Second cousins receive half less, out of one part.	
	(*a*) paternal	5
	(*b*) maternal	5
4.	Third cousins half less.	
	(*a*) paternal	$2\frac{1}{2}$
	(*b*) maternal	$2\frac{1}{2}$

The slayer's relatives are liable for the wergild in the same ratio. Presumably these sums are the maximum which may be exacted from *each* kinsman, and if the total falls short of 18 pounds some near kinsman becomes liable for the difference. This, as we shall see, is the case at St Omer. The subsequent paragraph (§ 3) describes a wergild of 100 pounds, regarded from the *plaintiff's* side:

		s.
Each brother pays to the principal (the representative of the slain)		40
„	first cousin (*ooms of moeyen kint*)	20
„	second cousin (*anderlinc*)	10
„	third cousin (*derdelinc*)	5

A rhymed law from Bruges, dating from the fifteenth century, divides the wergild into *moetzoene* and *maechzoene*, the former being equally shared by all (male) relatives nearer than first cousins (*nare danne rechtzweere*). Of the *maechzoene* first cousins have twice as much as second cousins and these twice as much as third cousins[1].

All over the Netherlands wounding, as well as slaying, was an injury involving the participation of kindred on both sides.

Many other towns also, outside Flanders, mention wergild, but we lack the details of distribution. Thus at Malines we,

---

[1] Warnkönig, III. 2, Anhang, p. 83. The proportions for first, second and third cousins are 4 : 2 : 1. (Cp. Brunner, p. 63.)

hear that the *mondzoender* kept half the wergild, the other half being equally divided among the maternal and paternal kindred[1].

In Antwerp it would seem that all the wergild went to the plaintiff, who is either the eldest son or the eldest kinsman[2]. It is however in Antwerp that we find the rule, similar to that prevailing in Utrecht and Dordrecht, that no two persons as near as third cousins once removed (*ten derden halven lede*) may hold office among the *Schepen* (magistrates or assessors) at the same time[3].

We find the curious feature that the kinsmen of the slayer are still bound to pay wergild for him even when he has been executed in the course of justice for his slaying[4]. This leads us to deduce that the kinsmen of the slayer were in the ordinary course liable for the same proportion of the wergild as was received by the kindred of the slain. Such is certainly the case at Lille[5]. In 1330-1 Count Ludwig of Flanders annulled the *legal* liability of the kindred for wergild, but we may suspect that it was still customary to pay it, for in 1464 a man claims a contribution to wergild from his brother. (The Court decides that the brother need not pay it unless he had promised to do so.) In Cassel, however, the legal liability of the kindred is only abrogated in 1613[6].

Various late *Keuren* maintain, as if it were a novelty, that wergild contributions cannot be forced from the kinsmen. So at Ardenbourg, in 1330: "When a man has killed another, he cannot constrain his kinsmen or friends, by law or otherwise, to pay *zoene* for his reconciliation, if they will not do it of their own free will[7]." The relatives of the victim, however, are to continue to receive their share. Fortunately we are in a position to judge more directly of the question, in Hainault at least, thanks to the

---

[1] Poullet, "L'hist. du droit pénal dans l'ancien duché de Brabant," *Mém. couronnées de l'Ac. roy. de Belge* (4to), XXXIII. 1865-7, p. 309.
[2] De Longé, *Cout. de Brabant*, Quartier d'Anvers, I. p. 122.
[3] Stallaert, *Glossarium*, 2, 171.
[4] Keure des Dorfes ten Hamre (1193), § 8 (quoted by Warnkönig).
[5] See p. 186, infra. [6] Brunner, pp. 64 f.
[7] *Cout. des petites villes*, II. p. 218 (quoted by Petit-Dutaillis, who also refers to the Keuren of Damme, of Mude and of Alost). Cp. also Keure des Dorfes Saffelære (1264), § 2. Warnkönig, III. 2, Nachtrag, p. 39.

preservation of a thirteenth century "register of reconciliations" from the town of Tournai[1]. One of the records runs thus:

"Let all those who shall see this deed know that on a day which is past Libens Gillart killed Clais Barisiel in the jurisdiction of Tournai, for which death this Libens Gillart and his kinsmen (*amis*) on the paternal and maternal side have made good terms (*pais*) with the brother of Clais Barisiel and with his common kindred on his father's and on his mother's side, in such manner that Libens Gillart, Watiers Gillart, Teri Gillart, Cholart le Lormier, Gheron de Has, Jehan de Grimaupont,...[2], Jakemes et Gille, brothers of Estievenes of St Martin, have agreed: To give to Watier of Poperinghe as compensation for the death of Clais Barisiel 50 pounds tournois and 30 shill. tournois for (instead of?) the pilgrimage to Saint Gilles, if Jehans Barisiel will take it by the advice of his kindred, if he likes better the 30 shill. than the pilgrimage....[3]"

We see that eight persons agree to pay the fine.

In another case, of 1344, one Rasson Delcourt fought with Jehan Haveron, in which 'piteous happening' the latter was wounded. He subsequently died, but Rasson was acquitted of having killed him. Yet Rasson longs for "the friendship of the near kinsmen of Jehan, and for the honour of God and the advancement of Jehan's soul he sent on divers occasions a goodly number of worthy folk to Jacquemon of Haveron, Jehan's brother, and his kinsmen, (asking) that he and his kinsmen might come to terms with him, and (intimating) that though he was acquitted and cleared of the deed by law, he would willingly amend it to the brothers and his kinsmen, and for the advancement of Jakmin the eldest son of Jehan..." Jacquemon yielding to the prayers of the good folks who plead for this, and also in order to relieve the soul of his brother Jean, received Rasson, on his own behalf and on that of his kinsmen, into good friendship (*pais*), and the said Rasson and Jakemes kissed each other. Rasson pays money which is to go to the orphans, but with the proviso that if these two, on attaining their majority, prefer feud with him, the money is to go to their uncle Jacquemon[4].

Here, a century later, there is no mention of actual financial participation of either kindred, but the kinsfolk on both sides take part in the reconciliation[5]. This, however, is occasionally

---

[1] Printed in full by Benary, in *Romanische Forschungen*, XXV. (1908).
[2] 'quermes demi Escault.' Possibly an error in transcription?
[3] From *Bulletins de la Soc. hist. et litt. de Tournai*, XXIV. pp. 131–2.
[4] Printed in *Bulletins de la Soc. hist. et litt. de Tournai*, XXIV. pp. 133–5.
[5] Defacqz, "De la paix du sang...dans les anciennes coutumes belges," *Bull. de l'Ac. roy. de Belgique*, XXII. 2ème série (1866), pp. 73–95, quotes two early Belgian jurists as saying that it is prudent to make all the kinsmen join in the composition, even if the victim forgave the murderer before his death.

characteristic of a much later date: thus in 1459, after a quarrel between two kindreds, "the slayer...together with his brothers, kinsmen and friends...have several times sent notable persons to the kinsmen and friends of the said Laurens, deceased," to ask for reconciliation, but complain that the latter refuse[1].

As late as 1500 Philip I. forbids the authorities of Flanders to pardon a malefactor unless he had come to terms with the interested parties. In 1619 the High Sheriff of Hainault received the right to pardon slayers, but only if they had previously made the *paix à partie*, and the Prince-Bishop of Liège declared as late as 1685 that a slayer could not claim his grace unless he had obtained the favour of the injured party[2]. These survivals are interesting from a juridical point of view rather than from ours, for probably by this date the 'interested parties' were only the near family of the slain.

In the 13th, 14th and 15th centuries feuds are extremely common, and seem usually not to have been confined to individuals[3]. It is not, however, to the feuds themselves that we would go for our evidence, but to the *truces*, which are frequently mentioned. They are imposed by public authority, with the object of granting a breathing-space during which negotiations for a permanent reconciliation can be carried on. In these truces the 'kindreds' of both sides are invariably concerned. In Liège the bishop could impose truces, but these only included the members of the slayer's kindred, not the slayer himself[4]. The custumal of Bruges (1461) declares that the persons bound by a truce were: the principal delinquent and the injured parties,

---

[1] Petit-Dutaillis, pp. 179-181, XXXVIII. March 1459. Cp. also XLIV. (pp. 194-5), Brussels, July 1460: "grant guerre et débat entre ledit suppliant et ses parens et amis d'une part, et lesdits Danel, Woutre de Bouchout et leurs amis d'autre."

[2] Defacqz, op. cit. p. 88.

[3] In the county of Namur a judicial record of 1439 speaks of a *conseille des amis* choosing a *chief dele guerre* (Brunner, p. 72). In this district feud or reconciliation remained possible alternatives, but in most other districts at this date feuds were promptly put down by means of *asseurements*. It is in Namur too that one Jehennin, who has slain Henri, is set free on its appearing that he had killed Henri in a legitimate feud, Henri's *cousins* having killed his father. This in 1477 (Brunner, loc. cit.).

[4] Poullet, Essai sur l'hist. du droit criminel dans...Liège, *Mém. cour. de l'Ac. roy. de Belgique*, XXXVIII. (1874), p. 139.

those who meditate vengeance, and the kinsmen or connections (alliés) up to the third degree inclusive, whether on the paternal or maternal side[1]. In the Tournai register we find:

"Colart of Callenelle has given truce on his own behalf and on that of his kinsmen (*les siens*) for the death of Capelain his brother to all the kindreds of those who were implicated in the slaying of his brother; and the actual persons implicated have none of it (the truce), nor the kinsmen of Floket on the father's side. Jehennet Tiebegot received it (the truce) as *kievetaine* (chief) for his brother Jakemin. And Lotar Gargate has pledged the truce and made it good on behalf of the strangers (? *sauvages*) for Jehennet Floket. And Biertrant Warison has received it as 'chief' for Jakemin Wisse on the maternal side. And Watelet de la Cambe has received it as 'chief' on the paternal side. And Druiel del Ausnoit has received it on behalf of his branch (*coste*), for Jakemin his son[2]."

Such a document gives some indication of kin-solidarity, but not very much, as it does not tell us how many kinsmen each individual represented. Oddly enough, by far the most striking evidence for cohesive kindreds is furnished by the *fourjurements*, peculiar it would seem to Hainault and the neighbouring French districts. The *fourjurement* is a public and collective repudiation, on the part of the whole kindred, of one of their number. The following is the first example in the Tournai register:

"The year of the incarnation 1273, on the ninth day of March, on a Friday, Jehan Moriel dou Mortier, in the hand of Williaume Castagne, Provost of the Commune, in presence of Provosts and assessors (*jurés*) in full assembly in the Town Hall, forswore Jehan his son, clerk, in such sort that Jehan Moriel promised and swore on holy relics that he will not support (*confortera*) nor aid Jehan his son, clerk, henceforward, neither with his person nor with his property, neither against death nor maiming nor bodily injury, nor against any chance that might befall his son aforesaid, on account of the bodily injury he inflicted on Jakemin, the son of Jehan de Rongi, during truce.

"And in exactly the same fashion as Jehan Moriel has forsworn his son, so all these hereinafter named have forsworn him with pledged faith and with oath, in the presence of the Provost and assessors:

"Colin, the son of Moriel dou Mortier, and Moriel has taken Jakemin('s oath) upon himself until he comes of age, when he will bring him to (ratify) this repudiation...."

---

[1] Petit-Dutaillis, p. 58. Cp. p. 64: in Bruges two persons are taken by the police out of each of the four branches of the family concerned, as 'otages' until peace is concluded.

[2] Benary, op. cit. p. 19, No. 51.

Then follow 70 other persons. Then

"Here after follows all those who have forsworn Jehan Moriel dou Mortier, clerk, of those who are related to him on his mother's side, and they have all forsworn him in the very same fashion as his father has forsworn him. To wit: Jehan Flamenc de Bauwegnies, and he has taken the oath of his two sons upon him to make them forswear (Jehan) when they come of age...."

Then follow 53 persons. Then

"These are those excluded from the peace of the party of Flamenc: Jakeme the brother of Flamenc, Gilles Mainbuede, Jakeme of Valenciennes and his two sons Henri and Jakeme, and the son of Colart the younger of Bauwegnies, Mathias de la Mote, Rogier his brother, Jehan of Lignette, the son of Gillion dou Pire and Monart Cavol of Lille[1]."

In all, 129 persons swear the oath.

In this case the repudiated kinsman has been guilty of what Scandinavian custom would call a 'nithing's deed,' but there are so many cases of repudiation in so short a space of time that we can hardly attribute them all to serious breaches of faith[2]. It is possible that in certain towns this formal and public repudiation by the kindred automatically followed the outlawry of one of its members. But whatever the origin of the custom, it is a striking illustration of the solidarity of the kindred that 129 male relatives can be suspected of a desire to harbour or shelter an outlaw. It is interesting to observe that some of the persons mentioned at the end are domiciled in such comparatively distant towns as Lille and Valenciennes.

Another case, in which 67 persons forswear their kinsman, is interesting because the first actor is no nearer a kinsman to the delinquent, Watier Maughier, than nephew. Some light is thrown on this by the following paragraph:

"Jakeme de la Buirie has forsworn by pledged faith in full assembly in the Town Hall all those who are related to him who have not forsworn Watier Maughier, and (has sworn) that he will never concern himself,

---

[1] Benary, pp. 99–101, No. 615.

[2] There are 27 cases in seven years. They usually seem to follow a slaying. That the *fourjurement* was common all over Hainault, at least, seems clear: the Hennegauische Pax of 1171 ordains that the ceremony must take place in the Count's Court. (O. Goldast, *Die Gerichtsbarkeit in den Dörfern des mittelalterlichen Hennegaues*, Leipsic 1909, p. 19.)

whatever may happen, with regard to the death of Gillot Kieville whom this Watier killed[1]."

We may perhaps deduce that some of the nearer kinsmen of Watier Maughier could not be induced to repudiate him.

In view of the above cases, we are perhaps justified in considering the solidarity of the kindred in these districts as beyond question. The *fourjurement* of a kinsman by over 100 persons at the end of the thirteenth century may be taken to prove the existence of large and cohesive kindreds.

The accounts of the fourteenth-century chroniclers Jean d'Outremeuse and Henricourt fully bear out the picture of cohesive kindreds traced for us in the laws and charters. In both the word *lignage*, kindred, occurs almost on every page[2]. Jean d'Outremeuse shows us the Bishop of Liège summoning his vassals to military service, and getting none, "car li lignages soy guerioient adont tous li uns à l'autre en paiis del evesque de Liège, si qu'il ne pot avoir nulluy[3]." In this district persons would often deny their relationship "en disant qu'ilh n'estoient point de linage," in order to avoid being involved in a quarrel, and would even go so far as to change their armorial bearings[4]. "The sire de Hermalle summoned all those of his kindred, and demanded their aid in order to have vengeance, and they all remained with him," says Henricourt[5]. Thus it is not a mere question of the immediate relatives.

---

[1] p. 105, No. 628 *a*.

[2] Cp. *Chronique de Jean des Preis det d'Outremeuse*, ed. A. Borgnet (Brussels, 1867), Tome V. (Chroniques de Liège):—

p. 543. "li linage des Preis qui estoient nobles et puissans, et les Malhars del Salvenier soy gueroient l'un l'autre...la guerre fut mult felle et fort, si en morut mains hommes. — Encore oirent les Malhars I. forte guerre à cel temps meismes encontre les Yerteis, qui estoient des Preis del costre de Nuefvis, acomblé de Waroux. Et encore al temps dedont avoit une grant guere entre les Malhars et cheaz de Sains-Servais en Liege, et enssi avoient guere les Malhars à III. fors linages."

p. 547. "Ly evesque...mandhit à li (sangnour d'Awans) et *à tous ses cusins* qu'elle li amendent dedens VIII. jours leurs meffais...."

[3] Quoted by Poullet, *Hist. du droit crim. dans l'ancienne principauté de Liège*, p. 130, cp. p. 134.

[4] ib. p. 135 (Polain, II, pp. 25, 31).

[5] *Miroir des nobles de la Hesbaye* (p. 341) : "Le sire de Hermalle mandast tos

The evidence of the popular epic of Reynard the Fox is not to be despised in this connection, for we may fairly consider that the Flemish version depicts the manners and customs of the Netherlands in general. The various versions are not all slavish translations of their Old French original, and perhaps we may be pardoned for digressing sufficiently to note their divergences in the matter of references to the kindred. Thus where the cock brings forward his suit against Reynard for the slaying of one of his family, the French Roman de Renart shows him accompanied by his mate and three daughters[1]. Willem, the thirteenth-century Flemish translator, depicts this scene as if it were an illustration of the custumal of Briel, for the bier is accompanied by four male relatives (no doubt the representatives of the kin), one at each corner of the bier[2], as is laid down in that work[3]. The Low German version, printed at Lübeck in 1498, follows what we have seen to be Schleswig-Holstein custom, and shows the cock surrounded with his kindred, his *geslecht*, as the bier is borne into the king's court of justice[4]. In the High German version of the poem, on the other hand, though it dates from the twelfth century, there is no trace of the kindred, and Chantecler is accompanied only by his wife[5].

In the same scene the French version makes the wolf Isengrim prefer his suit against Reynard alone[6]. The Flemish version shows the custom

---

ceaz de son linage, et requist leur ayde par avoir vengement, et ilh demoront tos deleis ly" (quoted by Poullet).

[1] *Le Roman de Renart*, ed. E. Martin, Strassburg, 1882, l. 279 ff.:
"Chantecler et Pinte
Qui a la cort venoit soi qinte
Devant le roi de Renart plaindre," etc.

[2] *Van den Vos Reynaerde*, uitg. W. L. van Helten, Groningen, 1887, ll. 275–6. So also in the 16th cent. chap. book, E. Martin, *Das niederl. Volksbuch Reinaert de Vos*, Paderborn, 1876, p. 14.

[3] *Het Rechtsboek van den Briel*, uitg. d. J. A. Fruin ën M. S. Pols (1880), p. 179: "dat die vier achtersusterskinder sullen gaen staen elcs an een hoeck vander baren."

[4] *Reinke de Vos*, hrsg. A. Lübben, Oldenburg, 1867, I. 3, ll. 294 ff.:
"Quam hane Hennink mit sinem geslecht
in des konninges hof gevaren," etc.

[5] *Reinhart Fuchs* (supposed to be the work of an Alsatian), hrsg. K. Riessenberger, Halle, 1886, ll. 1458 ff.:
"Schanteclêr quam dô
und ver Pinte zwâre
si truogen ûf einer bâre
ir tohter tôt."...

I do not quote from the 15th century Danish and English versions, as neither of these show any individuality of their own, but appear to be careful translations.

[6] Martin, ll. 27 f.: "Et Ysengrin qui pas ne l'eime
Devant toz les autres se cleime."

of Flemish law-courts: Isengrim *and his kinsmen* came before the king to make their plaint[1]. On this the Lübeck version enlarges:
"Isegrim de wulf begunde de klage
sine vrunde, sîn slechte, sine negesten mage
de gingen al vor den konnink stan[2]."
In the High German the kindred is narrowed down to the immediate family:
"Ver Hersant unde Îsengrîn
quâmen dar und die süne sîn[3]."

Worthy of note, too, is the form of the king's threat in the Flemish and Low German versions. In the former, the king declares that if Reynard continues to be recalcitrant he will not be summoned again, but that vengeance will be taken on all his kinsmen[4]. The Low German version makes the king say that disobedience will mean the ruin of Reynard and of all his kindred[5]. There is no similar passage in the High German version. Even there, however, we find a kinsman making a faint objection to serving the king at the expense of a kinsman[6].

The Flemish and Low German versions diverge characteristically from the French in depicting the part played by Reynard's kinsmen at the time of his duel and subsequent disgrace and condemnation. In the *Roman de Renart*, Reynard's defeat merely causes his kinsmen great shame[7], and they take no action when they see him bound[8]. The Flemish Willem makes Reynard's nearest kinsmen leave the court on his condemnation[9], while

---

[1] Helten, ll. 55 f.: "Isingrin ende sine maghe
Ghingen voer den coninc staen."

[2] Lübben, ll. 33 ff.   [3] Riessenberger, ll. 1359 f.

[4] Helten, ll. 926 ff.:
"Ne comt hi niet, hets hem quaet:
Men salne derdewerven niet daghen,
Maer rechten le lachtre alle sinen maghen."
Cp. *Reinaert*, hrsg. E. Martin, Paderborn, 1874, ll. 2537 ff.:
"Alle di hem ten tienden lede
sijn belanc, sullent becopen."

[5] Lübben, ll. 915 ff.

[6] Reinhart, ll. 1649 ff.:
"Dô sprach Diepreht ze stunt
daz lantreht ist mir niht kunt,
herre, er ist mîn küllinc."

[7] Martin, l. 1351: "li parent Renart ont grant honte."

[8] *Roman de Renart*, ed. Méon, ll. 11,637 ff.:
"Ses parenz ert et ses amis
Liez le voit et entrepris."

[9] Helten, ll. 1750 ff.:
"Do Reynaert verordeelt was
Orlof nam Grimbert die das
Met Reynaerts naeste maghen."

Isengrim on his side is urging his kinsmen to hold their prisoner fast[1]. In the Lübeck version Reynard's kinsmen keep vigil with him the night before the duel, and accompany him to the field[2]. Reynard, on his defeat, offers their perpetual service to Isengrim[3], and when his plea for mercy is refused, threatens him with the vengeance they will exact[4]. On his condemnation they leave the court, to the embarrassment of the king, who realizes that he can ill spare them. More characteristic still, perhaps, is the circumstance that when the tables are turned, and the king begs Reynard to pardon his enemy, Reynard insists on asking the consent of his kinsmen before he will yield to the king's request[5].

II. *France.*
A.

In French Flanders we find customs of wergild and of reconciliations of the same type as across the border.

Wergild-regulations exist for the town of Lille, in the 13th century *Livre Roisin*[6], which remained the recognized custumal of the town until Charles V ordered a revision of the customs of Flanders. The chapter in question runs thus[7]:

For the information of the '*paiseurs*' (pacificators) of this town, concerning the death of a man: a man owes a full payment of 24 Artois pounds, and the party of the delinquent shall raise this from his kindred as follows below:

			sous	deniers
1.	From the brother	20
2.	„ „ uncle, paternal or maternal	15
3.	„ „ nephew, son of brother or sister	15
4.	„ „ first cousin[8]	10

[1] Helten, ll. 1816 ff.   [2] Lübben, IIII. 6, ll. 6187, 6244 ff.
[3] Ib. IIII. 8, ll. 6397 f.:
"Dar to al mine angeborne vrunde
scholen ju denen to aller stunde."
[4] Ib. ll. 6457 ff.: "So mote gi alle tît vruchten dan
vor mîn slechte, vor mine vrunde."
[5] Ib. ll. 6551 f.: "Doch bidde ik, de konnink mi wille gunnen,
dat ik minen vrunden des ersten vrage."
[6] Brun-Lavainne, *Roisin, Franchises, Lois et Coutumes de la ville de Lille* (Lille and Paris 1842), p. vii f. The MS. dates from the second half of the 14th century, but seems only to reproduce legislation previous to 1295. Cp. Dubois, *Les Asseurements au 13ᵉ siècle* (Paris 1900), p. 132. In 1617 the collection was copied, presumably for reference, by order of the magistrates.
[7] *Roisin*, p. 107, c. IV.
[8] It may be pointed out that, exclusive of classes 2, 3, 4*a* and 5*a*, which are probably later additions, each more distant *parentela* pays half the quota of the next nearer *parentela*: 20 : 10 : 5 : 2½. (There are 12 deniers to a sou.)

								sous	deniers
4*a*.	From the first cousin once removed (*demi point mains*)							7	6
5.	,,	,,	second cousin	...	...	...	...	...	5	
5*b*.	,,	,,	,,	once removed (*demi point mains*)				3	9
6.	,,	,,	third cousin	...	...	...	...	...	2	6[1]

"If anyone breaks this peace and these arrangements which are made and declared for the purpose of making peace, it is ordained that if he be a townsman he shall be banished from Lille and from its territory (*castelerie*) for ten years and ten days, with 60 pounds forfeit, and all his kinsmen who are townsmen must repudiate him by oath (fourjurer)...."

The limit of the kindred was evidently the same at Cambrai as at Lille, for in 1227 Bishop Godefroi enacts that the bishop may sell or grant to any one the right to rebuild the house of a slayer, which had been pulled down for a year, *except to those who are related to the slayer within the fourth degree*[2].

A wergild statement from the town of St Omer, from the end of the 13th century, reckons the liability of the kindred even further—to fourth cousins, adding "et là va hors li parages." This statement of wergild is particularly interesting. It is drawn up by one of the more or less official arbitrators, Ghis l'Escrine-werkere, who adds at the end that he has acted on these ordinances, in company with other worthy folks, for fifty years and more, and that he has set them down, with the collaboration of others, as they have been applied in his time. He gives not only a detailed wergild statement, but a full description of procedure after a slaying[3].

The slayer may seek peace himself, offering pledges for the sum of 24 pounds, but if he is absent, his 'amis' (kinsmen) must offer pledges for the sum, and he who acts on behalf[4] of the body of kinsmen (representative of the slayer), and carries the sword, should persuade his kinsmen—"those whom he can best ask on his father's side"—to act as sureties (for the whole payment); but there is an understanding that these sureties shall not suffer financially unless in the last resort. The slayer's representative pays one-third of the wergild, and the children of the slain, whether sons or daughters, receive it. The other two parts are handed over to the four arbitrators,

---

[1] The total is only 3 livres 18 sous 9 den.: no doubt the slayer is entitled to take the sum stated from *each* uncle, nephew, etc.
[2] P. Dubois, *Les Asseurements au 13ᵉ siècle* (Paris 1900), p. 106.
[3] Giry, *Hist. de St Omer* (Paris 1877), pp. 576 f. (XXIX. 791).
[4] Kievetaine.

chosen by the injured kinsmen, and these have to distribute it to the kindred, 'member by member,' within the year. They receive 12 pence out of every pound themselves in return for their services. The representative of the slayer must demonstrate to the magistrates (*eskevins*) of the Town Hall that he has paid his instalment, and ask for a sergeant to accompany him to all his kinsmen, announcing the peace and demanding their legal contributions. The kinsmen of the slain receive similar proportions:

			sous	den.
A.		son, $\frac{1}{3}$ of total		
B.	1.	each brother	15	
	2.	each nephew, of either side	10	
	3.	first cousins	10	
	4.	,, ,, once removed	7	6
	5.	second cousins	5	0
	6.	,, ,, once removed	3	9
	7.	third cousins	2	6
	8.	,, ,, once removed	1	10
	9.	fourth cousins	1	3

It will be seen that the total will vary according to the number of brothers and nephews. Probably also each cousin pays the sum indicated. If the contributions fall short of the total, the father of the slayer's representative becomes liable[1]. If he is dead his (other) sons have to make up the total; or, in the last resort, the sureties. The actual *zoene*, or reconciliation, also involves the whole kindred:

"To make the *zoene*[2] for the death of a man the slayer must carry the sword, in his shirt, bare-legged and unshod, bare-headed. Item, the sons of the slayers, the brothers of the slayers, the nephews of the slayers, the first cousins of the slayers and their sons, must go in their shirts, bare-legged and unshod, without a hood. Item, the second cousins and their sons shall go with bare feet, in their tunics, ungirt, without a hood. Item, the third cousins and their sons shall go in their tunics, ungirt, without a hood, and shod. And all the slayers shall walk together after that one of them who carries the sword, in their shirts, bare-legged and unshod, and without a hood[3]."

The scribe adds that a *zoene* as described above took place in the town hall in 1374. An ordinance of 1593 still assumes the presence of kinsmen and friends on both sides[4].

---

[1] Giry says the representative himself, but: "se...li peires del vallet ki l'espeie portast vesquit encore...on devroit...prendre sour tout le sien...tout chou k'il i defauroit." [2] Giry writes this *zoeve*.

[3] Giry, op. cit. XXIX. (from Registre des Bans Municipaux).

[4] Bled, Le Zoene ou la Composition pour homicide à St Omer jusqu'au XVII.

The town records of St Omer have yielded some very remarkable documents of the 14th century, which show wergild still being received and distributed among relatives up to second cousins. Thus for 1381 there is a record of a *zoene*[1] "for the death of the late Jean Lamps, glazier of the town, son of Jehan Lamps: Jehan Martin called Mahieu, who killed him, carried the sword, and the said sword was received by Bauduin Cloez, of Rubroec, second cousin of the said deceased on the father's side, and the said treaty was sworn by: Luy le Poirele, bourgeois, second cousin of the said deceased through his father's father, George le Hoccre, bourgeois, second cousin of the said deceased through his father's mother, Jehan Fiebe Ysercoich, bourgeois, second cousin of the said deceased through his mother's father, and Thomas Fièbe, bourgeois, second cousin of the said deceased through his mother. And twenty-four livres were placed in the hands of messieurs the magistrates (*eschevins*) for the said peace."

The magistrates are of course to distribute it among the kindred, as the custumal prescribes. More often, however, they hand the sum over to four relatives of the slain, who are to distribute it among the various branches of the kindred. In this case there are sureties to see that the distribution actually takes place.

Thus there is a record of a *zoene* in 1389, at which 24 pounds (*livres*) were duly paid, "of which 12 pounds were handed over to the aforesaid Thomas Vidor (first cousin once removed), and Jehan Pasquiez (second cousin): the surety for them being Baudin Cokempot, bourgeois; item, 6 pounds of it were handed over to the said Willem le Bye (second cousin through his father's father): surety, Tassart Gaetoc, bourgeois; and the other 6 pounds were handed over to the said Jehan le Vinc (third cousin): surety, Michel Gougebent, bourgeois[2]."

siècle, in *Mém. de la Soc. d'Antiquaires de la Morinie* (St Omer), XIX. (1885), p. 231-4.

[1] Bled, Le Zoene, p. 341: ..."à la zoenne de la mort de feu Jean Lamps verier de la ville, fils de Jehan Lamps, porta l'espée Jehan Martins dit Mahieu qui l'ochist, et rechupt le dicte espée Bauduin Cloez, de Rubroec cousin en aultre audict mort de par le père, et jurèrent le dicte pais Luy le Poirele bourgois cousin en aultre aud. mort de par le père de sen père, George le Hoccre bourgois cousin en aultre aud. mort de par le mère de son père, Jehan Fiebe Ysercoich bourgeois cousin en aultre aud. mort de par le père de se mère, et Thomas Fièbe bourgois cousin en aultre aud. mort de par sa mère. Et furent vingt quattre livres par. mis en la main de messieurs Eschevins pour lad. zoene...13 nov. 1381."

[2] Bled, op. cit. p. 244, note 1: "...Et furent xxiiij l.p. [livres parisis]...dont douze livres en furent baillié aux dessusdictz Thomas Vidor (cousin germain demy) et

The money is thus handed over to four kinsmen, representatives of the various branches of the family, and the duty of each surety is to see that the money is actually distributed among the group of kindred concerned [1].

A case of 1482 is interesting as showing a rare generosity:

> "And as to the 24 Parisian pounds which from the oldest times have been paid by him who makes peace, the said kinsmen and friends of the said deceased, on their own behalf and on that of all the other kinsmen of this deceased, having regard to the poverty of the said Girard [the slayer], count themselves content in that matter and have promised to acquit Messieurs [the magistrates] and entirely remit the payment thereof [2]."

It was the magistrates' duty, as we have seen, to receive the payment from the slayer's kinsmen.

The practice of treaties after slayings continued in St Omer until the 17th century [3], but long before this they had been narrowed down to the immediate families of those concerned. Of the documents printed by Bled, the latest to show a real solidarity of the kindred dates from 1577:

> "At the zoene and reparation of Jehan Marissal, at the time of his decease a labourer living at the Nart outside the Boullizïenne gate, Loys Malbrancq, ironmonger (*cancaillier*) and bourgeois of this town of St Omer, carried the sword for the slaying committed by him on the person of the said deceased Marissal: peace was sworn by Charles de Lattre, son of Jehan, attorney by right of special powers inserted in the deeds of appointment for this occasion, recognized and acknowledged in the presence of royal notaries of this residence, on the 14th of June last, by Jehenne de Fosse, widow of Jehan Marissal, both in her own title and as having the care and guardianship, as mother, of Jehan, Charles, Gilles, Robert, Philippe, Vincent and

---

Jehan Pasquiez (cousin en aultre), plaiges pour aux Baudin Cokempot, bourgois; item en fut baillié six liv. aud. Willem le Bye (cousin en aultre de par le père de son père), plège Tassart Gaetoc, bourgois; et les aultres six livres furent baillié aud. Jehan le Vinc (cousin en tierch), plège Michel Gougebent, bourgois. 10 Oct. 1389."

[1] Cp. also p. 243, note 3: "lesquels xxiiij furent bailliées au [sic] quattre personnes dictes qui jurèrent lad. paix, *pour distribuer et payer aux cousins dudit mort de quattre costés...*" (1383).

[2] Bled, p. 243, note 2: "Et quant au xxiiij l.p. que de toute anchienneté se paient par iceluy qui faict zoene, lesd. parens et amys dud. deffunct pour eulx et pour tous les aultres amys charnelz d'iceluy feu, regardans la povreté dud. Girard, se en sont tenus contens et en ont promis acquittier et du tout déchargier messieurs."

[3] Bled, op. cit.

Chrestienne Marissal, her children ; Robert de Fosse, Bailly of Tatinghen, maternal grandfather, maître Arnoult Marissal priest, *curé propriétaire* of Longuenesse, Vincent Marissal labourer, these acting and answering for Lambert of Lattre and Jacqueline Marissal his wife, Flourens Bonnerue, Gillette Marissal, and Marie Marissal *fille à marier*; the above-mentioned of the surname of Marissal, brothers and sisters of the late Jehan Marissal, themselves acting and answering for all other kinsmen and friends of the said late J. Marissal, promising, through the attorney before named, to hold and cause to be maintained for ever, firmly and immutably, the said peace made between them touching the said homicide[1]...."

We see that in spite of the great number of names only the widow, brothers and sisters and brothers-in-law actually appear, though they vaguely undertake to answer for all other kinsmen. But this is in the last quarter of the 16th century.

St Omer is singularly fortunate in its archives, but it was not the only town in which the "kinsmen and friends" still appear in wergild treaties as late as the 15th century. Both parties are still concerned in the following case of 1458 from Lille :

About forty years before the date of this document[2] Parceval de la Woestine had killed Jehan Willays, as the sequel to a complicated feud. Parceval then took refuge in a church, and meantime "the Lord of Merckem and other kinsmen and friends of the said suppliant (Parceval) did so much and negotiated so eagerly with the kinsmen and friends of the above-named deceased, that a satisfactory peace and reparation were made and brought about for the said death and homicide, in such fashion that the said kinsmen and friends of the before-named deceased held themselves then, and have since always held themselves, well satisfied and content[3]."

The institution of truce enforced on the two parties by public authority is characteristic of a very wide area in France. St Louis seems to have originated the *quarantaine,* or automatic truce of 40 days for both kindreds, and later kings do their best to maintain it[4]. The towns frequently have a similar institution.

---

[1] Bled, op. cit. p. 343.
[2] These family feuds were of long duration, cp. Petit-Dutaillis, No. XXXI.
[3] Petit-Dutaillis, op. cit. pp. 173–4, No. XXXII.: "le seigneur de Merckem et autres parens et amis dudit suppliant firent tant et traicterent si avant avec les parens et amis d'icellui defunct, que bonne paix et amendise fu faitte et accomplie de ladite mort et homicide, telement que iceulx parens et amis d'icellui defunct s'en tindrent lors et s'en sont adèz depuis tenuz pour bien contens et satisfaiz."
[4] Dubois, *Les Asseurements au* 13e *siècle* (Paris 1900), pp. 74–8.

"All persons are within the truce, unless they are named and expelled from the town-hall, as they should be," says the custumal of Douai[1]. "When truce is taken, as it should be, by the law of the town for any of the kinsmen, all who are outside the town must hold the truce as firmly as those who are in the town when truce is taken[2]." At Valenciennes there is a 'respite': "all the kindred of either side, wherever they are, are in respite for the day or night during which the 'incidents' took place, and for the whole day and night following, except those who were actually involved in the deed[3]."

At Lille: "It is law that if one takes truce from a man who is wounded, and he die, the truce is none the less firm and immutable for all the kindred...," and we hear of truce being taken "from the folk of his kindred on both sides, that is to say on paternal and maternal side[4]." A truce between bourgeois of Lille cannot be repudiated, though a truce between bourgeois and 'forains' (outsiders) can, if the repudiator is accompanied by his 'kindred' (lignage) in the town-hall. If the *lignage* do not appear, three officials must fetch them, but are not bound to go further than fourteen leagues in search of them[5].

In many French towns, as in Flanders, there are *paiseurs*, pacificators, with authority delegated by the *échevins*. So at Lille, at Douai, at Valenciennes, at Amiens, at Hénin-Liétard[6] (in the Pas-de-Calais). The function of these officials is the specialized one, in other towns still performed by the *échevins*, of arbitrating between two kindreds with a view to imposing a permanent treaty. This is a preventive measure taken after some act of violence has occurred. St Omer furnishes a good example from 1339:

"Let all remember that Bauduin Cloet, Henri Cloet, Wautier Cloet, brother of Sire Mikiel Cloet, in that he was the son of Thieri Cloet, Jehan Cloet, the son of Wautier Cloet, Thieri Cloet, the son of Bauduin,

---

[1] Espinas, Les Guerres Familiales dans la Commune de Douai au XIII. et XIV. siècles. *Nouv. Rev. hist. de Droit*, XXIII. (1899), p. 443.
[2] ib. pp. 450–1 (1245).
[3] Dubois, op. cit. p. 133.
[4] ib. p. 136.   [5] ib. p. 150.
[6] For evidence of kin-solidarity in this town, cp. Dancoisne, *Recherches historiques sur Hénin-Liétard*, Douai, 1847, a book which I have unfortunately not been able to see.

Wautier de Lent, and Jehan Lernel, cousins of the said Sire Mikiel on the paternal and maternal side, have granted on their own behalf and that of their kinsmen, sound, firm and complete peace to Willaume de la Bruyère, the son of Gillon, and his kinsmen, as for the deed and slaying perpetrated by the said Willaume on the person of the said Sire Mikiel. Which peace the above mentioned have sworn, their hands laid on holy relics....[1]"

For Douai we have singularly tantalizing records of these reconciliations between kindreds, for a space appears to have been carefully left by the clerk in which to insert the number of kinsfolk present, and has never been filled up.

Thus in 1262-3 we find the guardians of treaties making known that Huet Boine Broke, in order to come to terms with Gerardin Goulet, must swear on holy relics with...men of his kindred that he and they deplored and repented the occurrence which took place between him and Gerardin Goulet. This is a preliminary to an oath of peace in which "Gerardin Goulet and his kinsmen...and Huet Boine Broke and his kinsmen...pledge their faith and swear on holy relics...that each party pardons the other for everything, and they add in the oath that they will not give up speaking, drinking, eating and bargaining each with the other[2]."

This swearing to repentance with a number of kinsmen is the only survival of the oath-helpers of the kindred in France. The institution exists in the Salic law, but seems to have disappeared very early.

The *fourjurements* so common across the border seem rare

---

[1] Bled, op. cit. p. 253: "Ramembrance soit à tous que Bauduin Cloet, Henri Cloet, Wautier Cloet frères à sire Mikiel Cloet par se que fu enfans Thieri Cloet; Jehans Cloet fil Wautier Cloet, Thieri Cloet fil Bauduin, Wautier le Lent, et Jehans Lemel, germains au dit sire Mikiel de par peire et par meire ont recognut de aus et des leurs bone, ferme et entière pais à Willaume de le Bruyère, fil Gillon, et as siens, comme du fait et de l'homicide perpétré par ledit Willaume en le personne dudit sire Mikiel. Lequelle pais li dessus-dit ont juré, leurs mains tendues as sains...."

[2] Espinas, op. cit. pp. 450-1, No. xv.: "C'est li pais de Huet Boinebroke et de Gerardin Goulet. 1. Li eswardeur des pais dient en leur dit tout au commencement, ke Hues Boine Broke, por venir a boine pais, a boine amour a Gerardin Goulet et a ses amis, doit fiancher et jurer sor sains en ceste piece de tere a...homes de sen linage, se il prendre les veulent, ke quant li aventure fu avenue de lui et de Gerardin Goulet, ke il et si ami, quant il le seurent, en furent dolant et repentant et sunt encore et seront tous jours....ke Gerardins Goule's et si amit...et Hues Boine Broke et si amit...fiancent par foit et jurent sors sains...ke il le pardonent tout li uns els autres, et mecent en leur sierment ke il ne lairont a parler, a boire, ne a maignier, ne a markaander li uns as autres."

in France: only at Lille does the Livre Roisin give the regulations for the repudiation of a kinsman by his whole kindred in the event of his having broken a treaty[1].

The 13th century custumal of Amiens seems also to expect that after a fight the kindred of either party will take an active part in the resulting feud, for we read that the authorities of the town can insist on an *asseurement* being given between the two parties and their kinsmen:

"but if it should happen that one of the two parties should desist, or that both parties should desire not to give a mutual *asseurement*, for the fear of some member of the kindred who was not in the town, or who was a clerk or a crusader, whom they could not include in the *asseurement*, they should quite fully grant security on behalf of all except those kinsmen who were absent or were clerks or crusaders." These should be named 'by name and surname,' and the kinsmen should pledge themselves on oath that they would do their best to induce the others to join[2].

Certain transactions of the year 1290 between one Robert Latruie, squire, and the authorities of the town of Amiens, show that kinsmen received compensation for injuries which did not involve death. Robert had had his right hand struck off as penalty for an attack made by him on the Mayor. He appeals against the sentence, and an amicable arrangement was made between the Mayor and Council on the one hand and Robert and his kinsmen on the other, the former being condemned to pay one thousand livres as damages, in consideration of which sum Robert and his kinsmen give an *asseurement*. But there are two other documents in which Guy Robert's brother, and a Jean de Beaumont respectively acknowledge the receipt of 200 livres, in reparation of the injury done to Robert[3]. As far as these documents go they bear out Roisin, who gives a scale of kindred compensation for *afolure*, maiming, as well as for slaying[4].

---

[1] *Livre Roisin*, pp. 108–9.

[2] A. Thierry, *Recueil de Mon. inéd. de l'hist. du Tiers État* (Paris, 1850), I. pp. 132–3. In 1417 Bishop Louis of Thérouanne ordains that under such circumstances clerks are to be obliged to join in the oath of peace: cp. Bled, *Mém. de la Soc. des Antiquaires de Morinie*, XIX. (1885), p. 207.

[3] Thierry, op. cit., pp. 262 ff., Nos. XCI.–XCIII.

[4] Brun-Lavainne, *Livre Roisin*, pp. 106–7.

For the districts further west, the old Neustria, Beaumanoir gives a striking picture of organised feuds between the kindreds, with their consequent truces and treaties, though he has been suspected of denying to the bourgeois a right of feud which they actually possessed[1]. Writing in 1283, he tells us that among his sources for his *Coutumes de Beauvais* were the customs and usages of the country and the decisions of the Court of Clermont. He says:

"it used to be the custom that one could take revenge by right of feud as far as the seventh degree of kinship[2] and this was not strange in the days of yore, for marriages could not be made within the seventh degree[3]. But as the degree for marriage has been made closer, beyond the fourth degree, so also one ought not to attack in feud any one who is further removed from the kindred than the fourth degree, because the kindred stops there in all cases, since matters have been so relaxed that marriages can be made; except in claiming inheritance, for one can still claim inheritance on the score of kindred as far as the seventh degree[4]."

"If peace is made between the parties at feud, it is not convenient that all the kindred of the one side and of the other be (present) to make or assure peace: but it suffices if it is made or assured by those who were chiefs of the feud. And if there are any of the kindred who do not wish to assent to the peace made and accorded by the captain of the feud, they must make it known that (the other side) should beware of them, for that they do not wish to be in the peace[5]." Exiles, and persons away travelling, are expressly

---

[1] Cp. Dubois, op. cit. IIe partie, p. 45. As late as 1361 King Jean at Paris forbids 'les deffiements et les coûtumes de guerroier' both among nobles *and roturiers*, in peace and war. So also Charles V. in 1367; and the Parlement in 1386 (Ducange, *Gloss.* ed. Favre, Vol. X. Diss. XXIX. Des guerres privées, p. 106).

[2] Cp. Viollet, *Hist. du droit civil* (2nd ed.), p. 435.

[3] Charlemagne's law (and Pope Gregory's).

[4] ed. Salmon, Art. 1686. "Il souloit estre que l'en se venjoit par droit de guerre dusques au setisme degré de lignage et ce n'estoit pas merveille ou tans de lors, car devant le setisme degré ne se pouoit fere mariages. Mes aussi comme il est raprochié que mariages se puet fere puis que li quars degrés de lignage soit passés, aussi ne se doit on pas prendre pour guerre a persone qui soit plus loingtiene du lignage que ou quart degré, car en tous cas lignages faut puis qu'il s'est si alongiés que mariages se puet fere, fors en rescousse d'eritage, car encore le puet on rescourre dusques ou setisme degré par reson de lignage."

[5] Art. 1678. (ch. lix.) "Se pes se fet entre les parties qui sont en guerre, il ne convient pas que tuit le lignage de l'une partie et de l'autre soit a le pes fere ne creanter; ainçois soufist assés s'ele est fete ou creantee par ceus qui estoient chief de la guerre. Et s'il sont aucun du lignage qui ne se vuelent assentir a la pes fete et

excluded, and so are bastards, "because according to our law bastards have no kindred[1]."

The principle that there shall be no feuds within the kindred is limited in Beaumanoir to a prohibition for a man *equally* related to either side to join in a feud at all[2]. Clerics, women and children are excluded from feuds. There are all the proper concomitants of peace-making: 'arbitres,' 'garants' or 'plegii' and the distinction between 'truce' and 'peace.' The 'garants' were relatives, and could be drawn from within the seventh degree of kinship[3].

There is a modified form of *fourjurement*: any individual kinsman may claim security from the opposing kindred by summoning them to a court of justice and there 'forswearing' his kinsmen: i.e. undertaking not to help them in the hostilities[4]. This must presumably be done during the 40 days' truce.

"For," says an early 15th century jurist[5], in discussing *quarantaine*, "whenever any quarrels, frays or mêlées, chanced to occur, as a result whereof not a few slayings, maimings and other injuries most constantly used to happen, the kinsmen of those concerned remained in security and had to remain so, from the day of the conflict...for 40 days. And if meanwhile, before the lapse of these 40 days, any of the *parentela*, stock, kinship or affinity of either of the principal delinquents dared to act otherwise in any fashion, sentence and judgment were passed on them."

The ordinance of St Louis was neither the first nor the last attempt to deal with the organised feuds and other manifestations of kindred-solidarity throughout the Frankish Empire. Already Clovis (481–511) made the way easy for the individual to cut loose from his kindred and its liabilities[6], and there can be no doubt that Childebert II. attempted to put a stop to the

---

accordée par le chevetaigne de la guerre, il doivent fere savoir que l'en se garde d'aus, car il ne vuelent pas estre en la pes."

[1] Art. 1697. "Car bastars, par notre coustume, n'ont point de lignage."

[2] Art. 1667. "Quiconques est aussi prochiens de lignage de l'une partie comme de l'autre, de ceus qui sont chief de la guerre, il ne se doit de la guerre meller. Dont si dui frere ont contens (dispute) ensemble et li uns mesfet a l'autre, cil qui se mesfet ne se puet escuser de droit de guerre, ne nus de son lignage qui le vueille aidier contre son frere."

[3] *Etabl. St Louis*, 11.

[4] Art. 1684. "Nepourquant se aucuns se veut oster de la guerre, fere le peut en une maniere, c'est assavoir s'il fait ajourner ses anemis par devant justice et les fet contraindre tant qu'il viegnent avant et après, quant il sont venu, en leur presence et par devant justice, il doit requerre qu'il ne soit pas tenus en guerre comme celui qui est apareillies de forjurer ceus qui firent le mesfet...."

[5] Boutillier, *Somme Rurale*, L. I. ch. 34 (quoted by Ducange, loc. cit.).

[6] Lex Salica, Tit. LX. "De eum qui se de parentilla tollere vult."

whole custom of composition for slaying in the enactment of 599, which ordained that "not by any price of redemption shall he [the slayer] redeem or compound for himself," and that "should it by any chance happen that anyone shall stoop to payment [wergild], no one of his *parentes* or friends shall aid him at all, unless he who presume to aid him shall pay the whole of the wergild; because it is just that he who knows how to kill should learn how to die[1]." We know that this was not the last royal decree which tried in vain to check the inconvenient manifestations of kinship-solidarity.

Various later kings issue decrees aimed against the solidarity of the kindred, with a view to checking feuds, and confining them to those immediately concerned. Thus Philip Augustus[2] promulgates an edict decreeing that when any 'incident' (*fet*) occurred those who were actually present should look to themselves, but that all the kindred (*lignages*) of either side were to have 40 days in which to purchase truce before becoming liable to attack[3]. St Louis repeated this decree in 1245 and again in 1257[4], but as his successors had to reiterate it, we may suppose that it was persistently disregarded, though Beaumanoir duly gives the edict in his *Coutumes de Beauvais*.

For Champagne we have some evidence that unless the kindred of the slain proceeded against the slayer, it was impossible to bring him to justice.

The Red Book of the Echevinage of Reims gives a case from 1303, in which two persons, Miles and Renaut, were seized by the archbishop as concerned in the death of one Anselet, a tailor. They were duly 'cried' in

---

[1] Pertz, *Leg.* I. 10 (Seebohm's transl.). Cp. Charlemagne, *Capit. Car. M.* I. 5, § 180: "Neximus qua pernoxia interventione a nonnullis usurpatum est, ut hi qui nullo ministerio publico fulciuntur...indebitum sibi usurpant, in *vindicandis proximis* et interficiendibus hominibus," etc. Ducange, loc. cit. p. 106.

[2] Or Philip the Bold? See Dubois, op. cit. p. 73.

[3] apud Beaumanoir, Beugnot's ed. IX. a. 13. "li bons Rois Phelipes fist un etablissement, tel que quant aucuns fes est avenus, cil qui sunt au fet present se doivent bien garder depuis le fet. Mais toz les lignages de l'une partie et de l'autre qui ne furent pas au fet present, ont par l'etablissement le Roi quarante jours de trives, et puis les quarantes jours il sunt en guerre."

[4] Cp. Dubois, op. cit. pp. 73 f. and Luchaire, *Manuel des Institutions Françaises*, pp. 230 ff.

13—2

public places in the city, four times, "and in addition the Provost sent to the father, son, brother, wife and to the other kinsmen (*amis*) of the said Anselet" to invite them to take proceedings. But no one came forward, whereupon Miles and Renaut demand to be set free, and the Echevins declare that their demand is in accordance with the ancient custom of the city[1].

The custom is more clearly stated in a later record, of 1333. Robert Ingrant and his brother Jesson are accused of slaying Gontier of Unchar, sergeant of the 'baillie' of Reims. When they appeared in court the widow and son of Gontier were summoned, with the latter's guardians, and further several of Gontier's brothers and sisters and cousins[2]. Altogether 18 persons are named. These declare in court that they believe the Ingrant brothers to be innocent, and the case is dismissed forthwith[3].

That *asseurement* still included a considerable number of kinsmen is vouched for by the following case of 1255:

"There was dissension between Wautier Buiron on the one side and Prioul le Martier on the other. The said Prioul le Martier complained of the said Wautier and desired that he should give him surety on his own behalf and on that of his kinsmen, because he did not trust him. The said Wautier gave him surety on his own behalf and on that of his kinsmen, with the exception of six whom he named, and he was to include them in the *asseurement* by a certain day if he was able, [acting] in all good faith, to do so. He returned on the day and told them on his honour that he could not include them. Judgment was given that he should stand warranty for them (?) or include them in his *asseurement*[4]."

A register of judgments given in 1288 at the chief assizes of Troyes contains a deed of reconciliation of considerable interest:

This is the peace of Raolin d'Argées, and of his children and of their kindred, on the one part, and of the Hermit of Sethenai, and of his children, and of their kindred, and of all those who aided him, on the other part, brought before the court of Champagne. The Hermit swore on holy relics,

---

[1] Varin, *Doc. inéd. de l'hist. de France*, II. 1, pp. 43 f.

[2] 'Cousins charnez.'

[3] Varin, loc. cit. II. 2, pp. 666, 685 f.

[4] *Livre Rouge de l'échevinage* (in the Municipal Archives at Reims), p. 37: "Descors estoit entre Wautier Buiron d'une part et prioul li marlier d'autre. Cil prioul limartiers se plaignoit de celui Wautier et voloit qu'il laseurast de lui et des siens pource quil se doutoit de lui. Cil Wautiers laseura de lui et des siens areis de. VI. quil nomma et les dut metre en l'aseurement tres qua I. jour. se il pooit par sa foit il reuint au jour. et dit lor sa foi quil nes i pooit metre. Droiz en fu diz quil les fournirat ou il les meist en son asseurement." For the (somewhat hypothetical) rendering of *fournirat* cp. Ducange, ed. Favre, s.v. *vadium*, p. 230 *b*.

with seven of his kinsmen, that no good had accrued to him through the death of Raolin d'Argées: that, on the contrary, he got grief rather than joy out of it: and the Hermit has given 100 livres to the kinsmen (*amis*) of Raolin for the slaying, to build a chapel where mass will be sung for the soul of the dead; and Girard, son of the Hermit, is to go across the sea, and start in the week in which St Remi's Day falls (Oct. 1), and return when he will, but let him bring back letters [to show] on the testimony of worthy folk, that he has been across the sea. And through this deed, good peace is granted by the children of Raolin d'Argées, and by their kindred, and by all their supporters on the one part; and the children of Raolin ask the court that if the children of the Hermit, or the kinsmen, demand deeds of witness from the court, that the court should grant (them) to them[1].

We may rest assured that one such document from Champagne vouches for the existence of many more. Indeed, with regard to the whole of Northern France, exclusive of Normandy and Brittany, it would be safe to say that it is rather a lack of sources than any absence of the customs we are describing, which has caused the almost complete neglect of the subject noticeable in works on French history and legal institutions.

In Burgundy there are only the faintest traces of kin-solidarity in the Middle Ages. We find arbitrators negotiating an *effaitement* or treaty[2], as in the case between

"Jehan de Baissey, escuier, frère du feu Guillaume de Baissey et plusieurs de ses amis, d'une part, et Jehan de Saulx...escuier et plusieurs de ses amis d'autre part," but only the slayer, Jehan de Saulx, offers compensation[3].

---

[1] From Ducange, loc. cit. pp. 103–4: "C'est la paix de Raolin d'Argées, et de ses enfans, et de leur lignage, d'une part: et de l'Hermite de Sethenai, et de ses enfans, et de leur lignage, et de totes ses aidans, apportée en la cour de Champagne. Li Hermite jura sur sains li vuitiesme de ses amis, que bien ne li fu de la mort de Raolin d'Argées, ains l'en pesa plus, que biau ne l'en fu: et a doné li Hermite cent livres as amis Raolin le mort pour faire une chappelle, ou l'en chantera pour l'ame dou mort: et en doit aler Girard li fils l'Hermite outre mer, et movoir dedans les octaves de la Saint-Remi, et revenir quand il voudra: mais qu'il aport lettres qu'il ait esté outremer par le temoing de bones gens: et parmi ce fait, il est bone *pais des enfants Raolin* d'Argées, et de leur *lignage*, et de tous leur aidans d'autre part, et requerent li enfant Raolin à la court, que se li enfant l'Hermite, ou li ami requerent lettres de tesmoignage à la court, que la court leur doint...."

[2] G. Valat, *Poursuite privée et composition pécuniaire dans l'ancienne Bourgogne* (Dijon, 1907), p. 108.

[3] Ib. pp. 121–3: "je lediz Jehan de Saulx suis tenuz de faire à faire l'obsèque d'icelluy Guillaume..." etc.

The brother of the slain, however, does include the other kinsmen (*amis charnels*) in the reconciliation: "Further, I, the said Jehan de Baissey, will hereupon grant and consent that good peace be and remain between my friends and the friends of the said Jehan de Saulx. And herewith I will and do answer for all the blood-friends of the said deceased Guillaume, who make demands of the said Jehan de Saulx on account of the said slaying and misdeed [committed] on the said Guillaume de Baissey[1]."

This is in 1389. In the *Ancien Coutumier* of Burgundy we find it provided that in the case of a feud between vassals in consequence of a slaying, their lord can order them each to choose two or three of their 'amis' as arbitrators[2]. But the wergild goes only to the children of the slain; and in the same chapter we find the slayer warned to beware of the *father and brother* of the slain. A little further north he and his kindred would have to beware of the whole of the injured kindred.

At Sens, in 1200, we find the husband paying compensation, on behalf of his wife, to the Abbot of St Colomb for a vassal[3]. This document does not however exclude the possibility that he also paid wergild to the relatives.

For traces of kin-solidarity among the noble classes we do not depend entirely on the picture drawn in the legal compilation of Beaumanoir. Literary evidence—for a somewhat earlier time, it is true—is also at hand in the older *Chansons de Geste*. In especial, the Song of Roland gives a lively picture of the responsibility of kinsmen in the story of the trial of the traitor Ganelon. When the latter stands disgraced before the court, thirty of his kinsmen rally round him[4], and one of them, Pinabel, declares that he will challenge any knight who dares to condemn his kinsman to death—a threat which prevents all but the bravest, Thierry, from giving an adverse verdict. On its pronouncement, the kinsmen of Ganelon plead their right to

---

[1] G. Valat, loc. cit. p. 123: "Item sur ce, ottroyerai et consentirai je lediz Jehan de Baissey que boine pais soit et demeurat entre mes amis et les amis dudit Jehan de Saulx. Et avec ce, je me feray et fais fort en ceste partie de tous les amis charnelz dudit feu Guillaume qui aucune chose vouldroient demander audit Jehan de Saulx à cause de ladite mort et meffait dudit Guillaume de Baissey."

[2] Marnier, *Ancien Coutumier de Bourgogne*, ch. XXIX. (quoted by Valat).

[3] Valat, op. cit. p. 105.

[4] Chanson de Roland (ed. L. Gautier, Tours, 1872), l. 3766 etc.

take up Thierry's challenge, and the Emperor consents to the duel but demands sureties. Instantly the thirty kinsmen pledge themselves to the righteousness of Ganelon's cause[1]—no light responsibility, as the sequel shows. Before the duel Thierry offers Pinabel peace, but the latter refuses, declaring that he intends to uphold (the honour of) his whole kindred[2]. Pinabel is killed by Thierry, and the Franks declare: "Now it is right that Ganelon should be hanged, and all his kinsmen who have pleaded for him[3]," and the thirty sureties are all hanged forthwith upon one tree[4]. Hanging is perhaps an extreme form of penalty, but these incidents would not appear in the story if there were not some basis for them in contemporary judicial procedure. We may suppose that the thirty were put to death as a punishment for having sworn a false oath of compurgation—for that is about what their action amounts to[5].

None of the other *Chansons de Geste* afford quite such striking evidence as this. However, in the *Chevalerie Ogier*, we find Ogier the Dane offering 'self-doom,' as the Icelanders would express it, to the kindred of the man he has slain:

"Si ai mort ton fil, ferai toi amendage
Com jugeront la gent de ton lignage[6]."

And we even find Charlemagne depicted somewhat in the guise of a *paiseur* of the northern towns, summoning the kinsmen of Ganelon and the kinsmen of Aimon, and commanding them to make peace, which they do in the orthodox fashion:

"Charles a fait la pais, si sont entrebaisié[7]."

In the *Chevalerie Ogier*, Ogier's numerous kindred are represented

---

[1] Ib. l. 3846: "xxx parenz li plevisset leial."
[2] Ib. ll. 3905 f.: "Dist Pinabels: 'Ne placet Damne Deu! Sustenir voeill trestut mun parentel.'"
[3] Ib. ll. 3932 f.: "Asez est dreiz que Guenes seit penduz Et si parent ki plaidet unt pur lui."
[4] Ib. l. 3958.
[5] Cp. v. Amira, Zur Salfränk. Eideshilfe, *Germania*, N. F. VIII. (1875), p. 64, "Das altfränkische Gottesurtheil ist Bestärkungsmittel des Unschuldseides."
[6] ll. 8753-4. Quoted by Flach, *Origines de l'ancienne France*, from whom the following examples are also taken.
[7] Renaus de Montauban (H. Michelant ed.), p. 441.

as interposing between Charlemagne and the hero[1]. But kin-solidarity is represented as going further than this, for it induces the kinsmen of Girard de Viane, whom the Queen has affronted, to fight against her[2]. It is very instructive to note that in spite of the prevalence of feudal ideas, duty to one's kinsmen still comes before duty to one's lord. Thus when Charlemagne reminds Ydelon that he is his liege man, and bids him avenge his Emperor on Richard the son of Aymon, Ydelon does not hesitate to refuse:

> "Sire, dist li Baiviers, en moie foi je non.
> Cousin somes germain, près nos apartenom.
> Jà n'aura Richars mal dont garder le puison[3]."

And Ogier goes even further in his reply to a similar proposition, declaring that he will aid Richard with four thousand companions, and will fail him for no man on earth[4].

In other cases, in order not to break openly with his lord, the kinsman has recourse to stratagem, as Turpin to save Ogier, or as when the kinsmen of Renaus urge Roland to strike one blow only at him 'por sa foi aquiter[5].' It is instructive to compare this attitude with that of Hagen in the Waltharius poem, written in Germany in the 10th century. Hagen sees his nephew killed by Walther, and yet refuses to fight his old comrade; it is only when the honour of his king is at stake that he flings aside the claims of friendship and enters on the fight[6].

This painfully incomplete survey of the duration of kin-solidarity in Northern France seems to justify the following conclusions. In the North-East districts, at any rate in the towns, cohesive kindreds continued to exist and to play no small part in local affairs until the 14th and even the 15th century. Further west we have little direct evidence save for the noble classes, and of them it may be said that the principle of kinship-solidarity survived in a very marked degree until the end of the 13th century. Such scraps of evidence as we have amassed for

---

[1] Chev. Ogier, ll. 9530 f., 9560 f., 9586, 9590 f., 9680, etc.
[2] Girard de Viane, l. 53.   [3] Renaus de Montauban, ll. 16 f.
[4] Ch. Ogier, pp. 388 f.   [5] Renaus de Montauban, p. 239, l. 30.
[6] Ekkehards Waltharius, VII. and IX.

Champagne and Burgundy suggest that a certain degree of kin-solidarity survived to about the same period. For an earlier time it has even been maintained that feudal power was founded, not on feudal ties but on kinsmen. " Le baron est, avant tout, un chef de famille ou de clan. Il a comme alliés naturels, comme 'charnels ou naturels amis,' les autres seigneurs de sa parenté, il a sous son autorité directe ses fils et ses petit-fils, des collatéraux, frères, neveux, parents plus éloignés[1]."

In his study of the 13th century treaties between kindreds Dubois took occasion to propound the question : " Pourrait-on établir un rapport de filiation entre les préscriptions des capitulaires et les bans des échevinages du XIIIe siècle?" He answers it thus : "Ce serait séduisant mais bien audacieux. Il serait préférable d'attribuer les ressemblances de ces dispositions pénales à l'analogie de l'état social qui les a nécessitées les unes et les autres, plutôt qu'à une succession juridique très hypothèque," and he thinks it safest to draw the conclusion that kinship-solidarity had lapsed in the centuries that intervened between the Carolingian period and the 13th century[2]. It may be possible to hold this view if France be considered entirely apart from the rest of Northern Europe, but when we have approached French institutions by way of North Germany and the Netherlands, it is impossible for us not to recognise in the towns of the North-East the lineal descendants, in an unbroken line, of the ancient Teutonic kindreds. There are extraordinarily close resemblances between the Lex Salica and the Capitularies on the one hand, and the actual practice of the 13th and 14th centuries on the other, and we cannot really attribute these resemblances to a critical study of the former on the part of mediaeval antiquarian lawyers. But there is another and more cogent reason for postulating an unbroken development. Neither history nor ethnology justifies us in assuming that when individuals find themselves in an anarchical state of society, they will even attempt to form cohesive kindreds for mutual protection. They may segregate themselves into artificial groups, such as gilds or

---

[1] Flach, op. cit. pp. 445 f.   [2] Dubois, op. cit. p. 5.

secret societies, or they may submit themselves to a lord, but there is no evidence to support the theory that they will bethink themselves of their relatives, and decide that they might do more for their third cousins, let us say, than they have hitherto done. Other countries suffered equally, or more, from an anarchical state of society without the slightest trace of any such consequences. The cohesive kindred is no mushroom growth, but a heritage from prehistoric times, and when once it is disintegrated there is nothing to make it cohere again. From this point of view the strength of the kindreds in the towns is of great importance, for it implies that the immigrants who formed the nucleus of the towns in Picardy and the Netherlands did not enter them as individuals, one by one, but in groups of kinsfolk. Whether we may connect the *conjurati* and *congildones*, against whom so many enactments of the capitularies are directed, with groups of kindred which had perhaps entered into special agreements, it is impossible to say; but it seems that the strength of the great merchant families, whom Luchaire terms 'l'aristocratie populaire,' was founded on kin-solidarity[1].

B. *Normandy.*

In Normandy a search for traces of the solidarity of the kindred is but meagrely rewarded. As in Denmark, we are told that a slayer cannot be re-instated by the Duke unless he has first made peace with the 'friends' of those whom he slew[2], but this may mean no more than the immediate family. And this is repeated in the second part of the laws, with 'King' for 'Duke.' On the other hand it is added that this reconciliation with the 'friends' is of no use to the slayer unless the Duke's pardon can be obtained[3]. That the relatives of the slain family

---

[1] Luchaire, op. cit. p. 357.

[2] *Coutumes de Normandie*, ed. Tardif (Paris and Rouen, 1900): Très Ancien Coutumier. xxxvi. "Des pes fuitis. Li dus ne puet fere pes d'omecide envers celui qui l'a fet, se il n'est avant reconciliez as amis a celi qu'il ocist." So also in the second part of the laws, with 'King' for 'Duke': lxxxix. "si que il face pes o les amis al mort."

[3] xxxvi. 4. "Se li homicides puet aquerre la pes as amis a cels que il a ocis, ce ne vaut riens se il n'a la pes le duc." In the treatise on procedure in the Exchequer Court (first half of 15th century), the slayer is directed to summon the kinsmen of

did not invariably take an active part in bringing the slayer to justice may be deduced from the following:

"If a strong man kills and maims someone, and none of the *lignage* (of the slain) pursues him, the law will seize the culprit, and he will be in the prison of the Duke so long as he does not clear himself by the ordeal of water[1]."

The following passage throws perhaps more light on the arbitrary methods of the Duke than on the solidarity of the kindred:

"The bailiffs of the Duke used to take the kinsmen of anyone when he had committed some wrong....So it happened with Uede le Manc and his sons at the hands of the *forestiers* of Bertrand of Verdun, who had captured no culprit but had put in prison several of his 'lignage' who had committed no wrong, and who were acquitted on judgment[2]."

On the other hand we must note one or two cases in which the responsibility of the kin is ignored or set aside. There are guarantors who are kinsmen, but there are no oath-helpers of the kindred; on the contrary it is expressly stated that the 'jurors' who most nearly answer to them, shall not be related to either party[3]. But more remarkable for its deliberate setting aside of the claims of kindred is the paragraph "Of the care of orphans," where the theory of guardianship runs so totally counter to all tribal ideas that it is worth quoting in full:

"Who shall have charge of the orphan heir whom it behoves to be in another's charge? The mother shall not have charge of him. Why? Because if she took a husband and had children by him, those children for envy of the heritage would slay their elder brother and be heirs

---

the slain to the next assizes, there to set forth their objections, if they have any, to the pardon already (conditionally) granted by the King. "Coustume, Stille et Usage" etc. ch. xxx., in *Mém. de la Soc. des Antiquaires de Norm.* XVIII. (1851).

[1] xxxix. "Se uns forz hom[s] ocit aucun e mehange, e nus del lignage ne le suit, la justice prandra l'omecide" etc. If the plaintiff in such a case is incapacitated by youth or age the 'Grand Coutumier' (c. 1275-1300) allows the suit to be taken up by any relative on whom the *lignage* agrees: Bourdot de Richebourg, *Cout. général*, t. IV. cap. lxx.

[2] lxi. "Li bailli le duc souloient prandre les paranz a aucun quant il avoit fet aucun mesfet...ainz avoient mis en prison plusors de son lignage qui n'avoient rien mesfet, qui furent quite par jugement...."

[3] xxvii. 1. "Li jureeur soient esleu lealment par la justice sus la veue de la terre, tel que ne soient del lignage a l'une partie ne a l'autre, ne leur home" etc.

[themselves], or the husband himself would slay his step-son in order to give the heritage to his sons. Who then shall have charge of him? His cousins? Nay. Why? Lest they perchance should ardently desire his death and covet his heritage, for that cause slaying the innocent. To avoid then such treachery and to eschew such cruelty it was established that the orphan be in the charge of him to whom his father was bound by (act of) homage[1]."

The ancient power and solidarity of the kindred must have been sadly shattered before this triumph of feudalism could have been rendered possible.

Compulsory truces appear in the laws, but the kindred is not mentioned in connection with them, and the truce seems to be merely between individuals[2].

The Court of the Exchequer has left on record a large number of cases from the 13th century[3], of which however very few allude to manslaughter[4]. From these few cases it would seem that the slayer is usually banished[5], and that his brother may by special leave receive the forfeited property[6]. In one case the slayer appears to make a payment to the brother of the slain[7]. There is here no trace of the solidarity of the kindred.

---

[1] xi. "Qui gardera l'oir orfelin que il covient estre en autrui garde? La mere ne le gardera pas. Por qoi? Por ce qe se elle prenoit mari e en avoit emfanz, li emfant per la covoitise de l'eritage ocirroient leur einzné frere e seroient oir, ou li mariz meismes ocirroit som fillastre por doner a ses filz l'eritage. Qui le gardera donc? Le garderont si cosin? Nanil. Por qoi? Que il ne beent par aventure a sa mort e covoitent son heritage, par que il ocient l'innocent. Por oster donc tel desleauté e por eschiver tel cruelté fu il establi que li orfelins soit en la garde a celui a qui ses peres estoit liez par homage."

[2] Grand Coutumier (loc. cit.), ch. LXII. etc. Cp. Cauvet, Des trèves établies entre particuliers, Mém. de la Soc. des Ant. de Norm. XXVIII. (1869), pp. 60 ff.

[3] L. Delisle, Recueil de jugements de l'échiquier de Normandie au XIIIe siècle, Paris, 1864.

[4] Nos. 4, 444, 579, 585, 599, 618 (648), 708, 747, 753.

[5] No. 599 (1236).

[6] No. 708. "Judicatum est quod Limare, miles, faciet adjornare dominum Johannem de Tornebu ad assisiam; et si ipse non potest assignare quatuor libras terre Renaudo Burnel pro morte fratris sui sine licentia ejusdem Johannis et de jure de terra quam tenet de feodo suo, ipse assidebit dictum redditum eidem alibi in terra meliori."

CHAPTER VII

ENGLAND

THE English legal evidence differs from most of the law which we have been considering, in that Anglo-Saxon legislation generally partakes rather of the nature of statutory than of customary law. Unlike the latter, which usually finds written expression once for all, the Anglo-Saxon laws are issued at many different times by a long succession of kings. It is necessary to insist on this aspect of most of the Anglo-Saxon law, as it makes it essential for us to proceed chronologically and with due attention to the political geography of the period.

The kingdom of Kent is the first to which we must turn our attention. In view of the nature of the impulse which set them down in writing, Æthelberht's laws, of the first three or four years of the 7th century, must surely be regarded as an attempt to state existing law, rather than an issue of new legislation.

The word used in the Kentish laws for wergild is *leod* or *leodgeld*, and the first reference of importance to us is contained in paragraphs 21–23[1]:

"If anyone slay a man, let him pay an ordinary wergild [the wergild of the ordinary free man], 100 scillings.

§ 22. If anyone slay a man, let him pay 20 scillings at the open grave and (let him pay) the whole wergild within 40 nights.

§ 23. If a slayer escapes from the land, let the kinsmen pay half the wergild."

Before we discuss these clauses we must go on to the only other which concerns us, § 30:

---

[1] Liebermann, *Die Gesetze der Angelsachsen*, I. p. 4.

"If anyone slay a man, let him pay out of his own property and with genuine currency whatever it may be."

Since this last clause clearly establishes the sole liability of the slayer for wergild, · § 23 can only refer to the *secondary* liability of the kinsmen[1], in case the slayer leaves the kingdom without paying the wergild. It is however to be noted that even in this case their liability is limited to *half* the wergild. In fact, as regards the *payment* of wergild, this law, attributed by Liebermann to the years 601–4, already exhibits a stage in the disintegration of the kindred almost as advanced as that of King Hákon Hákonarson for 13th-century Norway: "If the slayer escapes in his outlawed state, then let the kinsmen pay half payment...if his money does not suffice[2]."

With regard to the distribution of wergild we are told practically nothing, but we may guess that though the slayer's kin is generally the first to shuffle off its liability, by the time that the slayer stands alone the body of kinsmen on the other side has generally dwindled into a comparatively small group[3].

The other Kentish laws throw no light on our problem, although the laws of Hlothhere and Eadric (before 686) give the additional information that the amount of the noble's wergild was 300 scillings.

It is of course quite conceivable that these Kentish laws

---

[1] Brunner, *Sippe und Wergeld*, pp. 16 f., refers to § 23 as proving that the liability of the kindred was primary, but this view can hardly be maintained if the clause is read in conjunction with § 30.

[2] See supra, p. 50. In Denmark, as late as 1558, the kindred were liable for the *whole* wergild if the slayer fled (p. 83, supra). In the Siebenharde district of Schleswig the kinsmen pay a *whole* wergild for a kinsman who slays a man after truce has been made (his own property being forfeited, p. 104, supra). In a North Frisian charter the kin only appear to be liable for one-third of the wergild, unless the slayer fled, when they are to be liable for double the amount (p. 106, supra).

[3] In a Danish wergild case of 1567, at Helsingör, we find the kinsmen of the slain objecting to share the wergild with one of their number, a certain Iver Jörgensen, in Jutland, on the ground that when one of their kindred was so unfortunate as to kill someone, and they had asked a contribution towards wergild from this Iver, "he had always refused, and would not contribute towards the wergild with them." (Case of Michill Bagge, etc., 17 March 1567; given in P. V. Jacobsen's Uddrag of Helsingöer's Thingbøger, *Ny. Kgl. Saml.* No. 697 f. 4to.)

showing the limitation of liability to the slayer may be in the nature of revolutionary innovations, like that of Knut VI. in Denmark 600 years later[1], and that they may consequently not represent actual custom. There are however three points which should make us doubtful about accepting this hypothesis. Firstly, if Æthelberht, urged thereto by the Church, had been aiming at restraining feuds, would he not be likely to have followed the Frankish lead of Childebert II. in 599[2], and condemn the slayer to death? Secondly, already in the laws of Hlothhere and Eadric we observe that the kindred play no part in the oaths of compurgation, neighbours taking their place[3]. This does not look as if tribal custom could be very strong. Thirdly—though this is a small point—the laws of Wihtræd (695-6) show us wergild being paid to the king by a defaulter, as a mere fine for breach of law[4]—a phenomenon which only occurs, outside England, in the 13th century Sachsenspiegel and which indicates that wergild was not too large an amount for the individual to pay.

This appearance of the wergild as a mere fine, paid by the individual to the king, is extremely common in the Wessex laws, to which we must now turn our attention.

The laws of Ine (688-95) throw little light on wergild payments.

> We hear of the slaying of a stranger, met with off the highway, who can be killed as a thief, on suspicion, and his lord and associates (*gegildan*) may not prove the contrary. If however the slayer conceals his deed, the kinsmen of the slain may swear him clear[5].

This is the first appearance of the *gegildan*[6] in connection with

---

[1] See supra, p. 82.
[2] See supra, p. 195.
[3] § 5.
[4] § 26.
[5] c. 21.
[6] As far as the context is concerned, the *gegildan* in this passage could include kinsmen, but in view of the fact that the laws of Alfred regularly seem to regard *gegildan* as a substitute for kinsmen, this is a doubtful assumption. If we suppose that *gegildan* has the same meaning as in Alfred, we could imagine that though they might be responsible for wergild if one of their number committed a slaying, yet they are not yet regarded as legally competent to clear the memory of their associate from an accusation of theft.

wergild: we shall find that it is not the last. The next passage also refers only to the slaying of a stranger:

"If anyone kills a foreigner (i.e. not a West Saxon) the king has two parts of the wergild, the son or kinsmen the third part. But if the slain man has no kinsmen, half goes to the king and half to the *gesið*,"—which we prefer, with Schmid, to translate 'nobleman' rather than 'comrade[1].'

Of more importance for our purpose is c. 24:

"If an Englishman in penal slavery escapes, let him be hanged and not paid for to his lord. If anyone slays such a one, let him not pay wergild to his kinsmen, if they have not redeemed him [from slavery] within 12 months";

i.e. if his kinsmen have allowed 12 months to elapse without redeeming him from slavery, they are not entitled to compensation. The kinsmen of the wrong-doer are thus not under any compulsion to redeem their kinsman from slavery, and it is evidently conceivable that they will thus forsake him, since it has been found necessary to have a law regulating their claim to wergild.

The next clause of interest for us is c. 27, where it is laid down that if the father of an illegitimate child has not acknowledged his offspring, he does not get the wergild if the child is slain, but it goes to the lord (of the slain) and to the king. The clause seems to suggest that the father would have been entitled to the whole wergild if he had acknowledged the child to be his. Tribal custom however would surely have handed over the wergild to the child's maternal kinsmen.

We hear of oaths of reconciliation, but not in relation to ordinary feuds between kindreds. The relatives of a captured thief must swear *aðas unfæhða*[2] to the man who captured him.

C. 74 is often quoted as a proof of the primary liability of the kindred of the slayer:

"If a British slave (*þeowwealh*) slays an Englishman, his owner shall deliver him up to the lord and relatives of the slain man, or pay 60 shillings

---

[1] C. 23. Professor Chadwick points out to me that *gesið* is clearly used as interchangeable with *gesiðcund man*, nobleman, in c. 50. As the word in this sense soon became obsolete, the Latin translation, *congildones, consocii*, carries little weight.

[2] Orfeide, urfehde, oirvede in Danish, German and Dutch sources.

for the life of the slave. But if he will not give this sum for him, he must free the slayer, whose relatives shall thereafter pay wergild, if he has a free kindred (*mægburh*[1]) : if he has none his enemies may avenge themselves on him."

But since, as Toller, Schmid and Sweet concur in thinking, and as Liebermann seems inclined to assume, þeowwealh means 'British slave,' this passage is of no use to us in deciding the liability of Anglo-Saxon kindreds, for it must refer to the kindred-system of the Britons, which the dominant race would obviously exploit where possible. In this case the servile Briton is to be returned to his kindred, from which the penalty of his misdeeds will be exacted. The passage goes on to say that a free man need not join in (wergild)-payment with a slave, unless he wishes to buy off revenge from him, nor a slave with a free man; i.e., as long as a man is a slave he is not of the kindred, and none of his free kinsmen need help him. There is however a difficulty in the Anglo-Saxon, which runs: "Ne þearf se frige mid þam þeowan mæg gieldan, buton..." etc. There seem to be two alternatives. We must either read the dative, *mæge*, and translate: 'The free (man) need not pay with the slave kinsman' etc., or we must take *mæg gieldan* as a compound verb 'to pay wergild on behalf of a kinsman.' It is obvious that the existence of such a word would indicate a certain solidarity of the slayer's kindred at a previous date, even though it be a ἅπ. λεγ., used in a British context, and clearly misunderstood by at least one of the MSS.[2] But is *mæggieldan* a word? There are textual difficulties in both alternatives. In the former, it is odd that none of the MSS. should have the dative form. In the latter, though it is a common practice in the Anglo-Saxon charters to write a compound as two distinct words, this is not the practice of any of the texts of the laws; in fact, to judge by Liebermann's careful edition, this would be the only instance of such separation. Still, two of the MSS. do write it as one word[3], and the late Latin translation of the passage found in *Leges Henrici* (70, 5[b])

---

[1] It is perhaps worth noting that the first occurrence of the word *mægburh* 'kindred,' in the A.S. laws, occurs in this British context.
[2] Ld. has: "mid þam þeowan *men* gieldan."   [3] E, So.

evidently treats it as one word, Latinising it as *meggildare*. There is thus considerable textual evidence in favour of a verb *mæggieldan*. But perhaps the linguistic difficulties of such a form have hardly been sufficiently considered. Let us look at other cases connected with wergild where *gieldan* governs the accusative, as in this compound. In Ine, c. 24, we have: *ne gylde hine mon his mægum*, 'let him (the slayer) not pay (wergild) for him to his kinsmen,' and 54, § 1, also speaking of the slayer, *gif hine mon gilt*, 'if one pays (wergild) for him.' We see then that *þone mon gieldan* means 'to pay wergild for the (slain) man.' Therefore (*þone*) *mæg gieldan* could mean nothing but 'to pay wergild for the kinsman whom one has slain.' Yet we are invited to translate *mæg gieldan* as 'to (help) pay wergild on behalf of a kinsman who is a *slayer*.' I do not wish to minimise the difficulties of the text, but I cannot help thinking that it is easier to explain them than to make *gieldan* with the accusative mean something quite inconsistent with its invariable meaning. It would therefore be more than rash to attempt to deduce any liability of the kindred, in Ine's time, from the hypothetical occurrence of such a verb[1].

At the end of Ine's laws we do meet a term with a meaning analogous to that of the supposed *mæg gieldan*, but there is nothing hypothetical about the occurrence of this word—*mægbot* 'kin-compensation.' But it is a startling fact that this 'kin-compensation' only refers to the spiritual kinship between godfather and godson, though it must obviously once have had the same signification as the Scand. *ættarbót*:

"If anyone slays the godson or godfather of another man, let this *mægbot* be as high as *manbot* (the fine to the lord): let this *bot* increase in proportion to the wergild, just as the *manbot* does which is due to the lord. If however it be [a case of] the king's godson, let [the slayer] pay the wergild to the king as to the (slain man's) kindred." (Ine, c. 76.)

---

[1] Is it not possible that *mæggieldan* is an awkward translation, misunderstood by later copyists, of some British term? Or it would be possible to suppose that the original, correct reading was "mid þam þeowan mæg*gield* gieldan" and that a later scribe had omitted the *gield*. There is no objection to a noun **mæggield* (cp. Dutch *maechgelt*). *Mægbot* is however the form we actually find, though in a limited signification.

The word *mægbot* occurs twice more in the Anglo-Saxon laws[1], but there is nothing in either passage to indicate whether it means compensation to the spiritual or to the carnal kin. In any case, however, it is clear from the context that it only refers to compensation to the connections of the *slain* man. There is no trace of oath-helping kinsmen in Ine's law, in fact the existence of such an institution seems to be precluded, at any rate in slaying-cases, by the clause which makes the oath of a nobleman essential in every oath of compurgation for manslaughter.

Thus, but for the very doubtful word *mæggieldan*, there is no evidence in Ine's laws to show that the liability of the slayer's kindred was other than secondary, as in the Kentish laws. Incidentally, the use of the masculine pronoun in the 3rd person singular seems to imply that the slayer was expected to meet his liability alone. Thus, in c. 35, we read that if the slayer of a thief conceals his deed, "*he* shall pay wergild for him" (ðonne *forgylde* he *hine*). And in c. 54, § 1, if the man accused of slaying is found guilty, and pays the wergild, "then *he* may pay, in the place of each hundred (scillings) of the wergild, a slave and a byrnie and a sword, if *he* needs to" (through lack of cash[2]). If the kindred had been concerned the sum would probably be made up differently, and the use of *he* for 'they' would at least require explanation.

We must bear this use of the 3rd person singular in mind when we approach c. 27 of Alfred's laws, which runs as follows:

"If a man, kinless as regards his paternal kinsmen, fights and slays a man, and yet has maternal kinsmen, let these pay a third part of the wergild, a third part the *gegildan*: for the third part let him flee. If he have no maternal kinsmen (either), let the *gegildan* pay half, for half let him flee."

The passage is usually assumed to show a primary responsibility of the slayer's kinsmen; and it is certainly conceivable that it actually does so. But in that case the wording is, to say the least, remarkable. The passage does not say "the third

---

[1] Æthelred, VIII. 3 (in one MS. only), also Cn. I. 2, § 5, where however it is a repetition of the passage in Æthelred.

[2] "Gif hine mon gilt, þonne mot he gesellan on þara hyndenna gehwelcere monnan 7 byrnan 7 sweord on þæt wergild, gif he ðyrfe."

part let him pay," but instead it *assumes the outlawry of the slayer*. Yet Ine's laws, and passages in Alfred's own laws, forbid us to suppose that every slayer was invariably outlawed and that in normal cases the slayer paid nothing and the kindred paid all.

> Thus in c. 19, the man who lends a weapon for homicidal purposes can pay wergild jointly with the slayer, or pay a third of it by himself. So also in c. 29 : if a band of men commit manslaughter, let *him* pay the wergild and the fine who admits the deed ; if the supposed slayer denies the deed on oath, let them all pay the wergild together.

We cannot suppose that these persons both pay and are outlawed. Is not the real parallel to be sought in the Kentish laws, where the slayer pays the whole wergild, but if he leaves the country (*of lande gewite*þ), his kinsmen are liable for half the sum? We have several times had occasion to observe in the course of this work that the escape of the slayer involves his kindred in greater pecuniary liabilities than would otherwise be the case[1]. Both in Norwegian and Danish laws the kindred are declared to have no wergild liability unless the slayer escapes, but if he succeeds in this, they are in Norway liable for half the sum, and in Denmark for the whole. The ordinance of King Valdemar II. of Denmark furnishes an even closer parallel to our text. It dates from 1204 :

> "If a man slays another man, let him compensate entirely out of his own property, unless another kinsman will in his kindliness contribute somewhat thereto....If he does not offer compensation at the three (subsequent) *Things*, let him be outlawed and let him flee from the kingdom....After he has fled, let his next kinsman on his father's side, and another on his mother's side... pay two parts (of the wergild) and take two parts of the truce, and *let him flee with the third part*[2]."

It is thus unsafe to assume that the Anglo-Saxon passage means anything more than that the kindred become liable for part of the wergild (in normal cases for two-thirds) if the slayer is outlawed or has fled. But the slayer can only be outlawed if, presumably owing to lack of property, he has not paid the wergild himself. Incidentally we glean that whether a man has kinsmen or not, he is thought of as belonging to some kind of society

---

[1] Cp. p. 206, note 2, supra.   [2] p. 82, supra.

whose members are responsible for one another, but where the bond is not that of blood.

The next clause, c. 28, deals with the destination of the wergild of a kinless man if such should be slain: half is to go to the king, half to the *gegildan*. With regard to the receipt of wergild where there were kinsmen, we gather that it was at any rate not limited to heirs only: if a man slays the child of an escaped nun, let him pay the share due to the maternal relatives to the king, but let the paternal kinsmen receive the share due to them (c. 8, 3).

The part played by kinsmen in other connections must not be neglected, though there is nothing to lead us to suppose that the 'kinsmen' referred to are any others than the immediate family.

C. 1, § 2. A pledge-breaker while in prison is to be fed by his kinsmen if he himself has no means of subsistence. As so often in the Anglo-Saxon laws, the possibility of his being without kinsmen is taken into account.

C. 42, § 1. If a man is beleaguered by an enemy seeking rightful vengeance, and yields and gives up his weapons, he can be kept within for 30 nights, but his whereabouts and position must be announced to his relatives and friends (presumably in order that they may treat with the avenger). Similarly if he has sought sanctuary and has given up his weapons (§ 2). If under such circumstances the man is slain by his enemy, the latter shall pay wergild, and has 'forfeited his own kinsman'—i.e. has lost right to wergild for the kinsman whom he thus avenged (§ 4).

We see here some traces of greatly restricted blood-feuds, but we can hardly judge of their importance while we are in entire ignorance of the numbers of kinsmen who join in the negotiations.

It is perhaps a sign of the times that it is expressly stated that a man may fight on behalf of his own kinsman should the latter be unjustly accused—unless it be against his own lord[1]. A good many of Alfred's laws concern the relation between lord and man: thus a man may fight for his lord without involving himself in feud (42, 5): treachery to the lord is punishable by death (Introd. § 49, 7). But more remarkable is the indication that the lord pays for the misdeeds of his

---

[1] Cp. 42, § 6, the story of Cynewulf and Cyneheard, infra.

'man'; a man leaving a district in order to seek a lord must notify the ealdorman; if after he has changed his lord it appears that he had committed a crime while with the previous one, "*let him who has now taken him as man compensate for it*" (37, § 2).

As in Ine's laws, there is no mention of oath-helpers of the kindred.

The treaty of Alfred and Guthrum yields, as might be expected, no information regarding the kindreds, and we learn no more about the duties and privileges of kinship until we come to Eadweard's law promulgated at Exeter (924–5). Here (II. 6) as indicated in Ine, 24, the kinsmen can forsake a man guilty of theft, and refuse to pay compensation for him, so that he falls into slavery, in which case they have no claim to wergild if he is slain[1].

With Æthelstan's laws we have reached the period when Dane and Anglo-Saxon had settled down in peace. It is supposed that Danish administrative ideas had already begun to influence Anglo-Saxon kings by Alfred's time[2]. Among the 'duces' or 'ministri' whose names are attached at the foot of Æthelstan's charters not less than 13 bear Scandinavian names[3], and it is impossible to suppose that these members of the king's Council had no influence in legislation. When therefore we find for the first time in Anglo-Saxon law that the relatives stand surety for a kinsman convicted of theft (II. 1, §§ 3, 4) or homicidal witchcraft (6) (though they can give him up to justice if he commits a second offence); that the *mægð* is to find a lord for the lordless man[4] (II. 2); that the 'kinsmen' deliver the defaulting member of their family from prison by payment of a fine (6, § 1); that anyone taking in a kinsman from another

---

[1] Compare with this Ditmarschen: the kinsmen are forced, up to 1539, to pay compensation for goods stolen by a member of their kindred (p. 129, supra).

[2] Steenstrup, *Danelag*, pp. 76 f.: also Schmid, p. 614, s.v. *hundred*.

[3] Chadwick, *Studies in A. S. Inst.* p. 186.

[4] But cp. Pollock and Maitland, pp. 241–2: "We must resist the temptation to speak of the mægð as if it were a kind of corporation..., when the 'kindred' of a lordless man is ordered to find him a lord, we need not think of this as a command addressed to corporations, or even to permanently organized groups of men: it may well be addressed to each and all of those persons who would be entitled to share the wergild of this lordless man."

district must either deliver him to justice, if he is found to be a law-breaker, or pay compensation for him (c. 8); that 12 kinsmen go bail for the appearance of a peasant under suspicion (III. 7, § 2)[1]—all these new features must strike us as an administrative novelty, just as the orderly division of the country into hundreds appears to be an administrative novelty. Both are no doubt to be put down to the same source. Perhaps it is not fanciful to attribute the greatly increased frequency of the word *mægð*, where the older laws usually had *mægas* or occasionally *mægburh*, to the constant necessity for translating the Danish *ætt* or *kyn*[2]. It is true that very soon we find no more trace of the kindreds among the Danes than among the Anglo-Saxons, but there can be no doubt that men coming straight from a country where the kindred-system permeated society would at first expect all the old regulations and sanctions of kindred to hold good and to be effective in their new society.

Æthelstan's laws also contain an ordinance about clearing the name of a man slain as a thief: three relatives, two of the paternal and one of the maternal kindred, shall swear that they know of no theft committed by their kinsman. The slayer is to appear with 11 others, for a counter-oath, but it is not stated that these also shall be kinsmen[3]; and indeed there would be no point in such a provision.

There are two further passages of interest in Æthelstan's laws, and as they are somewhat similar we will consider them together. The first is from the Kentish ordinances (III.) from which we have already quoted, and is repeated in IV. (the Concilium Thunresfeldense), while what is usually taken to be a reference to it occurs in V. The first passage runs as follows (III. 6, practically repeated in IV. 3): "And if any man be so rich or be of so great a *parentela* that he cannot be punished, and if he will not refrain from the same (offence)—he is to be removed into another part of the kingdom."

---
[1] It is doubtful whether these provisions are more than a rough draft of no legislative force: Æth. V. repeated most of the clauses. It only exists in the Lat.

[2] I think I am right in saying that *mægð*, in the sense of kindred, only occurs once in all the chapters of earlier law (Ine, 76, § 1); *mægburh* once in Ine, 74, § 1, and once in Alfred, 41.

[3] Æthelstan II. 11. Cp. V. 1, § 5.

v. Prol. 1 seems to explain this further: "Now I have decided with the councillors who were with me at Christmas in Exeter, that those [disturbers of the peace] be ready, themselves with wife and movable property and everything, to fare whither I will—unless they will hereafter refrain (from misdeeds)—in such fashion, that they never afterwards come into the land (neighbourhood)."

All these ordinances seem to be aimed at certain definite malefactors who are defying the king's power. They can be supported either by wealth or by numerous or powerful kinsmen, probably by both, but we need not at once decide that a 'kindred' is banding itself together against the king, especially as we note that it is only the offender and his wife who are banished[1].

We now come to what is perhaps the most overworked passage in the Anglo-Saxon laws. It is in the Ordinances of Æthelstan for London. The Londoners declare (Æthelstan VI. 8, § 2):

"And if it should happen that any *mægð* should be so powerful and so large, whether in the land (London territory?) or out of it, whether it be 12-hynde or 2-hynde, that it refuses us our right and steps in to protect the thief, that we ride thither in full force" etc.

This is the *locus classicus* for those who wish to prove the solidarity of the kindred in England. Yet is it not almost impossible to suppose that 'kindreds' able to resist the armed forces of London could have existed in England and yet left no other traces of themselves than this solitary passage, no reference in repressive ordinances, or in charters? If we accept *mægð* as meaning 'kindred' in this sense, we shall have to suppose a far greater solidarity of the kin in England than anywhere else, for the Teutonic kindred has no local habitation to enable its enemies to ride out 'thither.' It seems to be forgotten that the Anglo-Saxon *mægð* has to do duty for 'family' (in the modern sense of the word), 'lineage,' 'house,' as well as for 'kindred[2],' just as *magas* alternates with *ieldran* for 'ancestors,'

---

[1] This is quite definitely stated; and we have not the least reason to include the rest of the kindred. Their inclusion would most certainly be expressly stated if it was intended: the paragraph carefully specifies the wife and the movable property and 'everything.'

[2] Anglo-Saxon also has the words *cynn*, *sibb*, but makes very little use of them. It is significant that outside the glossaries, Anglo-Saxon has extremely few words for

and also signifies 'descendants.' As a matter of fact we have no authority whatever, save the doubtful appeal to Continental analogies, for translating *mægð* as 'kindred' rather than as 'family.' In the Danish and North German laws there are plenty of passages which force us to translate *kjøn, slachte*, etc. as 'kindred' rather than as 'family,' but in England no passage, in the laws or out of them, gives the slightest indication of the limits of the *mægð*[1]; and there is no passage which would not make equally good (or better) sense if the word were translated 'family.' The only members of the *mægð* actually mentioned in the A.-S. laws are parents, children (brother and sister) and father's brother[2]. There is another feature of the Anglo-Saxon laws which should warn us of the danger of using the word 'kindred' with too great certainty. The frequency with which the laws consider the case of the kinless individual has hardly received the attention it deserves. The wergild clauses of Ine and Alfred, providing for the case of a man without maternal or paternal kinsmen, might be set aside on the hypothesis that they deal with an individual of serf ancestry on one side or both, but we cannot explain other cases in this manner—for instance the case of the man in prison (Alfred I, § 3) where provision is made for the event of his having no kinsmen, or Æthelred VIII. 22, or Cnut II. 35. In most Continental and

---

relationships, and never attempts, in the charters, to describe a more distant kinsman than "nephew's child" etc. Of the division of the kindred into four and eight branches, characteristic of Low German laws, there are only the faintest linguistic traces (cneow, etc.). These divisions are no longer groups of persons, but only a way of reckoning relationship (Bateson, *Borough Customs*, I. 274).

It is true that certain relatives, "inside the knee," are grouped together in the fragment *Be wergilde* (see below, p. 224), but as a matter of fact the father's brother, there classed as "inside the knee," cannot really be reckoned as inside it: he is obviously in the 'first knee' with other uncles, and with grandparents and grandchildren. 'Knee' is used in the ungermanic sense of 'generation' in the A.-S. poem *Daniel*, and in Ælfric, *Homilies*, II. 190; so also apparently in William of Malmesbury, I. 84: "Offa quinto genu Pendae abnepos": see Liebermann, II. 2, s.v. *Sippe* 12 a.

[1] Æthelred VI. 12 (Cnut I. 7) merely gives the limits of affinity from the ecclesiastical point of view.

[2] It is doubtless the feeling that 'kindred' implies more than we have any right to assume which induces Bosworth-Toller to suggest the translation 'a collection of magas,' 'kinsmen' for *mægð*.

Scandinavian laws we find clauses throwing responsibility on to more distant kinsmen in the absence of nearer relatives, but the assumption that a man is likely to have no 'kindred' is not made in any other laws unless in the Ribuarian. The most likely explanation of this phenomenon in England is that the *mægð* was of very limited extent. It is easily conceivable that a man may be without quite near living relatives, but it must be exceedingly rare for a man not to possess fourth, third or second cousins[1]. If, however, the *mægð* did not include these more distant relatives, a man could be called *mægleas* who merely did not happen to possess any relative within a narrow circle of kinship. This interpretation of these otherwise unexplained clauses must necessarily be hypothetical, but corroborative evidence is afforded by the absence of all regulations, so common in other laws, throwing the responsibility on to more distant kinsmen in the case of the absence of nearer ones.

But to return to the *mægð* in the London passage. There is no more need to interpret the word in this case as 'kindred' than there is to take 'an attack by the Sturlungs' in an Icelandic Saga, to mean more than that the force was headed by one or two 'Sturlungs' and was composed of their followers. We shall probably be nearer the mark if we translate *mægð* as 'house' or 'family' (with 'followers' understood).

There is one more point of interest in the ordinances for London. A man found guilty (by ordeal) of theft shall be put to death, 'unless the kinsmen and the lord' redeem him by paying his wergild (as a fine) and full compensation, and further stand surety that he will refrain from every misdeed in future (VI. 1, § 4). The inclusion of the *lord* is worth notice. But since there is no compulsion on the kinsfolk to come forward, we cannot regard this passage as evidence of strong kinship-solidarity, since no more is asked of the kindred than relatives of to-day would be willing to do to save a kinsman from a shameful death.

Eadmund's secular laws mark a notable advance in one

---

[1] Liebermann, regarding the *mægð* as a full *Sippe*, observes in this connection: "Dass jemandem niemand von der einen Seite mehr lebte, könnte nur Ausnahme sein" (II. 2, s.v. *Sippe* 8).

respect: private warfare between families, as a result of a slaying, is to be stamped out, and the slayer alone is to bear the feud, if feud there is to be.

II. 1. "If henceforth anyone kills any man, let him himself bear the feud, unless with the help of friends he pays full wergild within 12 months, whatever the birth (of the slain man)," i.e. however high the wergild be). It must be remembered that a slayer is not involved in a feud unless he cannot or will not pay wergild; and if he can pay wergild there is no feud. So here we must assume that the slayer has not been able to produce the sum out of his own pocket, and that his kinsmen have been unable or unwilling to help him. That even this secondary liability of the kinsmen is purely voluntary is seen from the next clause:

§ 1. "If the mægð forsakes him, and will not pay for him, then I will, that all the mægð be without feud, save the actual delinquent, if they give him thereafter neither food nor protection.

§ 2. If however thereafter any one of his kinsmen shelter him, then let him be liable to the king for all that he possesses, and bear the feud with the mægð (of the slain), for they (the kinsmen) had before forsaken the slayer.

§ 3. If however one of the other mægð takes vengeance on any other man than the actual delinquent, let him be outlaw to the king and to all his (the king's) friends, and lose all that he possesses."

In § 4 the king adds that he will have no shedder of blood taking refuge in his court, until he has submitted to ecclesiastical penance and has taken upon himself, as against the mægð[1] (of the slain), the compensation demanded by them (?).

C. 7 deals at length with the formalities of reconciliation between two kindreds, and shows undoubted Scandinavian influence in its wording, as well as probably in the ideas expressed:

"Wise men (witan) shall compose[2] feuds; first, according to folk-right, the slayer shall pledge himself to his representative (forespeca) by handsel[3], and this representative to the kinsmen (of the slain) that the slayer will compensate the mægð. § 1. Then it is fitting that (the injured mægð) should pledge themselves by handsel to the slayer's representative that the slayer may

---

[1] So text B: "wið ða mægðe gebet on bote befangen"—a difficult reading. H. has "wið þa ægðer gebet" etc.; Ld. "ðæm mægðe gebete"; B. "ðam ægðe." Quadripartitus omits the whole clause.

[2] sectan for 'sehtan,' Scand. sætta.   [3] on hand syllan.

approach in truce[1] and pledge himself to the wergild. § 2. After he has pledged himself to this, then let him find surety therefor. § 3. When this is done, then the king's *mund* (protection, i.e. peace) should be established : 21 nights from that day let *healsfang* be paid, 21 nights later *manbot* (fine to the lord), 21 nights later the first instalment of the wergild."

We note *sectan*, from the Scandinavian *sætta*, and the use of the Scandinavian word *grið*, actually in its right meaning of truce, and not in the derivative meanings which it eventually obtained in Anglo-Saxon ; and we are thus led to look for other traces of Scandinavian influence, but unfortunately we know so little of English procedure on such occasions that it is difficult to state categorically what is and what is not Anglo-Saxon. We hear a great deal of the composing of quarrels by arbitrators in Norwegian laws and in Icelandic sagas : we have never heard of it before in Anglo-Saxon records, but that may be due to their paucity[2]. Pledging by hand-clasp is a very definite feature of Scandinavian custom[3], and the English noun *handsel* is definitely a Scandinavian loan-word[4]. We cannot be certain that the Anglo-Saxons had not the same custom, but it is at least curious, in that case, that the only references to it in the post-Conquest Borough Customs are both in towns within the Danelaw[5].

We can hardly help remembering that Oda, Archbishop of Canterbury from 942 onwards, was of pure Scandinavian birth. We know that the reconciliation between two kindreds was of the nature of a solemn ritual in Denmark right up to the 17th century ; in England such reconciliations have left only the faintest traces, in strong contrast even to North French custom. Are we not justified in supposing that the Danish

---

[1] *grið* (Scand.).

[2] With regard to this passage, Steenstrup (*Danelag*, p. 300) says: "Man kan ikke hævde, at denne Række Regel om Wergilds Udredelsesmaade ikke er angelsaksisk, thi dertil mangler os fra engelsk side alle Hjælpemidler, men vi kunne fastslaa, at Reglerne i høj grad ligne de nordiske Love og at mange enkelte Udtryk ere laante fra Norden."

[3] For handclasp in Norway, cp. Appendix II. No. 1 ; for Iceland see Sagas passim.

[4] Skeat, *Etym. Dict.* s.v.

[5] Lynn (1388) and Grimsby (1259): Bateson, *Borough Customs*, II. 171-2 (note) and 182.

ritual of reconciliation, as practised by the Danes in England, would have had a considerable influence on native Anglo-Saxon practice; and is not this the most probable explanation of the Scandinavian features in the procedure just quoted? It is to say the least not usual to borrow foreign words to describe an entirely indigenous proceeding. But more of this later.

Eadgar's law contains nothing germane to the object of our search, and we pass on to the voluminous legislation of Æthelred. There is an obscure reference to the 'nearest relatives' in the Treaty with Olaf (c. 6), which we can safely neglect. In the law entitled *Be cyricgriðe* (VIII. Æthelred, 1014), we find the sanctuary-fugitive paying wergild to Church and King 'as well as *mægbot* and *manbot*' (c. 3)[1]. Whether *mægbot* here means payment to the godfather, as in the earlier passage (Ine, c. 76), cannot be definitely decided, but our knowledge of Æthelred's ecclesiastical sympathies will incline us to that view.

We can now devote ourselves to the case of the clerics of the various grades, the only class about whom Æthelred troubles to issue wergild-ordinances. Before examining these clauses in detail it will be well to recall that in Alfred 21 a priest is not expected to pay wergild if he slays a man (in this passage his lord may pay it for him). This is consistent with Continental practice[2].

C. 22. "If a friendless altar-servant is accused, who has no oath-helpers," he is to clear himself by a suitable ordeal. As there has as yet been no reference to oath-helpers of the kindred in the A.-S. laws, we need not suppose that the 'friendless' man means merely 'kinless[3],' and we can pass on to the next clause.

23. "And if a cleric is charged with manslaughter, and it is said that he

---

[1] If *mægbot* does refer to kin-compensation, it is worth while noting that it is only used for the *recipients*' kin, unlike the Dan. ættarbot, the Dutch maechzoen, etc.

[2] Jutish Law: § 26. "Clerks and women do not pay compensation, and they do not take compensation, however near they are in birth, because they may not take vengeance on any man nor any man on them." *A propos* of this ordinance it might be remarked that A.-S. law never considers the question whether clerics should pay or receive a quota of wergild for a kinsman's act or death.

[3] Liebermann, II. 2 (s.v. *Sippe* 1 c), "Den Gegensatz zum *freondleas* bildet wer *geferan* [comrades] hat, II. Cnut 35, 1; beides umfasst die Sippe mit, doch vielleicht auch andere Genossenschaft daneben."

was the actual culprit or incited others thereto, let him swear himself clear with his kinsmen, those who have to bear feud with him (?)[1], or compensate."

If we lose sight of the fact that a priest cannot bear feud or pay wergild, we shall of course jump to the conclusion that this passage shows participation of the kindred in all cases; in spite of Eadmund's express limitation of feuds to the actual slayer. But the true explanation is surely that, as a cleric cannot pay wergild for himself, his kinsmen must do it for him or suffer the feud. Whether more than father and brothers were implicated it would be hard to say; but in any case this passage gives no support to the idea that the kinsmen of *laymen* are liable to contribute towards the wergild or suffer feud. Clause 24 provides for the case of the cleric's kinlessness. Cap. 25 gives the same immunity to the monk, but adds that in entering the order he has definitely withdrawn from his *mæglagu*, so we may assume that his kinsmen do not have to pay either.

We must now consider the laws of Cnut. These differ from the preceding laws, since he does not content himself with issuing new ordinances, but makes an attempt at codifying the whole body of Anglo-Saxon law. With the repetitions of old law we shall not concern ourselves, but we may note in passing that while it is clear that everyone must have a *borh*, some one to stand surety for him (II. 20, 20 a), there is no repetition of Eadmund's clauses about the *mægð* acting in that capacity. Clause 35 speaks of "a friendless man and one come from afar" being "so oppressed by friendlessness that he has no one to stand surety for him," but it is surely rash to translate *freondleas* as *sippenloser*[2].

The only addition to previous wergild clauses is that of the slayer of an altar-servant: he is an outlaw unless he does much penance and compensates the *mægð* (II. 39).

The laws of Cnut are the last of the long series of pre-Norman legislation. But there are various stray documents, generally undated and even undateable, of which several can

---

[1] " þe fæhðe moton *mid* beran oððe forebetan."
[2] Liebermann's tr.

have had no legislative authority, but which are yet of importance in determining the customs of pre-Norman times. To these we must now turn. Those which bear some relation to the subject of our inquiry are: *Norðleoda lagu, Norðhymbra Preosta lagu*, and a fragment entitled *Be wergilde*.

The *Norðleoda lagu* is certainly not of native English origin, and its provisions do not concern us here, save the first, which enacts that wergild for a king is paid to his kinsmen, or as one MS.[1] has it, perhaps somewhat tautologically, it belongs to the *mægð* of the king's *cyn* or royal family.

The Northumbrian Priests' Law, from York, attributed by Liebermann to the 11th century, is of course equally Scandinavian, but it is of interest to us as containing a clear reference, the first we have so far come across, to oath-helpers of the kindred:

C. 51. "If a King's thane wishes to clear himself [of the accusation of heathendom] let 12 [oath-helpers] be appointed for him; and let him choose 12 from among his kinsmen [*or*, let 12 be chosen from among his kinsmen?] and 12 unrelated (? *waller wente*)."

It has been suggested that *waller wente* is a corrupted form of Scand. *valin vitni, for *valinkunn vitni*[2], in any case it is frankly admitted that the word is of Scandinavian origin, so that this passage does not help us to find oath-helpers of the kindred among the Anglo-Saxons. It is possibly significant that these oath-helpers of the kindred are only mentioned in the case of king's thanes, i.e. of the Danish conquering class. For other grades of society it is merely stated that the oath-helpers are to be the accused's peers (*gelican*).

We can now turn to the fragment *Be wergilde*. It is found in the MSS. as an appendix to Eadweard and Guthrum's Law (which probably dates from before the middle of the 10th century). Usually, however, the fragment is not considered to have any connection with that document. Liebermann dates it between 944 and c. 1060. It begins with what seems a somewhat

---
[1] Ld.
[2] Cp. Liebermann, p. 383, note ††. Steenstrup points out the resemblance to the Swedish Østgøtalag, Vaþamaal B. c. 13, § 5.

superfluous résumé of the elementary facts of wergild, known from Ine's day onwards, thus:

1. The wergild of a 1200-man is 1200 scillings.
1, 1. The wergild of a 200-man is 200 scillings.
2. When a man is slain, let him be paid for according to his birth.

After these commonplaces, it continues:

3. And it is right that the slayer, as soon as he has pledged himself to wergild, should find wergild-surety such as is right for it, that is: for a 1200-wergild twelve men are right for the wergild-surety: 8 of the paternal *mægð* and 4 of the maternal *mægð*.

4. When this is done, then the king's *mund* (protection, i.e. peace) is established; that is, that all they of either *mægð* jointly (lit. with joint hand) swear on one weapon to the mediator that the king's *mund* shall stand.

4, 1. After 21 nights from this day let 120 sc. be paid as *healsfang* in the case of the 1200 wergild.

5. *Healsfang* belongs to children, brothers and father's brother; that money is not for any kinsmen but those that are within the 'knee.'

6. Twenty-one nights after the day on which *healsfang* is paid, let *manbot* be paid, 21 nights later *fyhtwite*, 21 nights later the first instalment of wergild, and so on, until it is fully paid within the term settled by the arbitrators.

6, 1. Thereafter, if one wishes to receive full friendship [from the injured party] one can proceed 'with love' [Schmid: " mit Liebe vorschreiten "], (*or:* one can attain that by a private reconciliation, Liebermann: "das erlangen durch private Versöhnung ").

There is a close similarity between these regulations and those of Eadmund which we have already discussed. The additional information they afford can be summed up thus:

(1) The nature of the wergild-surety—8 paternal and 4 maternal kinsmen.

(2) The nature of the oath: sworn with 'joint hand' on one weapon to the mediating judge.

(3) The specification of the persons who can receive *healsfang*.

(4) The insertion of the *fihtwite* before the first instalment of the wergild.

(5) The fact that a completer reconciliation can be made 'mid lufe.'

We have already seen that Eadmund's wergild regulations showed Scandinavian influence, and certain of the points just enumerated are equally open to that suspicion:

(1) The oath of 12 kinsmen, in the pre-Conquest laws, appears only here, in the indubitably Scandinavian Northumbrian Priests' Law[1], and among the new regulations of Æthelstan, where 12 kinsmen go bail for the appearance of a delinquent.

(2) A *trygde-ed*, or oath of peace of 12 kinsmen after a slaying, is a feature of the Danish laws, and persists in Danish custom as late as the 16th century[2]. The expression *gemænum handum*[3] exactly corresponds to the 'samblet Haand' of Danish custom: thus a Danish wergild case of 1549 turns on whether the kinsmen did or did not swear (to pay wergild) 'met en samblitt Handtt[4]' or whether each swore for himself. These 'collected hands' are moreover placed on one weapon—which is known to be a Scandinavian form of oath, and which we do not meet again in Anglo-Saxon custom[5]. Perhaps it is worth while to quote from a case recorded at Helsingør in 1567:

"Then in God's name came forward the aforesaid Morthen Perssen, acting on his own behalf and for the said son of his deceased brother and for other common kinsmen on the paternal and maternal side who were not present, (and) Jens Krogermager, Frands Perssen, Christoffer Jörgenssen and Lass Kieldssen (came forward also)...and all together now this day here at the *Thing*, before God and the people, with mouth and hand, all holding (the) sword, gave and promised...peace to the aforesaid Michill Lauessen...and all their common kindred[6]."

---

[1] Here again it is only actually mentioned in the case of nobles.
[2] See supra, p. 92.
[3] The expression *gemænum handum* occurs in Alf. 31, 1: "if a band of men slay a man, let them all pay wergild gemænum hondum—jointly." This however does not refer to taking an oath 'with joint hand on one weapon.'
[4] Cp. Kolderup-Rosenvinge, *Gl. d. D.* I. No. 56.
[5] An oath on arms occurs in the Preston custumal, i.e. within the Danelaw. Bateson, *Borough Customs*, I. 30.
[6] From P. V. Jacobsen's Uddrag etc., *Ny Kgl. Saml.* No. 697 f. 4to. I am indebted to an unpublished treatise by Prof. Poul Jorgensen for references to similar oaths in *Næstveds Tingbøger*, 15 Mar. 1602, and 12 Sept. 1608.

(3) The relatives who are to receive *healsfang*, incontestably an English institution, are carefully specified.

(4) There is very strong reason for supposing that the term *fyht-wite* is only used in the Danelaw. No doubt there was a somewhat similar fine in Wessex (cp. Ine 6, § 4), but this appears to be called *mundbryce*. The significance of two passages in Cnut's laws seems to have escaped attention. In the first, in defining the dues to which the king lays claim, Cnut says: [II. 12] " These are the dues, which the king has over all folk *in Wessex*: that is, *mundbryce* and *hamsocne*, *forstal* and *fyrdwite*..." etc., and II. 14 he claims the same for Mercia. Then he continues, (II. 15) "And in the Danelaw he has *fyhtwite* and *fyrdwite*, *griðbryce* and *hamsocne*...."

The term does not appear until Eadmund's time, and it is doubtful from his reference whether it was then claimed by the king, for he seems to equate it with *manbot*, which fell to the lord: " And I will not, that any *fyhtewite* or *manbot* be forgiven " (II. Edm. 3).

(5) The 'full friendship' is difficult of explanation—as may be gathered from the lack of unanimity in the versions of Schmid and Liebermann[1]—unless recourse is had to Danish custom, when it can easily be explained as a reference to the *gjørsum* or 'additional gift' which we have seen in our study of Danish wergilds to be a varying sum or an object of value[2] given to the kindred of the slain by private arrangement between the parties[3], in addition to the wergild. This extra gift has many names in mediaeval Danish. We find it called *høveskhed*, 'courtesy,' and other terms which are less easy of explanation, such as *Feyring*, *Flining*, *Wandel*, etc. In Low German deeds from Schleswig it is sometimes translated *Minde*, 'love, friendliness,' which can

---

[1] Liebermann's translation shows that he considers this phrase to be a reference to *gjørsum*, for his version is almost a translation of the editor's note to *gjørsum* in the Danish laws, stating that *gjørsum* is given 'by private agreement.' Steenstrup regards the passage in the same light: *Danelag*, p. 300.

[2] Among nobles often a jewel, cp. Bilde-Hak orfejde, supra, p. 89, 'eth clenodie,' and the Støggy-Mogenssen orfejde, Appendix II. No. 4, 'tuende Klenody.' Among non-nobles it was often a piece of black cloth for mourning [hence its name Lediske, Leiden (cloth)]. Cp. Kolderup-Rosenvinge, *Gl. d. D.* I. 56 (1549).

[3] See supra, p. 89, a jewel to be chosen by 6 kinsmen of either side.

hardly fail to remind us of the A.-S. *mid lûfe* of our passage[1]. In 1635 a case occurs in which the kinsmen of the slain refuse to accept the wergild unless a *Mind*, 'friendly gift,' is handed over with it[2]. Of course it is perfectly possible that all these resemblances to Danish custom may be due, not to borrowing, but to a common origin. Still, when we count up the resemblances in the two sets of wergild regulations, we must admit that though the wording, at any rate in the fragment, is Anglo-Saxon, the number of Danish features *not otherwise found in Anglo-Saxon laws* is very considerable. And it is obvious that the two sets of laws must stand or fall together. In Eadmund's law we have the words *sectan* and *grið* (the latter in its proper Scandinavian meaning), the 'handsel' of pledges, and the expression *on hand syllan* with the meaning to promise, which does not occur till the Danish period[3]. In the fragment we have the oath of kinsmen, the *trygde-ed* with joint hand on one weapon, the *fyhtwite*, and a reference that is hard of explanation if it is not to the Danish *gjørsum*, the '*Minde*' of later custom.

We must suppose that the two sets of regulations are independent of each other, since each omits something that the other inserts. Eadmund has the *forespeca*, and the Danish terms *sectan* and *grið*; *Be wergilde* has *fyhtwite* and the reference to *gjørsum*.

A possible explanation of the fragment's combination of Danish and Anglo-Saxon elements would be furnished by the hypothesis that the compiler used two sources, of which one was the earlier Anglo-Saxon laws; and that, in points where he found no Anglo-Saxon regulations, he drew upon the customary law with which he was acquainted, which was of Danelaw origin and very likely not committed to writing[4]. It is to be noted in

---

[1] Schiller and Lübben, *Mittelniederdeutsches Wörterbuch*, s.v. *Minne*, 'Liebe, Huld, Zustimmung,...bes. Güte, *gütliches Übereinkommen, gütliche Beilegung eines Streitpunktes*.
[2] Stemann, *Schl. Rechts- und Gerichtsverfassung im* 17 *Jhdt.* (Schleswig & Flensborg, 1855), p. 67.
[3] Schmid, *Glossar*, s.v. *syllan* and *hand*.
[4] In view of its blending of Scandinavian and Anglo-Saxon custom, it is surely possible that this fragment really has some connection with Eadweard and Guthrum's Law, to which the MSS. attach it.

favour of this theory that every *new* fact he tells us either has a Scandinavian aspect, or else is an explanation of Anglo-Saxon terms, *healsfang, twelf-hynde* and *twy-hynde*. The last two must have had an archaic flavour by the Danish period, and it is improbable that they would be employed at that date by an Anglo-Saxon[1].

The resemblances between the fragment and Eadmund's law would be explained by the fact that both have certain Scandinavian characteristics grafted on to the original A.-S. reconciliation-customs.

On the other hand it is quite possible that the Danish influence observable in both sets of regulations is only indirect, i.e. that certain Danish customs concerning slaying-reconciliations had found their way also into Wessex, and that these two sources do represent Anglo-Saxon custom[2], but only as it was after the Danish invasion. All we would urge is that it is more than rash to look upon either or both of them as of purely Anglo-Saxon origin.

The private compilations of laws known as the *Leis Willelme* and the *Leges Henrici I.* have not, of course, the same value as evidence as the actual legislation of the Anglo-Saxon period. Of the two, the Anglo-French *Leis Willelme* is earlier (Liebermann 1090—1135), and, its author being perhaps a less accomplished jurist, it is perhaps also a more trustworthy reflection of Anglo-Saxon laws than the *Leges Henrici*. Like these, however, it contains inconsistencies due to the fact that its material is drawn from different sources[3]. It was probably composed in Mercia[4].

Unfortunately it tells us almost nothing about wergild. What it does tell us is rather surprising: c. 9, "Of the wergild

---

[1] We may also point out that the *raison d'être* of the oath of peace between the kindreds has departed with Eadmund's ordinance restricting feuds. But we do not lay much stress on this.

[2] For the fragment this explanation is more difficult, as it would hardly account for the *mid lúfe* clause, which is really only explicable as a direct translation from Danish.

[3] Cp. Steenstrup, *Danelag*.

[4] See Liebermann's ed. I. p. 492, note *a*.

10 sol. (shillings) shall first be given to the widow and orphans as *halsfang*[1]: and the rest the orphans and kinsmen divide among themselves." The substitution of the widow for the uncle may be considered to show a certain weakening of the bonds of kindred. The participation of the children in both the *halsfang* and in the rest of the wergild suggests that the latter also is becoming gradually restricted to the *heirs*.

Whatever the provenance of this passage, whether it be from Norman unwritten custom or from Mercian law, its very independence of all the older Anglo-Saxon laws known to us (and to the compiler) favours the supposition that it gives an accurate picture of the actual working of wergild customs at the time. This is emphatically not the case with the *Leges Henrici*. The compiler of this collection must have been an ardent jurist, and various clauses indicate that he had all a collector's delight in gathering together any passages, from whatever source, that could so much as illustrate an Anglo-Saxon ordinance. We can believe that provisions from Roman law and even from Salic law might come to be valid in Norman England, but it is impossible to believe that regulations out of the Ripuarian law[2] of the 6th and 7th centuries can have had any validity in the England of the 12th. These borrowings from Continental laws can however usually be recognized[3]: it is more difficult to trace to its source a Danish or, say, a Mercian law, since there remain for our guidance so few fragments of the former and practically nothing of the latter. Still in some instances an inference can be drawn with a fair degree of certainty. Thus we find Æthelstan's ordinance about clearing the name of a man killed as a thief, by means of an oath of one maternal and two paternal kinsmen[4], side by side with the following:

" If their kinsmen wish to clear those who have been put to death unjustly and without trial (sine judicio) it is permitted to them according to ancient law to clear them by *werelade*. If he (the slain man) were of £4 birth,

---

[1] As a matter of fact it is only the 14th cent. MS. (Pseudo-Ingulf) which has *halsfang*, the more trustworthy MS. Hk. has *hamsochne* (which must be an error): the Latin translation (of about 1200?) omits the word altogether.
[2] Cp. Leg. Hen. 70, 18.
[3] See Liebermann's edition.   [4] II. Æthelstan 11. Leg. Hen. 74, 2.

with 12 : let 8 be on the paternal side, 4 on the maternal. If of £14 [more probably £25[1]] (birth), with 16[2]."

These two passages are mutually exclusive and must be from different sources. We can put our finger on the passage corresponding to the first of the two (74, 2) in the Wessex laws, but the second we have not met before in any Anglo-Saxon law. We are thus led to deduce their non-Wessex origin. We have already, however, seen reason to suspect that the oath of 12 kinsmen, when it occurs in England, is of Danish origin; and we further note the similarity of the wording of this passage to the Northumbrian Priests' Law, c. 51, and to c. 3 of *Be wergilde*, which we hold to be Danish also. The Latin version of the latter even gives us the equation 12-hynde = £25 wergild[3].

In view of these resemblances as well as of the differences between it and the corresponding Wessex law, it does not seem unjustifiable to suppose that while the first passage we quoted, with its three kinsmen, represents Anglo-Saxon law, the second, with twelve, is from the Danelaw[4]. Certain passages relating to homicide can also be attributed to the Danelaw with a fair degree of certainty. After repeating an ordinance similar to Alfred c. 27, 1, regulating the wergild of a slain man who had no kindred on the paternal side, the *Leges* go on to say: "If anyone in a similar position (hujus modi) commit homicide, his kinsmen pay so much of the wergild as they would receive for him, if he were killed. If he have kinsmen on the paternal side and not on the maternal, and kills a man, let those related to him pay as much as they would receive for his death, that is, two parts of his wergild[5]."

It is possible that this passage may be intended as a sort of paraphrase of Alfred 27, omitting, however, the real point of that passage, the outlawry or liability of the slayer. It is quite possible that the paternal kinsmen of the slain should receive two-thirds of the wergild, and the maternal kinsmen one-third. But if the

---

[1] Liebermann, p. 591, note *n*.   [2] Leg. Hen. 74.
[3] The same as in Æthelred's treaty, II. 5.
[4] Presumably 64, 4 is also due to Scand. influence as far as the oath is concerned: "ut qui ex parte patris erunt fracto iuramento, qui ex materne cognacione erunt plano se sacramento iuraturos aduertat." We have seen that this oath is not of kinsmen in A.-S. law.   [5] Leg. Hen. 75, 9.

kinsmen of the slayer also pay at this rate, the slayer himself is not liable at all, which we have already seen to be contrary to Anglo-Saxon law.

Chapter 76 gives a series of wergild regulations, almost all taken from the fragment *Be wergilde*, though the recipients of *halsfang* are (possibly by a misunderstanding of the A.-S. *fæderan*), declared to be *father*, son or brother of the slain, or in their absence the nearest relative of the father. It agrees, however, with *Be wergilde* in devoting the sum to agnates.

We note that the whole wergild is paid in 4 instalments. Whereas Ine 54, 1 speaks of a sword, a slave and a byrnie as admissible wergild-currency in case of need, the *Leges* mention sheep and a horse.

We find the old law, that the 'men' of a lord could fight for him without becoming themselves subject to feud (Alf. 42, 5), but it is greatly expanded (88, 9, 9 *a*).

Cap. 88, 11 quaintly warns persons engaged in feuds that they must keep the proportion of 2 : 1 in their slayings of the paternal and maternal kinsmen of their enemy (!), otherwise the kinsmen of the slain can claim a surplus of wergild or feud, "*tam in generositate*[1] *quam in propinquiori pertinencia.*" We have not found this cold-blooded reckoning in any of our researches into feuds, nor can it be said to be practically feasible, unless perhaps among Welsh or Scotch clans. It probably originates in the laborious fancy of a jurist.

Strangely contrasting with this picture of cohesive kindreds, cap. 88, 17 observes that "it is better in every wergild that the kinsmen of the homicide make peace at the same time rather than singly." Individuals making peace separately, as this implies, would show a declension of the kindred as great as in Iceland. If this represents old Anglo-Saxon custom, and not merely the conditions of the 12th century, we were well advised to attribute to the Danes the solemn reconciliation and oaths 'with joint hand.'

We have already observed that laws are unsatisfactory evidence in the matter of kinship-solidarity, and especially in wergild-provisions, since they are liable either to preserve archaic and obsolete features, sometimes for an incredibly long period of time, or to mislead in the other direction, through our inability to distinguish statements of customary law from the

---

[1] Liebermann translates this "Geschlecht im weiteren Sinne."

innovations of kings. It is however probable that the Anglo-Saxon laws give on the whole a more correct impression in these matters than many of the other laws with which we have dealt in the course of this work. They are neither composed entirely of statements of custom, nor entirely of royal edicts; and yet we do not find the gross discrepancies between the two elements which are so common on the Continent. There may be archaic features: there may be royal innovations which never became custom, but the picture of the position of kinsmen is on the whole remarkably homogeneous. We gather that, in Kent and apparently in Wessex, the slayer alone paid wergild to the slain man's relatives, unless he had insufficient means, fled, or was outlawed, and we infer that the group of recipients would not be very large. In this connection we may note that in the Dialogues of Ecgbert (732—766) it is asked whether the slayer of a priest is to pay the *pretium sanguinis* to the Church or to the 'near relations[1]' (*propinquis*). The answer is also significant, for it gives the wergild to the Church. Seebohm considers this as evidence that the Church has succumbed to tribal custom, but it would surely be more correct to say that the Church succumbed to the barbaric custom of taking money for a slaying, but set aside the claim of the kindred by taking the whole sum. If the rulings of Ecgbert are founded on custom, this evidence would go to prove that the solidarity of the kindred was as much limited in the North, in pre-Danish times, as in Kent or Wessex.

It would also seem that there were in the earlier period no oath-helpers of the kindred (unless the three kinsmen mentioned in Æthelstan II., c. 11, can be counted as such). If we reject the evidence in favour of a Scandinavian origin for the fragment *Be wergilde*—which is difficult—we might claim that 12 kinsmen of a king's thane who has committed manslaughter act as sureties for the payment of wergild in Anglo-Saxon custom[2]; but even so the sphere of the kindred is very much restricted; for, from the time of the earliest laws, 'credible persons' or 'neighbours' or 'peers' have ousted the kindred from oaths of compurgation.

---

[1] So translated by Seebohm, p. 382. The passage is quoted by Schmid, s.v. *Geistliche*.   [2] This would be hard to reconcile with Leg. Hen. 88, 17.

In post-Conquest Borough Customs[1] compurgation is as favourite a method of proof as in any Continental laws, but only twice do we find kinsmen called in to act. In London six of them swear that a householder was only defending his house from an unwelcome guest when he killed an intruder[2]. At Dunwich (in the Danelaw) a man accused of murder clears himself with twenty-four of his neighbours and kinsmen[3]. This fact is the more remarkable because the oath of kinsmen was common in Danish law.

The only trace of a responsibility of the kinsmen for the maintenance of pauper relatives is contained in the ordinance of Alfred providing that if the imprisoned pledge-breaker has no means of subsistence of his own, his kinsmen are to feed him, if he has any[4].

The question of *odal* landholding is somewhat complex. Alfred's law, c. 41, says that if land is left by charter (book-land) with the express proviso that it is not to go out of the kindred (*mægburh*), this proviso must be respected, and anyone objecting to the alienation of such land must do so in presence of his kinsmen. The mention of the 'express proviso' seems to preclude the existence of any odal custom or *retrait lignager* in book-land. On the other hand, a claim of the nearest kinsman is suggested in the Ramsey and Ely histories, and is definitely provided for in a number of borough customs, not only in the Danelaw[5]. But the problem hardly concerns us here, for we have already observed (p. 5, supra) that the right

---

[1] See Bateson, *Borough Customs*, I. Index of Matters, s.v. *compurgation*; Ballard, *British Borough Charters*, pp. 137-9.

[2] In the London Libertas of 1133-54, cap. 2; Liebermann, I. p. 673.

[3] Ballard, op. cit., p. 139 (1215).

[4] Liebermann (II. 2 s.v. Sippe, 16) deduces a responsibility of the kindred towards a needy kinsman from the fact that they are forbidden to give an outlawed kinsman food or protection (II. Eadm. 1, § 2). But this hardly follows, for the giving of food or shelter to the outlaw is only expressly forbidden to kinsmen because they are the most likely to commit the offence. If we could reason in the way suggested, should we not have to assume that in Norway and Iceland everyone was bound to support a needy person, whether of the kin or not, for we find it expressly stated that *no one* is to give food or shelter to the outlaw? In any case, it is not the 'kindred' which is here spoken of, but only the individual kinsman (*hwilc his maga*).

[5] Ballard, p. cxxxiv (table).

of pre-emption does not involve cohesion of the kin. It is worth while remarking, however, that whereas it exists in Denmark, North Germany and France up to the 17th and 18th centuries, the sporadic evidences of it in English local customs disappear comparatively early. The Anglo-Saxon law of inheritance is chiefly remarkable for its testamentary freedom, which in itself affords strong evidence for the individual's independence of his kindred.

In what may be called the Danish period, by which I do not mean the period of actual invasion, but that of peaceful influence, there is a certain amount of evidence, in the laws of Æthelstan, that more was expected of the kindred, and this we attributed to Danish influence. But judging from the fact that Cnut omits these regulations in his re-issue of almost all the more important Anglo-Saxon laws, it would seem that the kindred had been found incapable of meeting the responsibility placed on it, even though it was of a kind which might rightly be demanded of a mere family.

We have further observed that in a few fragments of custom from the Danelaw the kindred shows itself very slightly more cohesive, but there is every reason to hold that this characteristic of the Scandinavian settlers was soon lost[1].

The real significance of the Anglo-Saxon laws with respect to the kindred consists chiefly in its omissions. We must emphasize the entire absence of any statement, or even hint, as to how far the *mægð* extended, and of any regulations for the distribution of wergild among persons more distant than the immediate family. There is also no sign of the usual Continental distinction between heir's compensation and kindred-compensation.

Let us now compare these results, gleaned from the laws, with such evidence as is afforded by the charters.

Firstly there is a remarkable paucity of references to the *mægð*. There seem to be no *Sühngerichte*, as on the Continent,

---

[1] Cp. Vinogradoff, *English Society in the 11th century*, p. 447: "Altogether it seems clear that tribal ties did not play an important part in those districts of England conquered and re-colonized by bands of warriors organized as military hosts and voluntary guild associations."

nor is there any trace of the forswearing of one member of the kindred by all the others, which Eadmund's law restricting feud (II. 1) would lead us to expect in England, if the *mægð* had been wider than the mere family.

The chief case in which the word *mægð* occurs is in the deed setting forth the terms made between Bishop Werferð of Worcester and one Eadnoð[1]. A previous bishop had given land at Sodbury to Eadnoð's ancestor, on condition that it should always be inherited by a cleric, or else should lapse to the see of Worcester. On the death of the second holder the family refused to give it up, though they were all lay, and according to the bishop "the *mægð* thus bereaved the spirits of their forbears of the land, as well as the bishop and church." The bishop pleads his cause against the 'kinsmen' (*magas*); and three persons, presumably these same kinsmen, promise to give up the land if they cannot find someone in their *mægð* to take orders and possess the land. "Then Eadnoð, who had the land, offered it to all the family, whether anyone would so obtain it." No one could be found, and the rest of the tale does not concern us. But it will be readily seen that there is nothing more in the tale than might happen if land were left on such conditions at the present day. Indeed it might probably be paralleled in the case of persons of, let us say, the 19th century, seeking to keep a living 'in the family.'

One would expect to find the *mægð* mentioned in wills, but this is not the case. Among all the wills which have come down to us, I only find one which notes the presence of kinsmen, and in this case ten relatives are witnesses to the deed[2]. But otherwise the wills are most discouraging to anyone seeking for evidence of the obligations of kinship. It is true there is only testamentary freedom with regard to 'book-land,' but this book-land can be bequeathed to churches without so much as a mention of the kinsmen's consent, which was obligatory even in France[3]. We even find, as a result of a suit by a son against his mother (in itself an illegal action in most Teutonic

---

[1] Birch, II. pp. 285 f., Thorpe, p. 166.
[2] Birch III. p. 373. Will of Byrhtric and Ælfswyð of Meopham, Kent.
[3] References in Brunner, *Deutsche Rechtsgesch.* 2nd ed. p. 126.

countries at this stage), that a mother leaves all her land and property away from her son and to a married kinswoman[1].

Of wergild we learn nothing, except that a sum described as 'my wergild' or 'my two wergilds' was sometimes bequeathed to St Peter[2] or to the church. Incidentally, from the story of Æthelstan of Sunbury, we learn that a man who had to pay wergild as a fine for breach of the law usually paid it himself, without the help even of a brother[3].

One other point must be noted. In the fragment entitled *Be wifmannes beweddung* the consent of the 'friends' seems to be necessary (c. 1), and 'friends' on both sides act as sureties. It is usually assumed, and seems probable, that these 'friends' are kinsmen, but in a marriage deed that has come down to us no consent of the kinsmen is expressed[4].

It is strange that England's great wealth of early charters should yield no single reference which could possibly be taken as a reference to cohesive kindreds. We are now driven back upon the literature, which is also fairly abundant.

From Beowulf we glean nothing that can serve as evidence for kin-solidarity[5]. On the contrary, we find Hrôðgâr, a foreign king, paying compensation on behalf of Ecgþeow for his slaying of Heaðolâf, one of the Wylfing dynasty (l. 470 f.). And from

---

[1] Thorpe, p. 336.

[2] Kemble, 235; Birch, II. 195, 6; Thorpe, p. 349. For these references I am indebted to Miss Harmer, who considers that 'St Peter' probably refers to a church in England, and not to Rome. Is it not possible that this was done with some idea of paying for burial, for which wergild would be a suitable sum as the price of a life? Cp. Kemble, IV. p. 303: Et ego Ærnketel uolo quod in *pretium sepulturae meae* et animae salutem prouenient aecclesiae Ramesiæ XV. librae....

[3] Birch, III. p. 282 (c. 960—962).

[4] Kemble, IV. p. 25 (Wulfric 1023).

[5] The passage, 2887—2889, where the faithful thane warns the cowardly companions of Beowulf:

" ...lond-rihtes môt
þære mæg-burge monna æghwylc
îdel hweorfan, syððan æðelingas
feorran gefricgean fleâm eowerne "

has been translated: "Every man of the kindred shall lose his *lond-riht*, shall be outlawed as soon as the ethelings from a distance shall learn of your flight" (cp. Brunner, *Deutsche Rechtsgeschichte*, 2nd ed., p. 119), but *mægburh* is usually translated in this passage as governed by *londrihtes*, and signifying 'people, nation,' i.e. the Geats.

the passage which describes Hrôðgâr indemnifying with rich gifts the companions of Aeschere, who had been slain by Grendel's mother (ll. 1053 ff.), we can only assume that it was the members of the *comitatus* rather than the kin, who received wergild for a warrior slain in his lord's employ, We are reminded of the participation of the *gegildan* in Alfred's laws (p. 211, supra). The famous entry in the Anglo-Saxon Chronicle under the year 755 reveals an attitude towards the obligations of kinship for which it would be difficult to find a parallel on the Continent:

> Cyneheard and his followers surprise Cynewulf, King of the West Saxons, and kill him. Cynewulf's companions hurry to the scene, scornfully reject Cyneheard's offer of peace, and fight with him until they are all slain but one. Next morning the rest of the king's party come up. To them Cyneheard offers 'self-doom' if they will but grant him peace, and he further points out to them that kinsmen of theirs are among his followers and will not be induced to abandon him. The king's party reply that "no kinsman was dearer to them than their lord[1]," and bid their kinsmen leave Cyneheard and depart unharmed before the fray begins. But these latter declare that they had made a similar offer to their kinsmen among those of the king's party who had already fallen, and that they will heed it no more than did these. So they fight until all Cyneheard's party falls save one.

Thus the followers of Cynewulf regard it as their duty to slay their kinsmen rather than to omit to avenge their lord, or as Plummer observes, "the tie of the comitatus supersedes that of the kin[2]." An attitude similar, if not quite so rigorous, is found in the Icelandic Sagas of the Sturling period, but hardly elsewhere.

An entry under the year 694 is usually regarded as dealing with wergild. The Kentians had burnt Mul, brother of Ceadwalla, King of the West Saxons, with twelve of his companions (687). Ceadwalla dies the following year in Rome, evidently without having extorted compensation. The record for the year 694 runs thus: "In this year the Kentians negotiated with Ine (now King of the West Saxons) and gave him '30 thousands' for that they had previously burnt Mul." The relationship between Mul and Ine is not mentioned in the Chronicle, nor is

---

[1] "þæt him nænig mæg leofre nære þonne hiera hlaford."
[2] *Two Saxon Chronicles*, II. p. 46.

Ine said to be a kinsman of Mul at all, but they would actually appear to have been third cousins[1]. Evidently Ine is exacting compensation, not so much for the death of a relative, as for an act of aggression committed by the Kentians against the West Saxons, and it is therefore doubtful whether the sum is really wergild in the strict sense of the term. No other relatives are mentioned.

A more definite case of wergild is recorded by Bede. Aelfwine was slain in a battle between his brother Egfrid and his sister's husband Ethelred. Egfrid and Ethelred were reconciled through the mediation of Archbishop Theodore, "and the due mulct was paid to the King who was the avenger for the death of his brother[2]." The brother alone is regarded as the avenger (on the Continent the whole kindred were potential avengers in the eyes of the law); and we must further note the violation of the old rule that there should be no wergild within the kindred.

Nor does popular tradition see anything amiss in the idea of wergild restricted to an individual, and that individual a woman.

In the *Leechdoms* there is a story of Thunor's slaying of the two young princes Æthelred and Æthelbriht, and their *sister* was allowed to choose wergild for her brother "in such things as she and her nearest kinsmen liked best. And she then acted thus that she chose the wergild on that island that is called Teneð, that is 80 hides of land in that place, which she received from the king[3]."

Here again only individuals are mentioned. It may be objected that the mention of these individual recipients does not exclude the possibility that they divided the sum afterwards among their kinsmen, or, in the last story, that other kinsmen also received shares which are not mentioned. This is true: but it is none the less strange that all the cases are silent about the kindred.

---

[1] Through their father's great-grandfather, Ceawlin; see under anno 685 (p. 38) and 688 (p. 40).

[2] *Hist. Eccles.* IV. 21 (Sellar's translation). The A.S. version has "ac hé mid feó wiþ *hine* gepingode, ðæt heora sib wæs."

[3] *Leechdoms*, ed. Cockayne, III. 426. "To ðam ðæt hió hyre bróðra wergild gecure on swylcum þingum swylce hyre and hire nýhstan fréondum sêlost lícode. And hió ðá swá dyde ðæt hió ðæt wergeld geceás on ðam íglande ðe Teneð is nemned, ðæt is hundeahtatig hîda landes ðe hió ðær æt ðæm cyninge onfeóng."

ENGLAND

In the Battle of Maldon Oswold and Ealdwold, two brothers, are represented as encouraging their 'kinsmen'—*winemagas*—to bear themselves well in the fight[1], but we can hardly found a theory on the occurrence of this word.

As far as the kindred are concerned, we must admit that Anglo-Saxon literature contrasts strangely with French and North German literature, though, as our sources are usually earlier than the latter, we might expect the contrast to be the other way. The *Chansons de Geste*, which we may equate with Beowulf, are very different from the latter with regard to this point. So are our early historians, Bede and the Chronicle, from the 13th and 14th century chronicles of Belgium and Friesland[2], with their wealth of allusion to kindreds: so, too, is the popular tradition enshrined in the *Leechdoms* compared with the far later popular epic of Reineke Vos[3]. Against these we have to set an almost complete silence as to the *mægð* in Anglo-Saxon literature. In the *Historia Eliensis*, we do, it is true, find a reference to certain evil persons making an attack, by the violence of their *parentela*, upon a farm called Berelea, and obtaining possession of it by force[4]. But as the attack was presumably unexpected, it would not need many armed individuals to obtain possession of it, and we can hardly regard this passage alone as sufficient evidence for cohesive kindreds in England.

In Wulfstan's address to the English we do, however, find the word *mægð*, and it is used with reference to wergild. Wulfstan was Archbishop of York from 1002 to 1023, and, in lamenting the consequences of the inroads of the Vikings, he observes bitterly that if a thrall fled from his lord, and became a viking, and in a subsequent fight killed his lord, the latter would lie 'unpaid for to all his mægð,' while if the lord killed the thrall, he would have to pay wergild as for a thane[5]. The passage is

---

[1] Battle of Maldon, l. 306. The lines 73 ff., where Wulfstan is bidden hold the bridge "cafne mid his cynne (he wæs Ceolan sunu)" appear to mean that Wulfstan, with the rest of his kin, was characterized by readiness in the fight.
[2] See supra, pp. 158 f. [3] Supra, pp. 182 f.
[4] *Hist. Eliensis*, Lib. I. cap. xlv.
[5] In Sweet's *A.-S. Reader*, xvi. l. 116 f.; gyf þræl þæne þegen fullice afylle, licge ægylde ealre his mægðe.

interesting from several points of view, but until we are sure that a *mægð* really means a full kindred, it does not throw much light on the number of recipients for wergild. Far more instructive is his twice-repeated lament over the decay of the closest family ties: "Too often now the kinsman spared (or protected?) kinsmen no more than the stranger, nor father his child, nor sometimes the child his own father, nor one brother the other[1]." And again: "We also know full certainly where that crime[2] happened that the father sold his child for a price, and the child his mother, and one brother sold another into the power of strangers outside this nation[3]."

We are reminded of the prophecy of the wise woman in the Icelandic Völuspá, as to the sins against near kin which would come to pass before Ragnarök. But Wulfstan's is no prophecy, and we may suppose that he was stating the facts, or something like them. It would need more than the one or two cases of the employment of the word *mægð*, which is all that Anglo-Saxon literature and charters offer us, to counteract the impression left on us by Wulfstan's statements. It is true that he is speaking of a country ravaged by enemies, but we see no trace of a similar decay of the bonds of kindred in other countries similarly ravaged. For a people sometimes supposed to fight in kindreds it is a strange result for warfare to bring about.

That the kindreds had left almost no trace of their survival in Normandy we have already seen, so that we need not look for a recrudescence of kinship-solidarity from that quarter. In fact it is generally assumed, even by those who hold that the kindreds were more powerful in Anglo-Saxon England than anywhere else[4], that this solidarity died out very soon after the Norman Conquest. The completeness with which it did die out seems to us to need more explanation than it has ever

---

[1] Sweet's *A.-S. Reader*, XVI. l. 78 f. Ne bearh nu for oft gesibb gesibbum þe mā þe fremdan, ne fæder his bearne, ne hwilum bearu his agenum fæder, ne broðor oðrum.

[2] *yrmð* might also mean 'poverty.'

[3] l. 105 ff. He also speaks of *mægræsas*, attacks on relatives.

[4] Nowhere else has it been suggested, I think, that a kindred could measure themselves with the king, or with such a town as London.

received, if indeed the kindreds were not at least moribund before the Conquest. That the new rulers, and even the lawyers, had no animus against them—(an animus which would have been reasonable if kindreds had really existed so powerful that they needed armed troops against them)—is obvious from the indifferent way in which they admit references to the *mægð* in the post-Conquest laws. Yet not one of the borough custumals yet collected shows any sign or trace of the kindred, save for the two cases of oath-helpers in London and Dunwich[1], for the very rare use of the expression 'slain man's kin' with regard to the receipt of wergild[2], and for two references, in Manchester and Preston respectively, to the advice or approval of 'friends' in connection with reconciliations after woundings[3]. There are no courts of reconciliation, no pledges of the kindred, no pleas for mercy by a kindred, no *orfejde* oaths to the borough authorities, no guardianship exercised by the kindred, and with the one exception of London (perhaps we should include Dunwich), no oath-helpers of the kindred. It would be hard to find a town in Denmark, North Germany, the Netherlands or Northern France where not a single one of these institutions is traceable: in England we can find none of them in any of the towns for which records have been published. There may be some way of accounting for this phenomenon, other than that there were no cohesive kindreds in England for some centuries before the Conquest[4], but it will be hard to find.

Nor do the deeds and Court records of post-Conquest times show more traces of these features than the borough laws. Wergild remains, however, and with it the necessity of using the phrase 'kinsmen of the slain'; but we may well believe that these kinsmen were no more than the immediate family. In 1202 we find one Hugh, son of Walter 'Priest,' having killed

---

[1] See above, p. 233.
[2] Bateson, op. cit. I. 30. The preceding extract from Archinfield refers to Welsh kins.
[3] Ib. I. 30, 31.
[4] Professor Vinogradoff, *Social England*, p. 218, speaks of the dismemberment of mægths as occurring in the 11th century (before the Conquest); but this would hardly account for the completeness of their extinction.

Roger Rombald and been outlawed, petitioning the sheriff to aid him in establishing peace between *him* and the kinsmen of the slain. There is no intercession on the part of Hugh's kinsmen, nor any hint of their joining in the peace.

A more interesting case is that of Herbert of Pattersley and Thomas of Ingoldthorpe. A man has been slain (presumably by these two): Herbert is to go on a seven-year pilgrimage, Thomas is to procure one of the slain man's family to be brought up in a monastery, and "further the said Thomas shall give the kinsfolk of the slain 40 marks[1]," to be paid in four instalments[2].

In none of the cases do we find more than one kinsman of the slain, or a husband and wife, appealing[3].

Bracton reports several homicides in his Note Book, but the slayer usually appears to be hanged[4], so that composition is not to be expected. The only case where wergild is paid is from Archinfield. In that district, it is declared, it is the custom for the slayer to make peace with the kinsmen (of the slain)[5]. Archinfield is a district of Herefordshire, on the Welsh border.

Such independent evidence as we possess thus more than bears out the conclusions we derived from the laws. It is of course possible that we have gone too far in ascribing to Danish influence passages which show a slightly greater degree of kin-solidarity. But even granted that every reference to the subject, including all those of the Leges Henrici, proved to be purely Anglo-Saxon, it would still be impossible to concede any real degree of kinship-solidarity to the Anglo-Saxons. The evidence from England need only be compared with that from the Continent to startle us into realizing how trifling the former is.

Except for the institution of twelve sureties of the kin in wergild-treaties—which we have seen cogent grounds for ascribing

---

[1] Maitland, *Select Pleas of the Crown*, I. p. 21 (Northamptonshire Eyre). Cp. also p. 54 (case 100; 1207).

[2] Ib. p. 56.

[3] Cp. pp. 1, 13, 17, 40, 75, 81, 118. See also Selden Soc. *Coroners' Rolls*, pp. 18–21, 32, 35.

[4] Bracton's Note Book, ed. Maitland, Nos. 1472, 1473.

[5] Ib. No. 1474: "bene potest concordiam facere cum parentibus."

to Scandinavian influence—the whole case for kinship-solidarity in England really rests on the not very frequent occurrence of the word *mægð* in the laws. When we reflect that neither the limits nor the structure of this *mægð* are ever stated or even hinted at, and that the word *mæg*, kinsman[1], unlike the *friund* of Old Saxon and Old Frisian laws, can and indeed usually does signify some relative within the first degree, such as son or brother[2], we must admit that this is a frail foundation on which to build so imposing a superstructure. But the negative evidence is much stronger than this, for we have to add the extraordinary fact that Anglo-Saxon literature appears to contain no word signifying 'cousin[3].' While Saxon, Frisian, Dutch, Flemish and Picard sources, whether laws or charters, can supply us with terms for first, second, and third cousin, together with terminology for expressing cousins 'once removed,' the whole range of Anglo-Saxon literature does not furnish us with one instance of the use of such a word. Nor can I find the Latin 'consobrinus' in the Latin charters. It is significant that English found it necessary to borrow the word 'cousin' from French.

Further, all our information with regard to the reckoning of kinship within the family is limited to the strange and almost certainly erroneous statement, that the father's brother is reckoned, with the brothers, as within the first 'knee[4].' It is hardly too much to say that there would have been no question of a solidarity greater than that of the immediate family among the Anglo-Saxons, but that students of our early institutions half-consciously sought the explanation of terms and of ideas

---

[1] In this point again there is a resemblance between England and Iceland: the Icelandic *frændi* is constantly used of son or brother.

[2] In Anglo-Saxon poetry *mæg* occurs 4 times for 'son,' 9 times for 'nephew,' once for 'uncle,' 3 times for 'brother,' once for 'father-in-law,' once for 'grandson,' and 26 times vaguely for 'kinsman.' (For this information I am indebted to my late pupil, Miss Rosa Schnabel of Vienna.)

[3] Several terms for 'cousin' appear in the Anglo-Saxon vocabularies to translate 'consobrinus' etc. (Wright, *A.S. and O.E. Vocabularies*, 2nd ed., col. 173-4, 210, etc.).

[4] Too much weight must not be laid on this error, however, for it may well have been committed by a Dane imperfectly acquainted with English terminology, see pp. 224 f., supra.

elsewhere than in England. Yet as soon as the Anglo-Saxon *mægð* is studied side by side with similar organizations on the other side of the North Sea or of the Channel, it becomes apparent how singularly flimsy, by comparison, is the evidence for its extent, its activity, its cohesion and its duration.

The evidence of place-names has often been adduced to prove that England was at any rate originally settled on a basis of kindreds. The place-names ending in *-ing*, it has been frequently urged, can only mean that settlement was largely effected by groups of persons descended from a common ancestor. This assumption has been half-discredited for some time[1], but it may be as well to point out that it has now received its death-blow from Professor Kluge[2], who proves its fallacy on philological grounds, after a survey of the Continental and English evidence.

---

[1] Round, *Feudal England*.
[2] "Sippensiedelungen und Sippennamen," in *Vierteljahrsshrift für social- und Wirtschaftsgeschichte*, Bd VI. (1908), pp. 73—84.

CHAPTER VIII

CONCLUSION

BEFORE proceeding to discuss our subject in its wider bearings, it will be convenient to summarize the results obtained in the foregoing chapters.

I. *Summary of previous chapters.*

In Denmark, signs of the partial survival of the kindred are not wanting even at the dawn of the 17th century, in spite of the hostility of powerful kings (from 1200 onwards), and of the Protestant Church. In Schleswig the old customs defy legislation levelled at them by king, duke or *Landtag* for another century still. In Holstein, though it is probable that the participation of the kindreds in wergild disappeared sooner than in Schleswig, they yet left their mark on other institutions, and certain of their functions continue to be exercised until near the end of the 18th, and indeed even into the 19th century. This is especially, but not solely, true of Ditmarschen, within whose territory alone we find the fixed agnatic kindred which can be loosely termed clan. In Friesland[1] the kindreds survive throughout the 15th century. In Hadeln and Bremen, and in the neighbourhood of Hamburg, they seem to have held out against adverse legislation until about the same date.

In the more northerly parts of Central Germany we find occasional traces of their existence throughout the earlier Middle Ages. In southern Teutonic lands the last trace of a real solidarity so far discovered dates from the 13th century. In Holland

---
[1] Friesland must be taken to include the Frisian districts of Oldenburg.

and Belgium the kindreds remain active throughout the 15th century, and indeed into the 16th, and hardly less long in Picardy. In Neustria, too, there are traces of organized feuds and treaties between kindreds until far into the 14th century, and so also in Champagne. Normandy, on the other hand, yields no evidence. In England the activity of the kindreds seems reduced to a minimum already in the 7th and 8th centuries, when we first catch a glimpse of Anglo-Saxon institutions. A slight revival of the solidarity of the family, which appears in the laws under Athelstan, is attributable to Danish influence, but it is not followed up, and the functions of the kindred are practically in abeyance long before the Norman Conquest. After that date no one has called their complete atrophy in question. In Iceland we have seen good reason to believe that the solidarity of the kindred was a thing of the past by the time the emigrants landed on the shores of the new country. In Norway we have caught a glimpse of a gradual disintegration of the kindred, beginning perhaps as early as the 9th, and consummated by the end of the 13th century. In Sweden, on the other hand, everything points to the survival of kinship-solidarity throughout the 14th century[1], and possibly for very much longer.

It is perhaps worth noting that in Holland, Belgium and French Flanders the *towns* were the strongholds of kinship-solidarity, and that the evidence for cohesive kindreds outside the towns is by no means strong. In Hamburg, Kiel, and Lübeck[2], on the contrary, the kindreds have been shown to disintegrate considerably sooner than in the surrounding districts, and the same is true of most of the larger Danish towns.

II. *The influence of the kindreds on social conditions.*

The importance of the *pre*-historic kindred-system is constantly recognized by historians, and has often been credited with more power than it can ever have possessed; but it is no

---
[1] Except in Gotland.
[2] These are Hansa towns, but so also was Briel in Holland—a town which was, as we have seen, a stronghold of the kindreds.

CONCLUSION

less constantly implied that such features of the system as survived into historic times had little or no influence on the body politic, and are only worth mentioning in connection with criminal law. It is true that the shifting nature of the Teutonic kindred precluded its ever having a chief, and asserting itself as a permanently compact body, so that its workings are bound to be obscure. Yet such organizations as existed in Denmark and Friesland, the Netherlands and Picardy, cannot have been without influence on the social conditions of their times. A man who can at any moment surround himself with a large group of persons, all of whom are willing to make sacrifices for him, is in a very different position to one who has to depend on his own efforts and on those of his immediate family for protection against aggression.

Not only would his position be better from the social and political point of view: it would also be far better from the economic point of view. It is generally agreed that the isolation of the small landowner was his undoing, since it rendered him unable to withstand adverse circumstances, such as a bad year, a fire, a plague among his beasts, or a piratical raid on his homestead. " In solcher Nothlage war es immerhin der einfachste und beste Ausweg, den Grundbesitz aufzutragen, ihn als Beneficium zurückzuerhalten und nun wenigstens eine sociale Stütze an dem Verleiher zu finden, die auch ihre ökonomische werthvolle Seite hatte[1]." This is all quite true of the isolated small landowner, but we cannot believe that it was at all true of the small peasant proprietor who was surrounded by a kindred. We have seen evidence to show that the cohesive kindred would rally round a member threatened with a lawsuit, and that it probably performed the functions of an insurance society[2], besides keeping a jealous watch on

---
[1] Inama-Sternegg, *Die Ausbildung der grossen Grundherrschaften in Deutschland*, p. 54.
[2] See supra, p. 140. With regard to this point I should be inclined to seek evidence in the North German *Dorfbeliebungen* or *Nachbarbeliebungen*, village enactments chiefly concerning the upkeep of roads and dykes, the conduct of agriculture etc. The provisions, usually of the 17th and 18th century, are frequently almost identical with those of the *Kluftbücher* of Ditmarschen, and it is at any rate possible that certain of their prescriptions embody the practices and ideals of the earlier

the inherited land belonging to its members. In regions where the kindred preserved its solidarity it would thus be far less easy for a wealthy landowner, or even for ecclesiastical foundations, to exploit the financial and social difficulties of a poor neighbour, by acquiring his lands or by extorting rights over him at a period of want. In such regions we might reasonably expect to find few great territorial lords, and few seignorial privileges, together with a preponderance of free peasant proprietors. This is exactly what we do find in Schleswig-Holstein. The 'nobles,' up to the 12th century, are peasant proprietors who perform certain military services to the king, and who receive certain immunities in return, but they are little wealthier than their fellows, and have no seignorial rights[1]. This class of noble disappears in the 13th century in Schleswig-Holstein, and somewhat later in the rest of Jutland, largely owing to poverty. The later class of nobles also sprang from the peasant farmers, but has a different history. In order to encourage colonization, the Count of Holstein granted fiefs in Eastern Holstein to persons of the peasant class, who thus became rich and powerful, with feudal rights over their dependents. Almost the whole of the later nobility of Denmark, as well as of Schleswig-Holstein, can be traced back to these colonists. Except in the colonized districts, the peasant farmers possessed their own lands, and continued to enjoy a high degree of local autonomy up to the 16th and 17th centuries. This independence is also characteristic of the Old Saxon peasants[2], until the country was overrun by colonizing nobles; and for a much longer period of time of

---

kindreds. The village of Gross Queeren in Angeln, for instance, enacts that neighbours shall help to bring in the harvest of a belated farmer (Hanssen, *Agrar-hist. Abhandlungen*, II. p. 127); and it is occasionally laid down that all the community is to make an appearance at the funeral of one of their number (ib. p. 112). Such provisions as these are surely more likely to have originated among groups of kinsfolk than in ordinary parish ordinances. Since it is impossible to find any traces of them in the judicial records of the 17th and 18th centuries, it is surely permissible to believe that similar customs among groups of kinsfolk might have existed a century or two earlier without leaving any trace.

[1] Sering, op. cit. p. 199.
[2] Fisher, *The Mediæval Empire*, I. pp. 90 f., p. 137; Guilhiermoz, *Origine de la Noblesse* (1902), p. 457.

CONCLUSION

East and West Friesland[1]. On East Frisian territory we must not forget that the districts of Wursten, of Stadtland and Butjadingen, and of Hadeln remained independent commonwealths, governed by their own peasantry, until the 15th and 16th centuries, and that it required repeated attacks by Dukes and Archbishops, with trained armies at their backs, to reduce them to subjection[2]. In West Friesland Westerwold, between Emsland and Drenthe, remained independent for hardly less long[3]. In Drenthe itself a 'Report of civil abuses' of 1557 complains that the persons administering justice in Drenthe are mere ignorant peasant farmers who favour their own class[4].

In non-Frisian Holland, too, free peasant proprietors continued to flourish until the rise of the towns, when it would seem that the free kindreds flocked thither, preserving their independence throughout the whole of the Middle Ages[5], and abandoning agriculture to a lower class[6].

In France, owing to the need for cavalry occasioned by the

---

[1] Ph. Heck, *Die Gemeinfreien der Karolingischen Volksrechte*, p. 234, goes so far as to maintain that in mediaeval Friesland "eine demokratische Bewegung, von der wir nichts Näheres wissen, die Standesunterschiede, wenigstens in ihren Hauptwirkungen, beseitigt," but the more moderate view of F. Swart (*Zur fries. Agrargeschichte*, 1910, p. 183) is to be preferred: "Im ganzen ist nicht zweifelhaft, dass trotz des Vorhandenseins reicher grundherrscherlicher Geschlechter der freie erbgesessene Hausmann während der zweiten Hälfte des Mittelalters dem fries. Wirtschaftsleben den Stempel aufdrückt....Die Rolle, die die Gerichtsgemeinde beim Abschluss von politischer Verträgen spielt, das Fortbestehen des bäuerlichen Fehderechts, die fast allgemeine Verbreitung des bäuerlichen Patronatsrechts, die Stellung, die den Bauern bei Ausbildung der Territorialgewalt in der ständischen Verfassung eingeräumt wird, sind überzeugende Beweise."

[2] Cp. G. v. d. Osten, *Geschichte des Landes Wursten*, Bremerhaven, 1900–2.

[3] Till 1316. G. L. von Maurer, *Einleitung zur Gesch. der Mark- Hof- Dorf- und Stadt-Verfassung*, p. 292.

[4] S. Gratama, *Drenthsche Rechtsbronnen*, Rapport van 1557 (van civilen abusen), VII. "In Drenthe is in de lottinge ende gerichte groot misbruick. Int yrste, datt sij gemeenlick den droste in der stemmen volge,...ten tweeden, binnen die etten buren, ongeschickt, die nyett een letter koenen scrijven; ten dardenn die eine buer den anderen favoreserende."

[5] Cp. I. A. Nijhoff, *Gedenkwaardigheden uit de Geschiedenis van Gelderland*, IV. Dl. (Arnhem 1847), p. cxiii: "Trouwens, het moge niet ontkend kunnen worden, dat vrijen, onderscheiden van de edelen, door het gansche tijdvak der middeleeuwen heen hebben blijven bestaan, en sich vooral in steden hebben nedergezet."

[6] Ib. pp. xciii–iv.

Saracen invasions, an immense impulse was given to feudalism, which naturally resulted in depressing the status of the ordinary freeman. Yet of the early Frankish kingdom it has been observed that "the prevalence of lordship is by no means so clear as in England[1]." In the north-eastern districts there is reason to postulate the same flocking of free kindreds into the towns which is characteristic of Holland[2].

Of our own country, on the other hand, Professor Vinogradoff has said that "in a sense, the feudal law of England was the hardest of all in Western Europe." The dependent state of the ceorl in the greater part of England (before the Norman Conquest) has been commented upon by many authorities, and is so marked that Seebohm found himself forced to contemplate a serf origin for the English village community[3]. Maitland attributes the ceorl's loss of independence to the exhausting efforts made by Wessex to keep off the Danes[4]. This would account for his poverty, if poor he was, but would it account for manors and seignorial rights? We must observe that the Viking raids (together with ecclesiastical influences, which should surely have been effective in England if anywhere) have been recently adduced as paving the way to an "Aufrücken der untersten Bevölkerungselemente" in Friesland[5]. Friesland suffered more than England at the hands of the Northmen, and it shakes our faith in the Vikings as the agents of social change to find them adduced in England as the chief cause of the prevailing serfdom, and in Friesland as contributing towards the rise of the agricultural classes.

Moreover even in Northern and Eastern England the only form of independence granted to free sokemen is the right to choose their own lord. Lords, it seems, they must have; and not only must they have lords, but for purposes of administration and police supervision they must be dragooned into groups (the *teoðung*)[6], whose function it is to guarantee their orderliness

---

[1] Chadwick, *The Heroic Age*, p. 351.
[2] pp. 200 f., supra.
[3] In *The Village Community*.
[4] *Domesday Book and Beyond*, p. 338.
[5] Ph. Heck, *Altfries. Gerichtsverfassung*, p. 238.
[6] Cnut II. 20, etc.

CONCLUSION

and produce them when required. In Wessex, too, feudal lords are frequently mentioned in Ine's laws[1], before the Danish invasions. Of course England was a military kingdom, won at the point of the sword, but it has been maintained that it was not until some time after the conquest that the status of the ceorl begins to fall[2], and in any case it is strange that the rigours of feudalism should be more pronounced in England than in the Frankish kingdom, which was also won by force of arms[3].

The real reason why the burden of the small landowner so soon proved too heavy for him to bear in England was not that the burden became so much heavier, but that it was a burden calculated for the backs of many individuals, not for one. Wergild for instance became a crushing imposition, leading to debt, serfdom, poverty, when the price was paid out of the cattle and household goods possessed by the individual slayer and his immediate family[4]: when dispersed among a whole kindred it was comparatively little felt.

Now let us compare England with a country which was not gained at the point of the sword. In Iceland individuals, not associated in kindreds, took peaceful possession of their land, and at the outset all landowners were on an equal footing. There were no Viking raids to repel, there was no national army whose officers might obtain over-lordship over their fellows; and yet, within a few years of the settlement, every landowner, unless himself a chief, had a lord to whom he owed military and other service, and the courts of justice were more seignorial than popular in character[5]. By the 12th century the small landowners were so crushed that the few powerful families

---

[1] Ine, cc. 21, 27, 39, 50, 76. Note also the *manbot*, fine paid to the lord for a slaying, as against the fine paid to the inhabitants of the district in Sweden, p. 70, supra.

[2] Cp. Vinogradoff, *Social Life in England in the 11th century*, p. 36 and elsewhere.

[3] It must be remembered that large seignorial estates need not necessarily put an end to the ownership of land by groups of free peasant proprietors: in Russia the two have co-existed for centuries. Cp. Grosse, *Die Formen der Familie*, p. 211.

[4] Cp. Lamprecht, *Beiträge zur Gesch. des französischen Wirthschaftslebens im 11ten Jahrhundert* (Leipsic, 1878), pp. 74, 94.

[5] This is noted by v. Amira, *Paul's Grundriss* (2te Aufl.) III. p. 101.

could demand what service and dues they liked. No resistance was ever made, despite the fact that the chiefs were always at war among themselves. Now if there is any fact agreed upon by all authorities, it is that these Icelandic settlers were no servile class accustomed to tyranny, but men with an extreme independence of character and traditions. Many of them, we are told, left Norway because they would not acknowledge Harald Hairfair's right to tax their ancestral lands, which they declared to be their own absolute property. And yet this is their history in Iceland, where they only needed protection against each other! If they had had kindreds to protect them, should we have found this absolute and speedy decline into dependence on a lord? It is not entirely the absence of a central executive which reduces them to this pitch, for in the commonwealth of Ditmarschen, which till the middle of the 15th century was governed by its kindreds[1], the noble class disappeared in the 13th century, and when Holstein nobles pressed in in the 16th century, after the subjugation of the country, the peasants united to buy them out[2].

As in Iceland, the chief feature of mediaeval Norwegian history is the enormous power wielded in the 12th and 13th centuries by the nobles and their followings, until the class was practically annihilated in their protracted civil wars against Sverri[3].

In Sweden, on the other hand, the aristocratic class does not make its appearance until the end of the 11th century[4], and when it reaches the summit of its power, in the 15th century, it admittedly owes much to its sense of kinship-solidarity[5], as the extensive genealogical tables in Swedish history-books

---

[1] Cp. Sering, p. 123. These kindreds were democratic, that is to say there were no chiefs.
[2] Ib. p. 157.
[3] Cp. Munch, *Den Norske Folks Historie*.
[4] Cp. *Sveriges Historia*, I. (O. Montelius) 1st ed. p. 461. It is to be noted that in the provincial laws fines are paid to the king, to the hundred or härad (district) and to "all men," i.e. the neighbourhood. There is thus no trace of seignorial justice.
[5] Op. cit. II. (H. Hildebrand), p. 244. "Det är redan (s. 30 o.f.) påpekadt, huru stormännens slägtforbindelser utöfvade inflytande på partigrupperingarna och dermed på Sveriges öden. Mer än någonsin tillförne eger detta rum under den tid,...då der uppstår mellan stormanslägterna en täflan om herraväldet i Sverige" (1434–70).

CONCLUSION   253

testify. Even then, however, the Swedish commons are still powerful enough to play a leading part in the struggle between king and nobles[1]. As late as 1608[2], justice is still administered in rural courts, with 12 doomsmen, and even cases of manslaughter are within their competence. We must note how very few traces of a hereditary class of nobles there are in the earlier period of the Viking Age, and indeed in the literary traditions from the Age of National Migrations. Kings there are in bewildering plenty, and it is they who lead migrations and Viking expeditions of every kind. Such nobles as there are seem to be officials of the king[3]. Round him are gathered an aristocracy of fighting men, often, it would seem, foreigners, to the wealth of whose equipment archæological finds testify. When these *comites*, as Tacitus calls them, reach a certain age, the king grants them land and they settle down. Professor Chadwick has shown us that in England this class soon formed a hereditary nobility, which early gained rights over the neighbouring freemen in return for protection. But if we suppose strong cohesive kindreds among these neighbouring freemen, for instance in the Jutish peninsula, is it so certain that the retired *comes*, unsupported by a kindred of his own[4], would obtain or maintain rights over his neighbours[5]? The absence of seignorial rights among the nobility of Jutland, Schleswig, and Friesland may thus well be due to the strength of the kindreds; just as the growth of these rights in

---

[1] Ib. p. 467 : "Att folket härvid icke hos oss, såsom i de flesta andra länder, alldeles förlorade sin betydelse, utan kunde ved medeltidens slut framträda med sådan kraft som det gjorde, torde väsentligen kunna forklaras af dens vana vid sjelfstyrelse, som i synnerhet i de smärre områdene tidigt rotfäste sig; i kommunalforvältningen deltogs bönderne jemte frälsemännen såsom likstälda."

[2] Cp. G. O. Berg, *Huru rätt skipades i Sverige för trehundra år sedan* (Upsala, 1908).

[3] Cp. Chadwick, *Heroic Age*, pp. 350, 360. It is noteworthy that it is the Swedes, Danes and Franks who have only one class of freemen.

[4] There is a Danish document of the 12th century which appears to represent the nobles of the kingdom organized, in groups, in an artificial brotherhood—a very significant fact. See Steenstrup, *Studier over Kong Valdemars Jordebog*, ch. 22.

[5] The absence of a strong landowning nobility in the Jutish peninsula before the conquest of Britain seems to follow from the fact that the Anglo-Saxon nobility is shown to rise out of a class of royal officials.

England and in Iceland has to our mind a common cause, and is bound up with the absence of cohesive kindreds in those countries, the military nature of the settlement in England having only a subsidiary influence.

These may be said to be hasty generalizations, and indeed the subject deserves a more exhaustive inquiry, but it seems that we must acknowledge this much: where cohesive kindreds persist into the later Middle Ages, there the peasant or townsman tends to be free. Where, on the other hand, the solidarity of the kindred disappears early, there the liberty of the individual suffers, and seignorial rights make their appearance. Further evidence pointing in this direction is not entirely lacking. Thus it is highly significant that wherever the kindreds survive the blood-feud remains a privilege of all classes, recognized, if deplored, by the law[1]. It is the unquestioned right of the slain man's kin in the Swedish law-books of the 13th century[2]. In France and the Netherlands it persisted until the same period and later, in spite of well-governed towns and powerful kings or nobles. In Namur we have seen a slayer acquitted in the 15th century, on its being shown that he committed the deed in a legitimate feud, the slain man's *cousins* having killed his father[3]. In England, on the other hand, there is no trace of legitimate blood-feuds after the time of Eadmund (c. 943)[4]. But the true significance of the survival of feud in France and the Netherlands is not fully apparent until we remember that in Iceland the blood-feud was never legally recognized, and that even the heir avenging himself on the slayer of his kinsman was as liable to penalty as the original aggressor unless he succeeded in killing his man before the next Althing[5]. There is only one way of accounting for this extraordinary discrepancy between the laws of anarchical Iceland and the comparatively well-policed Frankish towns and territories. In the latter large cohesive kindreds could stand on their rights, however disturbing to the community at large; in England and Iceland the feud was a

---

[1] It is noticeable that continental state-craft attempts rather to obviate blood-feuds by *asseurement* and similar devices, than to abolish them.
[2] p. 69, supra.
[3] p. 178 note 3, supra.
[4] p. 219, supra.
[5] Grágás, I *a*, 147 etc.

CONCLUSION 255

matter between a few individuals only, and it was easy to override their wishes in the interests of the general public.

We have already seen that kin-solidarity played a part in the rise of the early Frankish merchant families[1]. In late historical times its influence is easy to trace in the power wielded by the Dutch town officials, the Regents, who virtually ruled Holland until the end of the 18th century[2]. It is probable that the influence of certain families in other towns was also a result of their cohesion as units of a kindred[3].

It thus seems safe to admit that the kindreds of the early Middle Ages played no negligible part in the making of history. The countries where the kindreds did not survive—England, Norway, and possibly the States of Central and Southern Germany—avoided, it is true, a problem of government which gave other States some trouble, since among the difficulties in the way of a central government they did not have to reckon with the obstinate, if passive, resistance of the kindreds. Is it not possible, however, that they paid a heavier price for this immunity than their historians have ever quite realized?

In Iceland, it is true, there was no problem of a central executive, for in lacking a king, Iceland lacked also a nucleus round which a central executive could grow up. But since they further lacked the main cohesive principle of the ancient Teutonic State, the bond of kinship, the political efforts of the Icelandic settlers may be likened to the making of bricks without straw, and indeed the frail structure of their constitution, in some ways the most wonderful achievement of the Middle Ages, crumbled and fell through inner disintegration, before it was seriously threatened by enemies from without. But it is important to realize that theirs was a barren experiment, *not* because their constitution was an antiquated survival of a prehistoric Teutonic polity, but because it had lost both the factors, the kindred and the king, which made for permanence and cohesion in the ancient order, and had found no sufficient sub-

---

[1] p. 202, supra.   [2] p. 166, supra.
[3] Cp. C. Stüve, *Gesch. des Hochstifts Osnabrück* (1853), p. 303: "Im Rathe waren die Geschlechter herrschend, die ohne bestimmtes Vorrecht überwiegenden Einfluss besassen" (early in the 15th century). Cp. p. 241.

stitute. We must therefore beware of regarding the Icelandic commonwealth as a new Germania of Tacitus, miraculously appearing in the Northern seas to show us what 'Urgermanentum' was really like. Anglo-Saxon England is almost equally suspect from this point of view, for, if it has kept the king, it too has lost the kindred, probably a much more integral part of the ancient Teutonic State. In fact, if we want to seek after the *Urgermanisch*, would it not be safer to turn our attention to those regions where its two main elements remained longest in something like their ancient equilibrium, namely in Denmark and the old Danish provinces, and in Southern Sweden?

We may summarize what seems to have been the tendency of the kindreds by describing it as democratic[1],—that is to say that in discouraging the rise of petty local chiefs they tended to keep the status of all freemen equal, but we must believe that they achieved this result by refusing opportunities to the strong, as well as by protecting the weak against outside aggression. They were not democratic in the sense that the mediaeval Church was democratic. But though it seems that we must concede this quite considerable degree of influence to the kindreds, we must be careful to note that it implies no active organization, no conscious political aim, on their part. It was achieved as it were anonymously, by what we may call passive resistance. We still have no right to think of the Teutonic kindreds as 'organizing' themselves in any but the most temporary manner, or as combining for aggression. A kindred can only be said to exist at the moment when it groups itself round a given kinsman, and a large proportion of this group must merge into other groups if some other individual is in need. So long as kinship was recognized through both male and female— i.e. during the whole historic period—these characteristics of the kindreds must have set very definite bounds to their political power.

---

[1] It is perhaps worth while to note that various observers have commented on the unusual degree of social equality between the families of farmers and of day-labourers in villages in Ditmarschen at the present day. In Wursten, where the kindreds were powerful (v. d. Osten, p. 46), no native succeeded in obtaining seignorial rights until 1673, when the king of Sweden granted them to one family. Ib., Theil II. pp. 131 ff.

We need only compare the kindred with its offshoot, the gild, to realize the deficiencies of the earlier group in this respect. The gild is definite, organized, adaptable, transplantable—everything that the kindred is not. Yet it is a question whether the very indefiniteness of the kindred, its anonymity, its shifting outline, what we may call its Protean attributes, did not qualify it for its obscure workings towards social equality better than a fixed organization, more open to attack, could ever have done. There can be no question that the kindred, through a long course of centuries, clung far more closely to the democratic ideal than the gild. The gilds did a great work for the towns and the craftsmen, but did they achieve more than the kindreds, wherever they survived, accomplished for the rural districts or for the agricultural classes?

III. *Causes of the Decline of the Kindreds.*

We must now set ourselves to consider the causes of the disintegration of the kindred, but it is a task of unexpected difficulty, owing to the failure of the commonly-received explanations when confronted by the facts we have observed. For instance, the influence of Roman law has been considered to be the disintegrating factor: where the Roman law first took hold in Southern Germany, there, it was declared, did the kindreds first disappear. So long as the history of the kindreds in Germany was considered without reference to the history of the institution elsewhere, this explanation seemed sound enough. But if Roman law was the solvent, how was it that the kindreds were so tenacious of life in Northern France, the Netherlands, and North-west Germany—conquered by Romans, or by partly Romanized Franks, and during the later Middle Ages steeped in an atmosphere of Roman ideals of law—while in Norway and Iceland they disappeared before Roman law was even a name?

Then again the influence of Christianity has been invoked, and indeed its doctrine of the responsibility of the individual must to a certain extent have acted adversely on the kindreds, though perhaps not as much as has been sometimes assumed.

CONCLUSION

For the result of impairing the sense of corporate responsibility was too often to increase the temptation to take summary vengeance. That there was a tendency to sporadic and ill-disciplined acts of vengeance wherever the kindred was early shattered may well prove to be the case: Frauenstädt's collection of instances in South Germany[1], and the Icelandic Sagas, might go far to establish such a theory. So that the early Church in Northern Europe probably took the better part in profiting by the sense of corporate responsibility rather than in weakening it. Almost everywhere the Church mediates between the kindreds, and few would criticize her rôle[2]. But whatever the effect of the mediaeval Church in urging the acceptance of wergild rather than recourse to arms, it is obvious that neither Christian doctrine nor ecclesiastical influence can be the determining factor in the decay of the kindreds, when once we admit that they survived many centuries of Christianity in France and Germany, while their disintegration was complete in heathen Iceland by the year 1000[3].

A similar objection applies to the theory that a strong executive was the force which finally pulverized the kindreds. France and Denmark, at least, had as strong a line of kings as any mediaeval Teutonic state, yet in France the organized feuds of the kindreds were with difficulty checked in the 14th century, and in Denmark the kindred clung together for two centuries more. In Iceland, on the other hand, where the kindreds might have been a substitute for a strong executive[4], those ancient Teutonic organizations had but the feeblest hold.

Yet there can be no doubt that though Roman law, Christianity and strong executives cannot be made to explain the decline or predominance of the kindreds in the various parts of Teutonic Europe, they were nevertheless factors which actually had a mighty influence in pulverizing the kindreds in those

---

[1] Frauenstädt, *Blutrache und Todtschlagssühne im deutschen Mittelalter*, Leipsic, 1881.

[2] We even find the Church paying compensation on behalf of the delinquent: cf. Gregory of Tours, VII. 47 (in 585).

[3] The year of the introduction of Christianity.

[4] As they actually were in Ditmarschen and in Wursten.

CONCLUSION

regions where the institution had survived the earlier Middle Ages. It is the recognition of this fact which makes our task so difficult, for we have to account, not only for the disparities we have already noticed in the duration of the system, but also for the resisting-power exhibited by the kindred-organization all through the Middle Ages in just those regions where these three destructive influences were brought to bear on it, in strong contrast to its early disappearance where it had apparently nothing to contend against.

Our survey of the evidence in those countries where the kindreds showed marked vitality seems to suggest that the 14th century was the first in which their cohesion was really seriously threatened, and the date leads us to infer the possibility that the Black Death, which ravaged Northern Europe in 1349–50, may have had a more adverse influence on the kindreds than has been suspected. By killing off a very considerable proportion of the population, it may have helped to disintegrate the kindreds, both by encouraging migration[1] and by causing individuals to look to themselves instead of having recourse to the help of a wide group of kinsmen. There may well be an element of truth in this theory, but of course its uses as an explanation of the phenomena just described are but limited. It cannot, for instance, be made to account for the disappearance of the kindreds in Norway, England, Iceland, or even in Central and South Germany, since kinship-solidarity as a social factor of importance had entirely disappeared in these regions long before the visitation of the Black Death. Yet other explanations which have been put forward are no more satisfactory.

It has been maintained[2] that the Teutonic kindreds broke down as a result of their recognition of cognates. This theory, however, seems untenable in the light of our recent survey, for those regions where the most absolute equality between agnates and cognates prevails are the very strongholds of the system, while in Norway and England, where we traced a discrimination

---

[1] Cp. Hoeniger, *Der schwarze Tod in Deutschland*, Berlin, 1882, p. 94.
[2] Cp. Vinogradoff, *Zs. f. Social- und Wirthschaftsgeschichte*, Bd VII, and Sering, *op. cit.*, p. 141.

in favour of agnates, it disappears early. But we shall deal with this question again later.

Another suggestion is that the village-community form of settlement was favourable to the organization of kindreds, while a system of solitary homesteads tended to weaken them. This suggestion is attractive at first sight, since solitary homesteads are characteristic of Iceland and of most of Norway. But unfortunately they are equally characteristic of the greater part of Friesland and the Netherlands[1], where the kindreds show strong vitality, while the village-community system is prevalent in England, where the kindreds languished.

As far as the Norwegian kindreds are concerned, emigration, in the form of Viking expeditions, might be considered to have had an adverse effect upon kinship-solidarity, but this suggestion again is contravened by the fact that the kindreds were especially strong in the Jutish peninsula, whence emigration must at one time have taken place on a very large scale, and in the rest of Denmark, which took its full part in Viking expeditions. It would of course also fail to explain English conditions.

The disappearance of kindreds has also been ascribed to an increased density of population. "Sippenwirthschaft," it has been said, fails in intensive culture where that becomes necessary, and has consequently only survived where the population is of no great density[2]. This may be true in certain cases, though it is hard to reconcile with the fact that the wasteful system of strip-holdings survived in Teutonic countries long after the equal partition of land among the kindred, supposed to be its justification, had disappeared. But in any case, if there is a connection to be traced in Northern Europe between density of population and the survival of kindreds, it is of an almost opposite kind to that suggested. Probably the marsh-lands of Schleswig-Holstein, where the kindred survives longest, would be found to offer the best example of intensive culture, as also of density of population, while the sparsely inhabited Iceland and Norway, with their absence of kin-solidarity, do not encourage us to pursue this line of investigation.

---

[1] Meitzen, *Siedelung und Agrarwesen*, Atlas, Karte 66a.
[2] E. Grosse, *Die Formen der Familie* (Freiburg 1896), pp. 211–2.

CONCLUSION

There seems to be a growing tendency to regard the southernmost part of Sweden[1], Denmark, Schleswig-Holstein and the old Danish Duchies as the original home, at any rate from the Stone Age onwards, of the Teutonic race[2]. Certainly no other theory can so well be reconciled with the facts, both archaeological and philological. Now it is exactly these regions where the solidarity of the kindred persisted longest. The kindred-system of those tribes whose migrations did not lead them far afield, as the Frisians, shows a not very much reduced vitality. It is easy to imagine that the tribes which met with little resistance on their migrations, or who overcame it speedily, and settled down comparatively soon, would preserve the organization of the kindred almost unimpaired. Such a fortunate tribe were the Frisians; such, to an even greater extent, the Salian Franks, most of whom remained in the south-west regions of the basin of the Scheldt[3]. On the other hand, many of the South or Middle German peoples must have been in an unsettled condition for centuries, liable to the necessity of frequent migration, and constantly at war.

Yet the disintegration resulting from years of wandering and of warfare would not be very great except in extreme cases. But the analogy of the Icelandic settlers will incline us to accept the idea that a migration involving transport by sea was especially liable to impair the sense of kin-solidarity among those who venture on it[4], though the organization of those who remained

---

[1] On their arrival in Skåne it is quite probable that they had difficulties with another (non-Aryan) race: see Hansen, *Landnåm i Norge* (1904), and A. Brøgger, *Den arktiske Stenalder* (*Norges Videnskabl. Skrifter*, Christiania 1909, pp. 1—278).

[2] Hansen, *op. cit.*; Kossina, Die vorgesch. Ausbreitung der Germanen; *Zs. d. Vereins f. Völkerkunde*, VI (1896, p. 1 ff.); A. Kock, Är Skåne de germanske folkets urhem? (*Svensk*) *Hist. Tidskrift* 1905; *Cambridge Medieval History*, vol. I. p. 183.

[3] We shall presently observe that after Denmark and Sweden, the Frankish wergild laws seem to adhere the most closely to what we must suppose were old Germanic principles.

[4] The above does not apply with the same force to the case of clearly defined clans, each of whose members bears the same name as all the others, and regards himself as kin to him, however distant the actual relationship may be. Not only is such a clan more capable of undertaking a common venture, such as the building and manning of a vessel, but all the migrating members of the clan recognize each other and would tend to form a nucleus for a clan-group in the new country. In the case of the ordinary shifting kindred of the Teutons, the groups of kindred on the paternal and maternal side respectively are not in any way related to one another,

behind might not be appreciably affected. It is extremely unlikely that each group of kindred would build a vessel and man it exclusively, or even mainly, with their own kinsmen; on the contrary, all analogies show us that any individuals wishing to join an expedition would rally to the first ship that was sailing, and probably remain permanently associated with its crew in the new country. Professor Vinogradoff has pointed out that in the ancient Teutonic tribal system, which involved an equal claim to the ancestral estate on the part of a number of co-heirs, the danger of excessive subdivision of land was avoided by the renunciation of their claims on the part of the supernumerary heirs, who received an indemnity, calculated not according to the value of their shares, but to the ability of the estate to bear the outlay[1]. Where this system of co-heirs (the sons and daughters) still persists, in the moorlands of Schleswig-Holstein, these supernumerary heirs often leave home, permanently or for a time, to settle in the towns, since they have not the means to marry if they remain on the land. Professor Sering, in speaking of this custom, observes: "In welcher Ausdehnung es üblich ist, dass Geschwister beisammen bleiben oder auseinander gehen, hat von jeher wesentlich von dem allgemeinen Gange des volkswirtschaftlichen Entwicklung abgehangen. Steigt sie kräftig aufwarts, so wandern viele ab und gründen ein eigenes Heim; andernfalls bleiben mehr unverheiratet zu Hause. Auf diese Weise vollzieht sich seit Alters her die Anpassung der Bevölkerung an die vorhandenen Unterhaltsgelegenheiten[2]."

In prehistoric times in Denmark these supernumerary heirs no doubt went to swell the military followings of kings, who like themselves were very often in a landless condition[3]. The

---

still less have they a common name. There is no reason why my father's first cousin should consort with my mother's first cousin in a new country, if I am not there to form a connecting link.

[1] Art. Village Communities in *Encycl. Brit.*, 11th ed., vol. 28, pp. 69—73.
[2] Sering, *op. cit.*, p. 173 ff.
[3] Among royal families the centrifugal force must have been even stronger, since every member of a royal family was a king, and if he could not rule over the ancestral kingdom he was very likely to seek to obtain another kingdom for himself—a state of affairs of which Snorri seems to have preserved the tradition for Norway. Hence perhaps the absence of any suggestions of solidarity within the kindred in the oldest

historical sagas of Iceland and Norway give us the clearest insight into this process in Norway, and it is just these 'supernumerary heirs,' encouraged to seek other means of livelihood than agriculture, who join with others in the same position, and leave their country on permanent or temporary Viking raids[1]; in the earlier period under the leadership of a king, later under a noble. A classic example is afforded by the sons of Earl Hrollaug of Norway, one of whom, Göngu-Hrolf, is declared by Snorri to have founded the Duchy of Normandy; one lost his life in the Western Isles of Scotland on an expedition with Harald Hairfair; another became Earl of the Orkneys, while yet another settled in Iceland. It seems more than probable that the peoples of Schleswig-Holstein[2] lived under similar conditions in the 5th century, with Viking expeditions, and finally the permanent conquest of England, as the result. The settlers in England might therefore be almost as lacking in full kindreds as the settlers in Iceland a few centuries later. Before we make certain that the invaders must have come over *en masse*, in full kindreds, in order to achieve such a vast result as the conquest of England, we shall do well to remind ourselves that the feat was all but paralleled in a much shorter time and in the teeth of a resistance at least equally obstinate, by the Vikings of a later period; yet that no one thinks it necessary to assume a wholesale emigration of kindreds in this case, or to postulate that the organization of the Vikings, when they arrived in England, was on a basis of kindreds.

If we are to adopt the Danish theory that the Normans are mainly of Danish, and not Norwegian origin, we can point to Normandy also as affording corroborative evidence for the

---

traditions of the period of national migrations—a phenomenon to which attention has been recently directed (Chadwick, *The Heroic Age*, pp. 347–8, 373–4, 391).

[1] Some of the Swedish runic stones offer corroborative evidence: cp. Olson, *Yngvars Saga viðfǫrla*, Bihang, p. 51, No. 1 ("Thialfi and Holmlaug had all these stones erected in memory of their son Banki, who *himself alone* owned a ship and steered east with Yngvar's host").

[2] I do not see any reason to suppose that all the adventurers who won England were actually from Schleswig-Holstein, though the leaders were. We know that the invaders called 'Danes' by the English included Norwegians and probably Swedes, and that the 'Norman' conquest was largely effected by non-Norman mercenaries.

disintegrating influence on the kindred of a settlement by sea. According to this theory the invaders of Normandy came from the highly cohesive kindreds of Denmark. Yet the traces of kinship-solidarity in thirteenth-century Normandy are far fainter than in other districts of Northern France, which the Teutons reached by land.

So far as it goes, too, the evidence available for the easternmost and westernmost of Teutonic settlements bears out our contention. The laws of the Swedish kingdom in Russia, won by naval expeditions, show but a feeble conception of kinship: the slayer alone pays for his deed, and the right of vengeance is limited to brother, father, son and nephew[1]. On the other hand, West Gothic custumals in Spain show division of wergild between kinsmen, definitely organized blood-feuds between kindreds, and oath-helpers of the kindred: in fact, as Professor de Hinojosa observes: "Die spanische Familie der ersten Zeit des Mittelalters zeigt in dem Zusammengehörigkeitsgefühl, das sie beseelt, die eigenartigen Züge der germanischen 'Sippe[2].'" The West Goths travelled a long way, but they travelled by land[3].

Thus we are driven to the conclusion that the main disintegrating factor in the case of the Teutonic kindreds was

---

[1] Jaroslav's *Pravda* (from first half of 11th century) c. XXVIII. and I.—II. (in Ewers, *Älteste Recht der Russen* 1826, pp. 264, 306). In Oleg's treaty with the Byzantine Emperor in 912 it is laid down that if a Russ kills a Christian or a Christian a Russ, the slayer shall be put to death on the spot, but if he flees, his property is taken by the kinsmen of the dead (Dareste, *Études d'hist. de droit*, Paris 1889, p. 206). There is thus no liability of the slayer's kinsmen. I do not understand from what passage Dareste (p. 213) deduces the participation in wergild of distant kinsmen of the slain.

[2] Das Germanische Element im Spanischen Rechte, in *Zs. der Sav. Stift* (Germ. Abth.), XXXI. (1910), pp. 282—359.

[3] This particular instance suggests that the earlier the migration, the greater the cohesion of the kindred, and it is very probable that some connection of the kind might be traced. But there is hardly enough difference in time between the Frankish settlements in Gaul and the Anglo-Saxon conquest of Britain to account, on this theory, for the strength of the kindreds in the one country and their weakness in the other. Moreover the Vierlande, settled by Dutch immigrants at a late date, and Lübeck and other towns not founded until the 12th century, yet show considerable kin-solidarity. So do the records of the Silesian towns investigated by Frauenstädt, yet these only became German in the late Middle Ages.

CONCLUSION 265

migration, and especially migration by sea. Denmark and Schleswig are the strongholds of the kindreds: those of Friesland, the Netherlands and Northern France had vitality enough to withstand centuries of highly adverse influences, whereas the Icelander stood alone from the moment he set foot on Icelandic soil; and it may be questioned whether the Anglo-Saxon settler was in much better case in this respect. Here, too, we should find an explanation of the weakness of the kindreds in Norway, for much of the settlement of that country must have been accomplished by sea, and at a very late period[1]. No doubt the character of the country and the consequently often individualistic nature of the settlements were unfavourable to kinship-solidarity, and it may be that the small numbers of the invaders[2] and their relations with the aboriginal race were a partial cause of the weakness of the kindreds.

IV. *The pre-historic group.*

Throughout this book we have so far dealt with matters for which there is contemporary evidence in one form or another. It is surely pardonable if we now turn back to see how far the information we have gleaned in our researches will serve to throw light on the problems of an earlier time. With this end in view we will co-ordinate and tabulate the statements of wergild discussed in previous chapters.

§ 1. *Summary of wergild evidence.* The first point to strike us in the wergild schemes of the various Teutonic countries is their fundamental similarity.

Wherever there is any evidence at all that the schemes were actually in use, we find the sum paid in three instalments. In all cases the extent to which the individual participates is in the proportion of his degree of relationship with the slayer or the slain[3], and the liability of any given degree on the slayer's side usually corresponds in amount to the claim of that degree on the side of the slain. There appear to be two main methods of dividing that part of the wergild which goes to or is paid by the kinsmen outside the immediate

---

[1] The Trondhjem district and northwards does not seem to have been settled by the Teutonic invaders before the Iron Age; cp. A. Hansen, *Landnåm i Norge*.

[2] Hansen, op. cit., pp. 197 ff.

[3] Or, as in the North Frisian scheme, according to the degree of relationship between the slayer and the group of kindred to which the individual kinsman belongs.

family. The reckoning by thirds characteristic of the Salic Law is found again in the Oudenarde wergild scheme of 1300[1], and there are faint traces of it in the Norwegian wergilds[2],˙one of which however shows a certain predilection for reckoning small sums in fifths[3]. But far more widespread is the reckoning which gives to each further degree of kinship half the amount accorded to the degree nearer. It is obvious in the North Frisian wergild[4], and in the minor local schemes from both East and West Friesland[5], though there is, oddly enough, no trace of it in the full scheme given in the general custumal for Friesland west of the Lauwer[6]. And it appears in all Dutch wergilds[7]. If we abstract the classes of relatives of unequal degrees we find that it forms the basis of three more schemes: those from Lille and from Hunsingo (West Friesland), and that of the obsolete (Norwegian) Baugatal[8]. The principle is most clearly stated in the Swedish and Danish laws, which apply it consciously and consistently.

A point of more importance is the proportion borne by the heir's compensation to the kindred-compensation[9]. Here again the Norwegian wergilds elude us owing to their complexity, but for the other countries we can make out the following table:

	Heirs	Kindred
Iceland	all	none
Sweden (Vestergötland)	3	4
Denmark	1	2
Friesland	2	1
Holland	2	1
Belgium	2	2
France	2	2

We observe that Denmark rates the claims (or responsibility) of the kindred highest: Sweden comes next, Belgium and

---

[1] p. 174, supra.

[2] p. 59, supra (class III). Cp. also p. 51 (cl. II e), p. 58 (§ 228): the brother of the slain pays two-thirds of the sums paid by the slayer himself in II (1). The principle is definitely stated with regard to the *sakaukar* (IV), p. 60.

[3] p. 50 (cl. I v b) and p. 52, supra (V). In the case of small sums, fifths seem unnecessarily complicated fractions for an age when the precious metals could only be reckoned by weight. Possibly they were paid in cloth, or we may hazard a guess that there is a connection between them and the spiral arm-ring which is known to have been used as currency. It would be easy to reckon in fifths if these rings contained five (or two and a half) spirals.

[4] p. 106, supra.   [5] pp. 148, 152 (second and third cousins) and p. 153.

[6] pp. 149-50.   [7] pp. 160, 161, cp. p. 162 (Waterland).

[8] In Baugatal it is only approximately correct: brother 24: first cousins 12, second cousins $5\frac{1}{3}$, third cousins $2\frac{1}{3}$ (p. 12, supra).

[9] For the sake of simplicity I consider only the kindred of the slain.

CONCLUSION

France treat both alike, while Friesland and Holland exactly reverse the Danish ratio.

The next point to consider is the distinction between agnates and cognates. Perhaps even after all our studies of wergild it will still strike us as strange that so few Teutonic wergilds discriminate between persons related through males only and those related through women, whether on the paternal or maternal side. Except for South Germany, which does not concern us here, it is only in Ditmarschen, Norway and England that this distinction is observed[1]. In Ditmarschen the whole of the wergild probably went to agnates: in Norway[2] there is a distinctly preferential treatment of agnates, and in England a praecipuum, the *healsfang*, was definitely reserved for agnates, whatever may have been the case with the remainder of the wergild.

The peoples who ignore the distinction between agnates and cognates are however perfectly conversant with that between father's kinsfolk and mother's kinsfolk, and we find these participating in the following proportions:

	Father's kinsfolk	Mother's kinsfolk
Sweden: 1. All districts except Östgötaland	1	1
2. Östgötaland (later)	3	2
Denmark		
Holland		
Belgium		
France	1	1
North Friesland		
East and West Friesland: (1) local wergilds[3]		

---

[1] The later Vestergötland law in Sweden distinguishes between them, indeed, but treats them alike. The recognition of the distinction is presumably due to Norwegian influence.

[2] Including Baugatal.

[3] Brunner (p. 29, Anm. 1) suggests that though the mother's kindred is not stated to receive less than the father's kindred in the Hunsingo clause, this may yet be the case. He does not however deal with the Fivelgo wergild, which shows the same features. Moreover we have already noted that the local wergilds and the Westerlauwersche scheme are fundamentally inconsistent as regards the proportions paid to the degrees of kinship (p. 266, supra); so that it is unsafe to base theories on the probability of their similarity.

	Father's kindred	Mother's kindred
(2) *Allgemeine Gesetze des Westerlauwerschen Frieslands*[1]	3	2

The general prevalence of the fluctuating kindred, both in the original home and in the later settlements of the Teutons (with the exception of Ditmarschen), does in itself suggest difficulties in the theory of originally agnatic kindreds, and these difficulties increase in the light of our general review of the later evidence. If the agnatic kindreds had existed anywhere, it would surely be in Skåne, Denmark, and Schleswig, where the Teutonic race has been settled for a great period of time. Here then, we should expect to find the agnatic element strongest, or, if not, at least some clear traces of the struggle between the two elements. But what we do find is that in Skåne, Denmark, and Schleswig (including North Friesland), the kindred is not divided into agnates and cognates at all, but into father's kindred and mother's kindred, each of which receives the same sum in wergild, and has the same claim in inheritance. This latter feature is also characteristic of the Saxon law. "Es ist eine auffallende Erscheinung," observes Heusler, "dass das ostfalische Recht in der Seitenlinie jeden Unterschied zwischen Mann und Weib, Vater und Mutterseite scheint preisgegeben zu haben[2]," and he adds that the Magdeburg law resembles it in this respect. The old Holstein custom makes cognates and agnates equally liable for contributions towards the maintenance of pauper relatives.

Is not all this rather difficult to reconcile with the hypothesis of an originally agnatic society, which gradually, to its undoing, admitted the principle of cognation? Is it not vitally significant that the Danish peoples, the South Swedes, the Frisians and the Franks have not even grasped the distinction between agnates

---

[1] This is the ratio between the shares as far as uncles and second cousins are concerned, but the ratio between the shares of third cousins is as 28 to 27. The fact that the father's brother receives $\frac{1}{3}$ more than the mother's brother has occasionally been considered to show a preferential treatment of agnates, but it is clear from the fact that this proportion is maintained in the next class that it is based on the distinction between the paternal and maternal kindred, not that between agnates and cognates.

[2] A. Heusler, *Instit. des deutschen Privatrechtes*, II. p. 603.

CONCLUSION 269

and cognates, or, if they have, show absolutely no sign of it? They divide the kindred into father's kinsmen and mother's kinsmen, and treat the two exactly alike[1]. If agnation had ever been the rule among the Teutonic race, we should expect the institutions of these peoples, of all others, to have kept some trace of such a state of society. Where we do find discrimination in favour of agnation is where the kindred disappears early[2]: in England, in Iceland, in Norway, and probably among the Bavarians and Langobardians[3]—i.e. on the fringes of the Teutonic world. This description also includes the Saxons too, who do at least recognize the difference between agnates and cognates[4], and whose probably agnatic *Vetterschaften* appear to exist side by side with the kindred in Eastern Holstein[5]. It is obvious that there must be a strong tendency to an agnatic reckoning of kinship wherever there is a large alien and despised population, as among the Saxons, or indeed wherever a conquering race takes possession of a subject land[6].

The evidence we have just adduced thus tells heavily against the case for agnatic clans in the prehistoric period. Yet if the group of kinsfolk was originally a land-owning unit, as is usually assumed, the fluctuating kindred cannot be the original system of the Teutons, for such a group cannot hold land. When, in addition to the facts just stated, we remember that there is

---

[1] Except (for Friesland) in the Westerlauwersche wergild. No distinction is made in Friesland between the paternal and maternal branches in matters of inheritance.

[2] Except in Ditmarschen, which we will discuss later.

[3] Cp. Ficker, *Unters. zur Erbfolge*, I. pp. 236, 238.

[4] In the matter of *herwede*, war-gear, to which the *swertmac* or agnatic kinsman succeeds. It should be added however that *gerade*, the furniture of the house, descends exclusively through females (cp. Heusler, *Inst. des deutschen Privatrechts*).

[5] The vetterschaften of Eastern Holstein may possibly be agnatic, or they may be merely artificial groups. It must be noted that they are only mentioned by the side of the kindred, and that they appear in a district won back from the Wends. It is highly probable that they or their earlier prototypes were formed at the time of colonization, in which case they may perhaps be compared to the Teutonic Order which undertook the subjugation of the Slav population in Eastern Germany.

[6] Dr Rivers kindly tells me that his forthcoming work, *The History of Melanesian Society* (Cambridge University Press), will contain evidence showing that there is a tendency for patrilinear institutions to develop as the result of the interaction of peoples.

ample evidence from all parts of the world for transition from a matrilinear to a partially or wholly patrilinear society, whereas evidence for the reverse process is signally lacking, we must either deny that the primitive group was capable of holding land, or we must fall back on the theory, in favour of which other indications are not lacking, that membership of the primitive group was determined by descent through females.

We have not forgotten that Ditmarschen lies within the ancestral lands of the Teutons, and that it has a markedly agnatic constitution. It is a question whether Ditmarschen alone weighs as heavy in the balance as all the old Danish provinces. But in any case, is not agnation in this district susceptible of a very obvious explanation?

In 1559, as we have seen, the Duke issued a law for Ditmarschen which admitted daughters to a share in the family estate. In the following year the Ditmarschers submitted a plea for the repeal of the innovation. In this document they urge, not only that the subdivision of the farms led to impoverishment and to the emigration of their sons, but also that "*the upkeep of the dykes was endangered thereby*, for often the daughters were wooed [by men] in another parish; and before it could be shown to them and their husbands that the dykes and dams needed repair, it might happen that they had been completely destroyed[1]." Is it not possible that the work of con-

---

[1] Quoted by Sering, p. 142. Another passage in this same Ditmarschen document suggests a line of speculation as to one of the causes of the Teutonic migrations. There is some evidence that the principles of mother-right were still strong among the Teutonic peoples at the time of the migrations (cp. Chadwick, *Heroic Age*, ch. XVI.; *Origin of English Nation*, pp. 327 ff.). Could the intrusion of patrilinear succession be a contributory cause of the migrations? The document just quoted contains an interesting description of the results of forcing a measure of cognation on an agnatically organized society: "Not only are the farms (*hoven*) thereby torn from one another, but also the young men are in many ways hindered from earning their living, through the many subdivisions and diminutions (of their inheritance)...and they have been induced to seek their living and secure themselves maintenance elsewhere outside this land, and they will eventually leave the country desolate and forsaken." May not the unrest caused by the analogous process, the intrusion of an agnatic element into an agricultural community in which descent was reckoned through the mother, have been an indirect but none the less potent cause of the national migrations, by driving young men to the profession of arms, and thereby

structing and maintaining the great dykes, the names of which show that they were erected by groups of kinsmen[1], would result in an agnatic organization, for the reasons indicated by the Ditmarschers themselves in the foregoing passage? For this reason Ditmarschen cannot be adduced to prove the existence of prehistoric agnatic clans in the Danish peninsula.

§ 2. *The kindred and the cult-community.* It is still somewhat of a mystery why the migrating kindreds, which do show a distinct tendency towards agnation, never completed their development by evolving into powerful agnatic clans, with clanchiefs for leaders in war. A partial explanation of what we may perhaps call the arrested development of the migrating kindred may perhaps be sought in the religious history of the Teutons. It is obvious that ancestor-worship, so frequently found in connection with a clan system, must segregate the kinsfolk into organizations either on patrilinear or on matrilinear lines. Now we know that the warlike followers of kings

---

swelling the king's followings to such an extent that continual conquests became an economic necessity?

The influence of this unrest would be even more direct in the case of the early Viking expeditions by sea, if we are right in refusing to regard them as emigrations of whole tribes. So far as our information extends, chronology would bear out this suggestion. Our evidence for non-matrilinear succession among the Angli goes back at least a century earlier than among the Danes (Chadwick, *Origin of English Nation*, p. 334), and the unrest among them was also earlier. We can trace the succession through women in the royal families of Norway and Sweden to a still later date. If we might assume the persistence of mother-right among the other classes of the community for an equally long period, the intrusion of succession through males might have some connection with the earliest Viking unrest. (In some parts of the world the nobles are the first to abandon mother-right, as in Ashanti and Dahomey (cp. E. Mayer, *Deutsche und französ. Verfassungsgesch.* 1. p. 419, where it is maintained that father-right became the rule among the upper classes before it was introduced among the common people.) It may be remembered that Dudo, William of Jumièges and Saxo all attribute the unrest to an excess of population in Scandinavia, which they ascribe to polygamy. It is generally agreed that polygamy cannot be the cause, but the result of rival claims, both by agnates and cognates, on inheritance which had hitherto descended only through the female, would be very similar to the supposed effects of polygamy, since it would double the number of heirs to any given property.

[1] The basis of organization would probably be found in the already isolated groups of inhabitants of the *Wurten* or mounds, on which single houses or hamlets had been perched, prior to the erection of the great dykes.

worshipped Odin, the universal and anti-tribal nature of whose cult has been recently pointed out by Professor Chadwick[1]. As the influence of these warriors predominated among the migrating peoples, this cult must have exercised an adverse influence on the rise of tribal deities or deified ancestors.

This explanation can hardly account, however, for the impermanence of the Bavarian *fara*, and the Langobardian *genealogia*, for these appear to have been agricultural groups, not warlike clans. These groups seem to have survived the changes and chances of much wandering and many wars; and they must have been definite in outline, for they could own land. They seem to possess all the elements of permanence, and yet they disappear at the very dawn of history. Any attempt to account for their apparently sudden extinction must necessarily be little more than idle speculation, but is it not possible that the cohesion of each unit was due to a common cult, the worship of some ancestor, and that the introduction of Christianity, in shattering the cult, also destroyed the principle of cohesion within the clan? The kindreds of the north were not subject to this danger, for ancestor-worship is incompatible with the shifting kindred.

If we ask whether there are any traces of ancestor-worship among the Teutons, the answer is ambiguous but interesting. Such indications as exist for a cult of this kind come from Sweden and Denmark. Even here, however, there is little enough to enumerate. The Swedish ecclesiastical law from Småland speaks of the 'kindred's cairn' (*ættæ högher*), and mentions the penalty incurred by strangers who inter a corpse in it[2]. The practice of burying the dead in cairns or barrows was as a rule frowned upon by the ecclesiastical authorities, who considered it a heathen practice, so that the 'kindred's cairn' probably dates from pre-Christian times. In *Heimskringla* we are told how at the end of the heathen period (1019) the messengers of St Olaf were refused entrance at four farms one autumn night in Gautland, the inhabitants alleging that *álfa-blót*, sacrifice to 'elves,' was proceeding within[3]. Thus the sacrifice was offered by each household separately within its own four walls. The evidence that connects *álfr*, elf, with the spirit of a dead man, both in early Scandinavian and in North German belief, is sufficient to make the nature of this sacrifice quite clear[4].

For Denmark we happen to possess the regulations, dated 1440, for a yearly 'kinsmen's festival' in Ribe, at which the noble families Lange and Munk assembled. The regulations provide that a mass is to be said during

---

[1] *Heroic Age*, pp. 409, 425.
[2] *Sveriges Gamla Lagar*, VI. p. 110.
[3] Olafs S. helga, ch. 91 (in Magnússon-Morris translation, ch. 92, vol. II. pp. 145-7).
[4] Cp. esp. story of Ólaf Geirstaða álfr, Fornmanna Sögur X. pp. 211-2. The evidence is stated in *Cambridge Mediæval Hist.*, vol. II. ch. XV c.

CONCLUSION 273

the festival "for all the living and dead of that kinsmen's feast and assembly," for which purpose a chaplain is to attend the festival every year[1]. It is at least probable that this was not the only instance of the kind in Denmark[2], and that such definite honour to the dead dates back to the pre-Christian times.

There seem to be faint traces of ancestor-worship in Norway, where the custom is recorded of drinking toasts in honour of departed ancestors at the great festivals[3]. This toast-drinking, however, must have been a matter for the individual guest, though it may date back to a time when all the guests were kinsmen. In Iceland a belief was prevalent among a few of the settlers, that their kinsfolk died into a hill, which was sacred to them[4], but there is no trace of an actual cult. All over Teutonic Europe, however, except in England and Iceland, there is abundant evidence for a cult, not of ancestors but of the dead, in connection with which the Christian Church met with the most obstinate resistance[5].

The survival of ancestor-worship in South Sweden and possibly in Denmark, combined with the absence of all trace of a cult of the dead in Iceland and England, inclines me to think that we should not be far wrong if we regarded the evidence as pointing to the existence, among prehistoric clans, of an early ancestor-worship, which merged into a mere cult of the dead owing to the confusion arising from the intrusion of an agnatic element into the groups of kindred. It is obvious that the cult of ancestors could not survive in the 'shifting' kindred of historical times. Some such theory might explain the strange gulf between the faith of the multitude and that of the man who took up, even temporarily, the profession of arms, by supposing the latter to be cut off from the common cult of his kindred, and consequently adopting that of the royal court. It is worth noting that the cult of Odin itself shows features suggesting its affinity with the worship of royal ancestors.

§ 3. *Limits of the group.* We have so far not considered the extent of the primitive Teutonic group of kinsfolk. In historical times we find that the circumference of the kindred— if we may use the term—fluctuates between the third degree inclusive (in the Netherlands) and the sixth (in Sweden and perhaps in France)[6]. Scholars have made great efforts to

---

[1] Kinch, *Ribe Bys Historie*, pp. 308–12.
[2] When in Schleswig in 1912 I was informed that certain families of the old Schleswig nobility still keep up the custom of a yearly festival among themselves.
[3] *Heimskringla*, Hák. S. góða, ch. 14 [Magnússon-Morris transl., vol. I. p. 165 (ch. XVI.)].
[4] Cp. *Landnáma* (Hauksbók), ch. 56, 73, 164: Hæns. ch. 20; Eyrb. S. ch. 11.
[5] Cp. Saupe, *Indiculus Superstitionum* (Leipsic, 1891), under headings I to IV.
[6] Cp. p. 193 supra.

P. 18

show either that these variations are not original but are due to ecclesiastical influence, or (in some cases) that they do not in fact exist, the differences being merely due to variations in the mode of reckoning kinship. There is probably some truth at any rate in the latter contention, but the disparities cannot be wholly explained away, and the fact remains that it is useless to seek for the original bounds of the Teutonic kindred. If the original group was of the nature of a clan, recognizing kinship through the female only, it is easy to account for the divergences in estimating the limit of kinship among the Teutonic races, for there would be no primitive model to follow. A group organized on patrilinear or matrilinear lines will probably include much more distant degrees of kinship than a kindred recognizing descent through both parents. In the former case the whole group will have a name by which its members can distinguish one another, and the right to this name, i.e. descent, is the main factor determining kinship, rather than the actual degree of relationship between any two members of the group. But once kinship is reckoned through both sexes, we have to take into account the fact that the various branches of a man's kindred will no longer share a common name, will in fact no longer be related to each other as well as to himself, and the unwieldiness of the kindred will increase in proportion to the number of unrelated groups in it. This circumstance obviously sets a limit to the size of the shifting kindred. Thus it is easy to account for the divergences among the Teutonic races with regard to the extent of the kindred, for the necessity for limiting the group would arise naturally, and would depend in the last resort on the extent to which men took wives out of their own district. Where marriage within the district prevailed to any extent, the various branches of the kindred would be likely to be at hand and could be readily assembled; where this was not the practice the kindred would be unwieldy and its limits would tend to shrink[1]. On this theory, Östergötland and Vestergötland in Sweden, with kinship recognized to the sixth degree as late

---

[1] This refers of course only to the kindred as an effective and cohesive group : for purposes of inheritance kinship was frequently acknowledged as far as it could be traced.

as the 13th century, must have been the home of very much localized kindreds.

It has occasionally been stated that while kindreds organized on matrilinear or on patrilinear lines are to be found in various parts of the world, a cohesive kindred which should reckon kinship through both male and female not only did not exist, but was inherently impossible[1]. It is true that permanently organized kindreds on the double basis are unthinkable; but our researches have shown that the shifting kindred can persist for hundreds of years—probably it would not be an over-statement to attribute a thousand years of life to it in Schleswig—and that in spite of its lack of organization, of local habitation and name, it was able to exercise no small influence on the history of the nations which harboured it.

We have seen it manifest its solidarity in various ways: it appears in law-courts, now to support a kinsman by oath, now to pledge wergild or peace, now to sue the slayer or to insist on the proper distribution of wergild. Or again, we have seen it refuse to submit its internal affairs to judicial control, and this is perhaps its most characteristic and most primitive side. We have seen it maintain its own poor, and cling through centuries to the right to avenge its own wrongs. We may well doubt whether agnatic clans could have achieved more towards securing the independence of the settled agricultural classes. In Ditmarschen we have even caught a glimpse of the last shattered fragment of a clan owning and working land[2].

But it must be admitted that protracted migrations were likely to prove fatal to a group for whose continued existence it was necessary that the families of all the women who had married into it should be close at hand and willing to co-operate

---

[1] E. Grosse, *Die Formen der Familie*. Schrader, *Reallexikon*, s.v. *Sippe*.

[2] Swart, *Fries. Agrarhist.*, pp. 325 ff., describes an estate owned by a great number of persons divided into 'teeler' or 'teener,' which he considers to be originally *Geschlechter*. It is to be observed that inheritance is *only in the direct line*. The intention of this restriction was obviously to keep the property within the family. A more natural means of securing the same end would have been to limit succession to agnates, but we have no reason to suppose that the Frisians were acquainted with the idea of agnation.

with one another. Moreover the shifting kindreds were totally unfitted to serve as the organization of a migrating people. Everything would depend on the king and on his following of professional warriors, and in prolonged migrations this group would tend to increase very greatly at the expense of the disintegrating kindreds. Yet as long as the latter had not been entirely annihilated, they would tend to rally when a final settlement was made, the need being more urgent than before in view of the increased strength of the *comites* or nobles. Where however the migrating group is not a tribe, but a collection of warriors, as in the case of a migration by sea, there will be no nucleus round which a kindred can grow up, so that England and Iceland will lack the influences which the institution brings to bear on the social and political order. Yet even in these countries, the laws will still show clear traces of a system which had been the keystone of the social fabric before migration.

APPENDIX I

THE WERGILD OF A 'HUNDRED OF SILVER' IN ICELAND

At the beginning of his essay 'Das hundert silbers' published in 1856[1], Dietrich observes: "Es besteht also noch das schwanken zwischen einem werth von beiläufig 20 und einem von 120 speciesthalern." No doubt, like others before and after him, Dietrich hoped to have put the final interpretation on the term, but the fact remains that the words just quoted are as true to-day as they were when they were written.

It may be as well to recapitulate the points which are regarded as established. Besides silver, wadmal (homespun) was legal tender in ancient Iceland. Both wadmal and silver were reckoned in marks and aurar, thus:

Wadmal.	*Silver.*
6 ells one eyrir	3 örtugar one eyrir
8 aurar one mark	8 aurar one mark.
2½ marks (120 ells) one 'hundred.'	

It is obvious that in the wadmal reckoning the terms *eyrir* (ounce) and *mark* (8 oz.) are borrowed from the silver reckoning.

It is agreed that in the year 1000 an eyrir of 'legal' (i.e. alloyed) silver[2] was worth four times as much as an eyrir of wadmal. An eyrir of 'burnt' (i.e. refined) silver was twice as valuable as an eyrir of legal silver, or eight times as valuable as an eyrir of wadmal. Later the relative values of 'burnt' silver and wadmal fluctuated slightly, but this hardly concerns us here. 'Legal' silver disappeared early in the twelfth century.

---

[1] *Zs. f. d. A.* x. pp. 223—240.
[2] 'Old legal silver' (*lögsilfr it forna*) must be distinguished from 'legal aurar' (*lögaurar*) which refer to wadmal aurar of 6 ells.

Now we come to the point in dispute. What is a 'hundred of silver'? There are really three possible interpretations:

(i) The 'hundred' really refers to the wadmal reckoning, and the phrase 'hundred of silver' means 'the price of a hundred ells, paid in silver,' i.e. $2\frac{1}{2}$ wadmal marks or 20 wadmal aur. (5 silver aur.).

(ii) The term 'hundred' was borrowed from the wadmal reckoning, and as it meant $2\frac{1}{2}$ marks in that reckoning, so it also means $2\frac{1}{2}$ marks (of silver) in the silver reckoning; i.e. 20 silver aur.

(iii) 'Hundred' is merely a numerical term in either reckoning, and in the silver reckoning it means 120 aurar. Therefore the silver table should be completed by: '15 *marks* (120 *aur.*) *one hundred.*'

The first view is really held by Schive, in his *Norges Mynter i middelalderen*, published in 1865: " Hundrað silfrs = $2\frac{1}{2}$ marks or 20 aurar. The expression is in fact elliptical and signifies 100 ells of wadmal, that is a long hundred or 120 ells, reckoned in silver in 6-ell aurar; thus 20 aurar of silver = 6 × 20 ells of wadmal[1]." But we know that 5 aurar of silver = 20 aurar of wadmal or 6 × 20 ells; so the logical conclusion of this statement would be: a hundred of silver = 120 ells = 20 aurar of wadmal = 5 aurar of silver. Fritzner's Dictionary follows Schive: " *hundrað silfrs*, i.e. 120 ells of wadmal to be paid in silver at such a rate that 1 eyrir of silver is equal to 6 ells of wadmal." Zoega's Old Icelandic Dictionary, published in 1910, seems to follow Fritzner, but it indicates by a query that the question is still open: "hundrað silfrs ? the silver value of 120 ells (= 20 ounces)."

This theory can be seen to be untenable directly we follow it to its logical conclusion, that a hundred of silver = $2\frac{1}{2}$ marks *of wadmal*. For in this case the wergild for slaying would actually be less than the 3-mark (wadmal) fine for all sorts of breaches of the law, and would be less than half the amount of *réttr*, a fine payable for striking, wounding or insulting another. It will also be seen that this theory finds no support in the one passage which throws any light on the question, so that it may fairly be dismissed.

---

[1] p. xxii.

APPENDIX I 279

The second view (hundred of silver = 20 silver aurar) is that of Cleasby-Vigfússon's dictionary, and has since been urged by Arnljótr Óláfsson in 1904[1]. The main reason for it has been forcibly put by Professor Finnur Jónsson in an appendix to his German edition of Njálssaga in 1908[2], and by Professor Björn Ólsen, in the 1910 Year-Book of the Icelandic Archaeological Society[3], as well as in the periodical *Skírnir* of the same year[4]. The third view (hundred of silver = 120 silver aurar) has been held by various earlier Danish and German scholars, but its only modern upholder is Dr Valtýr Guðmundsson, who has urged it in two essays published in 1893 and 1909 respectively[5]. The two theories can be considered together, for they both turn on the same passage in the Icelandic laws, a little paragraph entitled *Frá silfrgang*, which we have in two recensions. The first (*Konungsbók*, ed. Finsen, I *b*. 192) runs thus:

"In that time when Christianity came out to Iceland silver was paid here in all large debts—'pale' silver" (i.e. alloyed or 'legal' silver)... "*þat var iafn micit fe callat. c. silfrs. sem iiii hundroð oc xx. alna vaðmala. oc varð þa at halfri mörc vaðmala eyrir.*"

The supporters of (ii) read this passage thus: "This was reckoned an equal amount of money: one hundred of silver and four hundred [and 20] ells of wadmal; and so an eyrir (of silver) is equal to half a mark of wadmal." Professor Finnur Jónsson regards the 'and 20' as an interpolation, while Professor Ólsen considers it to be an 'extra' sum, thrown in when large payments in wadmal were made at the rate of an inch per ell. Their justification is found in the other recension of the passage (*Skálholtsbók*, p. 462), where the 'and 20' is omitted. We thus get the following result:

---

[1] Um lögaura og silfurgang fyrrum á Íslandi. *Tímarit hins íslenzka Bókmentafélags*, xxv. pp. 1—26.

[2] Altnord. Saga-Bibliothek, *Brennu-Njálssaga*, pp. 422—4.

[3] Um hina fornu íslensku alin, *Árbók hins íslenzka fornleifafélags*, 1910 (Reykjavík, 1911).

[4] Um silfurverð og vaðmálsverð, *Skírnir*, 1910, pp. 1—18.

[5] Manngjöld-hundrað, *Germanische Abhandl. zum LXX. Geburtstag K. von Maurers*, Göttingen, 1893, pp. 523 ff., and in *Festskrift til L. A. Wimmer*, Copenhagen, 1909, pp. 55—63.

A hundred of silver = 4 hundreds, i.e. 480 ells, of wadmal.
= 4 times 2½ marks of wadmal.
A mark of silver = 4 times a wadmal mark.
Therefore a hundred of silver = 2½ marks (20 aur.) of silver.

(iii) It must be admitted that the third theory reads the above passage in a somewhat forced way. We are to take the 'IIII hundroð oc xx alna vaðmala' not as 4 hundred and 20 ells, but as '20 and 4 hundreds of ells,'—i.e. (24 × 120) 2880 ells.

On this plan a hundred of silver = 24 hundreds of wadmal, i.e. (24 × 2½) = 60 marks of wadmal.

One mark of silver = 4 marks of wadmal.

Therefore 60 marks of wadmal = 15 marks (120 aurar) of silver.

The other recension of this passage runs thus :

" This was considered an equal amount of money : C. of silver and iiij. c. of wadmal. Then half a mark (4 aur.) of wadmal is equal to an eyrir of silver."

Dr Guðmundsson reads this *iiij. c.* as referring to wadmal *aurar* (not ells as in the other recension). Thus he gets the result :

A hundred of silver = 4 × 120 aurar of wadmal.

Therefore a hundred of silver = 120 aurar of silver.

We should add that in his later essay Dr Valtýr Guðmundsson then proceeds to throw doubt on the value and accuracy of the whole passage, and in both contends that the wergild of a hundred of silver was paid in burnt silver. We will defer the discussion of this point and return to our main problem.

It is obvious that both theories are perfectly tenable as interpretations of the actual words of Grágás, though it would seem that (ii) has the advantage in this respect, as being a simpler reading. On the other hand it can be fairly urged for (iii) that it is equivalent to the wergild of Baugatal, and more nearly approaches the amounts of foreign wergilds. These are however points on which I cannot personally lay much stress, and were this all, there would seem to me to be no reason for deciding in favour of the one or the other. But fortunately there is another method of judging of their relative probability.

In comparing the wergilds of Saga times with those of the Sturlung period, it is essential to remember that much more distinction between persons was made in the later period[1]. It may also be regarded as beyond dispute that in the Sturlung times wealth had been collected into comparatively few hands. For these reasons the wergilds of *chiefs* in Sturlung times must be put out of court in any comparison between the two periods. Now the smallest wergild paid for any person in the Sturlung cycle of Sagas (for Böðvarr lítilskeyta, Sturl. I. p. 210[2], and to Hneitir's widow, I. p. 15) was 12 hundreds of wadmal = 1440 ells. But Thorgils Oddason claims 30 hundreds of wadmal for Hneitir (I. p. 16) and Hneitir had received a similar sum, 3600 ells[3], for his nephew Thorsteinn (I. p. 13). For Bjarni Arnason 20 hundreds, i.e. 2400 ells, are paid (I. p. 386). Now on theory (ii) a 'hundred of silver,' the normal wergild of the preceding period, contained 480 ells : theory (iii) would make it 2880 ells. The latter, it will be seen, corresponds very fairly to the smaller Sturlung wergilds, but before the supporters of the previous theory can persuade us that 480 ells was a reasonable wergild in 1000, while the *minimum* wergild for a small farmer in 1118 was 1440 ells, they will need to adduce some entirely new and unsuspected evidence for far-reaching economic changes in Iceland, or for a great increase in the value set on human life. Of the latter suggestion Sturlunga Saga itself is surely the best refutation.

But if we apply the results of Professor Ólsen's illuminating paper 'Um silfurverð og vaðmálsverð' to the wergild problem, the weakness of the 20-aurar theory is even more strikingly apparent. Professor Ólsen shows conclusively that at the time of the introduction of Úlfljót's law in 930, 6 ells of wadmal were actually equal in value to the eyrir of alloyed silver. He explains this state of things by the conditions of the newly-settled country, where, as in other new countries, the precious metals had a comparatively low purchasing power. Now in this case, the wergild of 20 silver aurar would be equal to 20 aurar of wadmal ; i.e. to 120 ells. Thus this theory is open to the same

---

[1] The largest wergild in Sturl., 2 hundred hundreds, is 24 times as much as the smallest—10 hundred.

[2] The edition quoted is that of Kålund.

[3] I.e. 10 hundred 3-ell aurar.

overwhelming objection as (1)—viz. the *réttr* of 48 aurar, for a blow or an insult, would in 930 be more than twice as much as a normal wergild. The latter would even be exceeded by the 3-mark fine (24 wadmal aurar) exacted for quite trivial breaches of the law.

We must thus conclude that the wergild of a 'hundred of silver' is equivalent to 120 aurar. In 930 this would be (120 × 6 =) 720 ells. As wadmal began to fall rapidly in value the recipients would insist on being paid in silver, and hence the stipulation constantly met with in the Sagas for a hundred *of silver*. By the year 1000, when an eyrir of alloyed silver was four times as valuable as an eyrir of wadmal, a wergild of 120 silver aurar would, as we have seen, amount to 2880 ells, or about the amount of the smaller Sturlunga wergilds.

There is much that is tempting about Dr Valtýr Guðmundsson's plea for reckoning wergilds in *burnt* silver, whereby a closer correspondence with the amounts of Continental wergilds is attained. But it is highly probable that Baugatal's 120 silver aurar, which had become a traditional wergild, may date back to a time when such a sum was really equal in value to the larger amounts of other Continental wergilds[1]. Moreover there is a difficulty in reconciling the burnt silver theory with the explicit statement in Grágás that payments may be made in alloyed silver[2]. Even if one surmounts this difficulty, it seems that one has to make another assumption, namely that Sturlunga always refers to aurar (of three ells) even where that word is not expressly mentioned. Now Sturl. itself equates ' 2 hundred hundreds' (of ells) with '80 hundreds of 3-ell aurar[3],' so that

---

[1] Professor Ólsen, in his paper Um silfurverð etc. quotes Holmboe, *Norges Mønter*, p. viii, as observing that it is a common phenomenon that traditional sums for fines etc. have been adhered to without regard to the fluctuations in actual value that the sum undergoes in the course of years.

[2] Dr Guðmundsson, Sølvkursen ved år 1000 (*Festskr. til Wimmer*, 1909), p. 62, throws doubt on this passage for various reasons into which we need not enter here. But surely he is unjust to the text when he refuses credence to its statement that base alloyed silver was legal tender in the year 1000, on the ground that Norwegian *coins* of that date are of refined silver. The passage does not say that alloyed silver was used for minting coins in Norway, only that it was legal tender in Iceland.

[3] Where Sturla demands the same sum that Hafliði got.

here at least it means *ells* not *aurar* where it mentions neither. Further arguments against the burnt silver theory have been adduced by Professor Ólsen in the above-mentioned paper (pp. 10 f.). The significance of the change from a silver to a wadmal reckoning must also be borne in mind. If wergilds had been reckoned in burnt silver from the beginning, there would have been no particular reason to abandon a silver reckoning for a wadmal one at the beginning of the 12th century. But it was just at this time that the supply of the old alloyed silver began to run short. It is surely not a coincidence that the abandonment of the old silver currency synchronized with the adoption of a wadmal reckoning in wergilds.

APPENDIX II

I. *Norway—Deed of reconciliation in a slaying-suit.*

17 April 1348. [From *Norske Samlinger*, III. Christiania, 1835, pp. 354–5.]

"Ollum monnum þæim sem þættæ bref sea æðr höyræ sendæ Symon Gudthormsson. Petær a Vpsalum. Ifuær j Oom. Olafuær Hakonærson. Sighurdr a Bö. ok Sigurdhr a Lökine. quediæ guds ok sinæ kunnigt gerande att a hælghæthorsdags æftan...varo mer a Fylkis-haughi hia. saam ok höyrdom aa att Arne Odzson sættis vidær Erling Ormssyne medr handzsale firis þætt att han hafde vordett att skada Ogmundi Pipprunghi vfirir syniu broder Erlings. medr þæim hætte att han fæk Erlinge halftt fimttæ öyris boll iærdær j Vræstodum ær liggær i Stumfnæ-dale till fulre æighu ok alz afrædis. var ok þætt skyllmale þeiræ j fyrirsogdu handszale. att Arne Odzson skall nu allungis sattær vera vidær Erlingh vm fyrnæmtt aftak Ogmunda brodr Erlings, sva sæm Arnne hæfde aldri brottett þætt værk motte Erlinghi ok þæn þæiræ sæm þennæ satmalæ ryfuær æðr rofzsmen till fær skal slika fyrir suara sæm gridnidinghun ligær vidær aatt rettom laghom. æffter þætt gaf Arnne Erlinghe æinæ hafzsældo smors."

"To all men who see or hear this letter: Simon Guthormsson, Peter at Upsölum, Iver at Umb(?)[1], Olaf Hákonarson, Sigurd at Bö and Sigurd at Lögr[2] send the greetings of God and of themselves, making known that on the eve of Maundy Thursday we were present at Fylkis-haug: saw and listened while Arni Oddsson came to terms with Erling Ormsson with clasp of hands[3], for having been so unfortunate as to kill, by misadventure, Ogmund Piprung, Erling's brother; in this wise, that he gave Erling a strip of land taxed at 4½ aurar at Orestadir, which lies in Stufnardal[4], [to be] his full possession and at his complete disposal; and it was their agreement upon the aforesaid hand-clasp that Arni Oddsson shall now be entirely at peace with Erling as regards the above-mentioned slaying[5] of Ogmund Erling's brother, just as if Arni had never committed that deed against Erling; and whichever of them infringes these terms of peace, or induces others to infringe them, shall be liable to the same penalties as those to which the nithing who breaks truce is legally liable. Thereafter Arni gave Erling a half-cask of butter."

---

[1] I cannot trace this name in the district with which this document deals. Umba occurs as a place-name in N. Norway.

[2] There is a place-name Lögr in Gudbrandsdal.

[3] As at the conclusion of a bargain.

[4] There is a Stufnardal in Heinafylki, west of Mjösen.

[5] Lit. 'removal.'

II. *Norway—Plea to the king concerning wergild,* 1585.

[From *Norske Herredags Dombøger,* udg. f. d. norske hist. Kildestriftfond. I. Række, Bd III (Tillæg), p. 223.]

A plea to the king from Thorold Asmundsen of Oddernes sogn in Manddals Lehn.

"...Aszmund Thorgiersen, wden skyld och brøde bleff ihielslagen aff Amund Endreszen j sit egett hus, for huilcken gierning hand [Thorold] med sine brødre och wenner fick Amund fangen, før end hand fick kongens dag i thend sag, och antuorde hannem foggitten, som thend tiid wor Hans Borre— och hand siiden wden hans minde slap hannem aff fengsell. att gaa ledig och løsz, huor hand midler thiid er død, och att hand och hans brødre ther effther ere worden forligt med for^{ne} Amund Endreszens arffuinge, saa the skulle haffue af thennom for theris faders død 60 daller,......effther thet forligelsze breff, thennom ther om er emellom gangen, huor aff hoesz cantzelliet findis en copie, siden haffuer laugmanden dømbt Amund Endreszen wdsleger, och hans godtz vnder kongen, huoroffuer hand och hans søskinde jntett fick aff thet thennom loffuit wor. Begierendis therefore...att kon. matt. naadigst for Guds skyld will ansehe hans och hans brøderis leylighed och betencke thennom med noggit effther hans matt. egen guode thøcke for theris faders dod, efftherthj att drabernis boe och godtz er optagen, kon. matts. thilhende."

Thorold Asmundsen complains that "Asmund Thorgeirsen (his father) was killed sackless and innocent of offence in his own house by Amund Endressen, for which deed he, with his brothers and friends, made a prisoner of Amund before he got the king's judgment in the case, and handed him over to the Provost (fogt) who at that time was Hans Borre; who later, without his approval, let him [Amund] out of prison, to go free, in which freedom he in the meantime died; and that he [Thorold] and his brothers thereupon made terms with Amund Endressen's heirs, in such fashion that they should have from them 60 florins for their father's death... according to that deed of reconciliation which passed between them in the matter, and of which a copy is to be found in the chancery. Since then the *Lagmand* has adjudged Amund Endressen to have been an outlaw, and has awarded his goods to the king, whereby he [Thorold] and his brothers and sisters got nothing of what was promised them. He therefore begs... that His Royal Highness will graciously, for God's sake, consider his position and that of his brothers, and grant them a consideration [in cash] for their father's death, according to his Majesty's own good judgment, seeing that the slayer's farm and goods are confiscated for the behoof of His Majesty."

III. *Denmark,* 1513—*The Bilde-Hak Orfejde.*

[From *Danske Magazin,* III Række, Bd II. p. 148.]

"Vii efftir[ne] Steen Bilde paa Liwngesgard, Nielss Hog paa Esker, Tyge Krabbe paa Brustrope, Axell Brade paa Krogholm, riddere, Hanss Bilde paa Egede, Knud Bilde, hoffuitzman paa Gladfaxe, Johan Oxe paa Nielstrop oc Holgerd Gregerssøn paa Torup, som aff waben ere, giøre alle vittherlicht met thette wortt opne breff, at wii haffue loffuit oc tilsagd, oc met thette wortt opne breff loffue oc tilsige erlig oc welbyrdug mend Her Henrich Krummedige, Knud Goye oc Anderss Hack paa welbyrdug mandz Anderss Bildes vegne, then bod, wander oc høffskhed for erlig oc welbyrdug mandz Nielss Hackes død, tess wer for[ne] Anderss Bilde ihiell slo, eth twsind marck vt at giffue i Lund inden ste. Mortens dag nw nest komendes, thre lester korn iordegodz, som gott er for sith landgilde, vd at legges i Skone, Sieland oc i Lolland inden Poske nw nest komendes. Ith twsend Marck at ste. Micaels dag ther nest efftir komendes i Lund vd at legges, oc saa halffannet twsende marck ocsaa vd at legges i Lund ste. Michelss dag eth aar ther nest efftir komendes, oc ther till eth clenodie effter sex theres venners seyelse paa begge sidher. Thii beplichte vii oss oc wore arffuinge at betalle oc vdlegge for[ne] Her Heinrich Krummedige, Knud Goye oc Anderss Hack, thennom eller theres arffuinge, paa for[ne] Nielss Hackes borns vegne for[ne] swm penninge oc godz inden for[ne] thiidher som forschreffuit staar, vthen allt hinder genseyelse eller hielperede i nogre mode[1]."

---

[1] Translated in text, p. 89 supra.

APPENDIX II

IV. *Denmark*, 1542—*Wergild for Niels Mogenssen.*

[From *Danske Magazin*, III Række, Bd IV (1854), p. 262.]

"Vii epter[ne] Erich Schram till Tielle Eyller Løcky till Torup Oluff Glob till Vellumgaard Kiendess och gøer witterlicktt for Alle att wi haffue lofuett oc tilsagdtt Och mett thette wort obne breff loffue oc tilsige Erlige oc welbyrdige mendtt Jacop Hardenbærigh till Sandhollt Eyler Hardenbærgh till Matterop Christopher Johanssen til Drenderop Anderss Johanssen till Faabitz Hartwiig Tammessen til Palsgaardtt Christopher Rosenkrandtz till Skierne Oc Christopher Rosenkrandtz till Heffringholm, Huilke for[ne] Riddermendtz Szom haffue loffuet oc fullsagdtt for Erlig oc welbyrdiigh Swendtt Peter Støggy till for[ne] Heffrindtholm For then Swm gwldtt oc pendinge Szom handt vdttgiffue skall till Nielss Maagenssens eptermaalssmendt huess Siell guudt haffue Szom for for[ne] Peder Støggy dess werre y hielsloo Szom ær fempten hwndritt marc y goidt mynt oc tuende klenody huertt Szaa gott szom ett hwndritt gyldene thette for[ne] guldtt och pendinge tilsige wii forbeneffnde forløfftings mendtt oc bekiende thet paa wor gode troff oc loffue att Per Støggy thette for[ne] vbrødeligen wiidt ordt oc alticle rider (*sic*) oc frunder vden [al hi]nder oc hielpe Reede vdttgiffue Schall Som thett breff indeholder oc vdtwisser [som] for[ne] gode Mendt for[ne] Nielss Maagensses eptermaalssmendt loffuet oc tilsagdtt haffuer oc schall handt holde thennom oc theris arffuinge thett vden aldt Skade kost oc tærendt y alle maade. Att Szaa ij Sandhudt ær tr[øcker w]ii waare Ingseygle neden for thette wortt obne breff."

"We whose names follow, Erich Schram of Tielle, Eiler Lykke of Torup, Oluf Glob of Vellumgaard, acknowledge and make known to all that we have promised and assured, and with this our open letter do promise and assure the honourable and well-born gentlemen, Jacob Hardenberg of Sandholt, Eiler Hardenberg of Matterup, Christopher Johanssen of Denderup, Anders Johanssen of Faabitz, Hartwig Tammesen of Palsgaard, Christopher Rosenkrands of Skjerne and Christopher Rosenkrands of Hevringholm; these knights just mentioned having (in their turn) promised to stand surety and bail on behalf of the honourable and well-born squire Peter Støggy of the aforesaid Hevringholm for that sum of gold and money which he shall pay to the plaintiffs in the suit concerning the slaying of Niels Mogenssen (whose soul may God keep), whom the aforesaid Peter Støggy unfortunately slew; namely fifteen hundred marks in good coin and two jewels each of the value of a hundred gulden. This gold and money aforesaid we the aforesaid sureties guarantee, and we declare on our good faith and word, that Per Støggy will pay the aforesaid faithfully, without fail, delay or excuse...[1] in such manner as the deed sets forth and shows, wherein the aforesaid gentlemen have given promise and pledge to the plaintiffs of the suit for Niels Mogenssen; and he shall compensate them and their heirs for all damage or incidental expenses of all kinds. In witness of the truth whereof, we have put our seals at the foot of this our open letter[2]."

---

[1] rider oc frunder, (? possibly riddere oc frunde).

[2] I cannot help thinking that in this copy of the deed (probably several were made), the scribe must have omitted some words or more probably a whole line, such as "a full true and irrevocable *sone* and *orfejde*," which the first three persons "promise and assure." Such a line would fit in after the first mention of Hevringholm. In this case the "we the aforesaid sureties" would refer to Jacob Hardenberg etc.

V. Denmark, 1602—Juul-Skeel Orfejde.

[From *Danske Magazin*, 1 Række, 3 Bd, Cop. 1747, pp. 318 ff.]

"Wii effterskrevne Ove Juel til Meilgaard paa mine egne og min Sl. Brøders-Børns Vegne, som ieg er ret Verge fore, saa og paa mine Søstere, som ieg og er ret Verge fore, deres Vegne, Iver Juel til Villestrup, Mouritz Stygge til Holbekgaard, Frue Anne Stygge, Salig. Niels Juels til Kongeslevlund, hendes Lav-Verge, Christopher Mitelsen til Lundbek, Hertvig Kaas til Hørupgaard, giør alle vitterligt og kiendes med dette vort obne Brev, at som Erlig og Velbr. Mand Albret Skeel til Jungergaardt haver (disverre) drebt og ihielsaget vores kiære Hosbond, Broder og Svoger, og Blods-Forvandt Erlige og Velbr. Mand Niels Juel til Kongeslevlund, for hvilket hand nu var indstevnet for kongelig Maj. og meenige Danmarks Riges Raad: Da epterdi hans Slegt, Biurd og Blodtz-Forvante, Svoger og Venner baade nu og tit og ofte tilforne paa hans Vegne hos os haver anlanget, at vi for deris og hans Hustru og Børns Skyld, som og er voris Slegt, Biurd og Blods-Forvante, ville afstaa, hvis Tiltale og Rettergang vi kunde have til hannem for samme Sæg, da efter deres flittige Begiering og Underhandling, og for deres og hans Hustru, Børns og deres Slegt og Venners Skyld, have vi samme Stefning og Tiltale afstaaet...da have vi nu der imod paa forneffnte Niels Juels effterladende Hustru, hendes Børns og Arvingers Vegne, som paa vores Egne Vegne, for os og vores Slegt og Byrd, paa Fæderne og Møderne Side, for baade føde og u-føde, opreist forneffnte Albret Skeel, og giort Hannem og nu med dette Vort Obne Brev giore Hannem og Hans Børn, Slegt og Byrd, baade paa Fæderne og Møderne, baade fød og ufød, en trøg veragtige uigienkallendes og uryggelige Sone og Aarfejde....

Dis til ydermere Vidnisbyrd...haver vi med forneffnte Niels Juels Hustru, Hengt vore Zigneter her neden fore, og underskrevet med voris Egne Hænder, og Venligen tilbeder med os at besegle og underskrive, Erlige og Velbyrdige Mænd, Christen Holch til Høygaard, Høvitzmand paa Hald, Niels Stygge til Søegaard, Thomas Malthisen til Tanderup, Erich Høg til Klarupgaard, Erich Lunge til Skovgaard, og Frantz Juel til Palstrup. Actum Viborg d. 20 dag Februarii 1602[1]."

---

[1] Translated, p. 94 supra.

VI. *Schleswig—Court record from the town of Hadersleben,*
    28 *Jan.,* 1693.

[From Schleswig, *Staatsarchiv,* Acta C. XIX. 5, No. 7.]

"Es erscheinet Niss Iferssen aus friedtstede, *nomine* fr. magdalenen Classen, vnd dessen Sohns hans Classen, producieret einen Vergleich mit S. Marren[1] Olufs nachgelassenen freunden wegen der Busse welches quantum laut ermelten Vergleichs auff 154 mark sich erstrecket, Und haben die freunde sich nochmals erkleret, bey dem Vergleich zu bleiben, ausgenommen Sören Sörensen in Falstrup, welcher *copiam* der von den Sandmennern abgesprochener Sententz begehret, von diesen Geldern aber nichts participieren wollen, Niss Ifersen aber hat die Gelder versiegelt in Gericht deponiret, und ist der *terminus distributionis* der gelder auff den 18 Feb. a. c. angesetzet, an welchem die angegebene freunde, so sich nochmahlen gerichtlich erkleret, bey diesem Contract zu verbleiben, und weiter keine *prætentiones* zu machen, auch *ratione graduum* mit einander friedlich gewesen ohn weiterer citation die gelder empfangen sollen.

Specification Seligen Marren Olufs angegebenen freunden und in welchem *gradu* Ein jedweder begrieffen—wie folget.

Von denen veraccordirten 154 Mark gehen ab an Unkosten 4 Mk. bleiben—150 Mk.

  darvon bekommen 4 persohnen in Andern gradu à 8 Mk.—32 Mk.
    20 persohnen in dritten gradu à 4 Mk.—80 Mk.
    19 persohnen in 4ten gradu à 2 Mk.—38 Mk.
             150 Mk.

	gradus		
	2	3	4
Bertelt Hansen in hiemdrup	2		
hat 3 Söhne			
Laur		3	
Andreass		3	
Siren		3	
Sören Bertelsen Sohn nahmens Bertelt			4
David Kuster in Sommerstede	2		
hat 4 Söhne			
der erste		3	
der ander		3	
der dritte		3	
der vierdte		3	
3 Sohns kinder			

[1] Marren = Marien.

	gradus		
	2	3	4
erste			4
ander			4
dritte			4
David Davidsen aus Riepen	2		
2 Söhne			
erste		3	
ander		3	
Erich Davidsen in Rincöping	2		
2 Söhne			
erste		3	
ander		3	
Hans Hansen in Tystrup		3	
2 Söhne			
erste			4
ander			4
Michel Paulsen in Stepping		3	
2 Söhne			
erste			4
ander			4
Jens Paullsen		3	
hat 2 Söhne			
der erste			4
der ander			4
Hanss Paulsen		3	
Bertelt Paulsen, welcher in Engelland ist		3	
Ein Sohn			4
David hansen in Segeling		3	
Ein Sohn			4
Andreas Persen in Faurwra		3	
Simon Peersen in Faurwra		3	
hat 2 Söhne			
der erste			4
der ander			4
Peter Nissen in Faurwra			4
Traulss Jenssen in Bayschau (?) hat 2 Söhne, welche wegen ihrer Mutter participieren			
der erste			4
der ander			4
Matz Mortensen in hiendrup wegen seines Sohns, welcher in[1]			4
Laurs Petersen in Jarup		3	
dessen Sohn knudt Laursen			4

---

[1] There is a lacuna here in the original.

VII. *Schleswig-Holstein—The Ranzow-Brockdorf Urfehde*, 1588.

[Printed in J. F. Noodt: *Beyträge zur Erläuterung der Civil-Kirchen und Gelehrten-Historie der Hertzogthümer Schleswig und Hollstein.* Hamburg 1744, p. 91.]

Edle, Ehrenveste und Ehrbare, freundliche, liebe Ohme, Schwägere und gute Freunde. Nachdem ungefehrlich vor sieben oder acht Jahren auf der Fürstlichen Huldigung zu Odensehe euer Gottseeliger geliebter Oheim, Bruder und Freund, Gerd Rantzow, und unser freundlicher lieber Bruder und Schwager Friderich Brocktorffen, zur Uneinigkeit und zur Wehr gerathen wodurch gedachter Gerd Rantzow von unserm Bruder, Vetter und Schwager Friderich Brocktorffen, zu leider entleibet worden, und also er Frederich Brocktorff, der gantzen seiner angehörigen Freundschaft zu Ehren, auch Verhütung mehrers Unheils und Weiterung, vieler guten Leute Gemeinschaft meiden, auch sich eine Zeit lang ausserhalb Landes begeben und enthalten mussen. Zudeme nicht allein auf unser seiner Freundschaft emsiges Bitten und vielfältig Anhalten, besondern auch durch Weiland des Durchleuchtigsten, Grossmächtigen Fürsten und Herrn, Friderich des Andern, zu Dennemarcken, Norwegen, der Wenden und Gothen Königs, unsers allerseits gnädigsten Herrn, Vorschriften und dazu verordneten vornehmen Räthe und Diener fleissige Unterhandlung, es bis daher zu keiner Aussöhnung gereichen noch kommen können: Und aber durch sonderliche Schickung Gottes des Allmächtigen, weil wirs demselbigen allewege, in unserm Gebete getreulich befohlen, und dann auch unser der Freundschaft vielfältiges Suchen, es nunmehro dahin befördert, woferne nach altem dieser Fürstenthüme wohlhergebrachten Gebrauch und Gewohnheit, durch 36 Personen von Adel, als 12 Männern, 12 Frauen, zwölf Jungfrauen, mit gebührlicher Abbitte eine christliche Aussöhne öffentlich ins Werck gerichtet und angestellet, auch in die Ehre Gottes zu dem Armen-Hause binnen dem Kiel, die vieff huse genandt, 1000 Marck Lübsch gegeben und überreicht wurde, dass alsdann dadurch aller Groll, Hass und Wiederwillen, wegen berührtes kläglichen und hochbetrübten Unfalls gedämpfet, beigelegt und vertragen sein solle. Demnach erscheinen wir 36 Personen allhie obangeregter maasse, und dancken erstlich Gott dem Allmächtigen, darnächst euch und der gantzen Freundschaft, dass es zu diesen christlichen billigen Wegen und Mitteln gerathen, bitten auch dienst- und fleissig, ihr wollet aus chi stlicher Liebe dem Allmächtigen zu Lobe, auch uns und unserer gantzen Freundschaft zu Ehren und Gefallen, gedachten unserm Bruder und Freunde Frederichen Brocktorff zugefügten Unfal, von Hertzen verzeihen und vergeben, dessen inskünftige weder mit Worten noch Werken feindseliger Weise nicht gewehren noch gedencken. Inmassen auch wir, wann uns solches von eurer Seiten begegnet und wiederfahren, zu thun gleicherstalt gemeinet, damit also die Gemüther beederseits Freundschaft wiederum christlich versöhnet und einer vom andern nicht anders, als alle Ehre, Freundschaft und geneigten guten Willen inskünftige zu erwarten haben möge, wie wir auch darob seyn, und befördern wollen, dass ab angeregte 1000 Marck Lübisch, dem genandten Armenhause zum Kiel erleget werden sollen. Solches um euch und der gantzen Freundschaft nach aller Möglichkeit zu verdienen, erkennen wir uns hiedurch schuldig, wollen uns auch solches jederzeit mit höchstem Fleiss getreulich angelegen und befohlen seyn lassen, mit erbieten, da sich in künftigen Zeiten, das der Allmächtige gnädig verhüten wolle, dergleichen Fall ihrer Seiten zutragen möchte, sich gleichfals aller christlichen Billigkeit und auf ebenmässigen Wegen finden zu lassen.

Frauen. Apollonia Brocktorffen zu Barn.
Oelgart von Qualen zu Koselau.
Catharina Brocktorffen, Friederichs Frau.
Anna Rantzow, Claus Frau.
Anna Brocktorffen, Pauls Frau.
Drude von Ahlefeld, Christophs Frau.

Ahlheit von Ahlefeld, Claus Frau.
Dorothea Wensin, Laurentz Frau.
Anna Sehestedten, Otten Frau.
Margarethe Rantzow, Claus Frau.
Ahlheit von Bockwolden, Jochims Frau.
Florentina von der Wisch, Claus Frau.

Jungfrauen. Catharina Brocktorffs, Friderichs Tochter
Lucia von Qualen, Josias Tochter.
Anna Brocktorff, Pauls Tochter.
Christina von Hagen, Henneken Tochter.
Ide von Ahlefeld, Wulffs Tochter.
Oelgard von Qualen, Josias Tochter.

Ida Brocktorffen, Pauls Tochter.
Abel von der Wisch, Claus Tochter.
Anna Brocktorffen, Jochims Tochter.
Barthe von Ahlefeld, Jürgens Tochter.
Catharina von der Wish, Otten Tochter.
Anna Rantzowen, Jacobs Tochter.

Junckere. Detlef Brocktorff zu Barn.
Hans Brocktorff zu Rosenhave.
Paul Brocktorff zu Eckernförde.
Friderich Brocktorff.
Detlef Brocktorff zu Windebüe.
Otto von Qualen zur Noer.

Otto von Qualen und Benedictus von Qualen, Josias Söhne.
Christoffer von Ahlefeld zum Nordsee.
Heinrich von Ahlefeld zu Sattrupholm.
Claus von der Wisch zu Glasow.

VIII. *East Friesland—Sums offered for the slaying of Ippo Meyen, who slew Enno Abekena.* 13 May 1443.
[Printed in Ehrentraut, *Fries. Archiv.* II. p. 369.]

Wy Syardus Curet wandaghes to ffyskwert, nv an duszer tiid to Pylsum, Enkenne openbaer an dusser scryfft vor den ghennen, den dussen opennen breff ghetoent wart, wo ick dar an ende ouer was, so ver als my to behoerde, bynnen Fiskwert vorscr. an der tiid als Enno Abekena saligher dechtnisse ghemene vrende to Dyken hues dar sulues, als hiir benamen nascreuen staen, de vastinghe makeden vp Yppo meyen to Pylsum umme de mysdaet, dar Yppo saligher dechtnisse an salighen Ennen hadde begaen, vnde loueden to sammede den ghennen, de Yppo vorscr. weder slaen kunden, dyt nascreuen guet vnde dar na van sammender hant schadeloes to holden, als oeck Ebbo to Pewesum ouer dat open graff sprack, als den Susteren to Dychusen kundich ys. Int erst louede dar to Tateke salighe Ennen huovrouwe en span vnde teyn grase landes bii lomken sloet. Item Ponptet to Hlerlten XX. grase landes. Item Gayko dar sulues XL. ar. gulden. Item Frerd VI. grase landes. Item Enno XL. ar. gulden. Item Mammo XX. ar. gulden. Item Vdo to Mydlum XL. ar. gulden. Item Poppo XX. ar gulden. Item Edo XII. ar gulden. Item Onko XX. ar gulden. Item Memmo to Vphusen XX. ar gulden. Item Yppo XX. ar gulden. Item Sybeko XX. ar gulden. Item Sebo XL. ar gulden. Item Hayo twe grase landes. Item Focko II. grase landes. Item Boel vnde Vlfart to Grimesum XXIIII. arnss gulden. Item Enneko sebensna XL. grase landes. Item Gayko lyursna XL. rynscher gulden. Item Ebbo II. hundert lichter gulden. Item Vdo vnde Sybrant to husum XXV. ar. gulden. Item Nyttart hayen XL. ar gulden. Item Meno to Manslyat IIII. hundert lichter gulden. Item Frederick habbena XL. ar. gulden. Item Hep folricksna hundert ar. gulden. Item Nonno reinkena hundert lichter gulden. Item Hero aptetzna hundert lichter gulden. Item Dyko XL. ar gulden. Dyt ys de rechte vastinghe, dar schach beide to Fiskwert ende Dichusen. In orkunde der warheit so hebbe ick Syardus vorscr. mynen Ingheseghel vm de rechte warheit hanghen heten bii neden an dessen breff. It yar vnses heren dusent verhundert XLIII. vp Sunte Seruacius dach des hillighen byscops.

"We Syardus, formerly incumbent of Visquard, now at this time at Pilsum, publicly acknowledge in this document on behalf of those to whom this open letter was displayed that I was present at the said Visquard, and presided so far as it behoved me, on the occasion when (in the nunnery of) Dyckhusen in that place, the common kinsmen of Enno Abekena of blessed memory, whose names follow here, made the agreement against Yppo Meyen of Pilsum on account of the misdeeds which Yppo of blessed memory had committed against Enno of blessed memory, and together promised to those who could slay the said Yppo in return, this hereinafter-named property, and also jointly (undertook) to see that they should not suffer thereby, as also Ebbo of Pewsum[1] declared over the open grave, as is known to the sisters of Dyckhusen...."

[The amounts promised (besides the widow's 'ox-gang' of plough-land and pasture-land for ten cows) are as follows :

    549 Arens gulden, by 18 men
    40 Rhenish gulden, by 1 man
    700 'light' gulden, by 3 men
    70 strips of pasture-land (each sufficient to pasture one cow[2]), by 6 men.]

"This is the true agreement, which was made both at Visquard and at Dyckhusen. In proof whereof I Syardus aforesaid have for the sake of truth ordered my seal to be suspended at the foot of this document."

IX. *Holland—Official adjudication in a slaying case*, 1392.

[From P. J. Blok, *Leidsche Rechtsbronnen uit de Middeleeuwen*, 1884, p. 35.]

Donderd. nae Paeschdagh anno 1392.

Dit is tsegghen, dat die burchgrave van Leyden ende tgherecht van Leyden als overmanne gheseyt hebben mit Gherijt Lam, Willem Foytgen, Hughe Claes soen ende Jan die Bruyn, die dadincslude gheweest hebben van Jan Hellebrekers doet, die God ghenadich si, daerin besculdicht waren Wolbrant Keysers soen, Floris van Rijsoord, Heinric Tier ende Jan van Renay, daer dat segghen of is twisken Wolbrant voirsz. ende sijn hulperen ende horen maghen an die een side, ende Claes Hellebreker, Jans broeder, ende sinen maghen op die ander side, op een pene van 500 ponden dat segghen te houden, ende te voldoen half den heer ende half den segghers. Nochtan dat segghen voert te gaen. In den eersten so sel Wolbrant voirsz. doen Jans ziel te rusten ende ter ghenaden twie hondert zielmissen, cloesterwinninghe te doen twisken Maze ende Zijp, alse costumelic is, ende dair betoech of te brenghen toten lesten daghe der betalinghe; ende want costumelic plecht te wesen, dat men voetval ende overeed plecht te doen, so is hoer segghen, dat die an beyden siden off sellen wesen.

Hierof sel costen die heel zoene 449 pont. hollns. paym., dertich grote, als ghenghe ende ghave sien, voir elc pont, welc ghelt verborcht heeft Jacop van Rijsoerd mid Floris sinen broeder voer een derdendeel, Jan van Leyden mid Dirc van den Werve een derdendeel. Item dat leste derdendeel beloept 149 pont. 13 sc. 4 penn. paym. voirscr.; daerof heeft verborcht Jan Costijns

---

[1] All the places mentioned are in the Emden district.

[2] For this explanation of 'gras' I am indebted to Geheimrath Dr Wachter, who also points out to me that the document has been more recently printed in Friedlaender's *Ostfriesisches Urkundenbuch*, 1. No. 548.

soen een vierendel, Nan van Lis een vierendel, Dirc Wolbrants soen mit Wouter Keysers soen ende mid Jan Loyaert een vierendel ende dat leste vierendel Wouter Keysers soen allien.

Hierof sel hebben ter erfsoen Claes Hellebreker 80 pt. Item ter voirsoene 130 pt.; daerof sel hebben sijn moeder 20 pt., sijn twie susteren elk 10 pt., sijn kint 20 pt., dat die doerne bi hem draecht, ende storve dat kint sonder blikende boort, so sout comen op Jan Hellebrekers recht erfnamen. Item sijn drie omen elk 10 pt.; item sijn moeyen kinderen ende oems kinder 50 pt.; te delen elc effen veel. Item ter maechssoene 213 pt. paym. voirscr. Item tgherecht, die nu sien, 16 pt., daer si se wisen; hierof sel wesen die eerste dach van der betalinghe tot sinte Louwerijsdaghe naest comende ende tot elken ses weken een derdendeel, te betalen opter stede huys : ende wes tgherecht hierof hebben sel, dat sellen si opboren van den eersten daghe.

Voert so sellen dieghene, die in den doetslach besaect sien, des Beliues ende des Burchgraven moede hebben mid ghevoeghe jof mit recht; desghelijcx so sel Claes Hellebreker mid sinen maghen oec den heer ende den Burchgrave stillen mid ghevoege jof mid recht; ende vel hier anders iet in, dat houden die segghers tot hore verclaringhe.

"This is the decision which the Burggraf of Leyden and the Court of Leyden as adjudicators have declared together with Gheryt Lam, Willem Foytgen, Hughe Claes' son and Jan die Bruyn, who have been arbitrators in the matter of the slaying of Jan Hellebreker (on whom may God have mercy), in which were implicated Wolbrant Keyser's son, Floris van Rysoord, Heinric Tier and Jan van Renay. The award is made between the said Wolbrant and his helpers and their kinsmen on the one side, and Claes Hellebreker, Jan's brother, and his kinsmen on the other, and is to be adhered to on a penalty of £500, half this sum to be paid to the lord and half to the adjudicators, and the award to be enforced notwithstanding. Firstly the said Wolbrant shall cause two hundred masses for the dead to be said for the comfort and pardon of Jan's soul: he shall cause him to be entered as a brother in all abbeys[1] between the Meuse and the Zijp, as is usual, and is to bring proof thereof on the last day of the payment; and since it is customary that persons should make a public plea for pardon or public reconciliation, it is their decision that both sides must be included in it[2].

Besides this the whole *zoene* shall cost £Holl. 449; thirty groats, such as are current, to each pound, for one-third of which sum Jacob van Rijsoerd with Floris his brother has stood surety, and Jan van Leyden with Dirc van den Werve, for one third. Item, the last third amounts to £149 13 scillings 4 pen. of the said money: for one quarter of this Jan Costijn's son has stood

---

[1] In order that his soul may benefit vicariously by the works of charity performed by the monks: cp. Verwijs en Verdam, *Mnd. Wb.* s.v. *cloosterwinning*.

[2] The translation of the words *off sellen wesen* is somewhat hypothetical.

surety, for one quarter Nan van Lis; Dirc Wolbrant's son with Wouter Keyser's son and with Jan Loyaert for one quarter, and for the last quarter Wouter Keyser's son alone.

Of this Claes Hellebreker shall have for heir's compensation £80. Item, £136 (shall be) for *voirsoene*: of this his (Jan's) mother shall have £20, his two sisters each £10, his child, whom the girl will bring into the world, £20, and if the child die at birth, it shall go to Jan Hellebreker's legal heirs. Item, his three uncles each £10, item his aunts' and uncles' children £50, to be shared in equal parts. Item, for kindred compensation, £213 of the aforesaid money. Item, for the Court (its present members) £16, to go as they shall decide. The first day of payment for this shall be on next St. Louwer's day, and one third every six weeks thereafter, to be paid at the Town Hall; and the part the Court shall have of it they shall receive from the first instalment.

Further, those who are prosecuted for the slaying shall secure the grace of the Bailli and the Burggraf by friendly arrangement, or else in legal course: similarly Claes Hellebreker and his kinsmen shall also satisfy the lord and the Burggraf by friendly arrangement or else in the legal course; and if there should be any dispute about any part of the compensation, the arbitrators shall have that part for their declaration."

INDEX

achtendeele 161
aðas unfæhða 208
Adolph, Duke 107
Æthelberht's laws 205
Æthelstan's laws 214 f., 229
Æthelred's laws 217, 221 ff.
ætt 215
ættæ högher 272
ættærbot 72 f., 210
aftersusterkynt 160
agnation 268 ff.
agnates 12, 50, 52, 59, 73, 126, 139, 141 f., 171
álfa-blót 272
Alfred, King 48, laws of 211 ff., 217
Alfred and Guthrum's treaty 214
alienation of land, see pre-emption
alimentation 7, 43 f., 67, 76, 140 f., 213, 233
Allgemeine Gesetze des westerlauwerschen Frieslands 149, 266, 268
Alost 173 f.
Als, island of 103
Altenwalde 145
älter leute 133
Althing 25
Amiens 190, 192
Amrum, island of 102 f.
Amsterdam 166
ancestor worship 271 ff.
anderlinc 175
anderzweers 174
Andreas Sünesøn 82
Antwerp 176
Appenzell 170
arbitrators 89, 124, 185
Archinfield 242
Ardenbourg 176
arfsal 97
aristocracy, merchant 202; Norwegian 47
Arröe, island of 103
artificial relationship 126
arvæbot 71
asseurement 192 f., 196
Augsburg 171
Austria 171

Bætr 11, 28, 41 f.

bails, see pledges
bane 128
barne bloet 105
Baugatal 11 ff., 50, 266
baugr 12 ff., 27
baugþak 12 f., 53
Be wergilde 223 f.
Be wifmannes beweddung 236
Beaumanoir 8, 193 ff.
Beauvais 193 f.
Bede 238
Belgium 173 ff., 246
Beowulf 236 f.
Bergedorf 146
Bjarnar Saga hitdælakappa 15, 21, 24 f.
Black Death 259
Blood-feuds, see Feuds
Blüting 122-3
Bordesholmer Amtsgebräuche 103, 136 f.
borgermesters 166
borh 222
bothe 106 f.
boyne bothe 105 f.
Borough Customs 220, 233
Bracton 242
bræðrungr 56, 61
Bremen 145, 245
Briel 8, 161 f., 182
British kindred system 209
brodertembte 126
brodertemede 128
brother as nearest kinsman 81, 174
Bruges 173, 175, 178
Burgundy 164, 197 f.
Butjadingen 249
Butjadinger Küren 148

Cambrai 185
capitularies 201 f.
Caroline code 125, 146
Cassel 176
Ceadwalla 237
Celle 168
Central Germany 168 ff., 245
ceorl 250
Champagne 195 ff., 246
Chancery, Ducal 133 f.
Chansons de Geste 198 ff., 239
Charles V 184

INDEX

Childebert II 194, 207
Christian I of Denmark 135
Christian III of Denmark 82 f., 104 f.
Christian IV of Denmark 99
Christian V of Denmark 103
civic authorities connected by kinship 166
clan 2, 126, 131, 245, 274
class distinctions 97
clerics 194, 221 f.
Clermont 193
Clovis 194
Cnut's laws 217, 222 ff., 234
comitatus 237
comites 253, 276
compurgation 6, 67, 71, 74 ff., 81, 99 f., 123 f., 128 f., 143, 154 f., 191, 199, 211, 215, 221, 223, 229 f., 241, 264
Concilium Thunresfeldense 215
congildones 202
conjurati 202
Count of Holland 160, 163, 167
cousin, in A.S. lit. 243
cross-payments in wergild 57 f.
cult-community 271
cult of the dead 273
custeet 166
custinghe 166
cyn 223

Danish period in England 214, 234
Danish features in A.S. law 227
Danelaw 220, 233
demi point mains 185
derdelinc, derdelingen 174 f.
distraint for wergild debts 81, 162
Ditmarschen 104, 125 ff., 252, 267, 270 f.
Ditmarschers in Fehmarn 137
Dordrecht 166, 176
Douai 190 f.
Drenthe 159 ff., 164 ff., 249
Droplaugarsona Saga 17, 22
Dunwich 233, 241

Eadgar's laws 221
Eadmund's laws 218 ff., 225 f.
Eadnoð 235
Eadric, *see* Hlothhere
Eadweard's laws 214
Eadweard and Guthrum's law 223
earls, Norwegian 47
East Friesland 147 ff., 155
Ecgbert, Archbishop 232
Edzard, Count 155
eerste lit 160
effaitement 197
Egilssaga 35, 48 f.
Eiderstedtische Krone der rechten Warheit 103
Eiderstedtische Landrecht 103
Ely 233

Emden 157
emigration 260
Emo, Abbot 158
England 246, 250
enhizkes bothe 106
erfzoen 161, 164
Erik Menved 82
Erik of Pomerania 137
eskevins 186, 190
Exeter 214
Eyrbyggia Saga 15, 18, 20
eyrir, pl. *aurar*, 12

Fachten 155
Falck 122
family ties, decay of 240
fangen 150
fara 272
father's kindred 69, 72, 79, 106, 267
fecht 106
fedethom 106
fedriethom 106
Fehmarn 104, 137 f.
festival, kinsmen's 272
feud 109, 111, 145, 164, 172, 178, 193 ff., 213, 219, 222, 231, 254, 258, 264
feudalism 172, 201, 250
feyring 115
'fist-law' 105, 108, 136
Fivelgo 153
Flanders 173 ff., 178, 184
Flensborg 109 f., 114
Flóamanna Saga 20
foðurbætr 39 f.
Föhr, island of 102 f.
forma bernig 152
Forty-Eight, College of the 125, 129
Fóstbræðra Saga 21
foster-brotherhood 24 f., 61
fourjurement 179 ff., 191, 194
frana 151
France 184 ff., 235, 249
frændbætr 52, 57
frændi 25
Franks 159, 250, 255, 261, 268
fratrueles 159
Friedrich, Duke 104
Friesland 147 ff., 245 ff.
Friesland, North 102 ff., 266
Frisian islands (North) 102
Frisians 159, 261
friund 151, 243
Frostuthing's law 44, 49 ff.
fründeschaden 108
'full oath' 128 f.
funeral of kinsmen 133
fünfharde 104
fyhtwite 224, 226 f.

Gegildan 207 f., 211 ff., 237

INDEX

Geldern 167
genealogia 272
Gerhard the Great 129
Geschlecht (slachte) 126
gesið 208
geslecht 182
Ghent 173 ff.
Ghis l'Escrinewerckere 8, 185
'gifts' 62; *see gjörsum*
gilds 201, 257
Gísla Saga 15
gjörsum 80, 226 f.
Glarus 171
Godefroi, Bishop 185
goði, goðar 22, 31, 33, 37, 46
Göding 146
Göngu-Hrólf 263
Grágás 11, 37 ff.
Grettissaga 19, 21 ff.
Groden 145
Groningen 156
guarantors, *see* pledges
guardianship 4, 155, 203 f.
Guðmundar Saga dýra 31
Gulathing's law 44, 56 ff.
Gunnars Saga Thiðrandabana 17
Guthrum 214

Haarlem 167
Habsburg, Count Rudolf of 171
Hadeln 145, 245, 249
Hadersleben 119 ff.
Hainault 176, 178 f.
halsfang, see *healsfang*
Hamburg 111, 114, 118, 143 ff., 245 f.
handclasp 220
handsel 220
Hanover 168 f.
Harald Hairfair 252, 263
Harðar Saga 15
hardesgerichte 123
hauld, höldr 61, 63
Hávarðar Saga 19, 22
healsfang 224, 226, 228 f., 267
heemrad 166
heirs 38 ff., 65, 83, 105, 111, 155, 161, 168, 171, 229, 262, 266
Helsingeland 68, 154
Helsingör 225
Hemricourt 181
Hénin-Liétard 190
hersar 47
Hesse 168 f.
Historia Eliensis 239
Hlothhere and Eadric, laws of 206 f.
höfuðbaugr 56, 61
Holland 159 ff., 245 f.
Holstein 102 f., 125 ff., 245
höveskhed 226
Hrafns Saga 30

hreppr 43, 45
Hrollaug, Earl 263
hundred, a district 70
'hundred' of silver 13; *see* Appendix I
Hunsingoer Küren 151, 153, 266

Iceland 246, 251, 254 ff.
Icelandic Sagas 218, 237
ieldstopa 154
illegitimate child, wergild of 208
illegitimate sons 12, 163
interfamily feuds 14 ff., 29 ff., 70, 238
Ine 237 f.; laws of 207 ff., 217
infants 82, 153, 194
Innsbrück 172
Itzelings 171

Jan Matthijssen 8
Jean d'Outremeuse 181
Johann, Duke of Schleswig-Holstein 135
justice, administration of 249, 251, 253
Jutish law 79 ff., 103
Jutland 248

Karr Harde 124
Kent 205 ff., 232
Kentians 237
Kentish ordinances 215
Kiel 141, 246
Kindred, causes of decline of 257 ff.; definition of 2; democratic tendency of 256; functions of in the social order 246 ff., 275; liability of abrogated 65, 76, 81 f., 87 f., 145, 164, 176; no litigation within 148, 235; not a corporation 3; secondary liability of 107 f., 206; limits of 63, 273 f.; structure of 106-7, 243; voluntary contributions of 87 f., 165
Kinlessness 213, 217 f., 221 f.
Kinship, denial of 181; mode of reckoning 274
Kinsmen, exclusion of on Councils 166, 176; new liabilities of 214 f.; secondary liability of 165, 211
Kjøn 217
Kjønseedt 123
Kjøns næfn 99
Kluft, Klufft 106, 126 f., 128, 132, 134
Kluftbücher 132 ff.
Kluftsvetter 133 f.
Knud VI of Denmark 80, 101 (*in this latter passage read* 'VI' *for* '*the Great*')
Kolding Recess 83, 104
Krone der rechten Warheit 103, 105 f.
Kyn 215
Kyns næfnd 99

Land, *see* pre-emption

Landholding, by *Klüfte* 134; by *teeler* 275
Landnámabók 11, 35 ff., 47
Landrecht, East Frisian 155
Langobardians 269, 272
laws, evidence of 8
Laxdæla Saga 15, 18
Leechdoms 238
Leges Henrici 209, 229 ff., 242
Leis Willelme 228 f.
leod, leodgeld 205
Letters of attorney 85, 119
Lex Salica, *see* Salic Law
Lille 176, 180, 184 f., 189 f., 192, 266
Ljósvetninga Saga 16, 19, 40
Liège 178, 181
lignage 181, 190, 195 ff., 203
Livre Roisin 184, 192
London 216, 233, 241
Loon 167
lord, responsibility of 213 f., 218
lordless man 214
loyalty, to lord 49, 200, 213, 231, 237; to kin 200
Lübeck 141 ff., 182 f., 246

Mægbot 210 f., 221
mægburh 209, 215
mægð 214 ff., 216 f., 224, 235, 243
mæggieldan 209 f.
mæglagu 222
mægleas, *see* kinlessness
maechtaele 165
maechzoen, maechzoene 161, 164, 167
Magnus, King, Eriksson 76
Magnus, King, the Law-Mender 65, 67
maintenance of paupers, *see* alimentation
Malines 175
manbot 210, 224, 226
manngjöld 14, 19, 20, 22, 27
manslaughter, death penalty for, 83, 109 f., 112 f., 130, 156, 195, 242; by misadventure or in self-defence, 83, 107, 130, 156
mark 12; of gold 63
Maldon, Battle of 239
marriage, consent of kin for 5, 70, 167, 236; persons connected by 12, 21, 61, 98, 131
medderthom 106
meggildare 210
meitel, meitele 149, 153
menteel 149, 151
merchant families 202
Mercia 226, 228
Metternich 170
migration 261 f., 271 f.
minde 226
moetzoen 161
moeyenkint 175

moeyensoen 160
mondzoene 173 f.
mondzoendere 174
Mosaic law 82 f.
mother 69, 131
mother's kindred 69, 72, 79, 106, 267
mundbryce 226
Münster 168 f.

Namur 178, 254
nefgildi 51, 52
neighbours 232
nemede 128
Neocorus 126, 129
Neumünster Kirchspielsgebräuche 103, 136 f.
Neustria 193, 246
niðgjöld 12, 14
niece 154
nithing 180
Njálssaga 17, 20, 22 f., 25 ff.
nobles 135, 153, 248, 252 f.
Norðhymbra Preosta lagu 223
Norðleoda lagu 223
Nordstrand 104 f., 122; Landrecht of 103
Norman Conquest 240 f., 246
Normandy 202 ff., 263
Nørre Rangstrup Herred 115 f.
North Friesland, *see* Friesland
Northern England 232, 250
Norway 246, 252
Nuremberg 170

Oath, *see* reconciliation
oath-helpers, *see* compurgation
Oda, Archbishop of Canterbury 220
odal 43, 67, 233
odalborinn 61
Odin 272 f.
ofledene 147
Ohthere 48
Oldampster Küren 151
olde torneye 107
Oldenburg, Counts of 147
Oldeslohe 139
oomskint 175
orfejde 91, 241; *see also* reconciliation
orkenen 155
orphans 154 f., 203, 229
örtug, örtugh 12, 13, 57, etc.
Oudenarde 173, 266
outlawry 18, 49 f., 212, 222

Pace-suchen 172
paiseurs 184, 190, 199
paix à partie 178
pardon, plea for 185, *see voetval*
parentela 159, 194, 215, 239
Pas-de-Calais 190

INDEX

paupers, *see* alimentation
perjury 129
Petreus 104 f.
pews, in church, of the *Kluft* 134
Philip Augustus 195
Picardy 246
place-names 244
plaintiff 38, 161, 173 ff.
pledge-breaker 213
pledges 34, 162, 193, 219 f., 224, 232
population, density of 260
pre-emption 5, 43, 67, 76, 100, 233 f.
pretium sanguinis 232
priests 153, 157
private treaties 83, 144
Protestant Church 83, 87, 111, 129 f., *see* Reformation
Public Prosecutor 144

Ragnarök 240
Ramsey Abbey 233
reconciliation, acceptance of 111 f., consent of *slachte* to 127; deeds of 65, 76 ff., 89 ff., 113, 117 f., 177 ff., 186 ff., 196 ff.; negotiations for 86 f., 193 f., 219 f., 224 f.; oaths of 208, 239, 241; *see also asseurement, orfejde*, private treaties. Cp. Appendix II
rechtzweere 174
rechtzweers 175
Reformation 96, 109
Regents 255
Reincke Vos, see Reynard
Reinhart Fuchs, see Reynard
renunciation of kindred 7; see *fourjurement*
repudiation of kinsman 7
réttr 41 f.
Reykdæla Saga 21 ff., 40
Reynard the Fox 182 ff.
Ribe 92, 272
Ribuarian law 167, 218
Roman Church 111
Roman law 229, 257
Roman de Renart, see Reynard
Russia 264

Quarantaine 189, 194

Sachsenspiegel 103, 136, 138 ff.
Saint Louis 189
Saint Omer 8, 185 f., 190
sakarbætr 11
sakaukar 12, 51, 55, 60
saker 56, 62
Salic law 174, 201, 229, 266
samfrænder ed 99 f.
samfreunde 124
sanctuary 213
Sandemend 84

Sandmänner 120
Saracens 250
Saxons 159, 248, 268
Schepen 176
Schildwolde 158
schlecht 135
Schleswig 102 ff., 245
Schleswig-Holstein 102 ff., 182
Schwyz 171
sectan 220
seignorial rights 248, 253
'self-doom' 16, 32, 237
serf 75 f.
Siebenhardenbeliebung 103 f.
Silesia 170
sister 131, 153, 238
Sjælland law 79 ff.
Skåne law 74, 79 ff.
skógarkaup 61
slachte 125 ff., 130; alliances of 130, 135
slachtes breve 157
slægt 86
slave 208 f.
slayer, flight of 50, 82 f., 206, 212; insolvency of 154; outlawry of 18, 49, 61, 212, 222; primary liability of 127; representative of 185; sole liability of 18 ff., 50, 65, 82, 155, 211
Sodbury 235
Södermanna law 70
sona 77
sonarbætr 22, 40
sone 171
Sonderburg 103
Spain 264
spear side 143; *see* agnates
spindle side 143
Staðarhólsbók 41
Stadtbücher 170
Stadtland 249
Staveren 159
Sturlu Saga 31
Sturlunga Saga 11, 29 ff., 40
succession 39
Sühngerichte 234
Sunbury 236
sureties 185, 199; *see also* pledges
susterbern 152
Svarfdæla Saga 21
Svinfellinga Saga 30
Switzerland 171
swertmac 139
swira 153
Sylt, island of 102 f., 111, 114, 118 f.

Tale 108
thale 105
thane 223, 239
theft 129, 214, 218

Thing 18, 21, 75, 81, 84, 86, 109, 115
thingman 21, 22, 33 f., 37, 46
Thorskfirðinga Saga 14
thrall 53
thrall-born kinsman 12, 51 f., 62
thredda halua knileg 152
thredda knileg 152
Thunor 238
Tournai 177 ff.
towns, solidarity of kindreds in 246, 249, 255
Trèves 170
truce 178 ff., 190, 194
truce-buying 53, 62
trygde-ed 92, 225
trygge 84
tryggva-kaup 62
twelf-hynde 228
twy-hynde 228

Upland law 70
upnám 56
Urfehde, see reconciliation
Utrecht 164, 166, 176

Valdemar II, of Denmark 82, 212
Valenciennes 180, 190
Vallaljóts Saga 19
Vápnfirðinga Saga 17
Vatsdæla Saga 16, 21, 36
Verden 145
Vestergötland law 72 f.
Vestmanna law 69 f.
Víga-Glúms Saga 16, 20, 23
Viking age 253
Viking raids 250
vígsakarbætr, vígsbætr 41 f.
Vígslóði 37 ff.
village community 260
Vetter 133
Vetterschaft 133, 136 ff., 141, 269
vierendeel 161 ff., 167
Völuspá 240

voetval 162, 167; *see* pardon
voorzoen 164
vrunde breff 157
vyfde lit 160

Wadmal 31; *see* Appendix I
waller wente 223
Waltharius 200
Waterland 162
Wends 103
werelade 229
Werferð, Bishop 235
wergild, abrogated 96, 105; bequeathed to churches 236; as fine 207; limited to heirs 38, 65, 76, 96; to near family 238; paid till 1751, 168
wergild surety, *see* pledges
Wessex 226, 228, 230, 251
West Friesland, *see* Friesland
Westerwold 249
West Saxons 237
Wetzlar 169
Wicht, Landrecht 155
widow 69, 110, 115, 117, 131, 154, 170
Wihtræd's laws 207
Willem 182 f.
wills 235
Wilstermarsch 140
wine-magas 239
Witte-Wierum 158
women, participation in wergild 12, 23, 62, 66, 97 f., 131, 142, 152, 154, 238; excluded 194
Worms 169 f.
wrield 154
Wulfstan, Archbishop of York 239 f.
Wursten 249

Zeeland 160 ff., 166
zoene 186 f.

þeowwealh 208 f.